America at the Ballot Box

POLITICS AND CULTURE IN MODERN AMERICA

Series Editors
Margot Canaday, Glenda Gilmore,
Michael Kazin, Stephen Pitti, Thomas J. Sugrue

Volumes in the series narrate and analyze political and social change in the broadest dimensions from 1865 to the present, including ideas about the ways people have sought and wielded power in the public sphere and the language and institutions of politics at all levels—local, national, and transnational. The series is motivated by a desire to reverse the fragmentation of modern U.S. history and to encourage synthetic perspectives on social movements and the state, on gender, race, and labor, and on intellectual history and popular culture.

AMERICA AT THE BALLOT BOX

Elections and Political History

Edited by

Gareth Davies

and

Julian E. Zelizer

PENN

UNIVERSITY OF PENNSYLVANIA PRESS

PHILADELPHIA

Published by
University of Pennsylvania Press
Philadelphia, Pennsylvania 19104–4112
www.upenn.edu/pennpress

Printed in the United States of America
on acid-free paper

10 9 8 7 6 5 4 3 2 1

A Cataloging-in-Publication record is available from the
Library of Congress
ISBN 978-0-8122-4719-0

To the pioneers of the fields of Policy History and American Political Development who inspired our generation of political historians.

CONTENTS

Introduction

Gareth Davies and Julian E. Zelizer

Mark Twain once quipped that "if we would learn what the human race really is at bottom, we need only observe it in election time." "If voting made any difference," he wrote elsewhere, "they wouldn't let us do it."[1] Such sardonic reflections aside, elections are, and have always been, the lifeblood of American democracy, embodying the bedrock assumption of American political culture that legitimate rule derives from the consent of the governed. Sometimes, when differences between candidates have been modest or during uncommonly quiet times, elections have been notable primarily for exuberant political theater and overheated invective. Other contests, though, have featured passionate debate about the character and destiny of the Republic. Either way, by the 1820s presidential elections had become a mass-participation affair; at a time when British elections, if often raucous and fiercely contested, were firmly an elite sport, the United States was already a mass polity, and nothing distinguished it more dramatically from the Old World than its approach to elections.[2] Early on in his 1842 American tour, steaming out of Boston, Charles Dickens remarked that "politics are much discussed" on an American train, that "party feeling runs very high," and that "directly the acrimony of one election is over, the acrimony of the next one begins, which is an unspeakable comfort to all strong politicians and lovers of their country; that is to say, to ninety-nine men and boys out of every ninety-nine and a quarter."[3]

The early centrality of elections to American politics—their pervasiveness—was also a function of a less obvious singularity, namely, their metronomic regularity (quadrennial for the presidency, biennial for the House of Representatives, similarly fixed in the case of state contests). Presidents and legislators alike have had to keep a constant eye on the electorate for fear of losing office, and it is not just in recent years that reelection has loomed as an early preoccupation. This regularity and frequency of contests, and the ongoing responsiveness to the popular will that it necessitates, have served to reinforce the majoritarianism of the American political process and helped make electoral participation a fundamental badge of equal citizenship—something for which those excluded from the franchise have fought with passion. Hence the central importance of the Nineteenth Amendment (extending the right to vote to women) and the Voting Rights Act of 1965 (strengthening voter protections for ethnoracial minorities) to the story of twentieth-century American democracy. The struggles over that right have been contentious and integral to the nation's development.[4]

The uniqueness of the American election was somewhat less marked by World War I, given the processes of political democratization that many other nations underwent during the late nineteenth and early twentieth centuries. What is more, by some measures elections were now somewhat less central to American democracy than had previously been the case: the United States had developed a stronger administrative state, and politics was conducted to a larger extent outside of the electoral arena—within federal agencies, for example, and by organized interest groups.[5] With each election, moreover, political institutions and established public policy acquired a certain rigidity, a greater resistance to change, diminishing the likelihood that electoral outcomes might trigger fundamental political change.[6] Meanwhile, elite political reformers evinced distrust at the corruption of ballot-box politics and disdain for its demotic, knockabout character.

Still, by other measures national elections mattered more than before; certainly, more was at stake, as government expanded by leaps and bounds, and as Americans looked to Washington for solutions to problems that had hitherto been thought of as local, private, or insoluble. Moreover, big government coexisted with a persistent antistatism; the more the state expanded, the more too conservatives were wont to construe elections as portentous opportunities to hold back the un-American tide of collectivism and reassert the core national values of individualism and localism. For these reasons, and because of the grand ructions, dramas, and tragedies that punctuated the twentieth century—war, holocaust, economic collapse, minority freedom struggles—elections since 1900, just like their predecessors, have seldom lacked drama or interest.

For all this, elections have received astonishingly little attention from academic historians during the past four decades. That reflects the parlous state of the subdiscipline of political history during years dominated by the writing of "bottom-up" social and cultural history. In that historiographical context, elections seemed redolent of the elite bias of older "Great Man" history. Many historians adopted a kind of cynicism toward elections, downplaying how much of a difference any single contest had on the national polity and pushing their colleagues instead to look at longer-term continuities that outlasted any particular presidency. And a generation of social and cultural historians who emerged out of the 1960s and shaped the profession in the 1970s and 1980s believed that scholars such as Arthur M. Schlesinger, Jr., Eric Goldman, William Leuchtenburg, Merrill Peterson, and even Richard Hofstadter incorrectly used elections and presidents as representative of American political eras.[7] In doing so they had downplayed conflict, missed the contributions and agency of African Americans, and ignored the struggles over power that took place in homes and communities and on the shop floor. Although the older work about political history in the 1950s and early 1960s had in truth been much more complex in its treatment of how politics evolved, this belief led younger historians to focus on issues other than formal politics, and elections tended to fall by the wayside.

The major exception to this work was the ethnocultural school of political history, culminating in the so-called New Political History of the 1970s, whose practitioners tried to study politics from the bottom up by understanding the voting behavior of the nineteenth-century electorate, using social scientific methodology. This trail was blazed by Lee Benson in his devastating critique of Schlesinger's economic interpretation of the antebellum period, *The Concept of Jacksonian Democracy*, followed up by historians such as Joel Silbey, Paul Kleppner, and Ronald Formisano.[8] For the most part, this literature focused on nineteenth-century politics. These scholars tested voting data to determine whether economic or ethnic factors motivated partisan attachment. They hoped to move beyond impressionistic and sporadic narratives by instead understanding the underlying, long-term trends that were shaping the polity. While this literature enjoyed a moment in the academic spotlight, the field soon faltered, as these historians became trapped in a circular debate over which factors mattered most. Additionally, their neglect of traditional forms of historical narrative constrained their ability to provide accessible and compelling arguments about the overall direction of politics. Their work also did not appeal as much to historians of the twentieth century given that so much of politics by then revolved around the development of government institutions and public policy: the American state. As a result, most social and cultural historians did not turn their attention to elections, focusing instead on other aspects of community formation and conflict throughout America.

The recent academic tendency to downplay elections has been as true for historical work in political science. To be sure, elections were not wholly neglected: Stephen Skowronek demonstrated how elections could help create new presidential regimes that structured "political time," while Theda Skocpol found that electoral pressures helped to explain the character of the welfare state.[9] And Scott James showed how the Electoral College system contributed to American state building.[10]

Yet, generally, elections have been used to tell another story rather than as the focus of inquiry itself, while the branch of political science most directly concerned with elections—realignment theory—withered on the vine.[11] Students of contemporary elections in political science were relatively consensual in their conclusion that the particularities of the back-and-forth between the individual candidates in each election were not as important as journalists made them out to be. Instead, the "fundamentals" of a period—the state of the economy, the balance of partisan electoral power, the organization and fund-raising capacity of the parties—mattered much more to the outcome.[12]

Meanwhile, the American Political Development school of political science, which studied the evolution of policies and institutions and the way in which institutional structures shaped political behavior, was more interested in the developments of bureaucracies, the courts, and administrative capacity. Implicit in this scholarship was the notion that over time elections diminished in importance as the "thickening" of the American state made it hard for new presidents and congressional majorities to transform government. When elections emerged in this literature, they were a small part of a bigger story rather than the story itself.

Calling for the rehabilitation of political history in 1986, William Leuchtenburg told the annual meeting of the Organization of American Historians that "while you may not be interested in the State, the State is interested in you," and subsequent policy historians have heeded his call.[13] Since that time, political history has undergone a dramatic revival with a new generation of historians who came of age in the 1990s and are studying the history of government institutions, public policy, and political culture. In some cases, including contributions to the present volume, elections have provided a central focus for this new writing, most especially under the auspices of the University Press of Kansas's U.S. Elections series.[14] For the most part, however, recent political history writing has focused elsewhere, favoring archivally based analysis of institutions and policy that complement the work of American Political Development scholars, or examining how social movements and cultural ideas have affected Washington—and vice versa.[15]

Why the comparative neglect of elections? Doubtless it owes much to the excitement of exploring new scholarly vineyards, and something too to a desire to avoid accusations of reproducing the real and alleged flaws of the "old" political history. Whatever the explanation, we feel that the time is now right for bringing elections back into the story of American democracy. One purpose of the present volume is to suggest a range of ways in which this objective can be accomplished without sacrificing the attention to institutional structures and public policy development that has been such a beneficial consequence of American Political Development scholarship, and without reproducing the simplistic focus on heroic leadership that diminished much past historical writing on partisan politics. New work on elections can treat these events in their appropriate social and cultural context rather than simply presenting them as embodiments of the national pageant.

Some of our contributors have focused on elections that manifestly resulted in dramatic political change (1800, 1860, 1980), but others have concentrated on contests whose importance lies more in the way that they illuminate broad, underlying processes of political change (the advent of television advertising in 1952, the wrenching controversies over corruption in 1884). A third set have taken a thematic approach (exploring the impact of foreign relations, Anglophobia, and revolutions in political communication over long periods of electoral time). What unites them all is a common conviction that elections are both exciting and entertaining, and that they offer a unique vantage point from which to view American political democracy.

As all this indicates, we have not sought to be in any sense comprehensive in our coverage, still less to rank and explore the "top ten" elections in American history. Rather, we began by approaching a dozen colleagues whose work exemplifies the recent renewal of American political history, invited them to pick an election, or a theme that might be explored across a range of elections, and respected their preferences. The result of that approach lies ahead of you. The wide range of elections covered (some landmark contests and others less clearly influential on the overall trajectory of politics), as well as the diversity of themes that are explored in this book, illustrates the substantial intellectual dividend that will result if we bring elections back into the study of American political, social, and cultural history. Our ultimate collective objective is both to stimulate a new generation of monographic writing that exploits this vantage point to the full and to reach out to the general reader, for whom elections have never ceased to exert fascination.

* * *

The organization of the collection is broadly chronological. In the first chapter, Jeffrey Pasley revisits the "revolution of 1800," urging us to take seriously the (albeit self-serving) Jeffersonian argument that it amounted to an important renewal and reconstitution of American constitutionalism, and marked the point at which elections became genuine decision points, moments of consequential choice, and not simply plebiscites on the existing regime. Whereas existing scholarship has often focused on the election's dramatic immediate aftermath (for example, the House's resolution of a tie in the Electoral College), for Pasley 1800 provides a vehicle for exploring the broad political crisis of the late 1790s and the grand ideas and principles that were at stake, including freedom of speech, the role of the judiciary, and the fundamental purpose of the Constitution.

Whereas Pasley is concerned with the apotheosis of the short-lived first party system, Sean Wilentz explores the strains to which its successor, the somewhat more enduring second party system, was already subject in 1844, at its seeming zenith: although the respective electoral performances of James K. Polk and Henry Clay suggested that party had trumped section, a longer historical lens suggests that this campaign was an important way station on the road to disunion. Using that lens, the central player in this electoral drama was not either candidate, but rather John C. Calhoun, who almost single-handedly managed to turn the election inside out, injecting the poisonous issue of the extension of slavery into the body politic despite the almost universal conviction of Democrats and Whigs alike that it should remain out of view.

Adam Smith complicates our view of the pivotal 1860 election, and simultaneously critiques two influential ways of understanding electoral history: the idea of "party systems" and "critical election theory" (or "realignment theory"). With the advantage of hindsight, it makes sense to see 1860 as having marked the inauguration of a third party system, but Smith suggests the greater advantages of understanding that year's election in its own terms. Doing so, one does not find very clear-cut differences between northerners who voted for Abraham Lincoln and those who voted for Stephen Douglas; rather, the two candidates were competing for ownership of a common set of principles, and they were the principles of the 1840s and 1850s rather than some new set of ideas forged by the climactic breakdown of the Union. To the extent that there is merit in construing the years from 1860 to 1896 as a stable political regime, Smith suggests that it was the war itself and the circumstances of life in a postwar, industrializing America that made it so, and that it is anachronistic to espy a fundamentally new party "system" in the charges and countercharges of the 1860 campaign.

The year 1884, like 1844, may be one of the less feted elections of the nineteenth century, even if the slogan "Rum, Romanism, and Rebellion" lives on. Richard John tells us that it should be better known. Partly, that is because it reminds us just how even party competition was during the late nineteenth century: the outcome of presidential contests was invariably determined by the same handful of states, New York foremost among them. In doing so John provides a compelling example of how a better understanding of the composition of the electoral map can provide the much-needed context of what shaped electoral decisions and, to some extent, outcomes. In that environment, the wooing of particular constituencies loomed large, as did third-party competition. He illustrates that the historian can focus in a forensic way on one state (New York, in this case) and just two or three issues (antimonopolism, corruption, alcohol) yet illuminate a very wide range of issues. In institutional and policy terms, the 1884 election helped to inaugurate the modern regulatory state. In ideological terms, it helps to complicate the simplistic portrayal of this period as a so-called Gilded Age: one has very little sense here that a small cabal of plutocrats were running the show; at the very least, they faced a diverse range of formidable opponents, coming not least from East Coast businessmen. And the campaign also marked an important landmark in terms of the way political arguments were advanced: thanks to important advances in print technology, political cartoons could now be mass-produced in newspapers (and not just, as before, in illustrated magazines), helping to create what John calls "a novel storytelling genre" that framed campaign discussion of both issues and candidates.

In the first of our broad, thematic chapters, Jay Sexton uses the persistence—indeed the ubiquity—of Anglophobia in nineteenth-century elections to illuminate both the distinct character of American political culture and the impact of elections on subsequent public policy. For all the vast changes that the United States underwent over the course of the century, and despite its growing strength vis-à-vis Great Britain, Anglophobia persisted and did not fundamentally change in form. Elections fueled the continued use of this rhetoric, even after the reality of international relations made the arguments somewhat obsolete. Sometimes candidates accused their opponents of morbidly pro-British instincts; on other occasions they vied with one another to demonstrate their determined opposition to John Bull's perfidious designs. Either way, the electoral politics of Anglophobia reveal both the demotic populism of American political culture and the complex admixture of insecurity and belligerent confidence that underpinned its attitudes toward the Old World. To some degree, though, this was primarily political theater: Sexton finds that election-time tweaking of the British lion's tail rarely led (let alone forced) the architects of American foreign relations to pursue what a later generation would call brinkmanship—pragmatism was the rule, and sometimes it even took the form of Anglo-American partnership.

The election of 1916, Elizabeth Sanders tells us, was remarkable for constituting the climax of the Progressive era and for having featured a tremendous popular mobilization against war whose climax came at the Democratic National Convention. Woodrow Wilson, Sanders argues, went into the convention a strong proponent of military preparedness, but a spontaneous eruption of pacifism forced him to recalibrate his campaign, embracing the slogan "He kept us out of war." Of course, that recalibration did not greatly derail the drift to war, but it did foreshadow the strong peace movement of the 1920s, and additionally highlights both the importance of conventions (unruly, hard-to-control affairs) to early twentieth-century electoral politics and Wilson's political vulnerability toward the end of his first term. That vulnerability was enhanced by the convention's continued appetite for domestic reform, despite the president's judgment that the New Freedom had now been fully implemented. The election, according to Sanders, also marked the last time a presidential candidate truly campaigned around the theme of peace, a message that she argues became much harder as a result of the marriage of militarism and presidential power in the twentieth century.

Bruce Schulman sees the importance of the 1924 election as residing not in its outcome (which was predictable and lopsided), still less in its policy discussions or its candidates, but rather in the new way in which it was fought. This was the first election in which a broad trend away from strong party affiliations was reinforced by the application to politics of the new profession of public relations and the revolutionary new technologies of radio, moving pictures, and recorded sound. In the nineteenth century, American electoral politics had possessed a very immediate character; that was the case in the

1920s too, but now this immediacy was increasingly achieved through these new techniques and media rather than through face-to-face contact. To some extent, though, the story of 1924 may be about incipient realignment rather than dealignment, in ways that at least dimly anticipate the New Deal order: Schulman notes that the Democrats were just starting to become the party of urban liberalism, while the estrangement of progressives from the Republican Party (already evident in the previous decade) was now accelerating.

When realignment theory was in its pomp, its political science exponents associated the later 1920s and the 1930s with what they termed a "rolling realignment," whose cumulative effect was to inaugurate a new Democratic order that would endure at least until the late 1960s. Gareth Davies, though, argues that scholars interested in the consolidation of the New Deal should also be interested in 1940. Superficially, this is surprising, inasmuch as the election was dominated by the war in Europe, and in that historians have generally associated this preoccupation with the waning of the reform impulse. For Davies, however, the Republican decision to nominate Wendell Willkie as its candidate, and his decision to embrace virtually the entire legacy of the New Deal during his campaign, illustrated the enduring transformation in American political culture Roosevelt had wrought. The absence of certain issues from the campaign was not a sign of how little impact the contest would have, but rather reflected the basic changes in public policy and government institutions that had resulted from the New Deal. The fact that certain questions were not off the table reveals a sea change that had occurred in politics. Americans now expected protection from what FDR had called the "hazards and vicissitudes of life," and no one could now be elected to the presidency without accepting this reality.

The significance of the 1952 presidential election lies in part in the Republican primary contest between rock-ribbed conservative Robert Taft and the ideologically indistinct Dwight Eisenhower, seeing in Ike's victory a Willkie-like GOP accommodation with the New Deal order. As for the general election campaign that followed, scholars have been interested, Kevin Kruse observes, in the Republicans' strategic formula, "K_1C_2," that is, in the party's decision to hammer away at the issues of Korea, communism, and corruption. However, this "formula" is largely a subsequent invention, and the campaign was less issue-based and less raw; rather, the historical importance of the 1952 election resides—as with that of 1924—in the new presentational techniques that candidates deployed. CBS journalist Eric Sevareid would identify 1960 as the moment when the "managerial revolution [came] to politics," with John F. Kennedy and Richard Nixon as "its first completely packaged products," but Kruse's chapter casts doubt on that quip, presenting 1952 as the first television election. Image, not issues, mattered most, with advertising agencies playing a dominant role both in crafting powerful new televised advertisements and in the staging of public events. Neither Dwight Eisenhower nor Adlai Stevenson was fully comfortable with this development, but the world of American electoral politics had changed for good.

Barry Goldwater versus Lyndon Johnson is among the most ideologically polarized presidential matchups in history. Not surprisingly, then, Julian Zelizer's chapter on 1964 focuses closely on issues. However, he is less concerned with how the two candidates debated the issues than with the way that the outcome of the election transformed the political arithmetic: some presidential landslides have remarkably little impact on congressional politics (with 1984 and 1972 as good recent instances); 1964, though (like 1932 and 1936) was an across-the-board landslide, one that fundamentally altered the political environment. Historians have often associated the legislative deluge of the Great Society with the bottom-up social forces that were pressing on Washington during the mid-1960s, or with LBJ's political finesse. Zelizer, though, urges us not to lose sight of the new calculus on Capitol Hill. For a quarter century, liberalism had been impeded by the strength of the Conservative Coalition in Congress; now, quite suddenly, that was no longer the case, and that created a window for reform. LBJ, to be sure, had the skill to force the window open and push a torrent of legislation through it before it closed again, but it was his two-thirds partisan majorities in Congress that made it all possible.

The 1980 election might be construed as the contest that slammed that window shut: certainly, numerous commentators have associated Ronald Reagan's presidency with a strong conservative counterreformation. Meg Jacobs, though, shows that this is not how even Reagan partisans viewed the political environment of the early 1980s. As with a number of other elections discussed in this volume (1844, 1860, 1884, 1964), she appraises the significance of 1980 in relation to what happened next, exploring the substantial barrier that what she has elsewhere termed "pocketbook politics" posed to the so-called Reagan Revolution. Historians have often been interested in the role that cultural (as opposed to distributional) issues have played in American politics after the 1960s, not least in relation to a "gender gap" in voting preferences. Jacobs, though, shows that Reagan's strategists recognized economic interests to be far more salient: moving into the workforce in ever-larger numbers, in an economically turbulent time, American women evaluated political programs in relation to issues such as jobs, child care, and welfare, not God, guns, and gays.

Andrew Preston, like Jay Sexton, explores the relationship between domestic politics and international relations, starting where Sexton left off, at the turn of the twentieth century. Just as nineteenth-century Anglophobia was often more about national self-definition than it was about geopolitics, so too the electoral politics of foreign relations since 1900 have sometimes had less to do with ideas about the United States' place in the world than with domestic considerations. In particular, the response of the electorate to presidential candidates' stances on international issues has often had less to do with policy substance (candidates have only rarely been sharply separated from one another in their foreign policy stances) than with the overall impression of resolution, responsibility, and statesmanship that their respective postures have conveyed. Foreign relations have not infrequently been central to election year politics, then—just not in the way that we might anticipate. But what about policy impact? Can it be said that the conduct of any campaign, or the outcome of any election, has made a policy difference? Here, Preston brings midterm elections into the equation, finding that they have not infrequently resulted in substantive redirection, reflecting both the importance of congressional elections as a pulse-taking moment and the significant role that Congress has occasionally played in constraining presidents or forcing their hand.

The overall importance that many of our authors have attached to image politics and to the political impact of new communications technologies culminates in Brian Balogh's concluding chapter. In the middle of the twentieth century, he observes, candidates for national political office took the pulse of the American people primarily through parties and interest groups, and sought to respond to (and influence) their preferences mainly through broadcast television. Because political parties were broad coalitions, because network television was aimed at Middle America, and because interest groups sought to wield political influence largely through deal cutting and "iron triangle" relationships, all the central elements in this now impossibly distant world of political communication tended to facilitate conciliation and governing. Since then, though, a series of profound changes have taken place in the world of political communication, and their cumulative effect has been to elevate "narrowcasting" over "broadcasting," that is, targeted pitches to particular constituencies rather than broad-gauge appeals to Middle America.

On the face of it, this is a story about democratization—about cutting out the middleman and facilitating greater responsiveness to and knowledge of voter sentiment. But, Balogh suggests, it is not anything like as simple as that, for the pollsters and consultants who now rule the roost invariably accentuate the divisions within the body politic, in ways that make campaigning more raw than before, and governing more difficult. Nowadays, the main role of parties and interest groups is to raise the vast sums that candidates need if they are to compete for office in the world of narrowcasting, and they raise those funds by stoking the flames of ideological enmity. Every aspect of this new communications regime militates against compromise and deal making.

This book seeks to stimulate additional historical work that analyzes presidential and midterm elections in a way that balances the benefits of a journalistic narrative, capturing the personalities and contingencies of each of these events, with the structural, economic, and institutional contexts that social scientists have shown play such a huge role in shaping the outcome. We hope to build on the scholarship in series such as that of the University Press of Kansas on elections with a conceptual and theoretical edge that connects these events to the broader evolution of the American state and the nation's communications infrastructure, as well as social and demographic changes. While the book does not provide a complete account of all elections, its contributors provide a bold point of departure for a new generation of scholars who share their interest in bringing elections back into the study of U.S. history.

CHAPTER 1

The Devolution of 1800: Jefferson's Election and the Birth of American Government

Jeffrey L. Pasley

American presidential campaigns have never been known for understatement, but one of the very first ones, Thomas Jefferson's victory over John Adams in 1800, has rarely been equaled for the epic sweep of its participants' rhetoric: "Republicans Rejoice! Our Country is saved from . . . counter revolution—from the fangs of an usurper," the New York *American Citizen* trumpeted. A song written to celebrate "Jefferson and Liberty" became an instant folk standard:

> The gloomy night before us flies,
> The reign of Terror now is o'er.

After several tense weeks of Electoral College deadlock, Jefferson's supporters threw boozy festivals and banquets in every major city and town, toasting their hero and the "bloodless revolution" they believed that his accession to the presidency represented. On the day of his inauguration, March 4, 1801, a holiday spirit was in the air. Some Jeffersonians toasted the day as a political Christmas, lifting their glasses to "the friends of liberty throughout the Universe, 'Peace on Earth, and good will Towards Men.'" Others, oddly, seemed to regard it more as Valentine's Day: "Our next administration, undefended by terror, but supported by love." Even in Connecticut, where Jefferson was righteously drubbed in the election, his acolytes held a "Republican Thanksgiving."[1]

In later life, Jefferson somewhat infamously took to calling his own election "the revolution of 1800." Historians and Adamses have scoffed at the phrase as an old man's tall tale ever since, pointing to the fact that President Jefferson did not immediately wreck the institutions that the Federalists had created (like the Bank of the United States) or forswear the use of his executive authority in dealing with unexpected foreign policy challenges such as extortion by North African pirates and Napoleon Bonaparte's offer to sell the French colony of Louisiana. Henry Adams, eager to vindicate his defeated ancestors, doubted that any Federalist president could have turned out "more Federalist than Jefferson himself." Even the devoted Jeffersonian Dumas Malone, author of a six-volume biography, thought the "revolution of 1800" was more semantic than anything else. Indeed, if one judges historical events by the standards of bloody social upheavals such as the French and Russian revolutions, as most scholars do in one way or another, then the election of 1800 is guaranteed to fall short. Cold War–era "consensus" historians like Malone were eager to disassociate Thomas Jefferson and James Madison from *that* kind of revolution, and later, more socially oriented scholars were no more inclined to accord that status to an event that directly involved relatively few people, no immediate social changes, and the rise of another slaveholder to the presidency. Hence it has become the custom to treat 1800 as representing little more than a slight power shift south from one faction of Founders to another, and to take a fashionably jaded view of Jefferson's "revolution."[2]

Yet considered in both a wider view and the narrower one recorded in toasts, speeches, and newspaper essays just after the fact, the term was neither an anachronism nor one that the candidate invented to aggrandize himself. Contemporaries agreed that a momentous event had taken place and really only disagreed on its polarity, whether it was a revolution accomplished or a counterrevolution thwarted, and how one should feel about either of those options.[3] Heads did not roll and society did not overturn, but the 1800 election was a revolution in political culture, the beginnings (if only the beginnings) of a popular if often not very admirable or honest democracy in which leaders tried to appear as friendly equals of the people who voted, rather than stern "Fathers of the State" like George Washington and John Adams. But while Jefferson certainly was the first president who came to power as "the People's Friend," what is striking upon returning to this campaign is how much about *government* it was; as Jefferson said, it represented "as real a revolution in the principles of our government as that of 1776 was in its form." The oppositions that the celebratory toasts and songs set up between love and terror, morning and night, and democracy versus monarchy (and "priestcraft") were all highly skewed and luridly colored encapsulations of two very real and very different visions of how the American government should operate under the Constitution.[4]

The emotional heat of Jefferson's Democratic-Republicans was directed especially at what they somewhat bombastically called the "Reign of Terror" under the John Adams administration. While relatively soft by French revolutionary standards (no guillotines), by American ones, the Federalist reign was a remarkable burst of "Hamiltonian energy" that seemed to its critics untrammeled by constitutional restraints and unreserved in its political and cultural nationalism. Fearing French invasion and subversion, Alexander Hamilton's followers in the Adams cabinet and Congress began building a navy, expanded the army and asserted national authority over the state militias, and created a kind of federal income tax, the Direct Tax of 1798, to pay for it all. This unexpected expansion of national power went along with a narrowing of national feeling, making citizenship and voting rights more difficult for immigrants and criticism of the government illegal. What seemed to be omissions or direct contradictions of the constitutional text were justified not only by the elastic clause that Hamilton had been using since the beginning of the government ("necessary and proper"), but also by using the rhetoric of the Preamble as a catchall, asserting the federal government's powers to do anything it needed to do for the "common defense" and "general welfare" of the nation. The new security program was put to immediate use. Troops were deployed against German tax protesters in eastern Pennsylvania, while a gadfly congressman and printers of opposition newspapers were thrown in jail. Dominated by men from the Bible Belt of the Early Republic, New England, the government's officials and supporters adopted an increasingly religious and nativist tone, declaring national days of prayer and smearing their opponents—often from the pulpit—as infidels, Illuminati, and "wild Irish."[5]

The inescapable and often stated crux of Federalist terror, as its victims saw it, was its apparent goal of establishing a submissive relationship between the government and the people, a relationship that critics described as essentially monarchical. Federalists had questioned the legitimacy of organized opposition to the federal government as soon as it appeared in the form of the *National Gazette* newspaper and the so-called Democratic-Republican Societies, political clubs that George Washington saw fit to officially denounce. None of the major Founders approved the idea of permanent, ongoing political parties, but the passionate debates over Hamilton's financial system and the proper American response to the French Revolution brought out starkly different approaches to opposition as a practical matter. Washington and most other Federalists took the position that in a government elected by the people, policy debates should be conducted by the people's representatives alone, and any effort to influence government from the outside, in the name of the people, was dangerous and inherently revolutionary. "Self-created societies" like the Democratic-Republican clubs lacked the standing to criticize duly elected officials, and when they did, it led to troubles like the Whiskey and Fries Rebellions in rural Pennsylvania. Federalists blamed these uprisings on Republican agitators in the city-based clubs and the press, even though the urban democrats had virtually no connection to the rebels or in many cases even much sympathy for them. "To Federalists," historian Johann Neem writes, "the rebels exemplified the danger of permitting organized opposition at any level," and they sought to "eliminate [that danger] altogether."[6]

The partisan intent of the Federalist crackdown on dissent was obvious. The Sedition Act targeting the opposition press was openly timed to coincide with the 1800 presidential campaign and set to expire just as the next president was inaugurated. By scaring off or silencing those inclined to speak, write, or organize against them, and fully using the constitutional leeway they gave themselves, Federalists allegedly hoped, as Democratic-Republican hyperbole put it, "to erect a Monarchy upon the ruins of [our] republican Constitution," in the sense of installing a national leadership that would be as stable and unchallenged as possible. Some Republicans used the monarchy charge quite literally, but their more sober comments indicate a more relatable concern about whether a democratic republic could arm and gird and empower itself so quickly without fundamentally changing its character: "Some honest men fear that a republican government can not be strong, that this Government is not strong enough," Jefferson said in his first inaugural address. Federalists had made their changes out of a "theoretic and visionary fear that this Government, the world's best hope" now that revolutionary France had collapsed into Napoleonic dictatorship, "may by possibility want energy to preserve itself." Here Jefferson had a point. Worried about a French invasion that never happened, the Federalists had convinced themselves that the opposition was the spearhead of a foreign conspiracy to engineer a bloody, atheistic revolution in the United States.[7]

What is particularly important for present purposes is the vindication that 1800–1801 represented for elections as a national institution. In question was just what presidential elections were going to be: genuine decision points where the voters rendered their judgment on the direction of national policy and the faithfulness of their constitutional officials or (in effect) plebiscites that reaffirmed the existing regime. Jefferson's followers took extreme pride in the fact that they had managed to make the election of 1800 the former, despite the Federalists' best efforts. "The Elective Franchise," they toasted, was "the high court of appeal for insulted freemen," and the Republicans had won their case, using only "representative democracy, with reason for its weapons and truth for its defence." The campaign had been largely conducted in the press and in the streets, with little overt participation from the candidates, and while the newly installed President Jefferson tried to distance himself from the vitriol of the campaign, he praised elections as a cornerstone of republican government, "a mild and safe corrective of abuses" that could otherwise only be changed by force, "lopped by the sword of revolution where peaceable remedies are unprovided." Jefferson and Madison liked the idea of ongoing political parties little more than Washington, Adams, and Hamilton—they hoped that the Federalists would fade away after they themselves took office—but they did not treat their Federalist critics as illegitimate participants in the political process.[8]

False equivalence can be as comfortable a myth for historians as it is for journalists, but it cannot stand in this case. The victorious Republicans largely stood by the First Amendment principles expressed during the 1800 campaign. No federal security legislation or sedition prosecutions were ever aimed at the Federalist opposition despite the overt disloyalty and obstruction that many New England Federalists displayed during the War of 1812. After the war, a Republican orator could boast with some accuracy that President James Madison had managed to get through a major foreign invasion (the only one any president has ever had to face) "without one trial for treason, or even one prosecution for libel." Localized violence against the press and a handful of state-level prosecutions did occur during the Jefferson and Madison years, but they involved both parties at various times, and the federal government asserted no authority over political expression. Later wartime presidents would show less restraint, but seditious libel, the doctrine that criminalized political speech during the 1790s, went into "a long eclipse" after 1800.[9]

The successful resort to electoral change devolved the duties of enforcing the Constitution, defending the government, and defining the nation (meaning the national culture) back on the people themselves and the institutions they were thought to have a more direct hand in, the state and local governments. Of course, one dimension of this devolution was protecting the ability of local elites in the South to manage their own "domestic concerns"—allowing slaveholders to protect slavery, in other words—but that was only occasionally mentioned in the 1800 campaign and not the principle being asserted. Nor was defending slavery the only purpose for which popular sovereignty could or would be used. Chief among the *stated* principles were equality before the law and tolerance of political, cultural, and social diversity. The government's watchword would be "equal and exact justice to all men, of whatever state or persuasion, religious or political," Jefferson said, a universalistic formulation that incorporated the racial and gender limits of the time without officially and explicitly enshrining them, an omission that proved crucial in the long run.[10]

The point of rehearsing all of this is to show that, as loud and empty and disappointing as they often are, elections have fundamentally shaped the United States, determining how the constitutional system works in practice and even some basic features of American culture. The rest of this chapter will look in more detail at some of the many ways that the election of 1800 redirected the country from the more authoritarian and monocultural path—unfriendly to dissent, unwelcoming to immigrants, and overtly Protestant—that the Federalists had embarked it on in the 1790s.[11]

Two Constitutionalisms

Despite the modern debates between proponents of the "living Constitution" and advocates of "original intent," Americans have long agreed that enforcing the Constitution is strictly a legal matter, something that lawyers argue and judges decide in the courts. But it was not so in the early years of the American Republic; before John Marshall, constitutional enforcement was a do-it-yourself project. (A Virginia Federalist appointed by John Adams just before the latter left office, Marshall began asserting the primacy of judicial review through the Supreme Court in direct response to the popular constitutionalism that had deposed his party, making the Court the Federalists' final and longest-lasting redoubt.) Though Americans had pioneered the idea of writing down the fundamental rules of their governments and treating these documents as a form of law, almost no one thought courts were or could or should be the sole means of enforcing those rules, as is the case in the twenty-first century. Following the unwritten British constitutional tradition and their own instincts, early Americans believed that keeping government within its constitutional limits was a duty that fell ultimately upon the people themselves. The people elected officials to various branches and levels of government. If the competition among these different representatives and institutions could not check violations of the Constitution, or if the representatives proved unfaithful, it was up to the people to defend their own rights with their votes, their voices, and their bodies if necessary.[12]

Along with these more popular ideas of how constitutions were enforced was a distinct notion of what they were for: to protect rights, of individuals and of the people as a whole. The world's first written constitutions were created by Pennsylvania and the other twelve original states at the beginning of American Revolution to replace a British regime the patriots believed had become abusive and tyrannical. These documents all included lengthy lists of the rights that their writers believed free governments were instituted to protect, but the unwritten British Constitution had not. With regard to the main rights at issue in the late 1790s, Pennsylvania's 1776 constitution had stated that "the people have a right to freedom of speech, and of writing, and publishing their sentiments; therefore the freedom of the press ought not to be restrained."[13]

If the early constitutions were all about asserting rights, the major purpose of the new federal Constitution framed in 1787 was quite different: creating a stronger central government that could finance itself and defend the country without depending on the states. The new goal of expanding the power of the national state—pushed by Alexander Hamilton and his coterie of wealthy, well-connected, mostly northeastern nationalists, later the core of the Federalist Party—led to a different, much less limiting form of constitutionalism. Hamilton did not believe in completely unlimited government or think that Americans would accept such a regime, but he and his allies deliberately erred on the side of strength. A bill of rights was intentionally kept out of the new frame of government on grounds that such protections were not needed: powers not granted, such as control over the press or religion, could not be exercised. That reassurance was undercut by the fact that some limitations on the new government *were* set in the Constitution, such as those against titles of nobility and ex post facto laws.[14]

More predictive of the future was Hamilton's argument in *Federalist* 84 that constitutional protections of individual rights, and indeed most textual limitations on government, would simply be ineffective in practice. It would be impossible, he contended, to define the people's liberties in any way that "would not leave the utmost latitude for evasion." Any real security that freedom of the press, freedom of religion, and other rights enjoyed, "whatever fine declarations may be inserted in any constitution respecting [them], must altogether depend on public opinion, and on the general spirit of the people and of the government." In other words, it was going to be politics, public debate, and elections through which Americans would have to "seek for the only solid basis of all [their] rights." This was a perceptive comment expressing a then-common understanding of constitutionalism quite different from the legalistic, judicial review–based approach that has come to be the dominant American mode. It was also not one that guided Hamilton in the way we might expect. For him, this insight led to, or perhaps sprang from, the conclusion that parsing constitutional texts was a waste of time unless challenged. The Constitution set up the broad framework of American government, but in terms of policies and working institutions, the federal government could do whatever it could accomplish and the people would accept.[15]

The Framers had inserted a clause to ensure that the new government had any powers deemed "necessary and proper" for executing the duties specifically mentioned in the Constitution. When challenged by Secretary of State Jefferson over the constitutionality of the proposed Bank of the United States, which required the use of a power to create corporations that the Constitution had not explicitly provided, Treasury Secretary Hamilton explained just how flexible he believed that elastic clause to be when he defined "necessary" not as indispensably necessary or absolutely required, but as "no more than needful, requisite, incidental, useful, or conducive to. It is a common mode of expression to say that it is necessary for a government or a person to do this or that thing, when nothing more is intended or understood, than that the interests of the government require, or will be promoted, but the doing of this or that thing." Hamilton took the view that the U.S. government enjoyed full sovereignty, and hence freedom of action, in any area it had been granted power over, including interstate commerce, public finance, foreign trade, and national defense. The Constitution did not explicitly prohibit national banks or corporations, so it must be assumed they were permissible. Restrictive textual interpretations that genuinely hampered or prevented "necessary" government actions would furnish "the singular spectacle of a political society without sovereignty, or a people governed without government."[16]

Simultaneously or even a little before Hamilton began arguing openly for his loose interpretation of "necessary and proper," promoters of the new federal Constitution were challenged by a popular constitutionalism that wanted the new government's limits more clearly marked out and rights protections reinstalled. Facing an outcry against the lack of a bill of rights, James Madison and other supporters of the federal Constitution were forced to promise in the ratification conventions and the first congressional election campaigns that explicit protections for freedom of the press, freedom of religion, and many other rights would be added as soon as the new Congress gathered. Madison fulfilled this promise himself as a congressman, but addressing Hamilton's critique of the state bills of rights in *The Federalist*, his constitutional amendments were worded very narrowly, avoiding vague, undefinable statements of principle in favor of relatively clear-cut prohibitions such as appeared in the First Amendment: "Congress shall make no law . . . abridging the freedom of speech, or of the press; or the right of the people peaceably to assemble, and to petition the Government for a redress of grievances."[17]

Appointed as the first Treasury secretary, Alexander Hamilton did not allow the inclusion of rights protection language (which he considered a sop to critics not meant to have any functional impact) to slow him down. Acting in effect as President Washington's prime minister, Hamilton proceeded to implement his financial policies and set a series of precedents about how the government would actually operate that skated over apparent limitations in the constitutional text. With little success, Secretary of State Thomas Jefferson attempted to fight Hamilton within the cabinet. As he told President Washington, Jefferson believed Hamilton's relaxed reading of the Constitution as allowing any government action that was conducive to its general purposes to be tantamount to no constitutional limitations at all. "To take a single step beyond the boundaries" that the Constitution specifically drew, he argued, was to "to take possession of a boundless field of power, no longer susceptible of any definition."[18]

Toward 1796: The Rise of a Democratic Opposition

Jefferson got very little traction with his constitutional arguments until a more public opposition developed, aimed at shaping popular opinion and using it to win elections. More successful than debating with Hamilton behind the scenes was Jefferson's turn to what I have called "newspaper politics," a phenomenon that eventually provoked the most flagrant constitutional violations of the Federalist "Reign of Terror," which itself became the major losing issue in the election of 1800. Trying to reach for public support outside the government without leaving it, and believing that newspapers had been the Americans' greatest political weapon during the Revolution, Jefferson and disillusioned nationalist James Madison arranged the founding of a Philadelphia newspaper, the *National Gazette*, edited by Madison's old Princeton roommate, the poet Philip Freneau. Saddled with a flawed business model that tried to rely on subscribers around the country instead of on advertisements, Freneau's *Gazette* lasted only two years, but it pioneered the formula that would be successful in 1800, emotionally framing the developing party struggle in Philadelphia as a desperately compelling one for every American, a battle between "the general mass of the people, attached to their republican government and republican interests, and the chosen band devoted to monarchy and mammon." Monarchy became the key thematic figure in the effort to popularize opposition to what seemed to its detractors a constitutionally unrestrained government, under the control of wealthy northeastern financial and mercantile interests and far too admiring of the political and economic model of Great Britain. Freneau's stated goal was getting readers into a "*phrenzy of thinking for themselves*"; and he did his best work in the form of satires such as his "Rules for changing a limited Republican Government into an unlimited hereditary one," which still circulates on the Internet today in mutated forms.[19]

Stepping in to fill the gap left by the failure of the *National Gazette* was the Philadelphia *Aurora General Advertiser.* Benjamin Franklin Bache founded the newspaper in 1790, using the printing facility his namesake grandfather built especially for him on Market Street. Bache's ardent sympathies with the Revolution in France (where he spent much of his childhood accompanying Ben Franklin on his diplomatic mission) made his newspaper a gold mine of information on European affairs but also led it to bitterly oppose what he and many others felt was the Washington administration's British-tilted foreign policy.[20] Meanwhile, the *Aurora* attracted a small network of like-minded Republican newspapers in Boston, New York, and other major towns, all of which republished each other's essays and satires and kept locals abreast of national political events. In a time when parties were completely uninstitutionalized, reading a party newspaper was the essence and only real embodiment of party membership.

As domestic opposition to the Hamiltonian regime grew, transatlantic pressures mounted along with (and augmented) them. When war broke out between Great Britain and the French Republic, both sides preyed on American trade and tried to influence American politics. One major form of

British influence was incidental. Faced with domestic reform movements sympathetic to the French Revolution, the British authorities cracked down harshly on political dissent and public assemblies, sending a wave of refugee radicals fleeing across the ocean to America. Many of them ended up working in the opposition press, greatly radicalizing its rhetoric and striking fear in Federalist hearts. Two of the most infamous ended up working at the *Aurora*. Scotsman James Thomson Callender wrote pamphlets lambasting the Federalists and the British, one of which both accused Alexander Hamilton of insider trading and exposed his bribery of his mistress Maria Reynolds's husband. Irishman William Duane, who became Bache's assistant and eventual successor as editor of the *Aurora*, arrived in America a refugee from British persecution twice over. A printer by trade, Duane had emigrated to India and started a successful newspaper there, only to be summarily expelled from the country and stripped of his property for mild complaints about the British East India Company. Finding work in London, Duane got swept up in working-class politics, becoming a leader in the London Corresponding Society and a writer for the London radical press just in time to be forced into exile again. Determined not to be bullied out of a third country, Duane naturally sided with the anti-British Republicans, publishing a pamphlet against President Washington soon after his arrival, and then joining the *Aurora*'s small staff.[21]

The opposition press came into its own during the 1795–96 controversy over the Jay Treaty, a trade agreement with Great Britain regarded in radical circles as a gross capitulation to the British and a betrayal of America's Revolutionary War ally, France. Though the Senate met in secret session to ratify the treaty, Bache obtained a leaked text, printed thousands of copies, and personally took some north to New York and Boston while a fellow Democratic Society member headed south. Giant political rallies met Bache at his major stops. When a rather contrived constitutional showdown in the House of Representatives failed, with the antitreaty forces trying to invalidate the ratified treaty by blocking appropriations needed to implement it, the *Aurora* and its allies turned to the goal of electing a different president in 1796, first by hounding George Washington out of office and then by electing Thomas Jefferson in his place. Among the high- or lowlights of the *Aurora*'s campaign was a vicious transatlantic anti-endorsement from Tom Paine, who accused Washington of (among other crimes and misdemeanors) having a "cold hermaphrodite" personality incapable of true loyalty or real friendships.[22]

With Washington on his way out, the Democratic-Republicans mounted a strong challenge to his belatedly revealed heir apparent, Vice President John Adams, but fell just short of electing Thomas Jefferson in 1796. As they had done to win final approval of the Jay Treaty, the Federalists mobilized the resources of what we would now call the business community (then dominated by all-purpose merchants who were often shipowners and financiers as well) to beat back the opposition threat. Following the lead of Hamilton (and to some degree Edmund Burke), pamphleteering Federalist congressman William Loughton Smith of South Carolina launched an anti-intellectual attack on Jefferson as an airy dilettante and moral lightweight whose speculative bent and physical cowardice suited him much better "for a professorship in a college" than the presidency. Smith and other Federalists also tried to shear off some of Jefferson's southern support by spreading the story that he had "cut and run" before a British invasion as war governor of Virginia and emphasizing the fact that his philosophical speculations included opposition to slavery.[23]

At the same time, the anti-Christian excesses of the French Revolution and Tom Paine's recently published deist tract *The Age of Reason* allowed Smith and Hamilton to label Jefferson and his followers threats to American Christianity, alleging that their advocacy for religious freedom masked their true agenda of "freedom *from* religion." Many Federalists had come to the conclusion that appeals to Christianity were the best means they had to rally ordinary Americans against the putative standard of democracy (a bad thing by Federalist lights, associated with French Jacobinism and mob rule), especially those who made up their New England base. Acting as President Washington's ghostwriter, Hamilton inserted several paragraphs into the Farewell Address extolling the crucial role of Christianity as "a necessary spring" in foreign policy, public finance, and basic social order. Jefferson's liberal views on religious toleration were depicted as both a character flaw and a failure of leadership, undermining the "indispensable supports" of social order and good government, religion, and morality: "In vain would that man claim the tribute of patriotism, who should labor to subvert these great pillars of human happiness."[24]

Federalist fear and anger were galvanized and somewhat substantiated by France's interference in the 1796 election. French minister Pierre Adet published an open letter to the government in the *Aurora* just days before the popular voting in the key swing state of Pennsylvania, hinting heavily at war if the United States did not abandon the policy of submitting to British trade regulations set by the Jay Treaty. The threats seemed to help Jefferson carry Pennsylvania, but the backlash elsewhere (along with the Federalist campaign) cost him enough southern electoral votes, including one in Virginia, to come in second to John Adams. The Democratic-Republicans had proved themselves a viable opposition party, but the Federalists ended up with the largest majority in Congress they would ever enjoy.

In "Defence of the Country": The Alien and Sedition Acts

By the time John Adams took office, the Federalist majority was ready for war against enemies without and within. The French had begun seizing American ships and grossly insulted American diplomats by demanding payment in advance of a meeting (the XYZ Affair). Revanche American-style was on. The one true presidential election cartoon of this whole era, "The Providential Detection," captures this spirit well (see Figure 1).

In May 1797, President John Adams called a special session of the new Congress to recommend "effectual measures of defense" and received authorization to call up eighty thousand troops from the state militias, outfit three frigates, and secure the harbors against attack. Adams's first annual message in November struck an even more alarmist posture, reaching back to the by then long gone French Revolution to give social and cultural heft to the foreign policy crisis: "The state of society has so long been disturbed, the sense of moral and religious obligations so much weakened, public faith and national honor have been so impaired," the president warned, that "permanent tranquility and order" would not be back soon.[25]

In response, congressional Federalists formed a Committee for the Protection of Commerce and the Defence of the Country, under the chairmanship of Representative Samuel Sewall of Massachusetts. The title turned out to chiefly mean defense of the existing regime against subversion and opposition. A committee report in May recommended "precautions against the promiscuous reception and residence of aliens," including stricter regulation of the movements and the naturalization prospects of immigrants based largely on assumptions about their politics. (There were a number of exiled British radicals working in the opposition press, but Federalists were just as worried about a much larger number of new arrivals not connected with politics, especially French who had fled from the revolution in Haiti but

Figure 1. Artist unknown, "The Providential Detection" (1797–1800). God watches as the American eagle protects the Constitution from Thomas Jefferson. Copyprint of lithograph. Courtesy of the American Antiquarian Society, Worcester, MA.

were themselves suspected as revolutionaries based on their nationality alone.) Collectively these became known as the "alien laws." The loudest of the Federalists made it clear that what many of them had in mind was a rethink of the whole idea of U.S. citizenship as a circle that would be extended to new arrivals through naturalization. South Carolina's Robert Goodloe Harper argued that "it was essential policy, which lay at the bottom of civil society, that none but persons born in the country should be permitted to take a part in the Government." Federalists envisioned a kind of guest worker or permanent resident status for immigrants, similar to how many ethnic and religious minorities—sometimes majorities—lived (and still live) in the rest of the world. This vision was not fully carried out, but the Naturalization Act of 1798 lengthened the probationary period and stiffened the legal requirements enough to raise the prospect that few adult immigrants would ever live to vote or hold office in America.[26]

The immigrants that the Defence Committee were most concerned about were the refugee radicals like Duane and Callender, and Sewall's committee took aim at them much more directly with a bill "for the prevention and restraint of dangerous and seditious persons." This measure authorized the banishment from the country of any immigrant who had been convicted of "seditious practices" in another country or fled from such a charge (therefore adopting in the United States, Great Britain's crackdown on dissent)—or whom the president simply "deemed" was "a dangerous person." Here the Federalists were grabbing for a war power before war had been declared, applying the practices used against enemy aliens to *all* immigrants based on their politics. Worse, they justified the measure constitutionally by citing the Preamble as a kind of blanket authorization, with Sewall reading it into the record at the beginning of the debate. Massachusetts congressman Harrison Gray Otis reasoned that if the United States had "a right to make war for the common defence and general welfare," it had the right "to do everything . . . necessary to prepare" for defense, such as neutralizing dissenters: "If we find men in this country endeavoring to spread sedition and discord; who have assisted in laying other countries prostrate; whose hands are reeking with blood, and who hearts rankle with hatred towards us—have we not the power to shake off these firebrands?" Taken aback by the storm of constitutional protest, Otis gave a puzzled but revealing summation of the two constitutionalisms, the newer Hamiltonian one that saw such documents as primarily frameworks for making government more energetic and efficient, versus the older popular understanding of them (reflected in the first wave of state constitutions) primarily as barriers or standards meant to measure and protect rights. Otis "considered and followed the Constitution as a lamp to his path," he said, whereas the other side "would make it a mere *ignis fatuus*, calculated to bewilder and mislead."[27]

The most worrisome thing about the émigré "firebrands" was that many of them were journalists. If Jefferson and his allies issued more paeans to the healing powers of publicity and truth, it was the Federalists who, like many conservatives after them, seemed to place the highest estimation on the press's influence. "Give to any set of men the command of the press, and you give them command of the country," Judge Alexander Addison lectured from the bench. "Dangerous men" could not be left in charge of it, and that included not just immigrants like William Duane and James Thomson Callender, but also homegrown incendiaries like Benjamin Franklin Bache. There was raw politics in this determination, the Federalist desire to shut down their critics, but also raw fear. The bloody "spirit of jacobinism" had acquired "a more gigantic body" and was "armed with more powerful weapons than it ever before possessed," Alexander Hamilton wrote after the Republican press forced him to publicly admit his sexual indiscretion with Maria Reynolds. "It threatens more extensive and complicated mischiefs to the world than . . . the three great scourges of mankind, WAR PESTILENCE and FAMINE" and "the political and moral world with a complete overthrow."[28]

The bill for "the punishment of certain crimes," a.k.a. the Sedition Act, had originally been introduced as part of the Sewell committee's omnibus measure against "seditious practices," but it was later spun off into its own infamous piece of legislation. It made criticism of the government a criminal offense, imposing penalties of up to $2,000 and two years in prison on anyone who should "write, print, utter, publish, or shall cause or procure to be written, printed, uttered, or published . . . any false, scandalous and malicious writing or writings against the government of the United States . . . with intent to defame the said government" or its officials "or to bring them . . . into contempt or disrepute; or to excite against them the hatred of the good people of the United States." As the Federalists well knew, this made it almost impossible for a democratic opposition to function: one could hardly protest a government policy or campaign against an incumbent officer without trying to bring one of them into some degree of public "contempt or disrespute." Following the most progressive legal standards of the day, the Sedition Act allowed defendants to exonerate themselves if they could prove their assertions were true. Yet, as Republicans pointed out, truth was useless as a defense in matters of political interpretation and opinion. In practice, and on the same grounds, most Federalist judges did not allow evidence of truth to even be presented in the Sedition Act cases.[29]

It would have been hard to invent a more clear-cut way to highlight the two constitutionalisms and pit them against each other. No one in the opposition needed a constitutional lawyer to tell them that the "Congress shall make no law" stipulation in the First Amendment obviously barred something like the Sedition Act. The Federalists had introduced the legislation "from excessive love of the constitution," the *Aurora* noted drily when the bill passed. Bache and Duane and their editorial allies had few illusions about what it would take to overrule the law. The courts would be no help. Instead, the opposition would have to stand and fight in the arena of public debate, and eventually at the ballot box. Without such active citizenship, "no Constitution however excellent, ever yet secured, or ever will secure the interest of the governed against those who govern," a widely republished item asserted. Continued political criticism and organization against men in power were the only things that could stop repressive, unconstitutional measures like the Sedition Act: "If through the fear of incurring the pain and penalties of this same sedition bill, individuals are deterred from animadverting on the conduct of those employed in public affairs, then farewell to Liberty." Luckily, most or enough of the Democratic-Republican editors were far from deterred, and particularly not the truculent duo of Bache and Duane.[30]

The Federalist drive to unite the country culturally—defining Americanism according to the homogeneously Protestant model of New England, where few immigrants had come since the seventeenth century and the old Puritan churches were still tax-supported—proceeded at the same time. While this campaign primarily sought to rally the Federalists' northeastern base, it had plenty of appeal to the pious Christians, nativists, and fearers of revolution who lived in other Federalist centers such as northern Virginia, the South Carolina Low Country, and the silk-stocking Quaker neighborhoods of Philadelphia. The Northeast's Federalist clergy were highly politicized and included such nationally prominent figures as the president of Yale College (Reverend Timothy Dwight) and the author of America's most popular schoolbook (Reverend Jedidiah Morse). They busied themselves promoting a popular European conservative conspiracy theory about the Order of the Illuminati, a long-suppressed Bavarian secret society posited as the secret instigator of the French Revolution and now said to be bent on destroying all world religions and active in America.[31] As John Adams's reelection approached, Federalists tried to rally good Christians against his "infidel" opponent, issuing sermon pamphlets with titles like *The Voice of Warning* and deploying what amounted to a new religious test for high officeholders. How could Christians claim to take their faith seriously if they voted for a "professed deist" like Thomas Jefferson? How could a United States ruled by Jefferson call itself a "Christian nation"? What did they think Lord Jesus would want them to do?[32]

Though undoing the separation of church and state was not part of the congressional Federalists' legislative agenda, the idea was in the air. New

England Federalists still bitterly defended their "Standing Order" of established churches and politicized clergy. Republican congressman Edward Livingston of New York raised the possibility that Federalist constitutionalism opened the way for the U.S. government to decree cultural uniformity in addition to the political kind. If "make no law" did not bar a sedition law, then there was nothing to stop the congressional majority from immediately establishing "a national religion . . . on the ground that uniformity of worship" promoted the general welfare better than "a diversity of worship." That bill was not introduced, but the thinking was there in the Federalist campaign. "Our difficulties and sins" as a nation, wrote Reverend John Mitchell Mason, "may be traced to this pernicious notion" that "religion has nothing do with politics." If American Christians let their religion guide them more, the Federalist clergy suggested, things would go much better.[33]

The High Court of Public Opinion Rules: The Election of 1800

The Republican opposition tried multiple methods of popular constitutionalism to bring the Federalists and their interpretations down. Jefferson and Madison themselves spent their time on an abortive effort to get the state legislatures to pass resolutions declaring the Alien and Sedition Acts unconstitutional. Only Virginia and Kentucky did so, with all the others rejecting the disastrous concepts of state interposition and nullification that would eventually spawn secession.

A free press, free speech, and a literal interpretation of the Constitution won out in the end because the *Aurora* and the Republican newspaper network it led were still standing in 1801 when Thomas Jefferson and a new congressional majority took office, self-consciously owing much of their victory to the press. In fact, despite the repression campaign, there were many more opposition newspapers by the end of the 1800 campaign than there had been before the Sedition Act was passed, and the *Aurora* had grown even more influential.

It was not that the Federalists didn't try. Led by glowering Secretary of State Timothy Pickering, the Adams administration carried out a strenuous program of harassment against Republican printers, speakers, and writers. Both *Aurora* editors and most of the other major Republican journalists in Boston, New York, and many other places were prosecuted under the new laws, and many were jailed, including Representative Matthew Lyon of Vermont. And the harassments went far beyond the Sedition Act prosecutions. Mobs attacked the *Aurora* building (also the Bache family home) repeatedly, and the editors were assaulted in the streets and in their offices. The government charged Bache with "treasonable correspondence" in addition to seditious libel; he died of yellow fever in a September 1798 epidemic while awaiting trial.[34]

His successor, William Duane, endured an even more epic struggle with the authorities. Duane was charged with "seditious riot" for trying to collect signatures against the Alien Acts outside a Catholic church. Acquitted in a circus-like trial, he was immediately targeted again, for insinuations that British secret service money had been used to influence American politics. Unfortunately for the prosecutors, the *Aurora* had obtained a letter making the very same charge from the hand of John Adams himself, during his vice presidency. With Adams's encouragement, Secretary of State Pickering combed through the *Aurora* for more actionable items and had Duane indicted again for criticizing the newly expanded federal military forces, which Republicans believed were being used to frighten dissenters rather than preparing to fight the French. A gang of soldiers returning from the so-called Fries Rebellion of 1799 took revenge for Duane's comments by pulling him from behind his desk for a pummeling and whipping in the street outside, mayhem interrupted only by the intervention of his teenaged son. At the same time, machinery was set in motion to have Duane banished as an undesirable alien, a complicated matter since he was born in colonial New York![35]

The Sedition Act had been framed with the *Aurora* in mind, but far from quieting the opposition's journalistic ringleader, these tactics actually resulted in increasing the volume and political effectiveness of its output. Insulting George Washington and cheerleading for the French Revolution gave way to detailed accounts of the editors' persecutions that dramatized in real life and real time the dangers of the expansive powers the Federalists were claiming. Bache published a lengthy pamphlet about the attempted suppression of the *Aurora*, *Truth Will Out!*

The injured Duane answered his beating by the soldiers with a long narrative of the incident in the next day's *Aurora*, under the heading "MORE OF GOOD ORDER AND REGULAR GOVERNMENT!" The accounts of Bache's and Duane's sufferings were reprinted in Republican newspapers throughout the country, and when brother editors were victimized in their turn, their sagas were publicized in the *Aurora*. More Federalist repression and chicanery just meant more bad publicity and worse electoral fortunes. When a Senate bill that would have changed Electoral College procedures to lessen Republican chances in 1800 was leaked and published in the *Aurora*, Duane was charged with contempt of Congress and forced into hiding for a time. His paper continued to appear and kept up a steady barrage all the while, ever adding to its long list of Federalist scandals and outrages. Duane turned the religious aspects of the Federalist campaign back on his opponents as well, dubbing Timothy Dwight the "Pope of New England" and dredging up embarrassments from the Puritan past such as blue laws and witch trials.[36]

Provided with such excellent material, the Republican press became the crucial element in the defeat of John Adams that vindicated the constitutional protection of press freedom and religious diversity. This verdict was rendered by the electoral system and the court of public opinion, rather than courts of law. The Federalists' attempt to use monoculturalism and the force of government to suppress opposition completely failed as politics. As the Democratic-Republicans of New York City declared in a toast to the defeated incumbent in March 1801, presidents and congressional majorities needed to learn the lesson that transgression of popularly understood constitutional limits could be punished by the loss of their offices. "John Adams—May his merited fate for opposing the general will and sanctioning acts hostile to our free constitution, be a lasting *memento* to his successors," they proclaimed, and so it was.[37] The Constitution's limits would become a live and permanent impediment to the accretion of federal power and the invasion of individual rights, albeit in different ways at different times. The federal government would accomplish much in the nineteenth century, but only in negotiation with the states and with only the most intermittent use of the direct and flexible powers that Alexander Hamilton tried to establish. With the temporary exceptions of the Civil War and the very brief one of World War I, the federal government arguably would not return to the directly coercive, nationally centralized, and permanently militarized state that the Federalists had tried to build until the Cold War era.

Governing Without Government

The word"devolution" in the title of this chapter is meant to encapsulate the characteristic type of American government that emerged from Jefferson's election: a significant institution with real influence, but also one genuinely hemmed in by the Constitution and forced to operate with regard to voters more by persuasion and feeling ("love") than coercion. The emphatically national and freely acting U.S. government that Federalists envisioned would instead be part of a truly federal system where the governments with the most effect on people's daily lives were those of the states and local communities they lived in. While this is not a development to be uncritically celebrated, it certainly does represent a devolution of power, and a dispensation more consistent with the constitutionalism of the American Revolution.[38]

Jefferson provided a mission statement for the new dispensation in his first inaugural address. The American Republic was an experiment, he argued, in a new and better form of government that would not exercise power in the forceful way that previous governments had. Hamilton believed that the only way a republic could be strong enough to survive was for it to partly embrace the old way, for the United States to be as rich and militarily powerful and sometimes as repressive as the British government was. As Jefferson saw it, the American Republic could and should do things differently. It could withstand criticism and opposition from within without becoming oppressive. It could be great without being a military empire. Democracy was the government's strength, Jefferson believed, not a source of weakness or a necessary evil: "I believe this, on the contrary, the strongest Government on earth. I believe it the only one where every man, at the call of the law, would fly to the standard of the law, and would meet invasions of the public order as his own personal concern." Like his followers, Jefferson kept returning to the figure of monarchy as a stand-in for all unlimited or authoritarian government. "Sometimes it is said that man can not be trusted with the government of himself. Can he, then, be trusted with the government of others? Or have we found angels in the forms of kings to govern him? Let history answer this question."[39]

At any rate, what Jefferson was announcing in his inaugural address was a serious effort to try this experiment for real. Adams family sour grapes aside, Jefferson's administration marked significant changes in policy and methods, even if not the irresponsible and dangerous ones Federalists warned about, such as defaulting on the national debts or closing the churches. While Hamilton had kept his congressional coalition together with aggressive agenda setting and bank stock, Jefferson relied on party loyalty and dinner parties: persuasion, in other words. Soft power was the order of the day, even in foreign policy. John Adams had bucked most of his Federalist allies and made peace with France in the last weeks of his administration, earning a furious pamphlet from Hamilton in return. Peace left Jefferson and the new Republican congresses free to reverse the expansion of the military and the income tax that had come with the expectations of war. To deal with the British and the French, Jefferson and Madison relied heavily if not very effectively on "peaceable coercion," especially trade sanctions like the 1807–9 embargo against all foreign commerce, meant to induce warring France and Great Britain to respect American neutrality. The example of Jeffersonian constitutionalism most heavily disputed by historians is the Louisiana Purchase of 1803, but it was actually quite consistent with his "soft," limited approach. When the Mississippi valley seemed about to fall to Napoleon, the Federalists called for an invasion, but Jefferson sought to purchase access instead. That option required a little constitutional embroidery, but also much more limited use of the president's and the federal government's powers than the alternative. Only a nation's "inherent right to acquire territory" had to be extrapolated, which seemed basic enough to Jefferson to present "no constitutional difficulty" with the purchase. The fact that Jefferson and his party paused to consider and debate the constitutionality of such a gift horse as the French offer to sell all of Louisiana showed just how much change had occurred. The constitutional text now provided serious impediments to government actions, ones that subsequent administrations would take even more seriously than Jefferson.[40]

Even Federalists started to throw up roadblocks, with Alexander Hamilton appearing in the unlikely position of free speech advocate. At the same time, Adams-appointed Chief Justice John Marshall began building up the court's power over constitutional interpretation, and influence over the federal government's conduct, with his decision against the Jefferson administration in *Marbury v. Madison*.[41]

Federalist-like efforts at forced cultural cohesion and the regulation of dissent were largely omitted, too. The Alien Acts were mostly rolled back, and having carried New York and Pennsylvania for Jefferson, the future Democratic Party began its lifelong romance with immigrant voters across most ethnic groups, a relationship that extended to the support of "alien suffrage," or the extension of voting rights to noncitizens, at various points in the nineteenth century. The Sedition Act lapsed the day John Adams left office, and the Federalist press (imitating Republican newspaper politics) raged even more bitterly and extensively than before throughout the Jefferson and Madison administrations. Yet Federalist printers remained untouched by the federal government, even during a real-life foreign invasion in the War of 1812. Meanwhile, Jefferson went out of his way to make it clear that church and state would remain rigorously divided by "a wall of separation" under his watch, inviting Tom Paine for an extended stay in the White House to show how little he cared for the rantings of Yankee divines. Neither Christianity nor Jefferson's popularity suffered at all. In the election years of 1802 and 1804, the Democratic-Republicans made heavy inroads into the Federalists' New England base, while religious revivals swept the South and the West. Federalist warnings turned out to be wrong as well as unpopular. Perhaps most importantly, and contrary to Federalist hopes, the use of competitive elections focused on seeking the favor of an expanding pool of voters never ceased, carrying forward even as the major parties fell, rose, and changed names. The decisive shift away from property requirements toward "universal" suffrage (meaning all adult white men before the Civil War) came in the wake of Jefferson's victory, and presidential elections changed too, with legislative selection of presidential electors becoming increasingly rare. The partisan press that the Federalists had tried to stamp out, having been credited with Jefferson's victory, multiplied across the country as competing parties and factions and social movements all sought to grasp that weapon for themselves. The era of mass parties, with Jacksonian Democrats squaring off against Whig counterparts, could never have developed without the changes that 1800 set in motion.[42]

The rise of political democracy did not make the nineteenth-century United States a paradise of social justice and effective governance. Slavery and its power grew, Native Americans bore the brunt of willy-nilly expansion, and the free, partisan press became a vast fount of invective and corruption as well as political information. What is certain, however, is that it was a vastly different place than it would have been had the election of 1800 turned out differently.[43]

CHAPTER 2

The Bombshell of 1844

Sean Wilentz

The presidential race of 1844 does not rank among the most memorable. Nor, judged by certain conventional academic standards, was it especially important, as compared with, say, the supposedly "critical" elections of 1828 and 1860. Aficionados of political trivia know that 1844 brought the first victory by a dark horse candidate, the Democrat James K. Polk. Arguably, it was also the first national election decided by a third party, in this instance the abolitionist Liberty Party. Among professional specialists, voting returns from 1844 helped inspire the once fashionable ethnocultural school's analysis of Jacksonian-era politics, but when that school's influence waned, so did scholarly interest in the 1844 election.[1]

In fact, the election of 1844, as a few recent studies have rediscovered, was profoundly important, and from numerous perspectives. A presentist interpretation comes to mind that likens the purposeful (alternatively, mendacious) James K. Polk to George W. Bush. By these lights, the extremely tight election of 1844 looks like the extremely tight election of 2000, the Liberty Party candidate James G. Birney looks like the Green Party candidate Ralph Nader, and the war against Mexico foreshadows the invasion of Iraq. Something of the intellectual impulse behind making those parallels informs recent reappraisals of the election's outcome. One major study, for example, portrays Polk's victory as a calamitous turning point that led to the unjustified imperialist, proslavery invasion of Mexico. Consequently, so the argument goes, if Polk's Whig opponent, Henry Clay, had won, the Civil War could at the very least have been forestalled—

and thus the 1844 election turns out to have been among "the most momentous in American history."[2]

To be sure, historians interested in the Civil War's origins have long recognized that Polk's defeat of Clay made an enormous difference. Yet 1844's importance extends beyond the election's portentous result. It was not, by any means, a realigning "critical" election in which one dominant party coalition gave way to another. Instead, 1844 might be called a consolidating election, one that affirmed the Jacksonian Democrats and the Whigs as evenly matched national organizations built on partisan instead of sectional loyalties. After a period of fluidity following Andrew Jackson's election in 1828, the Whig Party had come into existence over the winter of 1833–34. Not until 1840, though, did a rising group of new school Whig managers crush the Democrats with their Log Cabin campaign, which carried party organization to the county, township, and ward level throughout the country. The election of 1844 secured the Whigs' mass electoral base, just as it secured the Democrats' base. It helped to establish what an important study of Congress has called "the shrine of party" that some historians say dominated American politics in the 1840s and early 1850s.[3]

Here, though, lies a paradox. As hard-fought and balanced as the election of 1844 was, it also marked the beginning of the end of Jacksonian-era politics and the so-called second party system, destroyed by controversies over slavery and slavery's future—the very issues that the designers of the system had wanted to suppress. The Liberty Party campaign was a signal of the sectional breach. More important, dissension among the Democrats over the possible immediate annexation of Texas rattled the intersectional accord that had held the party together since its inception. The Texas annexation issue also bedeviled Clay and the Whigs, and contributed mightily to their defeat. For the first time in American history, conflicts connected to slavery transformed the dynamics of a presidential election. Thereafter, slavery would be important to every national election through the climactic contest of 1860. A stabilizing election also proved to be the pivotal election in setting the nation on the course to the Civil War.

This paradox complicates contending lines of interpretation about the war's political background. The parties' consolidation in 1844 jibes with so-called revisionist claims that cross-sectional partisan alliances remained sturdy and that slavery did not become a truly disruptive national political issue until the mid-1850s. The storm over Texas annexation, however, conforms to so-called fundamentalist claims that slavery, the basic cause of the Civil War, disrupted the Jacksonian party system as early as the 1840s. Apparently, political stability, defined as abiding partisan loyalties, could cloak increasingly fierce sectional divisions over slavery.[4]

This paradox, though, is still not the most remarkable thing about the political drama of 1844. Historians have richly chronicled the decline and fall of the formidable Jacksonian party system as the prelude to southern secession and civil war. But we have yet to appreciate fully how in 1844, just as that system came into its own, one man managed, as much as was humanly possible, to bend a presidential election to his will. The idea that a single political leader could have achieved as much seems mildly heretical, a return to discredited Great Man theories of history. But that is precisely what John C. Calhoun did. Any trustworthy account of the 1844 election must explain how and why Calhoun succeeded.

To be sure, except for the ambitions and the maneuvering of the accidental President Tyler and of numerous political factions, and except for a completely fortuitous shipboard tragedy, Calhoun would never have been in the position to accomplish so much. Nor was Calhoun omnipotent, the dictator of events. The importance of context, coincidence, chance, and unintended consequences in 1844 precludes turning back the clock to biographical Great Man history. Yet institutions, political symbols, and abstract social forces—the favored subjects of current scholarship—neither change historical contexts nor take advantage of those changes; people do. In 1844 one man did above all others, altering the election's significance as well as its outcome. He did so in part by driving the slavery issue like a wedge into the center of national politics. The political parties—and the nation—would never be the same.

Clay vs. Van Buren: A Sure Thing?

For a quarter of a century, the specter of the Missouri crisis of 1819–21 had haunted American politics. The battles in Congress over banning slavery in Missouri had raised virtually all of the issues and ideas that would eventually lead to secession and Civil War. "Here was a new party ready formed," John Quincy Adams famously wrote of the northern antislavery bloc, "terrible to the whole Union, but portentously terrible to the South—threatening in its progress the emancipation of all their slaves."[5] Only clever political maneuvering by moderates led by the Speaker of the House, Henry Clay, forged the compromise that calmed the fury.

The Democratic Party created several years later by Martin Van Buren and the supporters of Andrew Jackson, as well as the Whig Party of Clay that emerged a few years after that, was determined to prevent any such crisis from recurring. Michael F. Holt has summarized how, thereafter, partisan conflict over banks, tariffs, and internal improvements contained the sectional issues: "As long as the parties fought with each other over national and state matters, voters developed allegiances that often became their preeminent identification. . . . As long as men thought in old party terms, long-standing sectional differences over Negro slavery could not produce sectional disruption."[6]

In the early 1830s, states' rights, proslavery South Carolinians, led by then former vice president John C. Calhoun, tested the nation's will by trying to nullify the federal tariff, only to be forcefully checked by President Jackson. At decade's end, a band of northern Whig congressmen, led by John Quincy Adams, took up the antislavery cause in the name of defying the gag rule in the House of Representatives that barred debate over petitions received from the growing radical abolitionist movement. The abolitionists themselves divided in 1839 and 1840, as one frustrated wing of the movement broke away to form the Liberty Party, which aimed to squelch slavery using political means that included election campaigns.

Still, as the 1844 election approached, there was no reason to believe that slavery would enter in. The Liberty Party had won a negligible national vote in 1840; its highest statewide total, in Massachusetts, was just 1.28 percent. The slaveholder Virginian and crypto-Democrat John Tyler's accession to the presidency as a Whig after William Henry Harrison's sudden death in 1841 had scrambled the victorious Whig Party. Plunged into all-out war with the administration, the party's leading figure, Senator Henry Clay, found his popularity rise ever higher. Tyler, provoked and ambitious, planned to launch an independent campaign in 1844 with a pro-southern, states' rights platform, but he lacked a compelling issue, and he owned the backing of what Clay ridiculed as a knot of cronies too small "to compose a decent *corporal's guard*."[7]

By the end of 1843, state Democratic Party conventions were rapidly throwing their support to Martin Van Buren. The former president, a chief architect of the original Jacksonian coalition, had been building support among party leaders for years, hoping to avenge his loss in 1840 to Harrison and the Log Cabin Whigs. Clay, meanwhile, had a lock on the Whig nomination. The anticipated Clay–Van Buren matchup would highlight old party divisions over tariffs, banks, and internal improvements, to the exclusion, as ever, of slavery. But thanks chiefly to John C. Calhoun, it was not to be.

Calhoun had been trying to win the presidency for two decades, and he tried again in preparation for 1844. No party loyalist, he hoped to win the Democratic nomination in order to unite the slave South under his proslavery leadership. At its peak, Calhoun's campaign, trying to buy time against Van Buren, persuaded Democratic Party managers to postpone their national convention, originally scheduled for November 1843, until the following spring—a delay that would prove to be fateful. But Calhoun's campaign faltered, and he formally withdrew in January 1844. Disgusted with the Democrats and Van Buren, whom he regarded as a corrupt trimmer, Calhoun seemed to retreat into private concerns. Three months later, though, after some dramatic twists, he would return to the political scene, holding the second most powerful political position in the nation.

Intrigue over Texas

By the time Congress reconvened in December 1843, Tyler's new secretary of state, the reactionary Virginian and acolyte of Calhoun's, Abel P. Upshur, had already been in secret negotiations for the annexation of the Republic of Texas for two months. Almost a year earlier, Congressman Thomas W. Gilmer of Virginia, an ally of Calhoun's but also one of Tyler's political friends, had published a prominent public letter calling for immediate annexation. Gilmer's appeal played on an old Anglophobic theme: any delay, he warned, might drive the Texans into the arms of perfidious Great Britain, which had expressed interest in supporting an independent Texas while encouraging the Texans to abolish slavery—a direct threat, Gilmer claimed, to slavery in the American South.

Soon thereafter, annexing Texas, an idea already boosted by President Tyler, became popular in select southern circles. But it went nowhere as long as Tyler's imposing secretary of state, Daniel Webster (whom William Henry Harrison had appointed), remained in office. Among other objections, Webster thought that annexing an independent republic was unconstitutional. After crucial negotiations over the Webster-Ashburton Treaty had ended, though, Tyler pressed for Webster's resignation, which he received in May 1843. Two months later, Tyler named to the post his old friend Upshur, whom he had previously appointed secretary of the navy—and whom Upshur's mentor, Calhoun, had been quietly pushing for months to replace Webster.[8] Soon after, the administration began sounding out the Texans about annexation. On September 18, Tyler, in consultation with Upshur, ordered that secret talks be opened. Face-to-face negotiations commenced a month later.

Both the Clay and the Van Buren forces bridled at the mounting rumors that the administration meant to introduce what Clay called the "exciting topic" of Texas and cause "dissension, discord, and distraction"—solely, it appeared, in order to advance Tyler's presidential ambitions.[9] Since the Texas republic's birth in 1836, successive administrations, first Jackson's, then Van Buren's, had ducked annexation, certain that it would arouse enormous opposition in the North. Clay, meanwhile, had consistently opposed annexation. When Van Buren, during a canvassing tour in 1842, stopped to pay his respects to Clay in Kentucky, observers speculated that the two men agreed to keep Texas out of the coming campaign. A call by Tyler to annex Texas, Clay wrote late in 1843, "would be the last desperate move of a despicable traitor."[10]

Tyler, however, now a man without a party, believed that annexing an area as immense as Texas would glorify his administration, advance the expansion of slavery, and give him precisely the issue he needed for the coming election. To be sure, any annexation treaty would face an uphill battle to gain the required approval of two-thirds of the Senate, where the Whigs—likely loyal in this election year to the anti-annexationist Clay—held a significant majority. But pro-Texas leaders believed that there was sufficient support among northern Democrats and, they hoped, southern Whigs to ensure ratification. And by advocating immediate annexation in patriotic, expansionist terms, Tyler might just ally a united South with the sizable numbers of pro-Texas northern voters and form a winning electoral coalition. Tyler based his hopes on the almost certain expectation that neither the Whigs nor the Democrats would nominate a strong pro-Texas man.

A small group of prominent southerners from both parties, including the Democrat Robert J. Walker of Mississippi, joined Upshur, Gilmer, the Virginia Whig Henry A. Wise, and the rest of Tyler's huddle of friends in ardently supporting annexation. Calhoun and his supporters, at this point still very much in the presidential race, offered a great deal more than support. Calhoun had long enthusiastically supported Texas annexation, and Upshur, in need of strong guidance, verged on disloyalty to Tyler by directly, if quietly, consulting his hero. In London, Calhoun's old associate Duff Green, on special confidential assignment by the Tyler administration, sent dispatch after dispatch to Upshur warning of a British abolitionist plot to control Texas, with the larger goal of attacking slavery in the American South. In August, candidate Calhoun presented to Upshur, at Upshur's request, a three-point diplomatic strategy, which one measured and meticulous study of Texas annexation has called "a master plan, a blueprint for the Administration, by the master mind of the South."[11] Calhoun proposed pressing the British to cease their meddling, building support in the South with a newspaper propaganda campaign on the British abolitionist threat, and delaying formal negotiations with the Texans until public opinion had swung around.[12] Upshur followed the plan closely and, in late February 1844 all but the final details of an annexation treaty had been arranged. The secretary—along, it appears, with much of official Washington—was certain that there were sufficient votes in the Senate to ratify that treaty.[13]

Meanwhile, through the end of 1843, the political intrigue surrounding Texas annexation thickened. On January 23, the same day that Thomas Gilmer's pro-annexation letter appeared in a Washington newspaper, the Tennessee Democratic congressman Aaron V. Brown had sent a copy of it to Van Buren's most auspicious supporter, former president Andrew Jackson, asking Jackson to state his views on Texas. It was the normal way to get a leading political figure to speak on the record about a thorny issue; and as Brown was at this point backing Van Buren, Jackson would not suspect that there was anything amiss in his request. But Brown was also a determined annexationist, in close touch with Gilmer, Walker, and the rest of the pro-Texas agitators.

In soliciting Jackson's opinion, Brown knew the former president's basic views on Texas, and he knew even better how influential Jackson's opinions remained among the Democratic rank and file. Gilmer's letter cited British interference as the main justification for immediate annexation—which happened to be the eternal Anglophobe Jackson's chief concern as well—and so Jackson sent back to Brown a characteristically forceful endorsement. Brown, though, did not submit Jackson's letter to a newspaper editor, the usual procedure, but instead shared it with Gilmer, who in turn shared it with other pro-annexationists.[14]

Calhoun's supporters may have been privy to the scheme from the start; in any event, they obtained the text of Jackson's letter and planned to release it when the time was ripe during the coming presidential election. As it happened, though, in the fall of 1843 news of the plot leaked out and reached its projected chief victim, Martin Van Buren, as did the identity of the man who was, by now at least, the plot's projected beneficiary, John C. Calhoun. "[Jackson's] letter I understand is in the possession of the Calhounites," the Virginia Democrat John Letcher wrote to Van Buren in September, "and is to be used at the [Democratic] Convention." Supposedly, Van Buren would be asked for a public statement on immediate annexation, and (or so most observers anticipated) he would express his opposition. The Calhounites would then produce Jackson's letter, which they expected would instantly destroy Van Buren and secure the nomination for Calhoun.[15]

All along, unbeknownst to the naïve Tyler, at least two of the leading pro-Texas men, Gilmer and Upshur—men whom the president counted among his closest confidants—were playing fast and loose with the president and clandestinely aiding Calhoun. Upshur, in his secret messages, informed Calhoun about the administration's inner workings on Texas. In August, Gilmer quietly threw his support to Calhoun. Several weeks later, Upshur, working through Calhoun's confidant, Congressman Virgil Maxcy, sent word to Calhoun that he considered him the best possible candidate, "the only one" who could rally the South.[16]

While the pro-annexationists schemed, the Texas issue filled newspapers across the country and especially in the South, exactly as Calhoun, in his instructions to Upshur, had stipulated. Calhoun's closest supporters, who had been campaigning on annexation for months, now believed that only Texas could derail Van Buren. Yet agitation over Texas did not instantly change the electoral calculus. By mid-January, it seemed that, whatever annexation's fate, the election would proceed as forecast. Tyler and Uphsur's Texas gambit—which was just as surely, if unbeknownst to Tyler, Calhoun's gambit—had only reinforced Whig leaders' support for Clay. Soon after the new year began, Calhoun dropped out of the presidential race, leaving the isolated Tyler's band of annexationists to stir up the Texas issue virtually on their own. In mid-January, the prominent Virginia Calhounite R. M. T. Hunter reported that, even in his district, "the people are fast coming to the conclusion that Mr V B's nomination is inevitable." Van Buren, for his part, assured Jackson that the Democratic convention—now delayed, at the Calhounites' insistence—would be "very harmonious."[17] If not for that delay, Van Buren would already have won the Democratic nomination, but he professed that he was content to wait.

Calhoun Steps in

Into late February, Secretary of State Upshur worked with the Texans on the final details of annexation, but on February 28 he was killed when, during an official event, a gigantic gun exploded aboard a navy warship, the USS *Princeton*. On the brink of producing a signed treaty, the annexation effort temporarily halted. Tyler, possibly at the strong urging of Henry Wise, duly selected as Upshur's successor the man who, for reasons of his own, would handle the Texas issue in the most divisive manner possible—the sidelined former candidate John C. Calhoun. Having twice turned down cabinet offers from Tyler, and having lost his friends Maxcy and Gilmer as well as Upshur in the *Princeton* disaster (and nearly lost his own son), Calhoun, now sixty-two, at first professed reluctance. He gave way, ostensibly out of a powerful sense of duty and with a clear sense that Texas annexation would help secure slavery—but also with his advisers' assurance that the appointment would revive his presidential prospects, for 1848 if not 1844. "The beauty of the thing," Calhoun's friend Dixon H. Lewis of Alabama privately observed, "is that Providence rather than Tyler has put Calhoun at the head of this great question, to direct its force and control its fury."[18] Although he had no particular interest in helping Tyler, Calhoun immersed himself in Texas annexation. Perforce, his mind turned to the political situation, to Martin Van Buren, and to breaking what one of his several political correspondents now called "the shackles of party despotism."[19]

Calhoun took charge at the State Department on April 1; eleven days later, he and Tyler signed the negotiated treaty with Texas; and two weeks of backroom maneuvering followed. Word quickly spread that the pro–Van Buren Washington *Globe*, edited by the Jacksonian stalwart Francis Preston Blair, was about to endorse immediate annexation, which it did on April 15. The implication, worrisome to Calhoun as well as to Tyler, was obvious: Van Buren, who had been expected to join with Clay and oppose annexation, had changed his mind, and quickly gotten Blair to clear the way by having the *Globe* support annexation. By mollifying the South over Texas, Van Buren would foil Calhoun and Tyler and steal the Texas issue for himself. Annexation, now Calhoun's all-consuming interest, would wind up ensuring the reelection of his northern nemesis.

In fact, though, it was not Van Buren but Robert James Walker, presenting new documents from Andrew Jackson, who had beseeched the *Globe* to come out in support of annexation. Three weeks before, with Calhoun's presidential candidacy now dead, Thomas Ritchie's Richmond *Enquirer*, another pro–Van Buren (but also pro-annexation) paper, had published the letter that Aaron Brown had solicited from Jackson more than a year earlier. The unexpected pressure from the *Globe* to go along with Jackson's letter put Van Buren in a terrible position, but instead of crumpling, he objected to Blair's editorial and continued to ponder the Texas issue. Henry Clay, among others, still presumed that Van Buren would oppose immediate annexation. And all along, Secretary of State Calhoun, working in secret, was doing his best to ensure that, no matter what Van Buren decided, Texas would destroy the ex-president.[20]

Calhoun had detested Van Buren ever since the New Yorker had displaced him as President Jackson's anointed successor during Jackson's first term, but his animus was not purely personal. Never a party man, Calhoun the sectionalist had also been repeatedly thwarted in his efforts to sever intersectional partisan bonds, dating back to the nullification crisis. As gifted and tireless as he was, Calhoun had failed to turn American politics on its axis and create the only party that he believed could safeguard slavery, a party of the South commanded by himself. Not simply personally ambitious, Calhoun, by the mid-1830s, was a devoted pro-slavery sectionalist. But he did persuade himself, grandly, that his cause and slavery's were identical. And the party men, epitomized by Van Buren, were among his worst enemies.

Through the early 1840s, party managers had kept Calhoun at bay by blocking sectional issues from entering national politics. Calhoun's crushed campaign of 1843–44 marked his latest failure, made all the more galling because Van Buren was advancing to his third Democratic presidential nomination. Yet the Texas annexation strategy that Calhoun had devised behind the scenes was now causing Van Buren unexpected distress. And as secretary of state, Calhoun possessed the power to complete an annexation agreement while wrecking Van Buren's candidacy—and thereby upset all of American politics.

"Stipulations on the negro question"

Even before Calhoun took over at the State Department, other politicians perceived how he could destroy Van Buren. Frank Blair, for one, warned Van Buren that Calhoun might "insist on making slavery perpetual" and introduce into the treaty "stipulations on the negro question calculated to make [annexation] odious in the north & peculiarly a Southern question."[21]

If Calhoun could turn even moderate northerners against what looked like Van Buren's politic—and imminent—endorsement of immediate annexation, he might prevent Van Buren's nomination. Alternatively, making it impossible for a vacillating Van Buren to endorse annexation might arouse southern Democrats and compel the party to dump him in favor a slaveholder and take on the anti-annexationist Clay in the general election. Either way, the surest course, as Blair perceived, would be for Calhoun, explicitly and even stridently, to link annexation to a defense of slavery.

After he and Tyler signed the treaty on April 12, Calhoun delayed for ten days in sending it to Capitol Hill for the Senate's approval. Instead—with rumors flying about Van Buren's endorsement of annexation—he devoted nearly a week to composing a reply to an unanswered letter from Lord Aberdeen, the British foreign secretary, which the British envoy Richard Pakenham had forwarded to Upshur just before the latter's death. Much of the public pressure for speedy annexation had arisen from the continuing propaganda campaign's charges—encouraged by Calhoun—that the British aimed to turn Texas into a slaveless republic that would menace the American South. Aberdeen's letter affirmed his government's hopes for slavery's abolition the world over, but stated categorically that it would support an independent Texas with or without slavery. Aberdeen also renounced any effort to interfere with slavery in the United States. Observing that "much agitation" had given Americans false impressions, Aberdeen struck a strong conciliatory note.[22]

Aberdeen's letter received no response for nearly two months after Upshur's death. Finally, on April 18—six days after the Texas treaty arrived and three days after the pro–Van Buren *Globe* backed annexation—Calhoun finished an extraordinary letter to Pakenham that ignored Aberdeen's attempt to calm American fears. Instead, Calhoun upheld annexation with a sneer at Aberdeen's abolitionism and a lengthy defense of American slavery as a positive good—an institution that had provided "the negro race" with the highest standard of civilization it had ever attained.[23]

Calhoun had made sure that the British—and, more important, not just the British—would know that the annexation of Texas was officially a proslavery enterprise. He duly included a copy of his reply with the treaty documents sent to the Senate, ensuring that it would have the maximum political effect—which it did, possibly sooner than Calhoun expected, when the alarmed antislavery senator Benjamin Tappan leaked both the treaty and Calhoun's inflammatory letter to the New York press on April 26. Were Van Buren now to support annexation, he would look firmly proslavery and alienate his northern political base; but if he held to his original position, the South would reject him as a professed antislavery man. Frank Blair's warning to Van Buren had proved prescient.[24]

The Bombshell Explodes

"Never did I see such reprehensible sentiment, & unsurpassed nonsense, united," an astonished Daniel Webster wrote upon reading Calhoun's letter.[25] Whig Party strategists, however, seemed unconcerned. In mid-April, Clay had written an open letter from Raleigh, North Carolina, stating his firm opposition to immediate annexation. Clay wanted to beat Van Buren to the punch over Texas; with the treaty now signed, he also wanted to stiffen the resolve of southern Whigs in the Senate to reject it. Coincidentally, the letter appeared in print in Washington on April 27, the same day that the New York *Evening Post* published the treaty and Calhoun's letter to Pakenham. Four days later, the national Whig convention, unperturbed, unanimously nominated Clay for the presidency on a platform that mentioned Texas not at all. Some southern Whigs fretted over the Raleigh letter's possible impact, but the Whig congressman Alexander Stephens of Georgia spoke for most when, in mid-May, he dismissed the entire Texas effort as "a miserable political humbug," devised by Tyler and Calhoun to confuse southern Whigs, which "would avail them nothing."[26]

Martin Van Buren, meanwhile, had come under intense pressure to endorse immediate annexation well before Calhoun's letter to Pakenham became public. Van Buren knew of annexation's growing popularity in the South and also among pro-expansion Democrats in the North outside of New England. Had Van Buren, "the Little Magician," stuck by his career as the quintessential doughface, a "Northern man with Southern principles," he would have smothered the issue by releasing a noncommittal statement that appeared to support immediate annexation without provoking his northern Democratic base. Specifically, he would have heeded his sometime law partner and valued adviser Benjamin Butler and endorsed immediate annexation with the provisos that Texas would remain a territory, and that Mexico consented to the arrangement. In heeding Butler, he would also effectively heed the sterner pro-annexation views of Andrew Jackson, who for twenty years had been his political lodestar.[27]

Van Buren, though, was sensitive to the growing anti-Texas sentiment, especially in New York, aroused by a growing number of Democrats as well as abolitionists and antislavery Whigs. Endorsing annexation would risk infuriating voters across the North and then handing vital electoral votes to Clay in November. Van Buren also sincerely believed, as did Clay, that annexing Texas would provoke an ignominious war with Mexico. And he was concerned about the fate of the country, as well as his party, if arguments over Texas brought agitation over slavery to the center of national politics. Van Buren had habitually placated the slave South in order to preserve the Union and his party, but he had always stopped short at annexing Texas. Since 1840 he had begun to think that the slaveholders' price for party unity had become unreasonable, and the time might well come to draw the line against Tyler, Calhoun, and their minions. Finally, several of Van Buren's closest advisers, including New York senator Silas Wright, emphatically urged him, in Wright's words, to "take boldly the side of truth and principle" and oppose annexation.[28]

Either stance Van Buren might take on Texas carried potentially disastrous perils. Either way, he would have to take a position on a heated issue while also, somehow, at least appear to be splitting the difference. If he were to follow Wright's advice—stand firm for once against the slave South and oppose immediate annexation—he would have to do so on terms that would isolate the proslavery extremists around Calhoun, preserve his own southern following inside the Democratic Party, and stifle the annexation issue in the general election. It would be a difficult political trick—but it was precisely the kind of trick that the Little Magician had famously pulled off before.

On April 20, Van Buren declared his position in a letter intended for publication sent to the Mississippi congressman William Hammet. Hardly bold, customarily prolix, and sometimes baffling, the statement was also as courageous as any Van Buren would make in his entire political career. Favoring the eventual annexation of Texas as a territory, and conceding that he would acquiesce in immediate annexation if Congress willed it (an unlikely occurrence any time soon, to be sure), Van Buren tried to stake out a middle position between Clay's less measured opposition and those annexationists who demanded the new treaty's rapid ratification. In order remove annexation as a campaign issue, he had basically followed Benjamin Butler's reasoning, except that he presented his careful reply in opposition to, and not support of, immediate annexation.

Van Buren's calculations and his continued confidence over the coming weeks affirmed his belief that he could keep his political balance and finesse the Texas issue long enough to win the nomination, after which he and Clay would bury the renewed annexation controversy. The most courageous element in Van Buren's letter was its unstated but still glaring defiance of Jackson, whom he knew would be enraged by even highly qualified opposition to annexation. More than Van Buren understood, however, he was also defying a raging pro-Texas southern fever—one that Calhoun's letter to Pakenham was about to worsen by making annexation a litmus test on slavery.

When he finished revising his message to Hammet, Van Buren could not have known that, two days earlier, Calhoun had completed his incendiary letter to Pakenham.[29] Neither could Calhoun have known that Van Buren had declared his opposition to annexation. Both would be as surprised as anyone when Van Buren's letter, in a double irony, appeared in print on the very same day, April 27, as Calhoun's Pakenham letter and Clay's anti-annexation Raleigh letter did. The back-room strategizing had ended; everyone's cards were suddenly on the table; and Calhoun was joyous at the result. "Mr V B's letter has prostrated him," he effused to R. M. T. Hunter. "The annexation of Texas has become the absorbing question. It will probably control the presidential election."[30]

Van Buren Prostrate

The Van Buren camp did not understand its situation as Calhoun did. A few of Van Buren's strongest supporters, including the Massachusetts historian and politician George Bancroft, even judged the letter to Pakenham an extremist gaffe that (in Bancroft's view) would backfire disastrously on Calhoun and the proslavery cause. Other supporters failed to appreciate how, as the Virginian William Roane urgently tried to inform Van Buren, the Texas enthusiasm had rapidly grown across the entire South "to a size and extent of which you can form no just idea, and it is still increasing."[31] In fact, Van Buren's nomination, let alone his election, was now in mortal danger. Well before what Thomas Hart Benton called Calhoun's "Texas bombshell" exploded, many Democrats had doubted whether Van Buren could defeat Clay. He was too dull, some said, a loser; his views on banking and the currency were too rigid; he was unalterably linked to the economic collapse of 1837 and the ensuing depression. (Many Whigs agreed: "If we cannot beat Mr. Van Buren," Willie P. Mangum of North Carolina remarked, "we can beat no one.")[32] The old party chieftain had locked up a majority of the delegates, but even some of that support was soft.

Fortunately for Van Buren, several rivals opposed him, none especially distinguished, and only one a slaveholder, his controversial former vice president Richard M. Johnson.[33] With the opposition divided, Van Buren would almost surely conquer. Yet once he announced his views on annexation—costly enough in itself, but now branded, thanks to Calhoun's letter, as an antislavery outrage—efforts to unite behind and nominate a slaveholder instead began in earnest. In a swift opening strike at the party's national convention, Van Buren's southern foes, led by Robert James Walker and the Calhounite North Carolina congressman Romulus M. Saunders, won a rule that demanded a two-thirds supermajority of delegates to gain the nomination.[34] (The rule, ironically, had first been adopted in 1832 to buttress Van Buren's selection as Jackson's running mate.) Van Buren still commanded a strong simple majority of the delegates, but not two-thirds of them. After he fell short on the first ballot, his numbers steadily dwindled until, on the fifth ballot, he was trailing former secretary of war Lewis Cass, a northerner whom Van Buren and his supporters despised as one of the many intriguers unleashed by Calhoun's plotting.

The Van Burenites screamed themselves voiceless demanding that the convention rescind the two-thirds rule, but to no avail. Who, then, would replace their man as the nominee? Calhoun, who sent two friends to attend the convention on his behalf, had come to think that a Tyler candidacy as an independent Democrat might be "safest for the South."[35] He would consider a draft, but the number and the fury of Van Buren's delegates precluded that. Instead, a small group of powerful party fixers, including Van Buren's man Bancroft and some Tennesseeans, floated the name of former House Speaker James K. Polk of Tennessee, a protégé of Jackson's who had been firmly in Van Buren's camp but was also a pro-Texas slaveholder. The choice made sense; the fixers won over Van Buren's manager, Benjamin Butler; and after two more ballots, the convention nominated Polk by acclamation. Unity, of sorts, had been achieved—but no one doubted that Calhoun had demolished Van Buren (see Figure 2).

Figure 2. "Cleansing the Augean Stable." [June or July] 1844. Courtesy Library of Congress. A pro-Whig cartoon depicting the Whigs clearing out the Democrats in 1844. While Lady Texas gets shown the door, Andrew Jackson grows desperate, Henry Clay defenestrates James K. Polk, and Daniel Webster shovels out the hard money "mint drop" currency associated with the Jacksonian stalwart Thomas Hart Benton. John C. Calhoun appears to the left of Webster, a member of the cleaning crew; he holds by the tail Martin Van Buren (one of whose nicknames was "the Red Fox of Kinderhook") and prepares unceremoniously to throw him out the door. Calhoun's presence in the cartoon has perplexed archivists and curators, as the real-life arch-annexationist Calhoun was no Whig. But Calhoun's chief role in the campaign, to this point, had been to destroy Van Buren's candidacy—something the cartoonist, like every other political observer at the time, would have known.

"Every thing is completely satisfactory"

A political miracle had seemingly saved the Democrats from self-destructing over factional warfare, although grudges persisted. Many of the Van Burenites were heartbroken, and the entrenched anti-annexationists among them were incensed. When the convention, seeking amity, offered the vice presidential nomination by acclamation to Silas Wright, the New Yorker refused, infuriated at the delegates' rejection of Van Buren. But if Polk the slaveholder wanted Texas, he decidedly was not a Calhounite, which made an enormous difference. Most of the of Van Burenites, as John L. O'Sullivan, the editor of the *Democratic Review*, reported, were satisfied enough with Polk—"weeping with one eye while we smile with the other at the overthrow of the intriguers and traitors [that is, the Calhounites]."[36] And at the other end of the spectrum most Calhounites were pleased at Van Buren's rejection in favor of a slaveholder. The more radical Calhounites, lacking faith in the nominee, did depart the convention embittered, and called for a southern convention to meet in Nashville. When, in early June, the southern Whigs held firm and the Senate solidly rejected the Texas treaty, the red-hot South Carolinians, led by Robert Barnwell Rhett, threatened secession, declaring, as one of them put it, that "the safety if not the very existence of slavery" was at stake. But the radicals would get nowhere. "We have triumphed," Calhoun's agent Francis Pickens exulted.[37]

Polk, meanwhile, reached out to the defeated factions, starting with the Van Burenites. Pledged to serve only a single term (thus leaving open the chance that their man might yet to return to the White House), Polk reminded the New Yorkers that he had long been loyal to Van Buren and had remained so until the end.[38] Polk also supported the hard-money economic program that the ex-president championed above all else. These assurances soothed most of the Van Burenites: Silas Wright, fighting back his outrage, declared that if Van Buren could not run, he vastly preferred his old friend Polk, albeit in part, he noted incorrectly, because "[Polk's] selection would be as little palatable to the Calhoun clique, *per se*, as that of Mr. V. B."[39] Van Buren rallied and urged his friends strongly to stifle their pique and work hard for Polk.

Normal party politics revived and prevailed. Secretary Calhoun fell in line as soon as Polk offered assurances on patronage appointments and on slashing the protective tariff enacted by the Whigs in 1842. "*Every thing is completely satisfactory*," Francis Pickens reported to Calhoun in early September after meeting with the nominee for two days at Polk's Tennessee home.[40] Calhoun quashed the convention movement and the secessionist talk by Rhett and the other fire-eaters. Polk and his Tennessee friends got Jackson to help talk Tyler into ceasing his quixotic but potentially destructive campaign.

Polk's allure was easy to grasp. Although a slaveholder, he upheld not slavery but spread-eagle Manifest Destiny nationalism. Such, to be sure, had been the approach taken, disingenuously, by proslavery annexationists, including backers of Tyler and Calhoun alike, for much of the spring and summer; and in the South, Texas annexation never lost the powerful proslavery associations that Calhoun had fixed on it.[41] But one of the unforeseen effects of Calhoun's correspondence with Pakenham was to make Polk look like the truly Jacksonian nationalist he claimed to be, and not a slaveocrat sectionalist. In the North, Democrats soft-pedaled on slavery, repeating the specious argument, advanced most forcefully by Robert J. Walker, that expanding the institution would foster a "diffusion" that in time would hasten its extinction. When they emphasized annexation at all, northern Democrats focused chiefly on the great promises of Manifest Destiny, to open more land for settlement, enlarge the home market for American-made goods, and (not incidentally to Irish voters in the cities) twist the British lion's tail in Oregon as well as Texas.[42] In some closely fought northern states where the antislavery vote was strong, including New York and Ohio, Polk's supporters simply muted their advocacy of annexation or mentioned it sparingly. None of this, however, damaged Polk's standing with southern Democrats, for whom annexing Texas was by now virtually all that mattered.

Clay vs. Polk: A Close Battle

By end of the summer, annexation was chiefly vexing the once supremely confident Whigs. Clay, like Whigs generally, had initially thought Polk's candidacy a joke, which prompted the slogan "Who is James K. Polk?" If they thought Van Buren was a weak opponent, they considered Polk a nullity, his qualifications, one Virginian remarked, "small if not contemptible." But Clay quickly learned that his anti-annexation stance was hurting him severely in the South. To soften his position, he wrote open letters to two Whig editors in Alabama, but succeeded only in appearing unprincipled. ("Things look blue!" the Whig Party boss Thurlow Weed wrote to an associate after the second letter appeared. "Ugly letter, that to Alabama.")[43]

With most of the South against him, Clay focused on New York, Pennsylvania, Ohio, and Virginia, where his managers tried to win over niche constituencies. Polk's men fought just as hard over the same turf. Much of the campaigning had nothing to do with Texas or slavery. In Pennsylvania, for example, Polk's long-standing opposition to protective tariffs was damaging him badly, so he and his managers crafted an ambiguous public letter that seemed to support protection, at least in principle.[44] Ethnic and cultural issues also came into play. In New York City, a wave of anti-Irish prejudice had lifted nativist candidates into local offices; and in Philadelphia, anti-immigrant mob violence had accompanied intense nativist politicking. By nominating for the vice presidency the pious Presbyterian evangelical and former U.S. senator Theodore Frelinghuysen, widely known as "the Christian Statesman," the Whigs had practically invited big-city Democrats to attack them as anti-Catholic bigots. The Whigs responded, disastrously, by striking up alliances with political nativists in New York City and Philadelphia, and by planting stories that Clay would tighten up immigration and naturalization laws. By the time Clay, who favored restrictions on the naturalization of recent immigrants, gingerly distanced himself from the nativists, local Democrats had naturalized all the Irishmen they could round up and arranged for them to vote.[45]

The Texas issue chiefly helped Clay in the northern battleground states, and so the Liberty Party abolitionists concentrated their fire on him almost exclusively. Polk, in their eyes, was impossible, a small man committed to slavery. But Clay, they insisted, harmed the antislavery cause even more—a treacherous figure who hoodwinked northern voters into believing that he had antislavery feelings even though he owned slaves and upheld the Slave Power. The Democrats in turn abetted the abolitionists by spreading tales of Clay as a duelist, a gambler, and a sexual reprobate to unsettle the Whig vote among devoted evangelicals.

The Measure of Polk's Victory

Polk won the election, barely, with a popular vote margin of just under forty thousand out of 1.7 million cast, or roughly 1.5 percent. The results affirmed that the second party system had come into its own. Party loyalties proved amazingly strong. One statistical analysis suggests that at least 87 percent of those who had voted for the Whig candidate in 1840 did so four years later, while a whopping 95 percent of Van Buren voters in 1840 voted for Polk.[46] Both parties also showed considerable strength in every region of the county. Although Clay did not win any states in the Deep South, he came within a whisker of carrying both Georgia and Louisiana. Except for a shortfall of 5,100 votes (a little more than 1 percent of the total), Clay would have won New York, and with it the election. With an additional 7,000 votes in Pennsylvania and 2,300 in Indiana, Clay would have won even without New York. So evenly matched were the Whigs and Democrats that either party could now reasonably expect to prevail nationwide, at least in presidential politics.

The voting returns, however, could also give the misleading impression that the Texas annexation controversy made little or no difference in the election. Some historians have agreed with one embittered Whig editor's judgment that the "asinine fatuity of the abolition party," especially in New York, threw the election to the Democrats.[47] The case seems strong on its face: had even one-third of the nearly sixteen thousand New Yorkers who voted for Birney voted instead for Clay, the Whig would have won. Yet the Texas issue does not appear to have given Polk his margin of victory. As Holt has discovered from a close reading of the returns, the key to Polk's victory in New York, as in Pennsylvania and every other northern state that he won narrowly, was neither Whig defections to the Liberty Party nor Whig abstentions, but a dramatic rise in the size of the Democratic vote over that in 1840. Given the deliberate whipping up of ethnic and religious strife in New York City and Philadelphia, it appears that local cultural and ethnic politics and not sectional divisions over Texas tipped the election to Polk—a conclusion Clay himself drew several months later.[48]

Still, in subtler ways, the returns showed remarkable sectional differences that coincided with the struggle over Texas, especially among new voters who had yet to form partisan loyalties. In the South, new voters, like those who had voted earlier, disproportionally supported the Democrats, before and after the struggle over Texas began. Most likely, Holt concludes, "the Texas issue contributed heavily to the Democratic surge in Dixie" in 1844.[49] In the North, however, after the Texas issue broke, the Whigs suddenly began to capture the lion's share of new voters. The shift was especially dramatic in Massachusetts and New York, but the Whigs gained in every northern state except Maine, Indiana, and Illinois. Contrary to the Whigs' fears, the battle over Texas did not radicalize new voters by pushing them into the Liberty Party. As new northern voters stayed within the established party system, they abruptly began to flock to the party and candidate opposed to annexation.

In sum, even though the election consolidated the parties' respective existing electoral bases, the annexation controversy showed that debates over slavery and its extension could have dramatic sectional effects, at least among voters who had not yet acquired partisan loyalties. And there was much more to the election of 1844 than the voting returns.[50]

"A great political revolution"

The closeness of the result did not at all comfort the Whigs. Stunned that the great Clay had not crushed the pygmy Polk, some despairing insiders even suggested that the party change its name, as if that was the problem. But the Whigs' fears were exaggerated, something that became clear two years later, when a midterm electoral wave swept them back into the majority in the House. For the Whig Party managers, the main lesson of 1844 would come to be that, in presidential elections, they would be wise to remember the Log Cabin campaign, snub their traditional national leadership, and find an attractive figure (preferably a military hero like William Henry Harrison) who was blessed with a meager political record and a vague party affiliation. In time, a new generation of disciplined state party organizers, including Abraham Lincoln of Illinois and Alexander Stephens of Georgia, would steer the party in that direction—and, thanks to the Mexican War, which they would reasonably blame on Polk, they would find the figure they needed in General Zachary Taylor.

The Democrats had no such worries. At bottom, the outcome of 1844 looked like a great Democratic victory, no matter the slimness of Polk's plurality. The party had risen above vicious factional battles to avenge its defeat of 1840. It had survived the rejection of one of its founding fathers, and the substitution of an experienced but younger man, vaunted during the campaign as "Young Hickory." It had turned a six-seat Democratic deficit in the Senate into a commanding twelve-seat majority while sustaining the sizable majority in the House of Representatives it had won in 1842. Former president Van Buren, the loyal party man, responded to his rejection gracefully, throwing his energetic support to Polk. In all, among the triumphant Democrats but also among the more thoughtful Whigs, the drama of 1844, as Joel Silbey claims, "could be internalized as one more example of a bothersome sectional uproar that was subsequently tamed by the dominant processes of American politics."[51]

Beneath the surface, however, terrible damage had been done, the worst of it by John C. Calhoun. The sectional uproar of 1844 was not a congressional donnybrook that could be smoothed over with a patchwork compromise or be settled by marginalizing the dissenters. In 1844 the politics of slavery and expansion had become implicated, as never before, in presidential politics, where Calhoun's obsessive determination had dashed the hopes of powerful men in both major parties. The bitterness from the sectional combat, especially among the northern Democrats, receded but did not disappear. It would return, redoubled, when President Polk, upon taking office, proved to be more of a divider than a uniter.

Calhoun had failed to win ratification of the annexation treaty (although he and Tyler would soon enough achieve their goal with a joint resolution from both houses of Congress). The enduring strength of party allegiances continued to thwart his vision of a sectional realignment.[52] The man elected president was a foursquare pro-expansion southern Jacksonian Democrat, not a proslavery sectionalist. Yet by guiding the revival of Texas annexation, offering his protégé Upshur a master plan, and then, after Upshur's death, stamping annexation as a proslavery effort, Calhoun had succeeded brilliantly. The maneuvering over Texas and slavery had cost his greatest Democratic enemy, Martin Van Buren, almost certain renomination; and Van Buren's rejection in favor of Polk had almost certainly cost Calhoun's greatest Whig enemy, Henry Clay, the presidency. Van Buren the doughface found himself taking the antislavery side on what had become the burning issue of the day. Clay the supreme nationalist had had to grovel for southern support with letters that made him look unprincipled. Clay did not yet comprehend it, but he was finished as a presidential candidate once and for all. Van Buren would run for president one more time, but at the head of the sectional, antislavery Free Soil Party ticket in 1848.

The foremost victor in 1844, aside from Polk, was John C. Calhoun. Little wonder that Calhoun regarded Polk's election as "a great political revolution," which, if followed up with prudence and moderation, might at last "save the Government."[53] At one level, the dominant processes of the party system had indeed tamed a sectional uproar. But at another, more profound level, Calhoun had tamed the party system.

"The victory of the Slavery element"

Calhoun would soon be disappointed again, as President Polk—determined, he wrote, "to be *myself* President of the U.S."—went his own way.[54] What virtually no one else besides Polk knew was that the new president harbored territorial designs that stretched all the way to California—designs that would almost surely require a war with Mexico. Even if Polk governed as a Manifest Destiny nationalist, his aggressive expansionism would reopen all of the issues about territories and slavery that the Missouri Compromise had resolved for an entire generation. Soon enough, in 1854, that compromise would be repealed, placing the nation directly on the road to civil war. And pressing hardest for that repeal would be the members of Washington's so-called Calhoun party, including veterans of the Texas conflict like R. M. T. Hunter, who continued to advance Calhoun's sectionalizing politics after Calhoun died in 1850.[55]

The details were unknowable at the end of 1844. One shrewd observer of American politics, though, could sense that a dramatic change had taken place, despite the apparent stability of the political parties. John Quincy Adams recognized that many issues besides Texas had affected the election. "The partial associations," Adams wrote in his diary, "of Native Americans, Irish Catholics, abolition societies, liberty party, the Pope of Rome, the Democracy of the sword, and the dotage of the ruffian"—Andrew Jackson—produced Clay's defeat. Yet Adams also understood that Polk's election represented "the victory of the Slavery element in the Constitution of the United States." Worse, he wrote, even if the immediate future was uncertain, the election amounted to "sealing the fate of this nation, which nothing less than the interposition of Omnipotence can save." Adams had a deeply morose side, but this time events would eventually prove him correct. He certainly understood how a vigorous presidential contest between the evenly matched Democrats and Whigs, once manipulated by the leader of "the Slavery element," John C. Calhoun, augured a cataclysmic national crisis over slavery.[56]

CHAPTER 3

Beyond the Realignment Synthesis: The 1860 Election Reconsidered

Adam I. P. Smith

The Limits of the Realignment Synthesis

To the "New Political Historians" of the 1960s and 1970s, realignment theory seemed to describe the circumstances of the 1850s particularly well.[1] The election of 1860 (along with those of 1828, 1896, and 1932) became a paradigmatic "critical election," not so much, ironically, because it triggered the Civil War (which surely makes 1860 by far the most critical election in U.S. history in a non-jargon-laden use of the term), but because it brought to power the Republican Party for the first time and supposedly locked in the new political order, defined by a different set of issues than the one that had preceded it and with a differently constituted alignment of social and ethnocultural groups on each side.[2] The realignment synthesis reinforced the working assumption of the New Political History that long-term party affiliation was the most critical factor in explaining voter behavior. Stability was the defining feature of the political order in this view, and the 1860 election was "critical" because of the sudden stirring to life of voters' hitherto supposedly latent agency.[3] Since the 1990s, political history has been written in the shadow of the "cultural turn" rather than the social sciences, yet the language of party systems remains stubbornly embedded in historians' portrayal of the nineteenth-century political landscape. And consequently, the core problematic of antebellum history—explaining the origins of the Civil War—has been dominated for nearly half a century by the concept of the breakup of the "second party system."

There is now considerable evidence to show that electoral change in American history was more gradual and convoluted than the punctuated equilibrium model suggests, and that shifts in the fortunes of different political parties were to do with contingency and strategy as least as much as with structural changes in the economy. At the same time, rational choice theoretic models influenced some scholars to challenge the passive conception of voters implied by the realignment model.[4] In "the real world," David R. Mayhew observes (correctly, in my view), voters must make judgments not just during a periodic realignment but "all the time."[5] Although, according to the realignment model, 1860 was the decisive watershed between two stable phases of fixed partisan loyalties, it would be more accurate to see it as one in a sequence of elections through the 1850s and 1860s in which party identities and voter loyalties were malleable. Even the founding father of the realignment synthesis, Walter Dean Burnham, acknowledged that the second party system's "dramatic collapse" after 1854 "disclosed its essential fragility."[6] This is an understatement; the competition between Whigs and Democrats was not only fragile; it was also fleeting. If the second party system only coalesced in 1840, by 1848 it was already fragmenting.[7]

Most of Michael F. Holt's work on mid-nineteenth-century politics has been influenced by the presumption that voters' loyalties were not fixed, and that party identities were fluid.[8] And from a different angle, Glenn C. Altschuler and Stuart M. Blumin suggested provocatively that there was little more to voter engagement than the prospect of free beer and a hog roast: mobilization strategies were all.[9] Yet, on the whole, historical scholarship on the politics of the 1850s, and on the 1860 election in particular, has not yet taken account of the devastating critiques of realignment theory mounted by political scientists.[10] The purpose of this chapter is to consider whether, in the light of the theoretic disarray left by the assaults on the realignment synthesis, it is possible to make sense of this election and assess its significance within a larger framework.

Contingency

Elections are a challenging subject for scholars with a systematizing bent because it is hard to explain outcomes without taking into account contingent factors that can only be explained in narrative form. At first glance, the 1860 election may appear an exception to that rule: Abraham Lincoln's victory in the Electoral College was comfortable and was widely predicted several months in advance. "I hesitate to say it," wrote the ever-cautious Lincoln in August 1860, "but it really appears now, as if the success of the Republican ticket is inevitable."[11] This uncharacteristic sanguinity on Lincoln's part proved well founded, as it turned out, but it was the product of a series of events that in themselves need an explanation. Most important was the sectional split in the Democratic Party. The decision of the southern wing of the party not to support Stephen A. Douglas—the man who, back in the spring, was the favorite to win the election—meant that the 1860 contest became, in practice, two parallel elections: one between Lincoln and Douglas in the North, and one in the South between the candidate of the southern Democrats, John C. Breckinridge, and John Bell, who ran as a Constitutional Unionist.[12] Only one of these candidates—Lincoln—had any realistic prospect of winning a majority in the Electoral College. The refusal of southern Democrats to back Douglas made it almost impossible for him to win outright, given the strength of the Republicans in so much of the North. Breckinridge, the strongest supporter of the extension of slavery, could not hope to be a serious contender in the free states—and even if he won every slave state, that would still be insufficient. Some of Bell's more optimistic supporters dreamed of a national reaction against pro- and antislavery "extremism" which might sweep the old southern Whigs to power, but, realistically, with Douglas and Lincoln fighting to position themselves as the best defenders of the rights of free laborers in the North, and Bell's campaign lacking any clear statement on what to do about the slavery controversy, he was left, in the main, with the support only of southern moderates who could not stomach Breckinridge. Given this electoral reality, the other campaigns seem to have been focused on preventing Lincoln getting a majority rather than on building one for their man. Even Douglas campaign newspapers devoted lots of space to electoral analysis "proving" that Lincoln could not amass enough votes to win, rather than to arguing that the "Little Giant" would do so.[13] Although Douglas initially had hopes of winning New York, most political observers expected Lincoln to pick up the states Fremont had won in 1856 (plus Minnesota, which had recently been admitted and was, as Lincoln put it, "as sure as such a thing can be"[14]). The only question, then, was whether he would win sufficient numbers of Electoral College votes elsewhere.

If Lincoln had lost in the Far West (very possible), had failed to win any electoral votes in New Jersey (very possible), and narrowly lost instead of narrowly won Indiana and Illinois (entirely plausible), he would not have had the 152 votes needed to win in the Electoral College. And had Lincoln failed to carry Pennsylvania (which he did handily in the end, but which was by no means certain), his chances of winning would have been very slim. Maybe a less appealing Republican candidate—one perceived as being more radical, like William H. Seward—and a more northern-friendly Constitutional Unionist might have limited the very large number of northern voters who had supported Millard Fillmore in 1856 from moving into Lincoln's column.[15] In 1860 a different cast of characters may have influenced those crucial voters in Indiana, Illinois, and Pennsylvania who, in effect, put Lincoln in the White House. Candidates matter, as politicos at the time were very aware. Even given where things stood in August, Lincoln's confidence in his likely election might plausibly have been shaken if attempts to form anti-Republican "fusion" tickets had been more successful. Where there were fusion slates, voters often did not cooperate and split their tickets. This was one reason why Lincoln won some of the electoral votes in New Jersey that may otherwise have gone to Douglas. Had Lincoln fallen short, and the election been thrown into the House, it seems likely the Republican would have been blocked: Democrats controlled eighteen state delegations against the Republicans' fifteen in the Thirty-Sixth Congress.

And might the election have turned out differently had particular events not occurred? John Brown's dramatic attempt to incite a slave insurrection at Harpers Ferry, Virginia, in 1859, to take the most important example, shaped the contours of the election campaign profoundly. Democrats tried to tar the Republican Party with having fostered John Brown's extremism. The *Democratic Review* charged that William H. Seward's "Irrepressible Conflict" speech had "anticipate[d] the riot at Harper's Ferry as inevitably as night follows day." Lincoln too, with his "House Divided" speech, had launched a "war to the knife against Southern institutions."[16] Republicans responded that, on the contrary, Brown's violence was an outgrowth of the lawlessness, vigilantism, and "filibustering" of proslavery forces in Kansas and therefore a direct result of Douglas's "popular sovereignty" doctrine.[17] Furthermore, some of them welcomed Brown's execution on the grounds that it was a warning to disunionists of the consequences of treason. For southerners, both Bell and Breckinridge supporters alike, Brown's raid was the ultimate evidence of the threat they faced from northern abolitionists. The prominence of the issue in the campaign in both sections is a reminder of how the presentation and re-presentation of dramatic and essentially "random" news stories can be powerful elements in political discourse at a given moment. Had the raid not happened, the election would have been a different event.

Musings about alternative possibilities could be expanded almost ad infinitum, but where do they leave us? Was politics no more than a series of contingent events, with the agency of political actors generating constant flux? The specificity of the sequence of events that elections represent means that it is essential for them to be properly historicized; no determinative model can do full justice to electoral outcomes. Nevertheless, we can do more than simply tell the story. The significance of the 1860 election is not what the proponents of the realignment synthesis claimed. Although, for a while, the Republican Party did achieve a majority status, this was a product of war and Reconstruction and of postelection contingent events. On its own terms, what is striking about the 1860 contest is the similarity of the Republicans and Douglas Democrats in the North, and of the Bell and Breckinridge campaigns in the South. Rather than being the inauguration of a new political order, the 1860 election in fact exemplified some key characteristics of mid-nineteenth-century politics that are not captured by the realignment synthesis. These were (1) a *political culture* framed by republican ideological assumptions about the nature of power and liberty; (2) *electoral behavior* in which there were underlying continuities in the orientation of regions and social groups toward particular policies and political styles, yet in which voters were actively engaged in making choices, often *retrospective judgments* on perceived political performance; and (3) *campaign strategies* in which "valence" issues were more important than "positional" issues, in which political elites' responses to events were crucial, and which can be usefully imagined as a contest among competing *narratives*. I will take each of these characteristics of the election in turn.

Political Culture

Politics in this era, despite (or perhaps because of) wrenching social transformations, was characterized by continuity in the underlying assumptions made about the nature of power and politics. A republican frame—fear of subversion and conspiracy; a concern with protecting liberty from monopoly and tyranny; with manhood and honor—underlay most political choices.

And so too did preoccupations with the nation and with the threat from radical anticapitalist ideologies that testify to the embeddedness of the mid-nineteenth-century United States in a transatlantic political world. The continuing importance of republicanism in political culture ensured that Civil War Americans were quick to scent abuses of power, to worry about conspiracies to undermine the liberties of the people, to fear the corrupting effects of partisanship, and to condemn a love of luxury or pretentious airs as evidence of a lack of republican virtue in leaders.

Officeholders always faced insurgency from those who could successfully pose as "outs," representing the people against the wire pullers of corrupt parties. Republican electoral advances 1858–60 were due to their ability to pose as the antiestablishment insurgents as well as to their antislavery message. Like the Know-Nothing organizations that swept to dramatic victories in state elections in 1854 and 1855, Republicans claimed that their candidates were "fresh from the loins of the people." Republican campaign songs included the "Anti-party Glee," which contained the line

> I vote no longer for a name /
> pure principles are now my aim.[18]

The Constitutional Union Party also defined itself as the antidote to politics as usual (despite being led by a cobwebbed coterie of elderly ex-Whigs), denouncing the "spirit of party [that] raised its serpent fangs above them all."[19]

In *Democracy in America*, Alexis de Tocqueville, absorbing no doubt the presumptions of his informants, made a revealing distinction between "great" and "petty" parties, the former being "those which cling . . . to ideas, and not to men," and the latter being driven by a desire for power and pelf.[20] Like other nineteenth-century elections, that of 1860 was, on one level, a battle over which party represented great principles—such as the "eternal struggle between liberty and tyranny," as one (Douglas Democratic) newspaper put it—and which was merely the product of the "petty" schemes of "ambitious" or "fanatical" men. The Republican conspiracy theory about a scheming Slave Power was not just rhetorical window dressing; it was a powerful narrative, one that made sense of key events (the repeal of the Missouri Compromise, "bleeding Kansas," the Dred Scott decision, and so on). The Breckinridge campaign drew on similar tropes in its depiction of a Black Republican conspiracy to undermine southern rights. In both cases, a conspiratorial mode of presenting the world drew on a common republican political culture in which politics was about binary choices, pluralism was poorly developed as a concept, and liberty always had to be protected from those with power.

This was also the political cultural context in which anxiety about corruption was framed. A report by the Republican congressman John Covode on the corruption of the Buchanan administration was a widely circulated campaign document.[21] Corruption of the venal kind was bad enough, but in a republican political culture the pilfering by officeholders and the disreputable reputation of parties and wire pullers threatened to undermine the Republic by draining it of virtue and honesty. In the Republican Party imagination, corruption scandals were symptomatic of the existential threat posed by the Slave Power. There were two irrepressible conflicts, explained *New York Tribune* editor Horace Greeley during the campaign, one pitting freedom against "aggressive, all-grasping Slavery propagandism," and the second, "not less vital," between "frugal government and honest administration" on the one hand and "wholesale executive corruption, and speculative jobbery" on the other.[22]

Electoral Behavior

In this, as in every election in the middle decades of the nineteenth century, neither the appearance of new party labels nor the salience of new issues could obscure an underlying continuity in voting patterns. The Republican vote was strongest where Whigs and antislavery parties before them had always done well. It was regionally concentrated in New England (where Lincoln won every single county) and those parts of the North most influenced by evangelicalism and Yankee settlement: upstate New York and parts of Ohio, Michigan, Wisconsin and Iowa, plus northern counties of Illinois and Indiana. In 1860 Republicans did especially well in comparison with their predecessor parties in Illinois and Pennsylvania, states that had once been dominated by the Democracy. But the Democrats remained strong among their traditional supporters—Irish immigrants and working-class urbanites (the only major city Lincoln won was Chicago), and non-Yankee-influenced rural voters in the Midwest.

In the South, John Bell won in traditional areas of Whig strength—in his home state of Tennessee, plus Virginia and Kentucky. He also came in a close second in Georgia and North Carolina. Confirming his Whiggish appeal, some people supported Bell in the explicit hope that they might be able to create, as one Virginia Whig put it, a new, national "conservative Union party, somewhat resembling the old Whig party."[23] But this was, in the end, a purely regional, Upper South project. In the free states, the Constitutional Unionists failed, on the whole, to attract the support of former Whig and Know-Nothing voters; only in Massachusetts and the Pacific West did the old Whig vote gravitate to John Bell rather than Lincoln.[24]

Although in very broad terms, election results reflected historic cultural and socioeconomic political identities, these underlying patterns did not determine election outcomes, which were often shaped by relatively small margins. Politicians did not take the electorate for granted. On the contrary, they behaved as if defending and attacking the record of incumbents would swing votes. And corruption scandals, the fallout of the Panic of 1857, and the general sense that the nation was on the brink of disunion undermined the incumbents, the Democratic Party that had dominated national politics for thirty years. Despite his reputation, James Buchanan was not a vacillating and feeble president, but, on the contrary, ideologically driven and activist.[25] His most disastrous move was trying to drive the proslavery Lecompton Constitution for Kansas through Congress, at the cost of splitting his party, because he was convinced that only by acceding to southern demands could the controversy over slavery in the territories be "solved." The Democratic Party may well have split anyway, since, as numerous historians have shown, there was a powerful southern lobby that deliberately maneuvered to this end. Even moderate southern Democrats were determined to settle for nothing less than a federal slave code that was anathema to, and would have been electoral suicide for, the northern wing of the party. Nevertheless, at every stage of his administration, Buchanan took decisions that exacerbated the problem. And his loyalty to southerners in his cabinet meant that he overlooked the egregious corruption of men like Secretary of War John B. Floyd.

In the light of all this, many observers understandably saw the election as more a rejection of Buchanan and what he had come to represent than an endorsement of the Republicans. The *New York World*, which was not yet a Democratic organ, claimed in October 1860 that most Republican voters did not care "a broken tobacco-pipe for the negro question." The cause of Lincoln's likely victory, the newspaper suggested, was the popular belief that "the democratic party has been so long in power that it has become corrupt; that it understands too well the crooked arts by which partisan pockets are lined at the public expense; and that it is safer to try an experiment with new men and a young party, than to continue a set of old party hacks at the public crib."[26]

Chairman of the Democratic National Committee August Belmont agreed. "The country at large had become disgusted with the misrule of Mr. Buchanan, and the corruption which disgraced his Administration," he wrote. "The Democratic party was made answerable for his misdeeds, and a change was ardently desired by thousands of conservative men out of politics."[27] The "great idea" settled by this election, declared the Philadelphia *North American*, was "the overthrow of corruption." It made no mention of slavery extension.[28]

Campaign Strategies

Politicians' responsiveness to voters intensified sectional polarization by curtailing candidates' room for maneuver within each section. Since each party system is imagined to be oriented around a different set of issues, proponents of the realignment synthesis stressed the "positional" (that is, distinctive, new) issues of insurgent parties. However, my reading of the evidence is that so-called valence issues (that is, points on which the parties agree but compete to present themselves as best placed to deliver) were generally more important drivers of political debate in this period.[29] In 1860 the ideological divide (in Burnham's sense of "highly salient issue-clusters") *within* each section was *narrower than* in previous elections. On important matters of policy, Republican and Democrats were not so far apart. Douglas did not just endorse a Homestead Act, a Pacific railroad, and federal support for internal improvements, all policies that were championed by the Republicans; he claimed, not entirely implausibly, to have invented them all (although, to be fair, large sections of his party remained wary of all three).[30]

Both parties claimed to be the defenders of free white labor. Democrats were much more overt in their use of racism to warn of competition from freed slaves. But Republicans in Indiana and Illinois, where this was a major campaign issue, used similar arguments to make the case against slavery extension, albeit usually without the crude racism of the Democrats. Republicans attacked Democrats for favoring Cuban annexation on the grounds that it would lead to racial amalgamation. One such article, in the *Illinois State Journal*, may, according to Lincoln biographer Michael Burlingame, have been penned by the candidate himself.[31] As the Republican *New York Times* asked rhetorically, "How is the doctrine of negro equality to be 'forced upon the South' by the Republicans, when they scout and scorn it for the free negroes of the North?" Republicans do not "have any more love of the negro—any greater disposition to make sacrifices for his sake, or to waive their own rights and interests for the promotion of his welfare, than the rest of mankind, North and South."[32] Meanwhile, northern Democrats indignantly warned that if the consequence of southerners' "bolting" was Lincoln's election, they should no longer expect any support from northern Democrats in returning "a 'fugitive' which they have not a dollar's interest in." Douglas newspapers used the terms "slaveocracy" and "Slave Power," coinages associated with the Republicans, to describe Breckinridge.[33]

Both parties battled for the mantle of conservatism, with Republicans vigorously countering Democrats' claims to be the true Unionists. Lincoln's hometown Republican newspaper made this its consistent theme. The election, it stressed, was a battle between "conservative Republicanism [and] fire-eating, slave-extending Democracy."[34] One of Lincoln's supporters in 1860, a young ex-Whig, Manton Marble, later to become editor of the vocally anti-Lincoln *New York World*, was convinced that support for the Republicans was the only true "conservative" course.[35]

I do not mean to suggest that the differences between the parties were unimportant. Especially in its New England heartland, the Republican Party expressed itself in a political style colored by evangelicalism and a long reform tradition that was at odds with the laissez-faire approach and tolerance of cultural diversity of most Democrats. Almost everywhere the Douglas Democrats proved much more willing to use the nastiest forms of race baiting than did Republicans. And Republicans opposed all slavery extension on principle, whereas northern Democrats made much of their candidate's championing of "popular sovereignty." Yet while these were positions with divergent legislative implications, both were—overtly or implicitly—antagonistic to the Dred Scott decision, and both were expressed in terms of white settlers' opportunity in the West. Largely unnoticed by historians, powerful voices within the Republican Party even tried to neutralize the public appeal of Douglas's policy of congressional noninterference in the territories by denying that it amounted to a significant distinction between the parties. "The great mass of the people in all sections . . . recognize popular sovereignty as a fair, just and safe way of solving a very difficult problem," acknowledged the Republican *New York Times* in July 1860. "The slavery question *will* be settled on this basis, *whichever party may come into power.* This is, under any circumstances, to be the *practical solution of the difficulty.*"[36]

The key to the Republican Party's appeal in 1860 was its claim to be the most effective bulwark against an aggressive and destabilizing Slave Power.

Republicans presented themselves as the new broom that would sweep away years, if not decades, of rule in Washington by a corrupted national Democratic Party that was betraying the interests of the ordinary free white men it claimed to represent. The campaign made a conservative pitch to restore ancient liberties. There was a relentless focus in campaign speeches on the threat of the slave trade being reopened (this was mentioned by Lincoln in most of his 1859 speeches) and on Breckinridge's policy, backed by President Buchanan, of introducing a congressional slave code for the territories.[37] During the campaign, Lincoln newspapers reported random lynchings of northerners in the South, stories that fed their narrative about the barbarism of the Slave Power.[38]

Democrats had presented themselves as the embodiment of the common man for thirty years or more, but in 1860 Republicans worked hard to co-opt this Jacksonian language for themselves. Republican clubs held meetings to celebrate Jefferson's birthday, and Lincoln was hailed as a "Jeffersonian Republican" in campaign literature.[39] Republican campaigners argued that the "so-called Democratic party" was "false to its name" and was now the "aristocratic" party, its support for slavery extension being in effect support for land monopoly by slaveowners, securing "power to the few." Jefferson and Jackson were retrospectively enlisted as Republican spokesmen, since they had wanted to "give and preserve power to the people to enable them to become proprietors and secure them in their homes."[40] The candidate's carefully projected image as a "Rail Splitter" and as "Honest Abe," as an "obscure child of labor" who was "an apt illustration of our free institutions," was a core component in the project of presenting Republicanism as on the side of the workingman.[41]

The Douglas Democrats were left with a problem of differentiation. They too had the appeal of a popular candidate who had made his own way in the West. And they were the original party of the common man. Furthermore, Douglas's campaign was at least as enthusiastic as Lincoln's in trying to profit from the anti-incumbent mood of the electorate through excoriating and often very personal attacks on Buchanan's administration. Douglas's political feud with the president allowed his campaign to try to outbid Lincoln as the candidate of change. In 1860, Douglas Democrats, freed of their southern wing, ran against the Slave Power too—a high proportion of Democrats' campaign speeches framed the issue as a battle between the Union-saving Douglas and southern disunionists. Historians have sometimes assumed that "popular sovereignty" was a rather shallow fig leaf for a policy that benefited the South, but that is to underestimate the passion with which the Douglas campaign advocated it, on moral, economic, and nationalist grounds. So Douglas, like Lincoln, was presented as the defender of northern free labor values, with "popular sovereignty," an idea rooted in the American tradition, as the guarantor of that promise. What Douglas supporters tried to do was to tell a story about their candidate as the only true nationalist, the one man who could save the Union against "fanaticism," northern as well as southern. Douglas alone, the campaign asserted, would not only save the Union (in contrast to the "recklessness" of Lincoln and the "Disunionist bolter" Breckinridge), but would also transform the opportunities available to white northerners.

Back in 1856, the Buchanan campaign had some success in painting the Republicans as dangerous radicals, and Douglas tried the same approach in 1860. But circumstances had changed, the stakes now seemed higher, and the Republicans' warnings about southern aggression seemed, in the previous four years, to have been vindicated. Douglas supporters, meanwhile, tried to use Brown's raid as evidence of Republican extremism, but the charges did not stick, even with natural conservatives like Manton Marble. All the Harpers Ferry drama did, in the end, was to make it more difficult for Douglas to deny the severity of the sectional crisis. The case for the Republicans in 1860 was that if, as a northerner, one wanted to defend free institutions, why vote for Douglas, who was compromised by his association with the national Democratic Party and who probably could not win anyway, when one could vote for Lincoln, whose anti–Slave Power credentials ran much deeper?

In the slave states, Bell and Breckinridge supporters each presented their candidate as the one most likely to defend southern rights, albeit through different mechanisms. Bell's story was that he was a wise statesman in the tradition of Henry Clay. Breckinridge's was that he offered a specific and supposedly final plan to secure southern rights within the Union. A federal slave code would provide legislative backup to the Dred Scott decision; promises of Caribbean expansion offered a way of building the collective strength of the slave states within the Union. Explicit in this story was the idea that if the North rejected these demands, and Lincoln or Douglas became president, the South would have been finally vindicated in its assumption that Yankees were no longer prepared to respect their equal rights (by which they meant respect for slaves as legitimate property).

These campaign strategies were, in essence, aimed at creating "narratives" that connected an image of the candidate to a story about what was wrong, who the enemy was, and how it could be put right. The task of politicians—whether party managers, editors, or other opinion formers such as ministers and popular speakers—was to "make sense" of the world to voters, shaping, but by definition also being shaped by, voters' understanding of who their friends and enemies were and where their interests lay. Politics, especially at election time, was about synthesizing policy, political style, and underlying values into a plausible and compelling story. Whereas ideology is a way of describing longitudinal attitudes, it was the narratives constructed out of ideological components that mattered at election time. Such narratives were more or less compelling depending on context, events, candidates, and the effectiveness of mobilization strategies. Politics, as Robert Kelley once observed, often revolves around the "dramatic imagination" of its protagonists.[42] The drama lay in the acute consciousness of the choice confronting the nation and is often constructed, in a republican frame, around fears of conspiracy and threats to liberty.

All four campaigns told a story about how their man was best placed to maintain *order* and *stability*, how their man, and theirs alone, was the true protector of the legacy of the *Revolution*, the defender of *freedom*. Obviously the crisis over slavery, the threat of the Slave Power (to northerners), or of abolition (to southerners) was the immediate reference point. But the partisan political narratives in 1860 were given layers of additional meaning in the light of the fallout of the 1848 revolutions in Europe. When politicians talked about nation, revolution, freedom, power, government, the people, or order they were using terms reshaped over a dozen years by fears, and hopes, of social transformation and national transfiguration. So, for example, the prospect of disunion was equated in the northern imagination with civil disorder, anarchy, and violence, while antislavery politics was associated by its opponents with dangerous ideas about the confiscation and redistribution of property. When the Democratic *New York Herald* attacked Lincoln as an "abolitionist of the reddest dye," the implicit reference to revolutionary socialism was not accidental.[43]

The value to the historian of identifying the competing political narratives at play in an election is that it focuses attention on the practical process of political persuasion. It draws attention to how ideas, or abstract ideologies, were framed and expressed, and how perceptions of events were processed and manipulated. It cannot "explain" the election result in the sense of making alternative outcomes impossible to conceive, but it can identify the underlying assumptions that constitute the sources of political authority, and therefore how changes to them have implications for political development.

Conclusion

The 1860 election precipitated a highly consequential shift in party control with clear implications for public policy in some key areas such as banking, currency, tariffs, and, ultimately, federal-state relations. In rough correlation with Arthur M. Schlesinger, Jr.'s cyclical theory of American politics, the "outs" became the "ins."[44] Lincoln's victory, together with the withdrawal of southern congressmen as their states seceded, marked the ascendancy of a new group of men in Washington and the effective end of thirty years in which a distinctive Jacksonian variant of transatlantic liberalism had been the default setting in American politics. Since the Democratic ascendancy of the antebellum years had also been, to a greater or lesser extent, a southern ascendancy at the federal level, the shift in party control was more properly understood as a fundamental shift in the sectional balance of power.

But the relationship between this coming Republican ascendancy and the election was complex. The South, as it turned out, was excluded from national power because of secession and war rather than as a direct result of the rise in the Republican vote in Pennsylvania and the Midwest. And although around 7 percent of the whole electorate shifted toward Lincoln in 1860, the party's hold on these conservative voters was conditional. Apart from in Pennsylvania (where Buchanan's 1856 victory was the last in the state by a Democrat until 1936), Republican gains in 1860 were not wholly secure in the medium term, with Democrats making big gains in the 1862 midterm elections and beyond (although Lincoln held them all in the exceptional circumstances of the 1864 presidential election). In 1860 the Republican Party was still a very loose coalition of state machines, not all sharing the same name, let alone political priorities.[45] Even in victory, there were constant expectations that the party would cease to exist in its current form and under its current name. In 1864 Lincoln ran for reelection not as a Republican but as a National Unionist, which reflected, in part, recognition of the continuing toxicity of the Republican brand in large swaths of the country outside New England.[46] Just as the War of 1812 had—in popular memory—led to an "era of good feeling," the Civil War, argued *Harper's Weekly* in 1865, had taught Americans a valuable lesson: "Old party lines do not separate us. We are at the end of parties."[47] William H. Seward spoke enthusiastically of a "great coming together" of the parties once the divisive issue of slavery was dispensed with by the Thirteenth Amendment.[48] Expectations of continuing realignment, in other words, continued long after the late 1850s.

The Republican Party that was ascendant in the late nineteenth century was "made" during Reconstruction, building retrospectively on its wartime accomplishments to create a narrative about the "Grand Old Party" as the defender of the Union. A series of contingencies such as the assassination (and near sanctification) of Lincoln, the battle with President Andrew Johnson over early Reconstruction legislation, and the Panic of 1873 all helped to forge the institutional identity and characteristics of the party. It is difficult, if not impossible, as historians to deny ourselves the luxury of hindsight. But in order to understand a political event like this election on its own terms we need to try and isolate what happened in November 1860 from how subsequent events and subsequent political narratives retrospectively colored it.

Realignment theory presented the 1860 election as the moment when the party system readjusted to the underlying social reality. I have presented an alternative formulation: like other elections in this period, although with greater consequences in terms of war and a shift in party control, the 1860 election was a contest among parties to offer the most compelling narratives about how to save the Republic to voters whose political values had underlying consistency but whose partisan loyalties were more fluid. For a series of contingent reasons (to do with short-term party strategy and the impact of events like John Brown's raid), the parties that gained support (the Republicans in the North and the Breckinridge Democrats in the South) were those that most effectively dramatized the national crisis and offered the clearest solution to it.

Given the underlying political culture, campaign strategies that relied on fears of corruption and conspiracy were especially effective. As many historians have demonstrated, northerners did not vote for an antislavery party because they had all become abolitionists; they voted for the party that had the clearest solution to the threat posed by the Slave Power. The Douglas Democrats tried to offer their own solution to the national crisis by using Republican language about the Slave Power to show they knew who the real enemy was, and by presenting popular sovereignty as the most effective solution to the crisis. But they were also drawing, as were the Constitutional Unionists, on the "compromise" tradition, damning extremism on both sides. The balance was tipped against these compromisers in 1860. As is the way with most elections, the short-term losers did not regard themselves as having lost the argument, though, and, as events unfolded in the following years, both the Douglasite Democratic tradition in the north and the Whiggish southern tradition felt vindicated. They saw the 1860 election as just one battle in a bigger and ongoing contest.

CHAPTER 4

Markets, Morality, and the Media: The Election of 1884 and the Iconography of Progressivism

Richard R. John

The victory of Democrat Grover Cleveland over Republican James G. Blaine in the presidential election of 1884 is one of those events in U.S. history that once commanded broad attention but that has long since ceased to stir the blood. This was an epoch, after all, about which historians customarily play up the radical transformations being wrought by big business and downplay the influence of presidential administrations on public policy. In the conventional narrative—familiar to contemporaries, and updated a half century later for a generation of New Dealers by the journalist-turned-popular historian Matthew Josephson—greedy "robber barons" called the shots, while unscrupulous "politicos" did their bidding. This big-business-centric narrative has proved remarkably durable and helps explain why generations of historians have—misleadingly, in my view—borrowed a phrase from Mark Twain and called the period between the end of Congressional Reconstruction in 1877 and the emergence of the Progressive movement around 1900 the Gilded Age.

To the extent that the 1884 election lives on in the collective imagination, it is largely on account of a single incident that occurred in a Republican rally in New York City during the final, hectic week of the campaign. Exasperated by Blaine's Democratic opponents, an obscure pro-Blaine Presbyterian minister castigated the Democrats as the party of "rum, Romanism, and rebellion." Not until the following Sunday would Blaine issue a public statement disavowing the minister's derogatory characterization of the Catholic Church. By this time, the phrase had gone viral, galvanizing, if informed insiders can be believed, thousands of Irish Catholics to switch their votes from Blaine to Cleveland. Cleveland's margin of victory over Blaine in New York State was razor-thin, a mere 1,047 votes out of 1.2 million ballots cast. Even so, the margin was large enough to give Cleveland the state's thirty-six electoral votes and, with them, the election. Historians have long challenged the causal relationship between the minister's remark and the election outcome. Yet, in the annals of electoral lore, it lives on as one the most disastrous gaffes in the history of American politics.

The significance of the 1884 election is not to be found in its denouement. Rather, it lies in the emergence of a small yet determined voting bloc during the election campaign and in the role of this bloc following Cleveland's victory on the promulgation of public policy. At the core of this bloc of voters were antimonopolist merchants troubled by the conduct of giant corporations and anti-Blaine Republicans outraged at the moral failings of the Republican candidate. While this voting bloc existed in several northern and midwestern states, it was particularly influential in New York, the country's media capital, the home of the largest port, and its most important financial center. The legacy of this voting bloc extended well beyond the 1880s. By forging an alliance with journalists emboldened by novel forms of visual storytelling, it helped lay the groundwork for the early twentieth-century Progressive movement and the mid-twentieth-century administrative state.

Of the various issues to agitate the electorate in 1884, few proved more enduring than the public outcry over railroad and telegraph "monopolies." The rapid expansion since the 1850s of a nationwide transportation and communications network was one of the defining features of the age. Slowly yet decisively, the state-chartered corporation was supplanting the common-law proprietorship as the nation's dominant economic institution. While the emergence of giant corporations had a seeming inexorability, corporate expansion did not go unopposed. For a small yet articulate group of self-styled antimonopolists, the business practices of William H. Vanderbilt's New York Central and Hudson River Railroad and Jay Gould's Western Union, the nation's largest telegraph network provider, posed a fundamental threat not only to commerce but also to the Republic.

Antimonopolists objected less to the scale on which railroads and telegraphs operated than to their autonomy. Unconstrained by the regulatory mechanism of the market—a mechanism that, as all merchants knew, continued to regulate commerce on the high seas—these corporations had acquired the economic power to set prices for the conveyance of people, goods, and information at high speeds throughout the vast American interior.

Railroads and telegraph lines crossed state boundaries, making federal legislation a logical remedy. In the case of the telegraph, none was forthcoming. Though Congress repeatedly debated federal telegraph legislation during Cleveland's first administration, with the exception of an 1888 law outlawing the ownership of telegraph lines by land grant railroads (the Anderson Act), none of this legislation found its way into law.[1] In the case of the railroad, antimonopoly lawmakers were more successful. By the time Cleveland took office in 1885, Massachusetts and New York had already established state railroad commissions: Massachusetts in 1869, New York in 1882. Emulating their example, lawmakers in 1887 established the Interstate Commerce Commission (ICC) to regulate the nation's railroad network. The ICC was not the first federal regulatory agency, having been preceded by the Post Office Department and the Patent Office. Yet it was the first federal agency to oversee an economic sector in which the corporation had supplanted the proprietorship as the dominant mode of economic coordination.

Presidential elections in the late nineteenth century are best understood not as single events, as it has become customary to characterize them today, but rather as an aggregation of individual state elections, each with its own peculiarities. The outcome, of course, was *national*—one candidate won the majority of the electoral votes, and with it the presidency. The process, however, was *federal*. A typical late nineteenth-century presidential election revolved around a distinctive array of often idiosyncratic issues that had their own state-specific dynamic.

The great prize for party leaders was not the popular vote in the nation, but the popular vote in each individual state. Under the federal Constitution, the winning candidate needed a majority of the votes in the Electoral College, in which every state was allocated a vote total that was equal to the number of its U.S. senators and representatives. In accordance with a long-standing convention known as the "unit rule," the electoral votes of each state were awarded in a bloc to whichever candidate won a plurality of the state's popular vote. Whoever won the largest number of electoral votes—which was usually, though not invariably, the candidate who also won the popular vote—won the election.

As so often occurred in late nineteenth-century presidential campaigns, the 1884 election hinged on voting results in four states: Indiana, Connecticut,

New Jersey, and New York. The reason was simple. In each of these states, the electorate was more or less evenly divided between Democrats and Republicans, making it conceivable that, in a close election, the standard-bearer for either party might prevail. In a country that was as large and diverse as the United States, it might seem bizarre for a presidential election to be decided by such a relatively small number of voters. Yet that was how things worked in practice. Of these four states, none had more electoral votes than New York. In fact, New York, with thirty-six, had the largest number of electoral votes of any state in the country.

The outsized significance of New York in electoral politics was a by-product of the political compromises that an earlier generation of lawmakers had made to reunite the country following the Civil War. Terrified by the threat that ex-slaves posed to the political order, Democratic Party leaders had worked doggedly in the years since emancipation to deny them, and increasingly many poor whites, their constitutionally mandated voting rights. This strategy had an unmistakably partisan rationale. The vast majority of ex-slaves were Republican, and in several of the eleven southern states that had seceded during the Civil War, the Republican Party depended on African American votes to win elections. It took hard work to make the South "solid": persuasion, intimidation, violence, and even outright murder were among the tools that Democratic Party leaders deployed. Nothing any Republican ward heeler did to suppress the turnout in Democratic-leaning districts in the burgeoning industrial cities of the North was remotely comparable to the systematic disenfranchisement of hundreds of thousands of African Americans in the former Confederacy.

In short, the electoral map was biased in favor of the Democrats, and with each passing year it became increasingly clear that there was precious little that ex-slaves, Republican Party leaders, or, for that matter, high-minded ex-abolitionist civil rights activists could do about it.[2] It was, thus, no accident that all of the four swing states were located in the North. Party competition was the most intense in that part of the country in which the Democratic Party had the least control over the levers of power. Had the Democrats not systematically blocked southern blacks from participating in electoral politics, New York's electoral votes would not have loomed so large. Blaine would have won several southern states and, with them, the election. Yet the Democrats had rigged the system, making New York's electoral votes far more consequential than they would have been had the South been in play.

No seasoned political insider seriously doubted that once the final election returns had been tallied New York's bloc of electoral votes would be awarded to either Cleveland or Blaine, and not to a third-party independent candidate. Yet it was far from obvious who would win over the large cohort of independent voters who held the balance of power. "For more than twelve years," declared one political insider in July 1884 in seconding Cleveland's presidential nomination, the most critical voting bloc in the state of New York was the "large unattached vote"—one hundred thousand strong—"which belongs to neither political organization," and which was far less inclined to vote for the candidate, or the party, than for the positions on issues the candidate had pledged to uphold.[3]

The existence of such a large bloc of independent voters thrust into prominence two third-party candidates: John St. John and Benjamin F. Butler. St. John carried the standard for the Prohibition Party, Butler for the Greenback Party and the Anti-Monopoly Party.

St. John and Butler appealed to different segments of the electorate. St. John ran well among evangelicals in New York's upstate "burned-over district," a voting bloc that, had St. John stood down, would almost certainly have gone heavily for Blaine. Many evangelicals yearned for a total ban on the sale and consumption of alcoholic beverages and felt betrayed when Republican Party leaders refused to incorporate into their platform a strongly worded prohibition plank introduced by Frances Willard's Woman's Christian Temperance Union.[4] St. John shared the evangelicals' indignation and entered the race to protest the Republican Party's moral equivocation.

Butler, in contrast, could be expected to siphon votes away from Cleveland, given his popularity among urban workingmen, a constituency that typically voted Democratic, especially in New York City and Brooklyn.[5] Party leaders understood all of this perfectly well and responded accordingly. Republican operatives covertly funded Butler's campaign, while St. John's campaign received financial support from the Democrats.[6]

Butler's candidacy posed a particular challenge for Democrats, since he ran as a "fusion" candidate who had obtained the endorsement of two very different political blocs: the Greenback Party, an organization that drew the bulk of its support from midwestern farmers and laborers, and the Anti-Monopoly Party, an organization with close ties to influential New York City merchants.

The Anti-Monopoly Party had its beginnings in the rising protest of East Coast merchants against the business practices of railroad and telegraph corporations. One turning point occurred in January 1881, when the country's business elite was stunned by the unexpected takeover of Western Union by the notorious Wall Street trader Jay Gould. Gould's gambit crystallized the uneasiness that New York City's business elite felt toward financial practices associated with the emerging corporate order. Now that Gould controlled the nation's most important high-speed communications network, critics feared that he had it within his power to manipulate the prices not only of agricultural staples—and, conceivably, even the price of gold—but also of corporate securities.[7]

Gould's takeover of Western Union led directly to the establishment of the New York City–based National Anti-Monopoly League, an organization that would quickly establish itself as a force in electoral politics. The league drew its primary support from merchants, wholesalers, shippers, and the lawyers who represented their interests.[8] Its rationale, as founder Francis B. Thurber explained, was not to destroy the emerging corporate order, but rather to render it accountable to law: "Mr. Chairman and Fellow-citizens, *the Anti-Monopoly League stands simply upon the principles embodied in the Constitution of the United States, and as interpreted by the highest legal authority in the United States—the Supreme Court. If this is radical, we are radical; if this is the action of demagogues and Communists, we are demagogues and Communists, not otherwise.*"[9] So fervent was Thurber in his denunciation of the railroads that one critic sardonically called him the "bottom, top, rind, and the core" of the antimonopoly movement in New York.[10]

The legislative agenda that Thurber championed was broad and wide-ranging. Prominent among its goals was a ban on the informal agreements, known as pools, that railroad managers negotiated with each other to stabilize the flow of the goods they transported. Thurber also sought a restriction on the issuance of corporate securities in amounts that exceeded the actual value of a corporation's assets, a practice known as stock watering, and the elimination of rate schedules that discriminated against shippers who wanted to transport a relatively small quantity of goods over a relatively short distance, as distinct from shippers who transported in bulk and over long hauls. Finally, Thurber hoped to persuade the New York legislature to establish a permanent railroad commission, with rate-setting powers, that could authoritatively determine the actual cost of transporting a given item a given distance in a given period of time, making it possible to base railroad rate making on the actual cost of delivery rather than on whatever rates the railroad could obtain from the shipper, a practice that Thurber regarded as extortionate, and which he derisively termed "what the traffic will bear."[11]

Thurber's antimonopolism was grounded in his business experience. A highly successful wholesale grocer, Thurber was the coproprietor of Thurber, Whyland & Company, a sprawling commercial empire whose opulent six-story showroom in lower Manhattan was reputed to boast the "largest, choicest, and most comprehensive stock of food products in America." (The building still stands today; it now houses luxury apartments.) Thurber was one of the country's leading specialists in the global supply chains upon which his business depended, and filled his Manhattan showroom with exotic foodstuffs imported from East Asia and Europe as well as canned goods manufactured in his own Moorestown, New Jersey, factory.[12] To build a market for his wares among the retailers who were his primary customers, he capitalized on recent technical advances in multicolor printing to issue thousands of splashy, full-color chromolithographic trade cards, an innovation that historians of advertising regard as an important juncture in the transformation of advertising from a verbal to a visual medium.[13]

Hostility toward railroad and telegraph corporations was widespread in the 1880s, and not only in New York City. Upstate merchants, too, deplored the conduct of railroad and telegraph corporations and cried out for relief. The meteoric rise of Grover Cleveland from Buffalo mayor in 1881 to U.S. president in 1884 built on this popular groundswell. The most critical event in Cleveland's rise was his victory as New York governor in 1882, one that antimonopolists attributed to his endorsement by merchants disgusted with what they derided as the procorporate tilt in state government. Cleveland's immediate predecessor as governor, Alonzo Cornell, had been dropped from the ticket by Republican Party leaders for several reasons, including Cornell's refusal to veto legislation establishing a permanent railroad commission, a reform for which Thurber had diligently lobbied since 1879, and which would be duly established in 1882.[14]

Cleveland's tenure as New York governor divided the antimonopolists. Some admired his judiciousness in adjudicating the rival claims of corporations and their critics. Others—including Thurber—criticized Cleveland's appointees for the railroad commission and expressed outrage at his veto of a bill that would have capped at five cents the fare that a Gould-owned elevated streetcar line could charge off-peak-time commuters.[15] That Gould had bribed lawmakers to overturn the will of the people as it had been expressed through their legislators seemed to Thurber self-evident. Other prominent public figures concurred. Had it been permissible under U.S. law to issue a bill of attainder to bring Gould to justice without the necessity for a jury trial—or so declared the then little-known state assemblyman Theodore Roosevelt, in explaining why he too endorsed the rate cap—Roosevelt would do so gladly, for Gould headed up the "wealthy criminal class" that, through bribery, physical intimidation, and worse, was insidiously corrupting the political institutions that lay at the foundation of the Republic. A jury trial would only magnify Gould's perfidy: if legal proceedings were convened, Gould would almost certainly buy off the jurors.[16]

To the consternation of his critics, Roosevelt soon changed his mind. Cleveland's veto had been entirely proper, he now concluded; since Gould's franchise had been granted by a state legislature, the legislature had a legal obligation to uphold it.

Roosevelt was hardly alone. Among the antimonopolists to back Cleveland's veto of the five-cent bill was the prominent New York City lawyer Simon Sterne. Sterne, a Democrat, wrote widely on public policy topics and was the author of a respected history of the U.S. Constitution first published in 1882. Sterne's antimonopoly bona fides were unassailable. He had played a prominent role in the political crusade that had brought down the notorious Tammany boss William Tweed and had testified in support of the establishment of the New York railroad commission. Yet Sterne was a lawyer by training and shared his profession's veneration for legal propriety. Gould's overhead railroad operated in accordance with a legal charter, and the legislature lacked the authority to alter its terms.

Cleveland's nomination for president in 1884 did nothing to heal the rift in the antimonopolists' ranks. Moderate antimonopolists sided with Sterne and endorsed Cleveland as the antimonopoly candidate. Uncompromising antimonopolists like Thurber refused. Troubled by the appointments Cleveland had made as governor to the state's newly established railroad commission, and outraged by Cleveland's five-cent veto, he cast his lot with Butler.

Thurber's public endorsement of Butler underscored his dissatisfaction with Cleveland's tenure as governor. Everything in Cleveland's administration, in Thurber's view, revealed that his sympathies were "with corporations, and not with the people": "If the people want to be ruled by the wealthy criminal classes, and if they desire to see the National Government prostituted by the lusts of greedy and unscrupulous monopolists, let them vote for Gov. Cleveland. If they want honest government and the abolition of monopoly they will poll a heavy and independent vote, and leave Mr. Cleveland out in the cold." Only Butler, in Thurber's view, had the fortitude to challenge the powers that be: "The rights of labor and the opposition to the monopolies that are gaining ground day by day will be the rallying cries of the coming campaign, and the leading parties will learn when it is too late that the people are tired of machine misgovernment. There will be a conference of Anti-Monopolists later this month."[17]

Thurber freely conceded that he had voted the Republican ticket in the past and that his business partner and brother, H. K. Thurber, backed Blaine in 1884. But he would not. Unlike Butler, and in flagrant defiance of what Thurber regarded as the country's democratic heritage, each of the major party candidates preferred to "associate with" and "serve the interests" of the "rich and powerful few rather than the many who are poor and weak." It was an open secret, in Thurber's view, that corporations had come to wield enormous influence over many state governments and had proved equally successful in gaining a foothold in Congress: "The condition of things is truly alarming, for unless it be changed quickly and thoroughly, free institutions are doomed to be subverted by an oligarchy resting upon a basis of money and of corporate power."[18]

Sterne was more measured. Neither Blaine nor Butler, in his view, deserved the antimonopolists' vote, since neither candidate had ever "done anything" to "entitle him to the confidence of those who desire to see the growing monopolies curbed." A vote against Cleveland was a vote for Blaine, and Blaine's election would be a disaster for the antimonopolists: "[Blaine] dares not, if he now would, offend the monopoly powers, who hold the secrets and controlled his actions in the past."[19]

In the end, Butler's campaign failed to live up to Thurber's expectations or Sterne's fears. Despite a great deal of media hype, Butler polled far fewer votes than expected; in fact, in New York he did considerably worse than the Prohibition candidate, St. John. No one could deny that the workingman had grievances, explained one Brooklyn journalist in urging his readership *not* to bolt for Butler. Yet the electoral math was undeniable: any vote for Butler was a vote for Blaine. And the proposition that the workers' wrongs could be righted by putting Blaine in the White House, where he would be surrounded by a "crew of monopolists, corruptionists, tax eaters," and "openly confessed robbers" who had profited from high tariffs, which the journalist termed "surplus taxes," was "too manifestly absurd" to be made to "intelligent citizens."[20]

While Butler failed, the antimonopolists succeeded. By publicizing the challenge posed by the emerging corporate order, they popularized a morally charged reformist idiom that would shape American electoral politics for the next fifty years. "Like light, or air, or water," Thurber explained in a magazine article published in 1875—articulating a theme he would return to in the run-up to the election of 1884—steam and electricity were "God's gifts to the human race" and "should be possessed and enjoyed by everyone."[21] To Thurber's chagrin, in 1884, as in 1875, their benefits continued to be monopolized by the few.

For the antimonopolists the crux of the problem lay in the failure of the country's lawmakers to establish the necessary regulatory mechanisms to constrain corporate power. The critical dividing line was not rich versus poor; rather, it was proprietary capitalism versus corporate capitalism. Thurber's own business career was a case in point. The political economy in which Thurber had built his business was dominated not by corporations such as the New York Central Railroad and Western Union, but rather by proprietorships such as Thurber, Whyland & Company. Thurber had built his fortune as a proprietary capitalist, in markets defined by competition, rather than as a corporate capitalist, in markets structured by administrative coordination. A proprietor might well become wealthy—for Thurber had nothing against wealth. This was to be applauded, since he had earned his "accumulations" under the "regulations of the laws of competition," which he could not fix by charging an arbitrary price. Corporations, in contrast, set their own prices, unconstrained by the discipline of the market.[22] Even more disturbingly, they had no soul. And for Thurber, this was the nub of the matter. The fathers of the American Republic had abolished primogeniture in order to secure the country from the "evils" of the accumulation of "vast individual wealth" from "generation to generation." Corporations had discovered in their state-granted perpetual charters the "elixir of life": "A corporation can neither be hung nor sent to the penitentiary; that is to say, there is an entire absence of individual responsibility."[23]

The New York antimonopolists took it for granted that the recent rise of railroad and telegraph corporations owed more to bribery and corruption than to technological imperatives and market incentives. Many journalists concurred. The exposure of secret dealings made for a good story, and few disclosures could top the revelation that a politician had lavished special privileges on a corporation in return for inside information, money, or some other valuable gift. No other issue—not the tariff, civil service reform, Civil War pensions, or the disenfranchisement of the ex-slaves—offered up as much dramatic potential. The principal fault line was not the *people* versus *business*, as a later generation of progressives would contend. Rather, it was *business* versus *monopoly*, a very different polarity. "Monopoly is not business," explained an editorialist in a New York City periodical shortly before the election, in a particularly pithy distillation of the conventional wisdom. On the contrary, monopoly "kills business":

> The business of the country will probably have a good deal to say on election day. It is not the [money] princes who are to do the voting, but their somewhat disloyal subjects. It is not the monopolists, but the small dealers, the middle men, the men who used to make fair profits through the then established principle that opposition is the life of trade. Too much of the wealth of this country is in the hands of a score of men and too little in the hands of the people. That is the business issue that is to be settled now.[24]

The likelihood that a public figure would find himself implicated in a corporate corruption scandal was, all things being equal, roughly proportional to the length of time he had held public office. And here Cleveland had the advantage over Blaine. Cleveland's public career in 1884 was still pretty much an open book. Though Cleveland had served one term as a sheriff in 1871, he had held his first major public office—as the mayor of Buffalo—a mere three years before he won the Democratic Party's presidential nomination. Blaine, in contrast, had served in Congress from 1863 until 1881, including a six-year stint as House Speaker during the Grant administration. By 1884 Blaine had generated a long paper trail that could easily be used against him. Particularly damning was a cache of personal letters that Blaine had written to an Arkansas railroad contractor during the former's tenure as Speaker. These letters documented the brazenness with which Blaine bartered political influence for personal financial gain, a character trait that would haunt him throughout the campaign.

Had this cache of letters never existed, it would not have been surprising had some journalist found occasion to invent them. After all, they fit perfectly with what had become by 1884 a widely agreed upon narrative about Blaine. Notwithstanding his formidable intelligence, charisma, and ambition, the ex-congressman turned presidential contender had personally profited during his tenure in Congress from the back-room deals he had struck with railroad lobbyists. The consistency with which Blaine defended the massive federal land grants that Congress had bestowed on railroad corporations since the 1850s was, for Blaine's critics, compelling evidence that the Republican standard-bearer lacked personal integrity and, thus, that all men of conscience, regardless of party affiliation, had a moral obligation to deny him the power and patronage that he would inevitably command should he defeat Cleveland and become president of the United States.

Blaine's tarnished past posed a formidable dilemma for his fellow Republicans. Some, including the young Theodore Roosevelt, weighed their misgivings about Blaine's moral character against the personal and political costs of bolting the party, and chose the party.

Others did not. Prominent among the anti-Blaine Republicans were several of the most respected journalists in the country, including Carl Schurz and E. L. Godkin of the *Nation* and George William Curtis and Thomas Nast of *Harper's Weekly*. Troubled by Blaine's moral failings and outraged by the railroad land grants for which they held Blaine accountable, these journalists broke party ranks and endorsed Cleveland for president.

The anti-Blaine Republicans would come to be known as mugwumps, an epithet popularized by a pro-Butler New York City journalist who did not intend it as a compliment. Before 1884, to call someone a mugwump was to identify him as a holier-than-thou old-stock Massachusetts blue blood—a self-regarding group whom Butler had long despised, and who more than returned the favor. Whatever its origin, the mugwump label quickly became a badge of pride as well as a factor in the campaign. The often fervid oratory of anti-Blaine Republicans did much to give the Cleveland-Blaine campaign its melodramatic tone, while mugwump journalists churned out reams of anti-Blaine editorials and a gallery of visually arresting cartoons.

Historians long credited the mugwumps' bolt with Blaine's defeat, a conclusion that echoed, and was largely based on, the mugwumps' own assessment. Cleveland won the pivotal state of New York by a whisker, and mugwumps dominated the editorial page of several influential New York City newspapers, including the *Times* and the *Evening Post*. If, however, one analyzes New York's election returns using modern statistical techniques, then it would seem plain that this interpretation is mistaken. Blaine, as it happens, polled better in 1884 among several pivotal voting blocs than the previous Republican presidential candidate, James Garfield, had in 1880. In fact, Blaine outpolled Garfield among Irish Catholics—"rum, romanism, and rebellion" notwithstanding. Cleveland, meanwhile, polled more poorly than one would have expected of a Democratic candidate, given the composition of the electorate; indeed, he even failed to carry his hometown of Buffalo.[25]

If the mugwumps could not be credited with Blaine's defeat, then who could? If any single individual tipped the scales, it was almost certainly the Prohibition Party candidate, John St. John. Had Republican Party leaders prevailed upon St. John to take himself out of the running in New York, Blaine would have obtained many if not most of St. John's twenty-five thousand votes—far more than Blaine needed to win the state and the election.[26]

While the mugwumps failed to swing the election, they shaped its tone. Here, as in so many chapters in American electoral politics, the press took the lead. Well-educated, well-bred, and well-mannered, anti-Blaine Republican journalists penned countless editorials deploring Blaine's venality and extolling Cleveland's probity. For them, the election became, as it were, a morality play in which good and evil battled for the soul of America. In so doing, the mugwumps most emphatically did *not* strip American electoral politics of its raucous emotionality, as twentieth-century historians unfamiliar with the narrative conventions of the 1884 presidential campaign have mistakenly contended.[27] On the contrary, the mugwumps invested it with a burning sense of moral passion.

To render antimonopoly compelling for the masses, journalists devised a novel storytelling genre that combined words and pictures in a straightforward dramatic narrative. In so doing, they prefigured the eventual transformation of the presidential campaign from a face-to-face ritual that mobilized thousands of partisans in spectacular torchlight parades to a mass-mediated spectacle in which a sedentary, though not necessarily passive, citizenry consumed the news in the relative privacy of their homes.

The journalistic innovations of the 1884 campaign figured prominently in its final hectic week. At the behest of party leaders, Blaine agreed to attend a fund-raising dinner on the last Wednesday before the election at Delmonico's, a swank New York City restaurant. It was a high-risk gambit. In an age in which it was unusual for presidential candidates to openly campaign, it was even more unusual for them to appear at public events intended to fill the party's coffers. But Republican Party leaders were short of funds, and the gregarious Blaine obliged.

Most campaign funding in this period came not from corporations, but rather from wealthy individuals, and, most important of all—at least for the party in power—from the assessments that party leaders made from the salaries of government officials. To mount a credible election campaign in New

York City in the 1880s cost at least $100,000, a prodigious sum. Election Day expenses alone ran, at a minimum, to between $12,000 and $60,000, the cost of printing the ballots that party leaders distributed to their supporters so that they could register their preference at the polls.[28] Government-printed ballots remained in the future: every ballot in 1884 had to be paid for by one of the parties with candidates in the field. This total did not include the cost of vote buying, a ubiquitous practice for both the major political parties, or the staffing of polling places, a task that also fell primarily to the parties, having yet to be absorbed by the state.

The guest list for Blaine's Delmonico's dinner read like a who's who of New York City's movers and shakers. Prominent among them was Jay Gould, a circumstance that seemed highly consequential to several of the journalists who reported on the event. Never before, or so one journalist claimed, had the city's most notorious financial buccaneer fraternized so brazenly with a presidential candidate; in fact, the journalist added, it was hard to recall more than two or three previous occasions during which Gould had dined in public.[29]

The Delmonico's dinner received wide coverage in the press, almost all of it hostile. The fact that Gould would join Blaine for a fund-raiser less than one week before the voters went to the polls prompted anti-Blaine journalists to openly warn that the financier was brazenly undertaking to buy the election. Journalists remembered a similar banquet held a few years earlier at which Republican president Chester A. Arthur had reminded his audience about how, during the final frantic days of the 1880 presidential campaign, the last-minute infusion in Indiana of cash, or what Arthur euphemistically called "soap," had clinched the state and the nation for the Republicans. Arthur had toasted the "corruptionists" after the fact; the upcoming dinner would honor business moguls intent on "defrauding the nation" by stealing the election.[30] Five "money kings," including Gould, were alleged to have contributed $100,000 apiece to Blaine's campaign.[31] While it is unlikely that sums even remotely this large ever found their way to Republican Party coffers, the specter of electoral corruption remained. Gould's speculative coups were legendary and had furnished the theme for countless newspaper stories as well as a spate of cartoons, while his uncanny ability to predict the future movement of a particular stock had impressed his fellow traders with a combination of admiration, envy, and horror. How could it be, one reporter asked rhetorically, that so many respectable merchants permitted themselves to be seen in the company of such a moral reprobate? Why Gould had agreed to dine in public with Blaine seemed obvious. He stood to reap a rich financial reward from Blaine's election. Yet why so many honest businessmen had agreed to "join hands" with Gould by following his example was one of the "mysteries of the age."[32]

The single most effective piece of journalism to come out of the Delmonico's dinner was a rudimentary black-and-white cartoon drawn by Walt McDougall and engraved by Valerian Gribayedoff that ran on page one of the pro-Cleveland New York *World* on the day after the event (see Figure 3).[33] Entitled "The Royal Feast of Belshazzar Blaine and the Money Kings," the cartoon features Blaine and Gould at the head of a table of bigwigs, including at least one businessman—William H. Vanderbilt—who had not actually been present at the dinner. The confusion over the guest list may stem from the circumstances of the cartoon's composition. McDougall was reputed to have unsuccessfully pitched a similar idea earlier that summer to the editors of the mugwump humor magazine *Puck*. Following the Delmonico's dinner, he and Gribayedoff may simply have dusted off his mockup, updated it, and readied it for the next day's edition.[34]

The Belshazzar's feast conceit was hardly new. The "royal feast" to which it referred was an allusion to a legendary banquet in the biblical Book of Daniel in which the soon-to-be-deposed Babylonian tyrant Belshazzar is horrified to watch as a prophecy announcing his imminent doom suddenly materializes in plain view in his banquet hall. Yet McDougall and Gribayedoff gave it a distinctive twist. As it happens, a considerably more polished anti-Blaine cartoon by the renowned cartoonist Joseph Keppler on a similar theme had run several months earlier in *Puck* (see Figure 4). In Keppler's cartoon—entitled, appropriately enough, "The Writing on the Wall"—Blaine-the-King cowered behind a copy of the pro-Blaine New York *Daily Tribune* so that he might shield his eyes from the prophetic writing on the wall: "Republican Revolt."[35] In the *World* cartoon, in contrast, Blaine is confronted not by his Republican detractors, but rather by a humble workingman and his wife and child, who silently implore the monopolists to explain why they have been denied a place at the table.

"The Royal Feast of Belshazzar Blaine and the Money Kings" and "Writing on the Wall" were but two of the many hard-hitting anti-Blaine cartoons to be featured in the 1884 campaign. While these cartoons differed in many particulars, they had two things in common. Most obviously, they underscored Blaine's lack of moral fitness for the presidency, often, as in the *World* cartoon, by emphasizing his subservience to "money kings" like Gould. *Harper's*

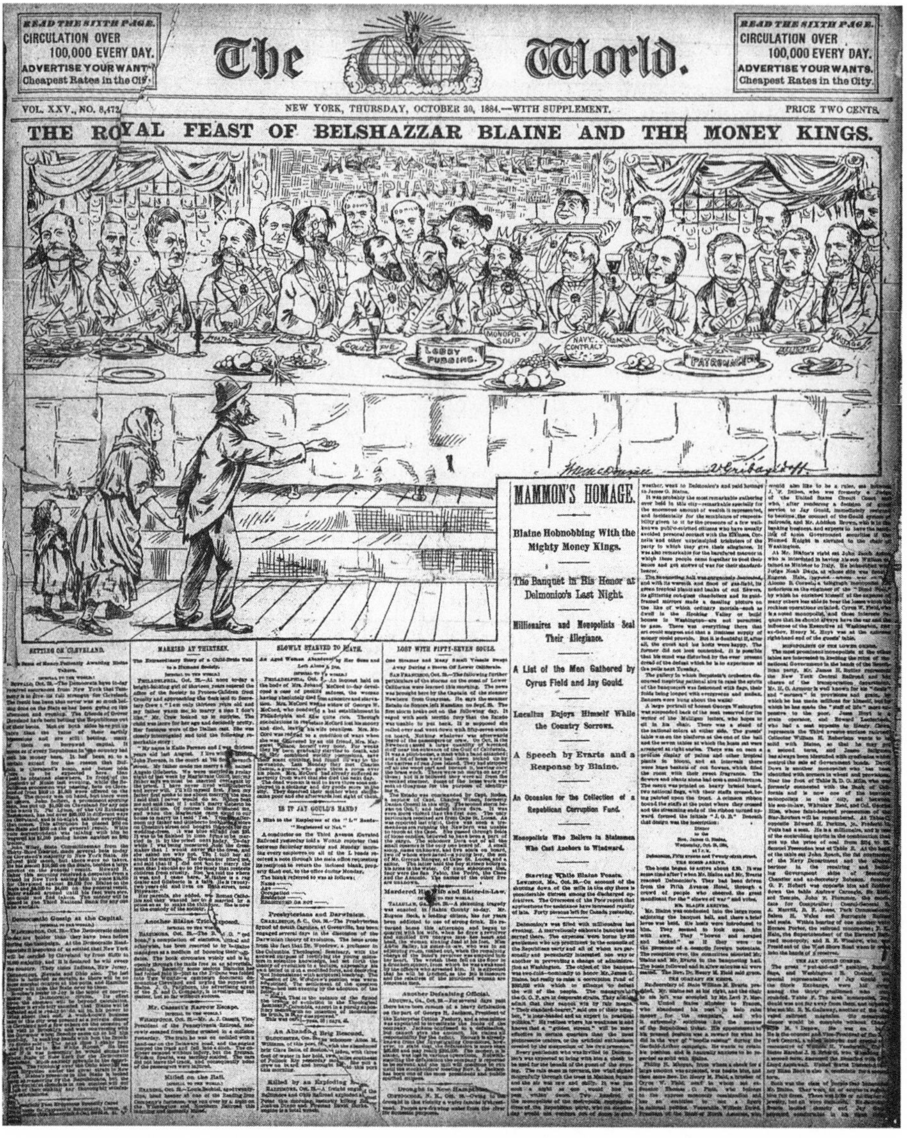

READ THE SIXTH PAGE. CIRCULATION OVER 100,000 EVERY DAY. ADVERTISE YOUR WANTS. Cheapest Rates in the City.

The World.

VOL. XXV., NO. 8,472. NEW YORK, THURSDAY, OCTOBER 30, 1884.—WITH SUPPLEMENT. PRICE TWO CENTS.

THE ROYAL FEAST OF BELSHAZZAR BLAINE AND THE MONEY KINGS.

MAMMON'S HOMAGE.

Blaine Hobnobbing With the Mighty Money Kings.

The Banquet in His Honor at Delmonico's Last Night.

Millionaires and Monopolists Seal Their Allegiance.

A List of the Men Gathered by Cyrus Field and Jay Gould.

Lucullus Enjoys Himself While the Country Sorrows.

A Speech by Evarts and a Response by Blaine.

An Occasion for the Collection of a Republican Corruption Fund.

Monopolists Who Believe in Statesmen Who Cast Anchors to Windward.

Starving While Blaine Feasts.

Figure 3. "The Royal Feast of Belshazzar Blaine and the Money Kings." New York *World*, October 30, 1884, 1. The willingness of Republican presidential candidate James G. Blaine to attend a lavish fund-raising banquet on the eve of the 1884 presidential election furnished the inspiration for this biting political cartoon. While Blaine and his wealthy benefactors dined on "monopoly soup" and "lobby pudding," a humble workingman implored the guests to leave something for himself and his family. The cartoon ran on the front page of the New York *WORLD*, one of the country's most influential newspapers. The ability of cartoonists to translate this dualistic worldview into a compelling visual idiom would shape the contours of political debate for many decades to come.

Figure 4. "The Writing on the Wall," *Puck* 15 (June 18, 1885): 199. This artful color lithograph by the celebrated political cartoonist Joseph Keppler dramatized the "revolt" within the Republican Party provoked by Blaine's nomination. Try as he might, Blaine and his running mate found it impossible to paper over this rift by hiding behind the favorable coverage in the New York *Daily Tribune*, a newspaper that remained loyal to the Republican Party. Like "The Royal Feast of Belshazzar Blaine," it was based on a biblical story. Keppler assumed that his readership would make the connection and recall that the writing on the wall—"Republican Revolt"—was a harbinger of doom.

Weekly cartoonist Thomas Nast proved particularly effective at exploring this dimension of Blaine's candidacy. In one cartoon, for example, Nast depicted Blaine as a gifted magician who relied on sleight of hand to fool the voters into regarding him as morally fit; in another Blaine became a medieval knight chasing after the "public purse" in the "railroad ring."[36] A second theme that these cartoons had in common was their marked pro-proprietary, anticorporate bias. Corporate kingpins like Vanderbilt and Gould were proprietary capitalists gone to seed. At their most harmless, they clogged the channels of commerce; at their worst, they were actively conspiring to destroy the Republic.

By far the most artful and elaborate of the anti-Blaine political cartoons ran in *Puck*, a weekly mass circulation humor magazine that featured three full-page multicolor chromolithographs in every issue. While *Puck* cartoonists caricatured Blaine in various unflattering ways, the conceit that made the greatest hit with audiences was the transmogrification of the candidate into the tattooed man, a sideshow attraction at a "dime museum" whom the promoter had put on display to satisfy the curiosity of spectators eager to learn about his sordid past.

The tattooed man had by 1884 become a familiar figure in popular culture. The original was a sideshow attraction whose body a savage oriental tribe had covered from head to foot with images of birds, fishes, and snakes. Like the body of the man in the sideshow attraction, Blaine's had been festooned with tattoos; unlike the tattooed man, however—at least, if one believed the showman's hype—Blaine's tattoos were self-inflicted and consisted of a catalogue of his dubious financial dealings.[37]

Few accounts of the 1884 election fail to mention its iconic political cartoons, yet almost never do they recognize them for what they were: a highly effective and largely novel medium for mobilizing public sentiment and articulating shared values. The political cartoon antedated 1884. Yet rarely before had it figured so prominently in public discourse or in popularizing highly polarizing—and, indeed, *cartoon-like*—archetypes: the "robber baron," the "politico." These archetypes would live on long after the issues that agitated contemporaries in 1884 had been forgotten. Indeed, to a remarkable degree they would remain staples of journalistic discourse about government-business relations for the next fifty years, and have been by no means entirely supplanted as a journalistic convention even today.

The influence of the political cartoon on the 1884 presidential campaign can partly be explained by recent technical advances in high-speed printing. The mechanical reproduction of woodcuts was, of course, old hat. Prior to the 1880s, however, their preparation ordinarily took at least two full days, making it hard for cartoonists to respond to rapidly unfolding events. "The Royal Feast of Belshazzar Blaine and the Money Kings," in contrast, was readied for the press in a mere two hours and would hit the newsstands the following day. Technical advances hastened the demand for new images, further increasing their proliferation. In 1880 only a handful of newspapers featured political cartoons with any regularity; a decade later, or so Gribayedoff would boast in a retrospective essay on the rise of "pictorial journalism," the total had increased to over five thousand.[38] Gribayedoff exaggerated. Not until the opening decades of the twentieth century would the political cartoon become a ubiquitous feature of the popular press. Even so, he was on the mark in underscoring the rapidly growing presence of the political cartoon in newspapers large and small, and not merely in trailblazers like the New York *World*.

Chromolithography was an even more fundamental technical advance. The mass publication of multicolor images was in 1884 less than a decade old, and the 1884 presidential election was the first in which two rival New York City–based humor magazines, *Puck* and *Judge*, ran dueling cartoons to boost rival candidates.

The highly conspicuous role that the political cartoon would play in the 1884 presidential campaign is a pointed rejoinder to the oft-voiced contention that the mugwumps had a principled aversion to spectacle. *Puck* was a mugwump periodical; so too was *Harper's Weekly*. Instead of taking the passion out of electoral politics, the mugwumps injected into the presidential campaign an insistent moralism, rooted in the worldview of proprietary capitalism, which translated often recondite issues into visually compelling imagery that fascinated contemporaries and remains today an enduring legacy of an often forgotten election.

* * *

The 1884 presidential election had enduring consequences not only for American journalism, but also for the American state. With Cleveland's victory, the Republican Party lost control of the administrative apparatus of the federal government for the first time since 1861, a significant shift that, paradoxically—since parties in power are ordinarily loath to give up the patronage that is at their disposal—accelerated the emergence of a permanent, nonpartisan civil service in several federal agencies, including the Treasury Department and the Post Office Department. Now that the Democrats were in power, they too had an incentive to ensure that their supporters would not be dismissed from office should the Republicans defeat them the next time around. For if there was one structural constant in U.S. national politics, it was the inevitability of the next presidential election and the challenge that an electoral defeat would pose for party leaders intent on retaining control of the levers of power. By expanding the number of federal officeholders covered by the Pendleton Act (1883) and, even more importantly, by championing the virtues of frugal, honest, and impartial public service, Cleveland helped lay the foundation not only for the ICC, established during his presidency, but also for the emergence in later decades of the administrative apparatus of the modern regulatory state.

"Liberty, Equality, Honesty!" trumpeted the headline for a page one cartoon by Walt McDougall that the *World* ran immediately following Cleveland's victory in 1884 (see Figure 5). McDougall, of course, was hardly impartial. Yet by depicting Cleveland as a morally upstanding statesman who had slain the "monopoly" serpent, he cast the spotlight on a dimension of the president's victory that was evident to contemporaries, yet that would be later forgotten. In the popular imagination, Blaine had much closer ties than Cleveland to the emerging corporate order, making Cleveland's victory a defeat not only for a political party, but also for the developmental vision that the Republican Party embraced. To make sure that no one missed the point, McDougall took pains, in the caption accompanying his cartoon, to spell out the moral: "The Government Again Belongs to the People and Not to Corrupt Monopolists."[39]

For most Americans in 1884, the corporation remained an exotic bit of flotsam in a sea of proprietorships. It was, thus, perhaps not surprising that the antimonopoly critique spearheaded by Thurber and Sterne would shape the legislative agenda of the Democratic Party's congressional leadership during the first Cleveland administration. The reason was simple. New York remained a swing state in the 1888 presidential election, elevating the importance of voting blocs that were not firmly committed to a particular political party.

Democratic Party leaders well understood the extent to which their party's future remained beholden to highly motivated, if numerically small, voting blocs such as the New York antimonopolists, and proceeded accordingly. Thurber and Sterne each received an invitation to testify before Congress on the merits of commission regulation, and their voices were heard. The Interstate Commerce Act of 1887 led to the establishment of the ICC, a federal agency with a broad mandate to ensure that railroad corporations did not abuse their power over rate setting. The ICC is sometimes assumed to have been a new departure. In fact, it built on several decades' experience at the state level and was directly modeled on the New York railroad commission for which Thurber and Sterne had lobbied since 1879, and which the New York legislature had enacted in 1882.

The solicitude of Democratic Party leaders for a permanent railroad commission represented a major compromise within the party's ranks. The Democratic congressional delegation in the 1880s included a large and vocal bloc of southerners who opposed the establishment of a permanent railroad commission as a dangerous augmentation in the administrative capacity of the federal government. As an alternative, they endorsed a detailed, rigid, and

The World.

NEW YORK, SATURDAY, NOVEMBER 8, 1884—WITH SUPPLEMENT.

LIBERTY, EQUALITY, HONESTY!

The Government Again Belongs to the People and Not to Corrupt Monopolists.

Figure 5. "Liberty, Equality, Honesty!" New York *World*, November 8, 1884, 1. Cleveland's victory in the election of 1884 was hailed in the Democratic press as a triumph of moral probity and equal rights over moral turpitude and special privilege. In this front-page New York *World* cartoon, Cleveland has just slain the "monopoly" serpent, saving the Republic from the corrupt alliance between business and government that antimonopolists deplored. Blaine's defeat was a setback for the Republicans' developmental agenda, which disparaged antimonopoly and idealized the emerging corporate order.

highly punitive railroad law championed by Texas Democrat John H. Reagan that mandated heavy criminal and civil penalties for the violation of its provisions and left its adjudication to the state courts. In the end, however, the New Yorkers prevailed and Reagan lost.[40]

Mindful of the imperatives of electoral politics, Democratic Party leaders subordinated a proposal that had broad support among the party's own congressional delegation to a minority proposal championed by the New York antimonopolists. The only significant concession that party leaders made to Reagan concerned the ban on pooling—and even here, it was the exception that proved the rule. On this issue, the New York antimonopolists were divided: Sterne favored pooling; Thurber did not.

Reagan's defeat is sometimes lamented by political scientists sympathetic to the anticommission, small-government antimonopolism that Democratic Party leaders rejected. Yet it is worth recalling that Reagan's proposal presupposed the same states' rights orthodoxy that had hastened the disenfranchisement of thousands of African Americans and that would remain an impediment to social justice until it would be finally be overturned by the Voting Rights Act of 1965. Reagan's favored regulatory mechanism—the state courts—was, after all, the same institution that had proved so effective in maintaining the racial status quo. For southern antimonopolists, any augmentation in the administrative capacity of the federal government raised the terrifying prospect that future lawmakers might threaten the Democratic Party's one-party monopoly in the South.

Blaine's defeat in 1884 was in no sense a rejection of the emerging corporate order. Yet it does raise questions about the commonplace characterization of the post–Civil War decades as a so-called Gilded Age. The "Gilded Age" catchphrase assumes that the period was unusually sordid, selfish, and corrupt. Yet was it? The phrase itself would not become widely used until after World War I, long after the period had ended. By that time, the antimonopoly political economy of Thurber and Sterne had been supplanted by the progressive political economy of Theodore Roosevelt and Woodrow Wilson. In the antimonopoly political economy, personal morality remained a core value. In the progressive political economy, in contrast, personal morality had given way to the moral claims of technological imperatives and economic growth. Might then it not be time to relegate the Gilded Age label to the historiographical scrap heap and to acknowledge the extent to which the 1880s were, in ways that have too often been underappreciated, an age of reform?[41]

Thurber himself lived long enough to reflect on this shift. Financially ruined by the Panic of 1893, he retooled as a lawyer and spent the final years of his life as a lobbyist for the U.S. Export Association. Contemporaries erred, Thurber reflected in 1897, when they personified giant corporations as the personal fiefdoms of grasping monopolists. On the contrary, these corporations, including those that had consolidated into trusts, should be lauded for their contribution to national prosperity: "The wholesale denunciation of Trusts is the denunciation of an economic evolution which is conferring enormous benefits upon the community in general." To explain why these wrongheaded ideas retained such currency, Thurber pointed his finger squarely at the "one-cent sensational journalism" of the country's mass-circulation big-city newspapers.[42] "Many good people have imagined a bogey monster that doesn't exist," Thurber elaborated two years later, in a pointed defense of the economic benefits of corporate consolidation. "They have accepted as facts the fancies of sensational journalism." In fact, the corporation had substantially cheapened the cost of goods and services, making it the most efficient economic institution in the history of the world.[43]

Thurber's mea culpa provides a perspective not only on the shifting character of the U.S. political economy, but also on the world that was lost. The 1884 election campaign had been fought in a world that remained defined by the market-oriented ethos of proprietary capitalism. Campaign funding continued to be dominated, as it had been in every campaign since Andrew Jackson entered the White House in 1829, by the contribution of wealthy individuals and the assessment of government officials. The influx of corporate money remained in the future. In fact, the specter that financiers like William H. Vanderbilt and Jay Gould might flood the coffers of the Republican Party—the subtext for the popular coverage of Blaine's Delmonico's dinner—inspired an outpouring of revulsion not only from journalists, but also from many businessmen. The new media of the day—including, in particular, the chromolithographic political cartoon—combined a high-toned ethic of personal moral responsibility with an almost Manichean good-versus-bad proprietary-corporate dialectic. The corporate capitalism of Vanderbilt and Gould pointed to the future, and it was a future that in 1884 the American people rejected when, by the narrowest of margins, they cast their ballots for Cleveland rather than Blaine.

CHAPTER 5

Anglophobia in Nineteenth-Century Elections, Politics, and Diplomacy

Jay Sexton

Bringing elections back into political history is a multifaceted project. The method pursued in most of the chapters in this volume is the investigation of important presidential elections, an approach that highlights contingent moments of political change or consolidation. This chapter, in contrast, connects elections across nearly a century by focusing on a recurring theme. Though elections provide a snapshot of political opinion at a particular historical moment, underlying structures, dynamics, and languages connect them across time, giving them their own internal logic and self-perpetuating mechanisms. The subject of this chapter is one of the most prominent threads running through the nineteenth century: Anglophobia, defined here as the aversion to or fear of things associated, however loosely, with Britain.

This chapter examines two aspects of the electoral politics of Anglophobia. First, it contends that the relationship between elections and Anglophobia was a two-way street. If America's anti-British culture shaped elections, the inverse was also true: elections played a key role in entrenching Anglophobia in American political culture. This point is illustrated by charting the spread of Anglophobia over time. Although Anglophobia was initially the tool of one political faction, politicians from across the spectrum soon competed to claim the anti-British ground during election years. Second, this chapter considers the implications of this electoral dynamic. The anti-British electoral cycle conditioned the congressional politics and foreign policy making of the period. Anglophobia was more than an electoral strategy; it was a broader political dynamic whose implications extended beyond Election Day. Yet if this dynamic conditioned policy making, it did not determine it, for the era's savviest statesmen found ways of balancing the imperatives of electoral politics with the realist pursuit of national interests, which often pointed toward collaboration with the hated British.

Anglophobia in Nineteenth-Century Elections

It should come as no surprise that nineteenth-century American political culture was deeply Anglophobic. "The young republic exhibited a set of anxieties not uncommon among nation-states that have emerged from long periods of colonial rule," the historian Sam W. Haynes argues in his 2010 study of Anglophobia in the early Republic.[1] Opposition to Britain derived from the experience of revolution and was embedded thereafter in nationalist practices such as Fourth of July celebrations. Election days ritualized antimonarchism into American political culture. Immigration, particularly from Ireland, injected new energy into American Anglophobia. The geopolitical context of British global power in the nineteenth century further fueled opposition to the world's greatest power. Notwithstanding bombastic claims of their national "manifest destiny," Americans feared deep into the nineteenth century that their republic remained trapped within the webs of an expanding and increasingly powerful British Empire.[2]

The persistence and pervasiveness of Anglophobia in American life, however, cannot be explained purely by reference to historical experience and geopolitics. After all, the nineteenth century witnessed a diminution of the threat Britain posed to the United States. Though rooted in memories of the Revolution and geopolitics, Anglophobia was not derivative of them. Like a genie out of the bottle, this phenomenon took on a life of its own in the century that followed the Revolution. A key to understanding its evolution and spread was its politicization. Americans condemned the political, economic, and cultural practices they associated with their former colonial master. But oftentimes Anglophobia was only loosely related to practices or policies that were identifiably British. Over time, American Anglophobia became unmoored from the "real" Britain, developing instead into an instrument of domestic political conflict, a malleable club wielded by office-seeking candidates in election years. Even admirers of Britain found themselves denouncing the former colonial master in election years. If Anglophobia illuminates the "postcoloniality" of the early Republic (as recently has been argued),[3] it also brings into focus how elections embedded a powerful and far-reaching dynamic into U.S. politics.

That electoral politics profoundly shaped nineteenth-century Anglophobia is evident in one of its key features: Americans were just as likely to direct their anti-British tracts at one another as at their former colonial master across the Atlantic. The origins of this dynamic can be found in the bare-knuckled politics of the 1790s. Those on either side of the spectrum deployed conspiratorial attacks that connected their domestic opponents to foreign influences. Federalists, particularly after the radicalization of the French Revolution, depicted their rivals as demagogues who plotted to import fanatical Jacobinism into the United States. Jeffersonian Republicans responded by presenting their Federalist opponents as crypto-monarchists who secretly worked to reestablish British rule in the United States. If both parties overstated the extent to which their opponents were subject to foreign influence—Federalist leader John Adams was no Anglophile, and many Jeffersonian Republicans moderated their pro-French views as events took their course in the 1790s—there is little question that the parties identified with opposite Old World powers.

It is fitting that the *Oxford English Dictionary* attributes the first use of "Anglophobia" to Thomas Jefferson in 1793, for if there was one indispensable figure in the entrenchment of Anglophobia in American politics it was he.[4] Jefferson and his allies exploited the unpopular Jay Treaty and the subsequent Adams administration's suppression of civil liberties to present the Federalists as the party of "Anglomen" who sought to roll back the achievements of the Revolution. In the minds of Jeffersonians, the political battle against the Federalists was merely a continuation of 1776. "There seems to have been a deliberate plan to exterminate liberty," declared one Jeffersonian in 1795, "and this was to have been effected by throwing off the connection with France and consolidating ourselves with Great Britain—in the arms of despotism."[5] When Jefferson wrested control of the presidency from the Federalists in the election of 1800, his supporters viewed it as a victory of no less importance than that of the revolution against Britain.[6]

Rather than marking the climax of Anglophobia in American electoral politics, the "revolution of 1800" kicked off what would become a nearly century-long struggle between politicians to claim the anti-British high ground in election years. Two factors explain the persistence of Anglophobia and the relative decline—though not disappearance—of Francophobia in U.S. politics. First, ongoing conflict and rivalry with Britain, which culminated in the War of 1812 but persisted long thereafter, kept alive fears of recrudescent British power, not least among Irish immigrants.[7] The reduced power of France after 1815, in contrast, helps explain the diminution of Francophobia. Second, Anglophobia became more pervasive in the years after 1815 because of its embrace by those who had been tarred as "Anglomen" by their opponents. Federalists hoping for a revival of their party had little choice but to distance themselves from the perception that they were pro-British elites—a perception strengthened by the 1814 Hartford Convention, in which leading New England Federalists flirted with pursuing a separate peace with Britain. Though the Federalist Party dissolved in the years after 1815, its successors would avoid falling into the trap of appearing to be a pro-British party.

The presidential election of 1828 illustrates this emerging anti-British consensus. Rather than being a contest between pro-French and pro-British parties, this election pitted two candidates who sought to capitalize on their anti-British records. Incumbent John Quincy Adams possessed a visceral hatred of British monarchy and colonialism, which found expression in the 1823 Monroe Doctrine, which he largely authored as secretary of state. There was perhaps no greater Anglophobe in the period than his opponent, Andrew Jackson, whose credentials included his triumph at the battle of New Orleans as well as his incursion into Spanish Florida, in which he hanged two British traders who collaborated with Indians. The supporters of Adams and Jackson did more than trumpet their candidates' anti-British credentials. They took the next step of hurling allegations of secret British sympathies at their opponents. In the eyes of Jackson supporters, Adams, whose wife, Louisa, had been born in England, harbored secret British sympathies as a result of the time he spent abroad in his youth and his alleged education at England's elite Eton school. Adams supporters responded by calling Jackson's nationalism into question by alleging that his mother was a British prostitute whose migration to America was overseen by British soldiers.[8]

The Anglophobic mudslinging of 1828 became a staple of the electioneering of the second party system. The Democrats possessed the advantage of having emerged out of the historically anti-British Jeffersonian tradition. They sought to capitalize on this by depicting their Whig opponents as the heirs of "blue light Federalism" and the Hartford Convention. Furthermore, the Whigs' opposition to territorial expansion and promotion of British investment made them vulnerable to Anglophobic lines of attack. But the new Whig Party did not concede the anti-British position to the Democrats.

Indeed, the name "Whig" itself conjured up opposition to Toryism, centralization, and monarchical rule. Whigs tarred Jacksonians with labels of "Tory" and "King Andrew."[9] They presented their program of political economy as the route to liberate the United States from the shackles of British economic imperialism. They put forward candidates with strong anti-British credentials during election years, avoiding the trap of nominating for president New England Anglophile Daniel Webster. When the Whigs nominated William Henry Harrison in 1840, they took a page out of the Jacksonian playbook in promoting a candidate whose reputation was built on fighting the British and their Indian allies in the War of 1812.

By midcentury Anglophobia had become a recurring feature of U.S. elections. Though this was most on display at the presidential level, it also shaped state politics, particularly in states that bordered Canada or had a large Irish immigrant population. New York, not surprisingly, was a hotbed of Anglophobic electioneering. Whig governor William H. Seward shrewdly established his anti-British credentials in the 1840s, not least by appealing to the state's rapidly growing Irish population. Anglophobia also appeared in territorial politics. It was a rare territorial governor who served his tenure without being equated to George III or some other symbol of British imperialism. "Our Governor is clothed with all the power of a British Nabob," complained a resident of the Ohio Territory. "The most infamous system of colonial government that was ever seen on the face of the globe" could be found in the Montana Territory in 1884—this was said not by a Native American, but by a white settler![10]

The battle to lay claim to the memory of the Revolution became entangled in the sectional politics of the antebellum period. In the famous U.S. Senate election in Illinois in 1858, both Abraham Lincoln and Stephen Douglas invoked the American Revolution on behalf of their candidacy. Lincoln portrayed his arguments as the outgrowth of the tradition of 1776; Douglas contended that Lincoln's position on excluding slavery from the territories by federal legislation was "the identical principle asserted by George III and the Tories of the Revolution."[11] Those on either side of the Mason-Dixon Line incorporated Anglophobic appeals in their political arsenals. Republicans viewed the so-called Slave Power as an alien infiltration of British aristocracy and corruption whose dangerous free-trade doctrines threatened to reduce the United States to a staple-exporting satellite of the British Empire. Meanwhile, southern slavers viewed northern opponents of slavery as the minions of British abolitionism and equated the new Republican Party to George III and the imagined British tyranny of 1776. "The Southern States now stand exactly in the same position towards Northern States that our ancestors in *the colonies* did towards Great Britain," asserted the South Carolina secession convention.[12]

The consolidation of the Union in the 1860s diminished the threat Britain posed to the United States. The long-feared nexus of internal separatism and British intervention did not materialize despite the efforts of Confederate diplomats. Yet, far from diminishing after 1865, the high tide of electoral Anglophobia lay in the decades following the Civil War.[13] Northerners and southerners alike felt betrayed by Britain's neutrality during the war. "I have always been Anglophile and Anglomaniac, but I am disillusionated [*sic*] now," George Temple Strong confided in his diary during the war. "I feel like repudiating the Archbishop of Canterbury and transferring my allegiance to the Patriarch of Constantinople."[14] The party machinery of the Gilded Age exploited such sentiments by carpet bombing the electorate with anti-British slogans and themes. Officeseekers and their allies connected the principal issues of late nineteenth-century politics to the perceived British threat: federal Reconstruction in the South became a reenactment of British colonialism; the suppression of Ireland became a matter no officeseeker could afford not to condemn; U.S. ambitions in Central America and the Caribbean reinvigorated rivalry with the old colonial master, leading to a steady stream of minor diplomatic confrontations that took on great significance in election years; the populist insurgency revived the old Jacksonian tradition of condemning British financiers and investment. Above all, Anglophobia conditioned the "great debate" concerning the tariff. Protectionists, led by Henry Carey, condemned their opponents as the stooges of British free-trade imperialism. Tariff reformers, led by Carey's onetime-disciple-turned-opponent David Ames Wells, countered with the argument that protectionism corrupted republican politics and mimicked the central tyranny of the very empire from which Americans had rebelled in 1776.[15]

The presidential contest of 1884 serves as an example of how Gilded Age candidates sought to undermine their opponents by hurling allegations of pro-Britishness at each other. In a change from the antebellum period, it was now the Democrats of Grover Cleveland whose policies of tariff reform and opposition to assertive foreign policies placed them at a natural disadvantage in the race to claim the Anglophobic high ground. James Blaine's Republican supporters lost no chance to press their advantage. "Cleveland runs well in England!" one Republican slogan asserted. Republicans even hoped that such appeals would peel away some of the Irish vote from their rivals, who long had profited from this constituency.[16] But rather than attempt to control the message and maneuver toward other topics, the Democrats' strategy was to fight fire with fire. The Republicans "have managed to surrender to Great Britain," declared the 1884 party platform. "Instead of the Republican party's British policy," it continued, "we demand on behalf of the American Democracy, an American policy." In case readers missed that last line, the platform repeated it verbatim a few paragraphs later.[17]

Anglophobia, in sum, was a versatile and recurring theme in nineteenth-century elections. What initially was the instrument of one political persuasion—Jeffersonian Republicans—came to be wielded by those across the spectrum. Politicians raced to establish their anti-British credentials during election years and to tar their opponents as "Anglomaniacal" tools of British power. The near ubiquity of Anglophobia, however, presents methodological and interpretive challenges to the historian. Chief among these is the question of whether Anglophobic tactics can be said to have determined election results. Did any candidate win an election because of the way he and his supporters played the Anglophobic card?

The most likely candidate for a presidential election being decided by the exploitation of widespread anti-British sentiments would be that of 1888. New York was the key swing state upon which this hotly contested campaign between incumbent Grover Cleveland and his Republican challenger Benjamin Harrison hinged. Cleveland had carried the Empire State in 1884, but lost it, and the election, four years later. One possible explanation was a letter penned by British minister to Washington Lionel Sackville-West, who fell for a plot hatched by Republican supporter George Osgoodby. When Osgoodby posed as a naturalized Englishman named Charles Murchison asking for advice on how to vote, Sackville-West took the bait and responded that a Cleveland victory would be in Britain's interests. The "Murchison letter" was widely reproduced in the weeks immediately preceding the election. It may have depressed Democratic turnout in New York, perhaps even leading some anti-British Irish American voters into the Republican camp. Yet it is impossible to attribute Harrison's victory in 1888 to a single factor like Anglophobia. One could just as easily argue that other factors, such as fraud, third-party candidates, and, most obviously, the other issues at stake in the election, determined the outcome in New York. It is revealing that scholars of this topic have stopped short of attributing Cleveland's defeat to the "Murchison" episode.[18]

Anglophobia as a Political Dynamic

The political significance of Anglophobia lies not in how it determined election results, but rather in how it created a dynamic that profoundly conditioned party politics and policy making. The ever-intensifying scramble to assume the Anglophobic high ground that took place in elections left its mark on politics more generally. The line between electioneering and policy making was in this regard blurred, not least because in the nineteenth century, election year was every year. As the century progressed, Anglophobia became more than just a campaign tactic. It developed into a broader political process with its own logic, keywords, and performative code.

Given the pervasiveness of Anglophobia, it is perhaps more appropriate to refer to it in the plural. Table 1 suggests that the taxonomy of Anglophobia should include at least seven species. Many of these Anglophobias overlapped. Furthermore, they all belonged to the same genus, which could be called "American nationalist Anglophobia." Or, to simplify, it could be labeled "American nationalism," which is impossible to imagine existing in the forms that it assumed without the foundation of what Peter Onuf has called "Anglophobic anti-imperialism."[19]

Like American nationalism itself, Anglophobia was simultaneously a point of consensus and conflict. Through negative self-referencing, it played a constructive role in the creation of a national "imagined community." The rising nationalism of the nineteenth century is impossible to separate from the

Table 1. Varieties of American Anglophobia

Species	*Representative Figures*
Republican Anglophobia	Thomas Jefferson; John Quincy Adams
Expansionist Anglophobia	Thomas Jefferson; James K. Polk
Economic nationalist Anglophobia	Henry Clay; James G. Blaine
Populist Anglophobia	Andrew Jackson; William Jennings Bryan
Proslavery Anglophobia	John C. Calhoun; John Tyler
Unionist Anglophobia	John Quincy Adams; William H. Seward
Hibernian Anglophobia	William H. Seward; James G. Blaine

process of "unbecoming British," as Kariann Yokota has called it.[20] Yet because it was so closely linked to national construction and formation—itself a highly politicized process that was contested in election years—Anglophobia became inextricably entwined with partisan and sectional politics.

The politics of Anglophobia had three components. The first entailed the identification and propagation of a perceived British threat. Table 2 highlights the threats identified by the proponents of the various species of Anglophobia. It helped if a politician could point to a genuine threat, especially if it involved British-backed Indians. But solid evidence of a British menace was not essential. More important were the public relations campaigns that politicians undertook with increased sophistication as the century progressed. Political speeches were adequate so long as they were widely reprinted in newspapers. Ones delivered on the Fourth of July were particularly effective.[21] Pamphlets, such as Robert J. Walker's brief on behalf of the annexation of Texas, were also used to good effect.[22] Sitting presidents had the advantage of exploiting their office. James Monroe, for example, selected his annual message of 1823 to announce what soon would be known as the Monroe Doctrine.

The best tactic, however, was to publicize or leak what originally had been private or official correspondence. This demonstrated that the politician's aversion to Britain was sincere. It further showed that he had the courage to publicly "look John Bull straight in the eye," as James K. Polk put it. The aim of this chest-thumping, it must be stressed, was oftentimes more domestic political than diplomatic. The best example of such playing to the gallery was John C. Calhoun's "Pakenham letter," a formal diplomatic note written by

Table 2. Step One: Identifying a British Threat

Species	*British Threats*
Republican Anglophobia	British monarchy/aristocracy/colonialism
Expansionist Anglophobia	British possessions in North America; pro-British Indians; the British Empire
Economic nationalist Anglophobia	British free trade/manufacturing/shipping
Populist Anglophobia	British investment in the United States; high-brow culture and religion
Proslavery Anglophobia	British antislavery
Unionist Anglophobia	British infiltration/recolonization
Hibernian Anglophobia	British rule in Ireland

Secretary of State Calhoun to British minister Pakenham. This correspondence subsequently was delivered to Congress and widely reprinted during the debates surrounding the annexation of Texas. Calhoun used this medium to denounce British antislavery as well as to present a robust case on behalf of the peculiar institution. His ultimate aim was to unify proslavery southerners into a single political coalition.[23]

The second component of the political script of Anglophobia was the key one: establishing a link between the British threat and one's domestic political foes. Table 3 highlights some of the domestic targets, which ranged across the political spectrum, of the various species of Anglophobes. This is where the politics of Anglophobia got dirty. Any statement a politician had once made, any vote on a treaty, any extended stays in England, any praise bestowed on a British policy—these and more were fair game. The most effective smears were those that connected a political opponent not simply to Britain, but to the worst of the worst in Britain—monarchs, aristocrats, and banks. Best of all was to connect a domestic opponent to the Anglophobe's trifecta: pro-monarch banking houses staffed by aristocrats. The veracity of these allegations varied. Daniel Webster, James Henry Hammond alleged, was "unprincipled and cowardly . . . [and] in the pay of the great English Bankers, the Barings."[24] This was true (the second part, that is; the first is open to debate). Grover Cleveland, Republicans alleged, was an Anglomaniac whose free-trade presidential campaigns were financed by British gold. This was untrue (the second part, that is; the first is open to debate).

Table 3. Step Two: Identifying Domestic Opponents

Species	*Domestic "Anglomaniacal" Collaborators*
Republican Anglophobia	Federalists/Whigs; territorial governors
Expansionist Anglophobia	Anti-expansionists; opponents of Indian Removal
Economic nationalist Anglophobia	Tariff reductionists, especially Democrats; anti-imperialists
Populist Anglophobia	Wall Street; cultural elites
Proslavery Anglophobia	Antislavery societies; the Republican Party
Unionist Anglophobia	Regional separatists/nullifiers; the Slave Power
Hibernian Anglophobia	Nativists; anti-Catholics

The politics of Anglophobia here became inseparable from the gendered politics of nineteenth-century American nationalism. Indeed, the terms "Americanism" and "anti-Americanism" (and its synonym, "Anglomania") frequently appear in the Anglophobic tracts of the period. A man who opposed the annexation of Texas, Walker asserted in his 1844 pamphlet, was "anti-American," "a monarchist" who "prefers the advance of monarchical institutions over our own great valley: he is also an Englishman in feelings and principle, and would recolonize the American States."[25] Theodore Roosevelt similarly did not mince his words during the 1895–96 Venezuela crisis. Those at home who questioned the assertive application of the Monroe Doctrine were "anti-American . . . Anglomaniacs . . . of the timid and flabby type" who would best serve their country "by relieving it of [their] presence" and migrating back to England.[26]

Having identified the British threat and tarred and feathered one's domestic opponents, all that remained to be done was to make the case for a policy that would remedy the alleged situation. This was the third component of the politics of Anglophobia. Table 4 provides a sampling of the policies to which Anglophobic appeals were deployed to advance. It is again worth noting how these policies spanned the spectrum—from proslavery to antislavery; from protectionism to tariff reform. Given the versatility of Anglophobia, the secret to success lay less in the substance of the Anglophobic appeal itself and more in the efficacy of the public relations campaigns aimed at mobilizing political support. It also should be emphasized that the formulation of a policy objective often preceded the identification of a British threat. In other words, rather than perceptions of the British threat shaping policy responses, fixed policy objectives often shaped threat perception. There is no better example than the expansionist Polk administration, whose desire to colonize California led it to imagine—and then publicize—the possible ways in which Britain might stand in the way.[27]

The political dynamic of Anglophobia was paradoxically both irrational and rational. It was a "phobia" in the sense that politicians overstated—if not altogether invented—conspiratorial plots hatched by Britain and its alleged American minions. The nightmare scenarios propagated by American politicians tended to be long on rumor and short on fact. The British bogeyman, particularly after 1815, did not lurk behind every tree in America.[28] Yet Anglophobia should not be seen purely as a manifestation of Richard Hofstadter's "paranoid style" in American politics. Two points should be kept in mind. First, Britain did possess power, particularly economic power, which it could

Table 4. Step Three: Identifying a Remedy

Species	*Policies Advocated to Counter British Threat*
Republican Anglophobia	Northwest Ordinance; Monroe Doctrine
Expansionist Anglophobia	Territorial expansion; Indian Removal
Economic nationalist Anglophobia	Protective tariff; economic pan-Americanism
Populist Anglophobia	Antibank; tariff reform; hard money (later bimetalism/greenbackism); cultural populism
Proslavery Anglophobia	Annexation of Texas; promotion of slave-holding interests
Unionist Anglophobia	Monroe Doctrine; Union war effort
Hibernian Anglophobia	Irish repeal movement / home rule; liberal naturalization laws

leverage to its advantage in relations with the United States. In some cases, there was cause for concern—one thinks here of southern anxieties concerning British antislavery.[29] Second, and regardless of the nature of the British threat, political calculations pointed toward overstating it. The rationality of Anglophobia, as we have seen, lay in its political payoff. It was not only a potent method of political attack, but also an agent of intraparty unity. The antebellum Democrats provide a classic example: opposition to England functioned as a cohesive force that brought together the party's disparate elements of northeastern radicals, midwestern expansionists, Irish immigrants, and southern slavers.

The rationality of Anglophobia extended beyond the narrowly defined political realm. One of its most powerful manifestations can be found in populist critiques of elite social formations, cultural practices, and economic institutions. The original Anglophobia of the Jeffersonian era, which targeted high Federalists from New England, in this regard conditioned what followed. It was elites who most often found themselves in the Anglophobes' crosshairs: Federalists; high Anglicans; New England intellectuals who looked primarily across the Atlantic for inspiration; the southern planter elite, the closest thing in America to the landed aristocracy of England; Wall Street financiers, the closest thing in America to the great capitalists of the City. The Anglophobic card enabled populists—not least the Populist Party of the late nineteenth century—to attack elites without calling into question their own patriotism. It was similarly used to great effect by Irish immigrants, whose

Anglophobia served both to oppose American nativism and to establish their claim to Americanness.[30]

The power and malleability of Anglophobia are revealed in how elites generally co-opted, rather than countered, anti-British critics. Both major political parties, for example, chose to at least rhetorically embrace Irish nationalism. But the pledges of officeseekers should not always be taken at face value. As one Democrat said of Republican James Blaine's professed Hibernianism, he hated England "just enough to get the Irish vote, but not enough . . . to do her the smallest harm."[31] Both sides of a social or political conflict could play the Anglophobic card. Indeed, it was often used by conservatives seeking to discredit radical political or social movements. Antiabolitionists, for example, sought to undermine those who advocated the end of slavery in America by highlighting their connections to British antislavery societies. If the substance of Anglophobia often appears irrational and paranoid, the political method and rationale underlying it were anything but.

Anglophobia and Foreign Policy

The domestic politics of Anglophobia inevitably collided with the formulation of U.S. foreign policy. The race among politicians to claim the patriotic high ground; the frenzy in election years to become the most severe Anglophobe; the political incentive to denounce compromise agreements of the past—all these pushed statesmen from across the political spectrum into pursuing harder lines as the nineteenth century progressed when dealing with Britain. Yet what was rational in domestic political terms was not always so when it came to foreign policy.

It took only a minor spark to set off a diplomatic controversy that produced an Anglophobic wildfire at home: a Maine lumberjack whistling "Yankee Doodle" on the wrong side of the border and ending up in a Canadian jail; British and U.S. consuls acting beyond their instructions in Central America; fishermen dropping their nets in disputed waters. Add to such incidents contested structural dynamics—British hegemony on the high seas; persistent British economic power in the United States; American settler colonization of disputed territories in the West; competition for the markets of Latin America—and it becomes clear why a series of confrontations characterized Anglo-American relations in the nineteenth century.

None of the options confronting politicians during a diplomatic dispute with Britain were risk free. One route was to attempt to brush a diplomatic controversy under the rug, thus buying time to pursue a long-term solution behind the scenes. This tactic had advantages: it could limit partisan attacks and sidestep a potentially disastrous and costly confrontation with the powerful British over something that might not be worth a fight. But it had its downsides. Political opponents might label it cowardly and Anglomaniacal, thus transforming the issue into a larger controversy that became both a greater domestic political liability (particularly if in an election year) and a more difficult diplomatic problem to resolve.

The post–Civil War *Alabama* claims revealed the risks of this approach. The Johnson administration sought to resolve through diplomatic channels the dispute concerning the construction of warships for the Confederacy in British shipyards. This approach did not yield the results required to assuage domestic critics. When the imperfect Johnson-Clarendon Treaty finally reached the Senate floor in 1869—six years after the *Alabama* escaped to sea down the Mersey—it was denounced by Charles Sumner, the onetime friend of England who now felt betrayed by Britain's allegedly insincere neutrality during the Civil War. In a notorious speech that sent stock markets plunging on both sides of the Atlantic, Sumner asserted that "with the lapse of time and with minute consideration the case against England becomes more grave."[32] The Senate rejected the treaty, complicating the already complex diplomatic challenge confronting the newly inaugurated Grant administration. Cleaning up this mess consumed Grant and his secretary of state, Hamilton Fish, for the next three years. The end result was an agreement more favorable to the United States than the Johnson-Clarendon framework. But it came at a domestic political price, as well as the cost of closing to the United States for several years the money markets of London, where the Treasury hoped to refinance at a lower rate its high-interest Civil War debt.

Given episodes such as this, it is not surprising that many administrations chose to pursue a more aggressive line in disputes with Britain. Truculence had potential payoffs both domestically and diplomatically. It could preempt Anglophobic attacks at home—indeed, it could mobilize political support in elections, as well as for controversial objectives like territorial expansion. Furthermore, by boldly asserting U.S. aims, aggressive diplomacy could bludgeon the British into accepting a quick resolution. Two classic examples of this strategy are James K. Polk's assertion in his 1845 inaugural address that U.S. claims to the disputed Oregon Territory were "clear and unquestionable" and Grover Cleveland's aggressive invocation of the Monroe Doctrine during the 1895–96 Venezuela dispute. In both cases an administration publicly took a hard-line position on a long-festering border dispute, setting in motion a chain of events that eventually led to a compromise resolution.

Both episodes, however, came at a cost, not least in that they rapidly escalated what had been containable diplomatic disputes. Polk's bluster ultimately alienated midwesterners in his party who believed that the administration would adhere to their slogan "Fifty-four forty or fight." These Democrats cried foul when betrayed by an administration willing to fight Mexico for territory in the Southwest but unwilling to go on the offensive against the hated British in Oregon. Grover Cleveland's bellicose diplomacy during the Venezuela dispute also came at a price. Recent scholarship has made clear that Cleveland's aggression in this episode was aimed at countering domestic opponents and advancing his vision of an anti-imperial foreign policy. Yet Cleveland's bid to "out-jingo the jingoes" on the Venezuela issue paradoxically contributed to the very development he hoped to counter—the emergence of a more assertive and interventionist foreign policy in Latin America.[33]

In such ways the domestic politics of Anglophobia conditioned U.S. foreign policy. Though the specific approaches of different administrations varied, the overall trajectory was one in which the range of politically acceptable diplomatic options narrowed over time. To generalize, there was more U.S. assertiveness—indeed, more aggression—as the nineteenth century progressed. This reflected, of course, the gradual geopolitical power shift in the United States' favor. But it also derived from the dynamics of the politics of Anglophobia, which ratcheted up the stakes in what might be minor diplomatic disputes.

The career of the Clayton-Bulwer Treaty provides an illuminating case study of this phenomenon. This 1850 agreement of the Whig administration of Zachary Taylor was in many regards a diplomatic coup for the United States. In the deal Britain and the United States pledged to cooperate in the construction of an isthmian canal in Nicaragua as well as to refrain from colonizing Central America. The treaty recognized the United States as equal to the British in Central America, advanced the U.S. goal of noncolonization, and provided the political settlement necessary for British capitalists to consider financing the digging of an isthmian canal—a massive project that American investors showed little signs of underwriting on their own. The

Whigs attempted to sidestep Anglophobic attacks at home by conducting the negotiations in secret as well as holding the discussions of the Senate Foreign Relations Committee in an unrecorded session. Furthermore, the treaty fudged the crucial issue concerning if its noncolonization clause related to preexisting British spheres of influence, particularly that on Nicaragua's Miskito Coast. "Words . . . which cannot but be more or less offensive to us, which will be alarming to Capitalists, and of which you can express the real value in other terms," Bulwer wrote Clayton during the drafting of the agreement, "cannot but be words that, on all accounts, had better be changed."[34] As was often the case in Anglo-American treaties in the nineteenth century when it came to the most contentious issues, Clayton and Bulwer kicked the can down the road in the hope that future negotiators could deal with it in a more hospitable political climate.[35]

The Whigs' attempt to sidestep domestic criticism did not pan out. Democrats immediately denounced the agreement as a "truckling to Great Britain."[36] "The Treaty altogether reverses the Monroe Doctrine and establishes it against ourselves rather than European Governments," James Buchanan declared.[37] The Democrats exploited this issue to great effect in the 1850s, going so far as to include a Monroe Doctrine plank in their platform in 1856—the first time the phrase appeared in a party platform. Clayton-Bulwer soon became the "dead man walking" of American politics, a punching bag that politicians, journalists, and historians queued up to take a swing at. By the late nineteenth century, it was the Republicans who sought to reap political gain from denouncing it. When Secretary of State James Blaine composed a truculent dispatch to Britain in which he made clear his dislike of the treaty, he did so with his presidential ambitions in mind.[38] Those who approved of Clayton-Bulwer in the late nineteenth century, principally devoted liberals like Hamilton Fish and Grover Cleveland, were smart enough politicians to avoid a full-throated defense of this widely condemned agreement. When the Senate finally smelled blood at the turn of the century, a frenzied shark attack resulted. Britain had to do more than acquiesce to a U.S.-constructed canal (the 1900 Hay-Pauncefote Treaty). The Senate went further than that, deeming it necessary to humiliate the old adversary by forcing Britain to consent to the formal abrogation of the 1850 agreement, thus allowing the United States to unilaterally fortify what became the Panama Canal (the 1901 Hay-Pauncefote Treaty).

The fate of the Clayton-Bulwer Treaty was in this way connected to the dynamics of the domestic politics of Anglophobia. Yet one could turn the tables and view this episode in the opposite manner: despite a markedly Anglophobic political culture, it is worth emphasizing that the unpopular Clayton-Bulwer formula persisted for half a century. In fact, this episode could be interpreted as an example of the gap between the domestic politics of Anglophobia and the realist statecraft of the United States. Throughout the nineteenth century, it was necessary for the United States to work alongside the British in Central America; the latter remained a key player in the region, not to mention the central source of capital for the envisaged canal. It was one thing for nationalist politicians to rail against an unpopular treaty in an election year, but it was quite another to formulate a viable alternative, especially when the obvious alternative policy of unilateral imperialism was certain to provoke resistance—in the region, in London, and among the anti-annexationist, antistatist lobby at home. In other words, the hated Clayton-Bulwer survived half a century of Anglophobic attacks because it was good policy: it contained British expansion, established the United States as an equal power in the region, sidestepped troubling political and diplomatic questions, and advanced in theory (though not in practice) the canal project. If electoral calculations generally led toward anti-British policies, diplomatic ones could point in the opposite direction.

This argument can be extended to nineteenth-century U.S. foreign policy more generally. The culture and politics of Anglophobia presented many challenges to foreign policy makers, but it did not prevent them from cooperating with the hated British when it was deemed to be in the national interest. A recurring theme in nineteenth-century diplomatic history concerned how best to harness British power on behalf of U.S. objectives. The precise formula here depended on the persuasion of the government in power, but it is worth stressing that statesmen of different stripes all sought to exploit British power in their own ways. The plans of economic nationalists like Henry Clay required British investment capital for their realization. They also drew inspiration from British models—they sought to overcome the success of British political economy through emulation, "to outdo England without fighting her," as Henry Carey put it.[39] It is difficult to imagine a more robust Anglophobe than Andrew Jackson. The Jackson administration, however, proved willing to cut a trade deal that opened the British West Indies to U.S. goods but discriminated against U.S. shipping. When Britain "violated" the Monroe Doctrine by colonizing the Falkland Islands in the 1830s, it did so with the acquiescence of representatives of the Jackson administration who believed that British ownership of the islands advanced U.S. commercial interests.[40] Proslavery men lost sleep at night due to nightmares of British antislavery, yet their vision of a prosperous South was predicated on access to Liverpool's cotton market—and, during the Civil War, on British diplomatic support. After meeting Confederate Robert Toombs, the London *Times* correspondent William Howard Russell commented on how the southerner was "something of an Anglo-maniac, and an Anglo-phobist—a combination not unusual in America."[41]

Architects of U.S. globalism, such as John Quincy Adams and William H. Seward, strategized about how to counter and eventually supersede the British Empire around the world. They were certain that the Declaration of Independence, as Adams put it in his 1821 Fourth of July oration, "was the corner stone of a new fabric, destined to cover the surface of the globe."[42] In the short term, however, their plans for overseas expansion relied on structures of British power: its commercial treaty system, its naval power, its system of global finance, its vastly superior consular and diplomatic network, and even its imperialist ideology. The United States was the great practitioner of "hitchhiking" or "jackal" diplomacy, arriving in new treaty ports in Latin America and the Far East as the cockboat in the wake of the British man-of-war.[43]

A central task for U.S. statesmen concerned how to harness British power toward their own ends without opening themselves up to domestic political attacks. George Washington's signature statement on U.S. foreign policy provides an early example of a politician walking this tightrope. The Washington administration's foreign policy tilted toward the British, particularly in the 1795 Jay Treaty. Yet in the famous 1796 Farewell Address, which is as much a campaign document from that year's election as it is a timeless statement of foreign policy principles, Washington glossed over this fact, emphasizing instead the alleged "great rule" of having "as little political connection as possible" with the Old World and the need "to steer clear of permanent alliances." The nationalist myth of nonentanglement paradoxically came from an administration that aligned itself with the former colonial master but hoped to distance the Federalist Party from that perception in an election year.[44] The 1823 Monroe Doctrine similarly balanced domestic and foreign objectives. The message boldly proclaimed that the Western Hemisphere henceforth would be governed by the U.S. principles of noncolonization, nonintervention, and republicanism. John Quincy Adams later revealed that this was a dog-whistle warning to Britain itself.[45] Yet the Monroe Doctrine was upheld by the powerful Royal Navy. Furthermore, despite the myth to the contrary, it was not a rejection of Britain's offer of joint Anglo-American action—it was British Foreign Secretary George Canning who first backtracked from this offer, and the Monroe administration continued to consider collaboration with the British after the pronouncement of the president's famous message.[46] The genius of the Monroe Doctrine lay in how it boldly articulated a popular nationalist policy while at the same time quietly harnessing British power on its behalf.

In sum, the politics of Anglophobia conditioned, but did not determine, U.S. foreign policy. The challenge confronting the era's statesmen was to find a way of balancing realist interests with the imperatives of a deeply anti-British political culture. The most successful politicians were those who maintained the appearance of opposing Britain—particularly during election years—while nonetheless cooperating with the hated former colonial master when it was in U.S. interests.

Conclusion

The politics of Anglophobia long outlived the real British threat to the United States. Its persistence owed much to elections, which ritualized and entrenched anti-British discourses. Anglophobic politics did not diminish until the turn of the century, largely because of changing geopolitical and racial contexts, as well as a gradual diminution of the cultural link between American elitism and old England. But entrenched structures never disappear at once. Anglophobic politics persisted deep into the twentieth century, not least among Irish Americans, rural isolationists, and cultural populists (indeed, the author can report that Anglophobic antimonarchism remains alive in his Kansas homeland to this day).[47]

If Anglophobia diminished in political importance in the twentieth century, the electoral and political dynamic that it created found new sources of inspiration. Anticommunism emerged as a twentieth-century successor. It was a similar political force connected to, but not purely derivative of, geopolitical rivalry. Like Anglophobia, anticommunism was a multifaceted phenomenon: it was a campaign tactic, a versatile political language, a foreign policy, and a culture. Just as nineteenth-century politicians raced for the Anglophobic high ground in election year, Cold War politicians elbowed each other aside to establish pole position in the anticommunist hierarchy. The electoral politics of anticommunism conditioned the formulation of foreign policy in ways similar to Anglophobia, generally thwarting attempts to modulate tensions, though not dictating diplomatic strategy. And, like Anglophobia, the language of anticommunism long outlived anything that could be construed as a traditional geopolitical threat. Indeed, this language persists to this day, despite the Cold War ending a quarter century ago and the fact that today's communists are mostly curious anachronisms.

Other parallels to nineteenth-century Anglophobia can be found outside of the United States. The anti-Americanism of recent times shares many of its traits. The structures and ubiquity of U.S. power—in both its geopolitical and cultural forms—fuel resentment and anxiety, even among foreign allies. Politicians scramble in election years to present their rivals as lackeys of the United States, but this does not stop officeholders from quietly finding ways behind the scenes of harnessing American power toward their own ends.

The example of nineteenth-century Anglophobia suggests that elections can tell us much about the entrenchment of these and other conspiratorial political dynamics in the United States and beyond. In the bigger picture, this chapter suggests that the project of bringing elections back into political history should focus its efforts not only on crucial elections, but also on the themes that connect different elections over time. Such an approach will highlight not only how recurring languages and dynamics bring together discrete days at the polls, but also how elections conditioned politics and policy making more generally.

CHAPTER 6

The War and Peace Election of 1916

Elizabeth Sanders

> There never was a time when, in my opinion, some way could not be found to prevent the drawing of the sword. I look forward to an epoch when a court, recognized by all nations, will settle international differences, instead of keeping large standing armies as they do in Europe.
>
> —Ulysses S. Grant

The American election of 1916 was remarkable for constituting the climax of the progressive era, a period of lasting and important legislative accomplishments; and it was also notable for a great emotional popular mobilization against war that reconfigured the election and delivered a popular verdict that could not be sustained. The election was a referendum both on American entry into the war and on the surge of domestic reform and government expansion of the Democratic progressive era. It marks a dividing line between reform and war, and thus might be seen to reside in a small class of post–Civil War elections, sharing the reform/war demarcation with 1896, 1940, and 1964.

But the most remarkable feature of this election was the upsurge of popular pacifism that managed to restrain war-prone elites, if only temporarily, even in the face of serious international provocations. A fitting expression of the Progressive reform era, the Democratic convention that nominated Woodrow Wilson departed from the script written by the president, its passions aroused by a speech that galvanized deep peace instincts and created a new frame for the election.

This episode did not, of course, stop U.S. entry into World War I. Its significance lies in what it reveals about public norms and elite and presidential inclinations in the period of emergence of a more active and internationalist presidency. In the shorter term, it presages the disillusionment with presidential foreign policy leadership and the reemergence of a broad peace movement that exerted a powerful effect on four postwar presidents. From a longer-term perspective, it raises questions about the inclination of presidents for war and the ease of arousal of nationalist passions when presidents acquire greater resources for communication and opinion manipulation.

In 1916 the Democrats met to renominate their president as the bloody conflict in Europe dragged on. The war had brought the warring European parties "nothing but enormous loss of life" in the two years it had raged. It had been

> a stalemate most of the time. . . . It was the costliest and most depressing sort of combat, without meaning, accomplishment, or sign of an end. A few months in the trenches produced a hopelessness of the sort described in Erich M. Remarque's classic "All Quiet on the Western Front." . . . One army would besiege the other with artillery, and the infantry would climb out of the trenches to capture however many feet of ground the enemy could be forced to yield.[1]

Would the United States join a slaughter that seemed to most Americans so meaningless? That was the great question faced by the delegates to the 1916 Democratic convention. Might a decade of remarkable, movement-led reform end in the trenches of Europe?

A Movement Era

Beginning in the 1880s with new and dynamic national organizations of workers, farmers, and women, their ranks greatly expanding in the first two decades of the twentieth century, collective action outside the major political parties grew to exert powerful influence on state legislatures and Congress.

The Farmers' Alliance, Knights of Labor, and women's suffrage organizations took their grievances to legislators, and even presidents, without giving up other political strategies such as demonstrations, lobbying, creation of producer and consumer cooperatives, and, of course, where enfranchised, the vote. The post-1890s decline in the size of the active electorate, which resulted from registration requirements, the Australian ballot, new suffrage restrictions in the South, and the decline of party competition in both the Northeast and the South, did not prevent the emergence of "the people's lobbies." New workers', farmers', and women's organizations were formed and gained some leverage with the internal democratization of party nominating processes via party primaries and the possibility of direct issue targeting through the initiative and the referendum.[2]

Thus the decline of the Knights of Labor and the 1896 defeat of William Jennings Bryan and the Populists did not signal a prolonged hiatus in organizing for reform. To the contrary, even after the displacement of the Knights and radical socialist factions by the American Federation of Labor (AFL), and of the Farmers' Alliance by the Farmers' Union, those more cautious organizations grew rapidly in the early 1900s.[3] The two major women's suffrage organizations that had merged in 1890 continued to experience internal contestation over strategy, but became far more effective with the return to the presidency of the National American Woman Suffrage Association (NAWSA) of Carrie Chapman Catt. The emergence of a more radical faction in NAWSA led by Alice Paul did not disrupt the women's movement, but rather attracted younger and more militant women to the cause of a constitutional amendment to gain the vote in every state.[4]

In addition to these three national organizations, the Socialist Party reached its peak in membership and voting share in 1912–14. The nine hundred thousand votes for Eugene Debs in 1912 (6 percent of the total, in an election where the winner, Woodrow Wilson, garnered only 41 percent) strengthened the possibility of political alliance between workers and farmers in support of legislation aiding both, or at least not injuring either: public ownership (especially of transportation, utilities, and armament makers); the eight-hour day; removal of government prosecution of labor unions and worker and farmer cooperatives; employer liability for worker injuries; better roads; public education; mechanisms of direct democracy; and above all, peace, a reduction of armaments, and an end to imperialism.[5] These issues, particularly support for public education, outlawing child labor, reducing armaments, and avoiding war, also yoked women's organizations with labor, socialist, and farmers' groups. Together they formed a powerful campaign for domestic reform and peace.

Congress and Progressive Reform

Movement pressure at the national level was felt first, and most strongly, in Congress in the first few years of the twentieth century. Midwestern and mountain state Republican progressives, who had fought with their party leaders over farmer and worker demands and electoral democracy, went from statehouses to the U.S. House and Senate, joining with agrarian and labor Democrats to push through early progressive reforms such as railroad regulation, food and drug regulation, new banking laws, modest labor measures within federal jurisdiction (a mediation board for railroad disputes, the right of federal employees to organize, an eight-hour day for contract employees on the Panama Canal, and creation of a Children's Bureau, seen as a preliminary step to the abolition of child labor). By 1909 the bipartisan progressive alliance had secured a weak tariff reform and passed a constitutional amendment for a national income tax law against Supreme Court objection. Two years later, Congress sent a senatorial direct election bill to the states for ratification.[6]

When the Democratic Sixty-First Congress took its seats in 1913, it was ready with a reform agenda, steeped in a half-century of Antimonopoly-Greenback-Populist demands: it lowered tariffs that burdened farmers and consumers of modest means; enacted an income tax to secure needed funds for government projects from wealthy citizens concentrated in a few industrial states; abolished the conservative Taft invention of a Commerce Court and greatly strengthened railroad regulation; and finally redeemed the Democratic pledge to labor by emancipating its core activities—strikes and boycotts—from prosecution as restraints of trade under the Sherman Act. A new, publicly controlled banking and currency system (the Federal Reserve) was created as a weapon against deflation and economic paralysis. Congress also amended and strengthened antitrust law, specifying which corporate abuses could be prosecuted. It inaugurated federal regulation of warehouses where farmers stored their crops and brought scientific knowledge to farmers in an innovative new "extension" system for learning, by doing, how to farm more productively. It was a remarkable two-year achievement.

President Wilson as Reformer

More conservative than the majority of his congressional party and their progressive Republican allies, Wilson saw less urgency in the situations of child laborers or seamen on merchant ships; and he saw no need for a national women's suffrage amendment opposed by city machines and southern patriarchs (for the latter of whom he had resegregated the federal bureaucracy). The president pulled teeth from congressional drafts of regulatory laws, insisting, for example, on a new bureaucracy (the Federal Trade Commission) with great discretion and weak enforcement powers to implement key sections of the new antitrust law; he rebuffed more radical proposals for currency expansion; and he introduced ambiguities into the 1914 Clayton Act that would be highly disadvantageous for labor unions.[7]

Then, having little involvement in the difficult last legislative stages of the antitrust and labor legislation, the president declared in 1914 that the New Freedom was complete. His wife had just died, he was exhausted with grief, and Europe was at war. To Wilson, having no wider domestic legislation in mind, the reform era was over.[8] When the Republicans, blaming a mild recession on the bevy of new regulatory, tax, tariff, and labor laws enacted by the Democrats, made large gains in the 1914 congressional elections, the end of reform seemed a safe prediction.

Progressivism in the Shadow of War, 1915–16

Despite the political backlash, the diminished reform ranks in Congress were not ready to throw in the towel. For them, the reform agenda was still glaringly incomplete: workers' accident compensation (employers' liability) had been on the legislative agenda since 1912 when it appeared in the Democratic platform, and remaining labor representatives and their agrarian supporters were eager to finally enact the program. The crusade to outlaw child labor had also picked up momentum in the North, with strong support from both women's groups and business interests outraged at the success of southern textile competition using child labor. Even in the South, the remaining opposition to a ban on child labor was concentrated in a few textile states, the others being divided or in favor of the ban. A third labor reform with strong support in Congress was a seamen's bill to outlaw the harsh working conditions of merchant sailors and impose manning requirements for merchant ships in U.S. ports. Farm states had pressed hard for a Federal Farm Loan Act, which had passed both chambers by early 1915 but died in conference. Finally, labor and farm groups and the American Association for Labor Legislation were pressing for a program of federal aid for vocational education in public high schools.[9]

All five measures had stalled in the economic crisis created by the European war and the disruption to American shipping (which particularly affected the cotton regions), but the five bills also suffered from presidential opposition or indifference. After the child labor bill passed the House in 1915, Wilson expressed constitutional reservations and refused to press for Senate passage. He also considered the proposed farm credit system to be a constitutional stretch and threatened to veto it. Supporters of the seamen's bill managed to win Senate passage, but the president opposed it on diplomatic grounds.[10] Reformers worried that the president's increasing attention to the war would redirect attention away from the domestic agenda.

Both the British and the German navies were harassing neutral merchant ships bound for the other's ports, but the British navy quickly commanded the sea lanes, establishing an unprecedented blockade of neutral ships bound for ports of the Central Powers. The UK blacklisted American and other companies dealing with its enemies, and censored the international mails. Much congressional time was consumed, with little success, on proposals for the government to purchase foreign ships marooned in U.S. ports and in dealing with the increase in tensions with both Great Britain and Germany as the United States worked through its position on the rights of nonbelligerents in the shipping lanes. As disruptive as the British blockade was, the lethal expansion of German submarine warfare against British and neutral ships carrying food and war supplies to the Allies particularly tested the determination of the president and congressional progressives to formulate and defend their neutral rights to commerce on the seas.[11]

In most American studies of World War I, President Wilson is portrayed as making continued, heroic efforts to keep his country out of the European war, facing down the Germans with outraged protests against submarine attacks that killed hundreds of Americans and persistently exerting diplomatic pressure on the arrogant British-led alliance to agree to peace negotiations.

The reality of Wilson's actions in 1915–16 is much more complicated. Although he publicly represented his country's desire to stay out of the war and spoke often and eloquently to that effect, he also led a campaign of military preparedness; acted through prowar subordinates to forge a secret agreement that contemplated taking the United States into war on the side of the Allies;[12] and did not strongly contest British predations on American and other neutral shipping or their highly successful efforts to prevent foodstuffs or materials useful for war from reaching the Central Powers. Wilson adamantly refused to entertain congressional proposals to forbid Americans to travel on passenger or merchant ships of belligerents, or even to strongly warn them against such travel, instead elevating to a major war issue and point of national honor the rights of ostensibly neutral countries' citizens to travel to Europe on belligerent ships laden with food and munitions for the Allies. He made only weak and belated attempts to use powerful American leverage—a threat to withhold further loans to the Allies—which might have persuaded them to endorse a 1916 "peace without victory" conference; and, most mysteriously, Wilson ignored the increasingly desperate efforts of the German chancellor and other Berlin civilian officials to call an immediate peace conference and cease-fire in the last months of 1916. The latter episode in the saga of Wilsonian diplomacy receives little attention in most American-centered accounts of World War I, perhaps because it is so difficult to understand and so out of step with the heroic Wilson narrative.[13]

For political scientists, generally more attentive to electoral/institutional incentives, some of the discordant aspects of Wilson's behavior in 1916 are perfectly understandable. As party leader and agent of national foreign policy, the president engaged in diplomacy that in its more public aspects conformed to the powerful peace tendencies of his political coalition, while at the same time being exquisitely sensitive to the criticisms of antagonistic Republicans. Below the surface, Wilson's private maneuvers can be seen as expressions of a complicated personality with strong affinity for the Allies and an obsessive desire to achieve a world-historical victory as the architect of a new world order. However, the presidential campaign for a military buildup in late 1915 and 1916, which Wilson defended vigorously in a presidential speaking tour of eight states in early 1916, calls up the most straightforward of election-year motives: as Wilson biographer John Milton Cooper writes, a patriotic campaign promoting increased military preparedness was recommended to Wilson by his advisers as a way to parry "repeated attacks by bellicose critics." His adviser Joseph Tumulty predicted that it would "pocket Roosevelt completely."[14] But more than an election-year gambit, Wilson's conversion to strong preparedness can also be seen as a part of his new internationalist vision. "If we are going to join with other great powers in a world movement to maintain peace, we ought to immediately inaugurate a big naval programme," Colonel Edward House wrote to the president as he prepared an important foreign policy speech.[15] Large foreign policy ambitions required a navy "ultimately equal to the most powerful maintained by any nation of the world," advised the Board Wilson appointed to help construct his naval expansion program.[16] Thus the president's Naval Act of 1916 provided for a three- to-five-year naval buildup almost six times as expensive as the navy of the Spanish-American War, totaling over $300 million. Speaker of the House Claude Kitchen, a strong opponent of the buildup, noted that it exceeded even the "extravagant, wild, and reckless program presented by the Republicans," an appropriations increase "over seven times more than the total increase by Great Britain in the ten years prior to the European war . . . [and] sixty times more than the total increase by Germany in the five years preceding the war."[17]

Great presidential pressure was required to sway Democrats to join Republican conservatives in passing legislation expanding army and naval appropriations and a bill to create a national professional army less reliant on the state guards. The latter proposal also drew fierce opposition from congressional Democrats, but was ultimately passed in more modest form in June 1916.[18] Wilson provoked the most bitter battle in his party over the issue of allowing Americans to travel on armed ships bound for the United Kingdom and Europe. The southern, midwestern, and mountain agrarian regions insisted on the maintenance of U.S. neutrality and were outraged at British disruption of export trade with Germany. As a Texas Democrat put it, Britain had allied with northeastern bankers and munitions makers supporting the Allies, "dragged our commerce from the seas," and "robbed the Southland of nearly $400,000,000."[19] Other important voter blocs—German American and Irish American—also opposed U.S. aid to the Allies when it raised the risk of war with Germany, and most members of trade unions were decidedly opposed to U.S. entry into the war. Thus Wilson's insistence on the rights of Americans to travel as passengers on ships laden with weapons went too far for them. It was a much more provocative position than the mere insistence on commodity export rights.[20]

During the fight over the Gore-McLemore resolution in Congress in February 1916, Wilson had candidly told three Democratic supporters of the resolution that if a German submarine sank an armed merchant ship carrying Americans, the United States would break diplomatic relations with Germany, and the Germans would then likely declare war. American entry into the war, he predicted, might bring the war to a much faster end than was otherwise possible. This admission was alarming to the delegation, though the president's protestations of his unflagging determination to avoid war, along with ferocious presidential lobbying, ultimately subdued the Democratic rebellion. Despite the conviction of antiwar Democrats that Americans "did not want to go to war to vindicate the right of a few people to travel or work on armed vessels" bound for belligerent nations, the resolution to warn Americans not to travel on such ships was ultimately tabled on a 276–142 vote.[21]

To build a coalition for preparedness in the face of opposition in his own party and among progressive Republicans, Wilson would need new allies. He hoped that the preparedness campaign would win over some independents, if not the more militant northeastern Republicans, who early began to clamor for a robust military buildup.[22] Wilson also began a courtship of labor leaders with whom he had not had a warm relationship before. By forging a new partnership with Samuel Gompers, who was abandoning his early labor pacifism and taking harsh positions against labor antiwar and antipreparedness advocates, the president may have hoped to undermine the strong pacifist tendencies in the trade unions. In the fall of 1916, Wilson appointed Gompers to the Council on National Defense, a national advisory commission promoting preparedness. The AFL leader became a major supporter of the president's foreign policy, and in turn received public visibility for himself and tangible benefits for his organization and its allies.[23] That did not, of course, significantly diminish opposition to war among northern workers, particularly Socialists and German and Irish Americans.[24]

Opponents of war, most of whom also opposed preparedness, were a numerous and diverse group, if generally less well placed and possessed of far fewer resources for lobbying and publicizing their message than the hawks. There were a few exceptions. Advocates of a conference of neutral officials and citizens to mediate an end to the war failed to gain presidential support, but did persuade Henry Ford to give generous support to their efforts—including the chartering of a ship to take the activists to Europe.[25] Journalists, labor activists, Socialists, social workers, and peace groups based in religious and educational institutions, women's suffrage organizations, and urban peace societies (such as the Chicago Peace Society) forged links with their counterparts abroad, and, of course, pressed their ideas on the American government. Among the most important and long-lived of the organizations energetically trying to stop the war, find ways to prevent war, and prevent U.S. entry into the war were the Woman's Peace Party (later the International League for Peace and Freedom), founded by dozens of women's organizations in January 1915. It claimed over forty thousand members, including well-known activists such as Jane Addams, Carrie Chapman Catt, and Charlotte Perkins Gilman, a prominent feminist, writer, and social reformer.[26] Another peace organization, the American Union Against Militarism (predecessor to the American Civil Liberties Union), dedicated its efforts to ending or preventing international conflicts, contraction of armaments production, and other legal scaffolding for permanent peace.[27]

Though the president did not endorse their international efforts and ultimately ignored their appeals to try to end the war through mediation or by brokering a peace conference, he did reach out to collect ideas from a variety of peace-promoting organizations and individuals who had come to share a faith in what they saw as the universal moral principle that war should, and could, be discouraged by human-constructed institutions. Jane Addams, energetically working to keep the United States out of the war, was a frequent visitor to the White House, through whose doors passed a great variety of peace advocates.[28]

At the invitation of former president William Howard Taft, Wilson on May 27, 1916, gave an important address to the League to Enforce Peace, a conservative organization with a distinguished membership that did not oppose increases in armaments or work to end the existing war, but did support a new international organization to keep the peace.[29] Wilson's speech underlined the U.S. commitment to international involvement in the service of peace, both in ending the current war and through the instigation of new collective processes to assure open diplomacy, the territorial integrity of nations, and self-determination of peoples. It was the first rollout of his still-developing plan for a postwar League of Nations.[30]

The 1916 Convention: "We Didn't Go to War!"

By the time of the Democratic convention of June 14–16, 1916, the Democrats had added only a few additional reforms to the legislative accomplishments of the first two years; others remained under desultory consideration because of pockets of opposition that could only be overcome with a mobilizing force from the top of the ticket. The fights over an army and navy buildup and the Gore-McLemore resolution had occupied much congressional time.

Wilson himself drafted the platform his party would run on in November, though with much input from the party. One of the most ambitious policy agendas came from Senator Robert Owen of Oklahoma, a progressive Democrat from a state that registered, in 1912 and 1914, the largest membership in the Socialist Party and the largest percentage of a state electorate voting Socialist.[31] Owen's letter to the president urged that the party move beyond its prior accomplishments to court former Progressives by, as Arthur Link put it, "drafting a plank approving everything that every social justice worker had ever proposed," an advanced progressivism that would secure social justice through ambitious legislation not constrained by the inevitable constitutional objections.[32]

Wilson, however, was not inclined to rely for reelection solely on celebrating and extending the party's unprecedented progressive achievements; it was also important to quiet the strident critics who still claimed he was doing too little to prepare for war. The loudest of these was Theodore Roosevelt, who had abandoned progressive leadership in favor of shrill condemnation of the president for weakness in the face of German aggression. Roosevelt became, after 1914, "the country's most obstreperous pro-Allied extremist and the administration's most wrathful (some observers said 'crazed') critic."[33] Thomas Knock quotes Taft's shrewd assessment of his onetime mentor thus: "The Truth is . . . he believes in war and wishes to be a Napoleon and to die on the battlefield. He has the spirit of the old berserkers."[34] But Roosevelt and his close allies were not the only advocates of hyper-preparedness in the Republican Party, and they were joined by some Democrats from the northeastern and upper midwestern industrial areas.

Wilson's platform draft of early June listed domestic legislative accomplishments but also pledged measures to protect American interests in the European war. It condemned disloyal "hyphenated" Americans and issued a stern warning to potential subversives and the organizations that supported them. The text advocated "adequate" military spending, "worthy to support the great naval traditions of the United States and fully equal to the international tasks which this Nation hopes and expects to take a part in performing." It affirmed "the duty of the United States to use its power, not only to make itself safe at home, but also to make secure its just interests throughout the world in securing settled peace and justice."[35]

And thus the balance of domestic accomplishments and resolute nationalism might have stood, but for an uprising on the convention floor on the first day, June 14. The delegates had gathered in a flag-bedecked coliseum in St. Louis, Missouri, and the opening of the convention followed Wilson's script. The president was "determined that his followers should outdo Republicans in their display of patriotism" and directed the singing of patriotic songs and a keynote theme of "Americanism.[36]

But for keynote speaker Martin Glynn of New York, "Americanism" had a rather different meaning. For him, and likely for the large majority of Democratic delegates in St. Louis, Americanism meant avoiding entanglement in foreign wars, even if that entailed suffering a bevy of indignities and even loss of American lives (which would be dwarfed by casualties in a war). In a speech remarkable for its philosophical reflections and historical detail, Glynn occupied almost an hour and a half proclaiming to a growing crescendo of delegate cheers and encouragements to continue, what he called "the doctrines of our Fathers"—pronouncements of revered presidents and statesmen—and many historic incidents in which the United States, though sorely provoked by humiliating and deadly encounters, refused to go to war with the offending nation. As the examples multiplied, the hitherto languid body of delegates came alive, and the "manufactured enthusiasm" and flag-waving directed by the president's Americanism script for the convention gave way to genuine passion, according to the *New York Times*.[37] The following examples convey the tone of the remarkable speech:

> So far the United States has held the flame at bay" and "saved its people from participation in the conflict . . . that now devastates the nations across the seas.[38]
>
> The policy of neutrality is as American as the American Flag.[39]
>
> Neutrality is America's contribution to the laws of the world.[40]
>
> And today in this hall, so that all the world may hear, we proclaim that this American policy of neutrality is the policy which the present administration pursues with such patriotic zeal and religious devotion; while Europe's eyes blaze red from fires of war, Europe's soil turns red from the blood of men, Europe's eyes see red from tears of mourning women and from sobs of starving children.[41]

> For this policy of neutrality, Thomas Jefferson was called a spineless poltroon, and yet today Jefferson is hailed as one of the wise men of the world and for millions his opinions are a political bible.[42]

> Is there any American so blind to our past, so hostile to our future, that, departing from our policy of neutrality, he would hurl us headlong into the maelstrom of the war across the sea?[43]

> [The president of the United States] stands where Grant stood when he said there never was a war that could not be settled better some other way.[44]

> Neutrality is the policy which has kept us at peace while Europe has been driving the nails of war through the feet of a crucified humanity.[45]

> In his policy of peaceful negotiations today, the president of the United States follows the example set him by the greatest presidents the Democratic party and the greatest presidents the Republican party ever gave this nation.[46]

> When Grant was president, during the war between Spain and the Spanish West Indies, a Spanish gunboat seized the vessel "Virginius" flying the American flag and a Spanish commandant in cold blood shot the captain of the Virginius, thirty-six of the crew and sixteen of the passengers. But we didn't go to war. Grant settled our troubles by negotiation, just as the President of the United States is trying to do today.[47]

The first nine statements are followed in the typescript of the minutes with "(Applause)." The *Virginius* anecdote, the first of many recitations by Glynn of historical occasions on which, despite great provocations, "we didn't go to war," was greeted by "Great applause," according to the convention record.

Subsequent historical anecdotes became a litany of speaker-audience interaction. Glynn would describe incidents involving dismal predations against Americans, and then the audience would ask, "And what did we do?" To which Glynn would respond, "We didn't go to war," and describe the negotiations that resolved the conflict. France led the tally of unreturned attacks with, according to Glynn, twenty-three hundred violations in the John Adams administration alone. Compared to all the cited episodes, "the present violations against our neutrality are insignificant," Glynn argued. Several times the former governor tried to stop the speech, worried that he had greatly exceeded his allotted time, but the delegates compelled him to continue. Cries of "give us some more," "Give it to them," "Yes, yes, yes," and so on dot the annotated minutes of the convention. "This policy [of negotiating our way out of quarrels] may not satisfy the fire-eater or the swashbuckler," Glynn remarked (to "Laughter and applause").

> But it does satisfy those who worship at the altar of the God of peace. It does satisfy the mothers of the land (applause) for whom (great applause)—But, my friends, this policy does satisfy the mothers of the land, at whose hearth and fireside no jingoistic war has placed an empty chair. It does satisfy the daughters of this land, from whom brag and bluster have sent no sweetheart and no brother to the moldering dissolution of the grave. It does satisfy the fathers of this land, and the sons of this land, who will fight for our flag and die for our flag, when Reason primes the rifle.
>
> (Long continued applause. A voice: "Say it again." "Repeat it." Cries of "Repeat it." "Repeat it." "Say it again." "Say it again.")[48]

And according to the minutes, Glenn does repeat the last litany.

After remarks in this vein, recorded in thirty-six pages of the minutes, Glynn moved to the discussion of Americanism and preparedness, as the president had instructed convention speakers, but added his own twist. He mentioned Wilson's support for the navy but added that "The Democratic party advocates and seeks preparedness, but it is preparedness for defense, not preparedness for aggression."[49]

Glynn then added a defense of Wilson's intervention in Mexico, which had received "a great deal of criticism" but was "inherited" and designed to restore a democratic government overthrown by force. The language of "inheritance" and defense of democracy and the absence of a pledge to remove American troops any time soon appear scripted, as does the boast of increased naval expenditures, of which the Democratic Party had in the past been quite skeptical. The language on both Mexico and naval appropriations is similar to that in the subsequent convention speech by Senator Ollie James, which again suggests compliance with the president's wishes.

There were no applause indications when Glynn defended Wilson's Mexican intervention.[50] The applause, and Glenn's enthusiasm, reappeared when he embarked on the last section of his speech, recalling the Democrats' domestic policy reforms and new trade policies, and the opportunities they opened up for Americans, especially for the poor, who now had work and could enjoy leisurely relaxation in the city and countryside and send their children to college. "Our skies are red from fire of furnace and of forge, not from fires of war." The new prosperity, Glynn intoned, "is a true prosperity" that results from helping every man stand on his own feet and gives him an equal chance in life, not a result of "munitions makers' accounts."[51]

Glynn ended his speech with a glowing assessment of an administration he called "the most progressive since the days of Jefferson, the most humane since the days of Lincoln, and the most responsive to the people since Andrew Jackson." He praised Woodrow Wilson for handling with prudence and dignity "the destiny of a hundred million people," despite being assailed by "the wolves of privilege."[52]

> [O]ne name will shine with golden splendor upon the page that is blackened with the tale of Europe's war, one name will represent the triumph of American principles over the hosts of darkness and of death . . . (Applause). . . . It will be the name of the student and the scholar who has kept his country true to its faith in a time that tries men's souls . . . the name of Woodrow Wilson, President, and President to be. (Great applause).[53]

The keynote speech of Martin Glynn was a masterful political performance. With more democratic instincts than Wilson himself, the former New York governor set the tone for the coming campaign. It would be a celebration of peace and domestic reform, not a carnival of patriotism and preparedness. The response of the thousands of Democratic delegates and alternates to Glynn's speech was confirmed by the subsequent speech of Chairman Ollie James, whose many references to peace were also wildly cheered, confirming that Wilson's model for a convention centered on preparedness and patriotism had been jettisoned for a celebration of peace—a "pacifist stampede," as the *Times* called it.[54]

The next day's speech by Senator James and the delegates' reaction to the dramatic appearance and brief address of Bryan[55] suggested, to Arthur Link, that "the delegates were entirely and permanently out of control." Senator James, like Governor Glynn, knew what the crowd wanted and sent them into a spontaneous, exuberant twenty-one-minute demonstration, cheering and parading, "waving hats, fans, and flags" in celebration of peace through diplomacy.[56] James's speech, more emotional than Glynn's, reached a crescendo of biblical references to love and the blessedness of peacemakers, all the more extraordinary for our inability to imagine such a speech today.[57]

Contrasting Wilson and his chief Republican critic, James argued that "It is a perfectly easy thing for the President of the United States to plunge his country into war if he is a politician before he is a patriot. He would seek his own reelection as he came upon horseback up the bloody highway of contending armies. The American people have never yet repudiated a war president and never will." Had Roosevelt been president, the Kentucky Senator argued, "today 500,000 brave American sons would be contending around the fort of Verdun in this mighty maelstrom of blood—thousands would have been buried in the ditches."[58] Instead, James continued, "Without orphaning a single American child, without widowing a single American mother, without firing a single gun, without the shedding of a single drop of blood, he [Wilson] wrung from the most militant spirit that ever brooded above a battlefield an acknowledgement of American rights and an agreement to American demands."[59]

The spontaneous move of the 1916 Democratic convention to abandon (or at least move well beyond) the president's script and make the convention a celebration of peace and social progress was said by the *Times* to have alarmed and dismayed unnamed Democratic Party leaders who were anxious about the broader public's response to the "peculiar emphasis" on the pacifist language of Glynn's speech. But those fears were not realized.

The party platform writers did take note of the exuberant reception of the Glynn and James speeches and revised their document significantly, according to Link.[60] Instead of focusing on preparedness and Americanism, the platform committee inserted a new theme: "In particular, we commend to the American people the splendid diplomatic victories of our great president, who has preserved the vital interests of our Government and its citizens, and kept us out of war."[61] This was the first appearance of the phrase "He kept us out of war," which became the main slogan of the Democrats'

1916 campaign. In a highly contested election, it seems likely that the shift to peace and diplomacy was effective in wooing a critical number of new women voters, labor, Progressives, and Socialists to the Democratic side on November 7.

The Last Surge of Reform, 1916

After the convention, and with the advice of many Democratic officials around the country, the president yielded to his party and finally threw his support to the child labor bill, the rural credits bill, federal aid for vocational education (the Smith-Hughes bill), the Workmen's Compensation Act, and a new federal roads program that delighted rural citizens. In a spontaneous move by congressional Democrats, a new Revenue Act was passed in early September 1916, making the income tax much more progressive. If elites wanted a military buildup, Democrats and other antiwar progressives reasoned, they could pay for it. "Conservatives were aghast" at passage of this landmark populist law.[62]

After attempting to mediate a threatened strike of railroad workers—which confronted the president with the possibility of economic paralysis on what might be the eve of U.S. entry into the war—Wilson endorsed an important and extremely controversial eight-hour day law for the nation's rail workers (the Adamson Act). It passed with only three Democrats in opposition in the House and two in the Senate.[63]

The record of Democratic progressivism that the party presented to the electorate in 1916 was now even stronger, and despite his late arrival at "advanced progressivism," Wilson, when he took to the stump, defended the domestic record as well as his party's emphasis on keeping the peace. Other party leaders had already begun to publicize these peace and reform issues before Wilson's turn, and the party organizations printed and distributed millions of copies of Glynn's convention speech as well as a late-conversion speech by Wilson eschewing war with Mexico. Bryan, who had resigned from the cabinet in 1915 to protest Wilson's insufficient peace efforts, now campaigned joyfully for his president and was a great asset to Wilson and the party. In the closely contested midwestern and mountain states, Democratic politicians followed Montana Senator Thomas J. Walsh's advice to play up the peace issue in their campaigns.[64]

The 1916 labor and income tax laws did, however, result in a significant drop in the volume of campaign contributions that Wilson and other party leaders had anticipated from better-off sympathizers. Bankers and businessmen opened their wallets to the Republicans with a level of desperate generosity not seen since 1896.[65] Still, the Democrats found funds enough to buy newspaper ads and distribute pamphlets hammering home the blessed benefits of peace and new social legislation. "More than all, our country is at peace in a world at war," concluded a pamphlet entitled *Woodrow Wilson and Social Justice.* Another, entitled *Children's Emancipation Day*, also brought the two themes together, "remind[ing] mothers that Wilson had saved their children from mines, mills, and sweatshops just as he had 'saved their sons and their husbands from unrighteous battlefields.' "[66] When the Republican candidate appeared to move closer to Roosevelt's bellicose position, the Democratic campaign headquarters exploited the opportunity and ballyhooed the association in a pamphlet entitled *Complete Accord with Roosevelt*, which bluntly charged that a victory by Charles Evans Hughes would be "notice to all the world that America repudiates her policy of peace for the Roosevelt-Hughes policy of war."[67]

The Hughes Campaign

Hughes, who won the Republican nomination on June 10, 1916, was a man remarkably similar to Woodrow Wilson. A straight-arrow Protestant, Hughes had been a reform governor of New York at roughly the same time (1907–10) that Wilson was a reform governor of New Jersey (1910–13). He was highly intelligent and accomplished, probably even smarter than Wilson (at least a better student, with a razor-sharp analytical mind), a man of highest integrity and great dignity.[68] His disadvantages compared to Wilson were his less-well-honed political instincts (after all, he had most recently been a Supreme Court justice, not a politician), his much less eloquent speech making, his more polarized party, and the fact that as a progressive himself he approved most of the Wilsonian program. But he had to be careful about that approval: the hard-core conservatives in the Republican Party did not like the income tax, the low tariff, the antitrust law, or the too-soft military policy of the Democratic Party. They particularly hated one of the most recent reforms: the Adamson Act limiting working hours for railroad workers.

Hughes thus talked a lot about how distasteful and dangerous the eight-hour law was. But the eight-hour law was popular with the public and Hughes's condemnation gave Wilson the opportunity to praise the law and other Democratic labor legislation.[69]

Hughes was the moderate, consensus choice of Republican Party leaders. His major competitor for the nomination had been Theodore Roosevelt, a man who had put domestic progressivism aside in favor of a strident militarism that particularly offended German Americans and midwestern antiwar Republicans. When he realized he had no chance to win the Republican nomination, and no future as the Progressive Party candidate, Roosevelt tried to persuade party leaders to nominate someone close to him—the patrician conservative Elihu Root or the military reformer and avid preparedness promoter Leonard Wood. Neither looked to former president Taft and other party leaders like good possibilities.

Hughes was surely the best choice for the Republicans. Had he been a better candidate, had he merely avoided offending California progressives by campaigning in the company of decidedly unprogressive California political bosses, he might have won. Despite the great problem of running against an inspiring Democrat who had an impressive legislative record and a unified and enthusiastic postconvention party campaign effort, in addition to (thanks to the war) a strong economy, Hughes almost won.[70]

Outcome of the Election

Wilson and his Republican opponent were running neck and neck as the election approached, and a number of states were won with small pluralities. The election was held on November 7 and the result not known for certain until two days later. Overall, Wilson won about 590,000 more popular votes than Hughes, and garnered 277 electoral votes to Hughes's 254.

He had achieved this narrow victory on the basis of his party's reform program and his own ostensible commitment to diplomacy over war. Hughes had opened his campaign with an attack on the eight-hour law; the Democrats had worked hard to remind industrial and transportation workers of their delivery for labor. Postelection analysis cited by Link indicated that Wilson had carried the labor vote, but according to a November 12 electoral analysis in the *New York Times*, the labor vote was not decisive in carrying any state but New Mexico.[71]

The offense to California progressives may have cost Hughes that state's thirteen electoral votes (and the election). Progressive gubernatorial candidate Hiram Johnson carried the state handily.[72] But the Socialist vote was also important in California. According to Arthur Link's analysis, about three hundred thousand Socialists and left progressives who had voted Socialist in 1912 shifted to Wilson in 1916.[73] They, of course, endorsed the progressive legislation of 1913–16 and also strongly approved the president's apparent reluctance to take the country into the European war.

According to the *Times*, the major factor in Wilson's victory was the women's vote, which was particularly important in the West, where most of the states with women's suffrage in 1916 were located, and where domestic policy approval and opposition to war reverberated strongly among both women and former Bull Moose progressives. Christine Lunardini and Thomas Knock also argue for the importance of women's peace votes in Wilson's victory, noting that ten of the twelve women's suffrage states (all but Oregon and Illinois) went for the Democrat.[74]

And women voted for Wilson despite the fact that the Democratic platform endorsed women's suffrage only through state action, not a national constitutional amendment. Hughes, for his part, went beyond his own party's similar platform statement and verbally endorsed a national amendment. On that basis, and the greater Republican support for suffrage in state referenda, the radical wing of the suffrage movement—Alice Paul's National Woman's Party—endorsed Hughes and worked to defeat Wilson and the Democrats in 1916; but that effort was dwarfed by the pro-Wilson women's vote.[75]

"He kept us out of war," then, was the decisive factor in the *Times*'s analysis. That need not be seen as contradicting Link's argument that broader commitments to progressive policies enabled Wilson to win substantial numbers of 1912 Republican progressive voters in New Hampshire, Ohio, and ten western states.[76] Progressivism outside the Northeast was both programmatic (in the domestic policy sense) and pacifist. In fact, the 1916 electoral map looked quite similar in its regional patterns to the map of 1896, demonstrating the populist legacy in progressivism; but where they differ, one sees the additional urban, labor, and female progressive appeal that enabled Wilson to carry California, Washington, Ohio, and New Hampshire.

In 1916 the Democratic Party had behaved in classic parliamentary fashion: it reined in a president it perceived as becoming too interested in the possibilities of war. In this paradigmatic example of party as information conveyer from the people to the government, convention delegates—most of them elected officials or party leaders—were responsible for promoting the strongly held policy preferences of their constituents.

Half a century later, after the party and presidential nomination reforms of the 1970s, conventions would fall under much greater control of sitting presidents. Delegates would no longer be elected officials close to those they represented; instead, mostly amateur activists chosen in low-turnout primary contests involving ambitious, self-selected presidential candidates (often with little experience in national or even state government) would go to conventions to represent those ambitious candidates with whom they identified.

But in 1916 a thousand seasoned politicians still filled the convention hall. They certainly cooperated with their president—but only up to a point. Instructed to demonstrate effusive "Americanism," patriotism, and preparedness, the main convention speakers gave lip service to the president's instructions and then boldly and creatively set out the achievements and goals of the party as *they* saw them: the Democrats had enacted a great and diverse program of reforms, some of them as old as Greenbackism and Populism, others representing new government programs to help the poor in all walks of life, from field to factory. The experienced politicians at St. Louis had supported their party leader in his seeming determination to rely on diplomacy to protect American trade routes in seas policed by belligerent parties. They wanted the president to keep doing that. They made their preferences very clear.

Was Wilson privately distressed to read what happened at the convention he and his allies had so carefully planned, realizing now how difficult it would be to convince Americans to go to war?[77]

Of course, he ultimately did get them to go to war, with the help of German submarine captains, a lot of presidential framing (and refusal to call for a peace conference of belligerents), and a bungling foreign minister named Arthur Zimmermann. Before the election, the country had put up with worse, and, as former governor Martin Glynn reminded the assembled delegates on the first day of the convention, other countries, even bandits, had in the past done awful things to us, and what did we do? We didn't go to war.[78]

CHAPTER 7

Farewell to the "Smoke-Filled Room": Parties, Interests, Public Relations, and the Election of 1924

Bruce J. Schulman

On the face of it, the 1924 presidential campaign seems an odd candidate for a study of pivotal elections. A glance at the electoral map hardly identifies 1924 as a momentous—or even a minimally interesting—contest. The incumbent, Republican president Calvin Coolidge, posted a majority of the popular vote and an overwhelming margin in the Electoral College while his opponent, the West Virginia–born lawyer and diplomat John W. Davis, captured no state outside the solid Democratic South. Only Wisconsin disturbed the otherwise conventional results; the Badger State gave its thirteen electoral votes to favorite son Robert La Follette running on the Progressive ticket. But while La Follette polled an impressive 16.6 percent of the popular vote, his insurgency had no effect on the outcome.[1] Predictions as late as a month before the election that La Follette would sweep the upper Midwest and the northern plains or that his appeal to German American voters would swing several states proved illusory.[2]

Still, the 1920s marked a crucial milepost in the three-decade-long transformation from the largely face-to-face politics of parties that had dominated nineteenth-century American elections to the mass-mediated politics of interests that emerged in force by the Great Depression. No single factor propelled this shift. It reflected demographic change, especially the huge influx of immigrants that forced parties to recruit outside their natural bases, as well as the political mobilization of voters outside parties (particularly a large constituency of women involved in reform activities hostile to party politics). But it also drew energy from the revival of antiparty sentiment and the diffusion of new communications technologies. Deeply embedded in the nation's founding, antagonism toward parties formed a key part of the Progressive agenda in the early twentieth century. This discourse, along with the mechanisms that reformers put in place to weaken the power of parties, really mattered. It was not any singular innovation—the Australian ballot, primaries, the direct election of senators, and so on—that did it. Rather, the combination of these reforms with a steady drumbeat criticizing the whole idea of parties undermined partisan attachments. At the same time, new technologies created alternate vehicles for political communication between politicians and ordinary citizens. They also narrowed the appeal of party affiliation. In the last part of the nineteenth century, politics had functioned as a form of mass entertainment as well as a tool of governance. The emergence of competition—films, recorded music, and radio—further damaged parties by uncoupling entertainment from politics.

During the 1920s, then, the political arena opened to new, different forms of mobilization. As industrial organizations swelled, the professions emerged, and the flood of immigrants challenged simplistic melting pot notions, specialization offered a compelling response to the growing scale and scope of American life. The United States could function as a nation if all of these parts—ethnic, racial, regional, and occupational—could find a place in the whole, but increasingly, day-to-day politics focused around ensuring adequate representation for specific interests. Rather than forming new parties and voicing broad-based demands, increasingly specialized interest groups made it possible to break public policy into component parts. Compare, for instance, the populist championship of "producers" in the 1890s with demands of the American Farm Bureau three decades later for crop subsidies. The election of 1924 did not produce these long-term changes, but the events of that memorable campaign brought them out into the open and clarified an irreversible turn in American presidential politics.

The significance of the election was not immediately apparent. Contemporary observers certainly found the campaign a mostly sterile nonevent, a contest with little of significance at stake and few differences between the leading candidates. Writing in the *Baltimore Sun*, John W. Owens spoke for many observers when he concluded, "The choice presented to the people by the two parties this year is between a conservatism which says that everything of importance is all right as it is, and a conservatism which says a few changes are necessary."[3] A drawing by Jay Norwood "Ding" Darling in the Republican-leaning *New York Herald Tribune* captured the prevailing boredom. Casting the voter as a dog clutching a bone marked "Coolidge honesty" over a caption that read "Remember the poor dog that tried too hard to better himself," the cartoonist warned his audience to stand pat; the dog overlooked a swamp containing a nearly identical bone labeled "Davis sincerity" and a menacing creature called "third party."[4]

To be sure, the contest generated its share of overheated invective and creative electioneering. Indeed, one issue both clearly dominated the rhetoric of the candidates (at least that of the two challengers) and eclipsed all others in the popular press: corruption. The Democrats built their campaign around the administration's connection to the scandals that had plagued the Harding presidency and only intensified this focus after Coolidge's running mate, the prominent banker and Harding administration official Charles Dawes, became enmeshed in a scandal of his own. "The Democratic leaders," one sympathetic paper explained, "intend to make of Republican corruption the principal issue in the campaign, overshadowing all others."[5] At the Democratic National Convention, not only did the keynote speech focus on Republican corruption, but the party brass also strategically named as chairman Thomas J. Walsh (D-MT), the senator who had played the lead role in the Teapot Dome investigation.[6] Declaring that "a vote for Coolidge is a vote for chaos," the Democratic platform identified the scandals as proof of the Republican Party's "inability to govern even itself."[7]

Even the campaign's most celebrated publicity stunt—the so-called Singing Teapot—reminded voters of recent Republican perfidy. Wrapped in canvas and adorned with a papier-mâché teapot to evoke the Teapot Dome scandals, the seven-passenger vehicle was escorted by the Women's Division of the Democratic National Committee on a tour of more than one hundred cities and towns. Accompanied by a saxophonist, the ladies passed out campaign literature and pasteboard teapots. "'The Singing Teapot' will boil with Republican corruption," Women's Division chairwoman Caroline O'Day told the *New York Times*.[8] Sadly for the tour's organizers, the biggest tempest it produced involved the outrage of a Democratic official, insulted when the "Teapot" drove off before he had finished his speech.[9]

The Progressive Party banged the anticorruption drum even harder (and much more plausibly) than the Democrats. Unsurprisingly, La Follette lumped together the two major parties as vehicles of graft, scandal, and self-dealing and drew frequent connections between the dirtiness of his opponents and the Progressives' main bugaboo—the illicit control of the Republic by private monopoly. The very first plank of the Progressive platform, numbered item one in its "Covenant with the People," called for "a complete housecleaning in the Department of Justice, the Department of the Interior, and the other executive departments."[10] On the campaign trail, La Follette explicitly tied Coolidge to the Harding scandals and warned that Americans could expect nothing better from the incumbent than "four more years of misgovernment." Mocking Coolidge's efforts to distance himself from his predecessor, "Battlin' Bob" insisted that "the acts of the Harding-Coolidge administration must be judged as a whole."[11]

For his part, President Coolidge ignored the issue of corruption. He never mentioned it except for an oblique reference in his speech accepting the Republican nomination when he suggested that a dishonest administration would not have cut taxes and trimmed spending as he had, but would rather have kept maximum cash on hand for illicit purposes. Coolidge's refusal to acknowledge the subject enraged his opponents. William Randolph Hearst's *New York American* noted "a strange and ominous omission" in Coolidge's rhetoric: "the name or the record of Warren G. Harding. . . . It is the more extraordinary because nearly every one of the achievements to which President Coolidge points with such pride are achievements of President Harding and not President Coolidge." Accusing the president of cowardice, the *American* fumed over the incumbent's efforts to dissociate himself from the scandals.[12]

Still, as much as the candidates and the press lavished attention on the issue of corruption, the charges of Coolidge's opponents gained little traction. They neither derailed his candidacy nor broke through the general torpor that, according to many commentators, surrounded the campaign. Relatively few Americans even voted; as a percentage of the voting age population, turnout fell below that of 1920 and far below that of other elections of the era.[13] Historians have not much altered those contemporary judgments. They have not taken the corruption issue seriously and have mainly ignored the 1924 election altogether. In *The Perils of Prosperity*, his classic 1958 survey of the United States between 1914 and 1932, William Leuchtenburg includes the campaign in a larger chapter on the eclipse of Progressivism. Lynn Dumenil's *The Modern Temper*, the 1995 book that replaced Leuchtenburg's as the standard treatment of 1920s America, barely mentions the election. Even the 2013 Coolidge biography by the conservative activist Amity Shlaes gives the campaign short shrift. A reader might expect so laudatory an account to dwell on its subject's greatest achievement in electoral politics, but

Shlaes depicts the contest as an unwelcome diversion from the essential work of cutting taxes and slashing wasteful government (she does, at least, mention the Singing Teapot).[14] To the extent that scholars of 1920s America analyze the 1924 election, they normally view it as evidence of the continuation of a long era of Republican dominance in national politics as well as the triumph of conservative business over the exhausted forces of reform. Addressing the question of the president's popularity, for example, David Burner suggested that "perhaps Coolidge offered the country the sedative the country appeared to need."[15]

For scholars of American politics more generally, the national campaigns of the 1920s have occasioned little interest on their own terms. They draw attention mainly as fodder for debates over the preceding era—arguments over the persistence or collapse of Progressive reform—or as harbingers of future developments, such as the emergence of the New Deal coalition. Those latter interpretations focus on conflicts within the Democratic Party. While the Republicans nominated Coolidge practically by acclamation, the Democrats split badly. During the party's 1924 convention—held in a roasting, unair-conditioned Madison Square Garden during a New York heat wave—the Democrats deadlocked for sixteen brutally hot days. Divided between its cosmopolitan, urban, ethnic wing, which opposed Prohibition and rallied behind Al Smith, the Roman Catholic governor of New York, who was of Irish immigrant stock, and the rural, Protestant, Prohibitionist southern and western bloc that supported William G. McAdoo, the two factions fought over whether to condemn the Ku Klux Klan and over who to nominate for president. Ballot after ballot dragged on for weeks, but the rival wings could not agree. On the 103rd ballot, after the main contenders had withdrawn, the still-divided party compromised on the bland Davis. Several historians have depicted the convention as a pivot, a point of equilibrium between the old Democratic Party, personified by McAdoo and William Jennings Bryan, and the New Deal coalition embodied by Smith and Franklin D. Roosevelt. In this view, the defeat of McAdoo and the nomination of an explicit critic of the Klan point toward the modern liberal, urban Democratic Party that would take shape a decade later.

That argument owes its origins to Samuel Lubell's classic study, *The Future of American Politics*. In that 1951 book, Lubell, a prominent pollster who had worked in federal agencies during World War II, suggested that Al Smith's unsuccessful presidential runs during the 1920s had planted the seeds for the assembly of the New Deal coalition and for an era of Democratic Party dominance in American politics. In particular, Lubell stressed growing Democratic strength in the nation's cities. In 1920 the Republicans swept the nation's twelve largest cities by a million and a half votes. Eight years later, however, the Democrats won the urban vote. Of course, this forward-looking account emphasized 1928 and Smith's presence on the top of the ticket, an election where the Democrats carried the big cities but lost a significant chunk of the "Solid South."[16]

In recent years, political historians have refined and deepened this notion of the 1920s as incubator of modern American politics, seeing the period as herald not merely of imminent shifts in partisan affiliation but of broader changes in the style and structure of American politics. Brian Balogh casts the decade as the critical juncture in a half-century-long transformation from a politics of parties to a politics of interests. For Balogh, however, as for Lubell, the decisive shift does not arrive until Herbert Hoover's 1928 presidential campaign. Unlike his predecessors, Hoover "rose to power outside of the party structure" and "was more beholden to interest group cues than partisan intelligence for his connection to voters."[17] With its parochial focus on corruption and internecine strife over whether or not to condemn the Klan, 1924 remains a relic of the vanishing past.

In his 2006 biography of Coolidge, David Greenberg tells a slightly different story of long-term political change. In this account, party organizations also cease to remain the principal mediators between politicians and ordinary voters. But rather than relying on interest groups to mobilize and communicate with constituents, Coolidge constructs the first modern presidential media operation. Drawing directly on the skills of public relations experts like Edward Bernays, advertising executives like Bruce Barton, and celebrity surrogates like Al Jolson, the Coolidge campaign made deft use of film as well as the new medium of radio, carefully placed magazine stories (including features about First Lady Grace Coolidge in women's magazines), and established campaign operations outside the normal party structure. Bernays, for example, founded the Coolidge Non-Partisan League, an organization dedicated to then still-novel practice of orchestrating presidential endorsements from prominent Democrats.[18]

Compelling as they are, these accounts of the 1920s in general and of Coolidge's 1924 campaign in particular as incubators of developments in the style and structure of national politics entirely ignore the obsessions of the press and the protests of Coolidge's opponents. For political historians, the concern about corruption and frequent calls on the president to denounce the Klan remain fascinating curiosities, amusing signs of the time no more significant than the rages for flagpole sitting and mah-jongg tournaments. But the specific conditions of 1924 played a key role in forwarding the larger transformations scholars such as Balogh and Greenberg have outlined. In particular, the corruption issue, the debate about the role of third parties in the La Follette campaign, and the controversy over the Klan accelerated the development of and helped to coalesce new forms of presidential politics. In these processes all three of the major candidates played an important role.

In hindsight, Coolidge's victory appears wholly unremarkable. It marks a midpoint in the "New Era" of Republican political supremacy and business-government fraternity that began with the repudiation of Wilson and the League of Nations, culminated in Hoover's 1928 landslide, and persisted until the game-changing onset of the Great Depression. Yet from the perspective of 1922, when the GOP suffered heavy reverses in state and congressional elections, the "Republican ascendancy" looked anything but inevitable. The party lost seven seats in the Senate and seventy-seven in the House. At the same time, the establishment of the Conference for Progressive Political Action, a motley collection of disgruntled farm, labor, and reform interests, threatened to sunder the party much as the Bull Moose had in 1912.[19] Prospects appeared little better the following year, when President Harding succumbed to a coronary thrombosis and the initial period of mourning gave way to revelations abut corruption in his administration and sordid tales of scandal, such as published tales of the president's sexual liaisons with his mistress in the White House. Soon after Harding's death, the Washington correspondent for the *New York Times* reported that "alignments within the Republican Party have become all awry." Assessing the presidential aspirations of half a dozen contenders, Richard Oulahan concluded that the national convention, "which will assemble in the early summer of 1924, will not be a ratification meeting. . . . Instead, it will be the scene of a stupendous battle in which every element of the party will take part."[20]

File that prediction in the "oops" folder! Not only did that convention turn into a stage-managed coronation of the incumbent, but by the fall of 1924, Coolidge turned his election into a forgone conclusion. He even co-opted the taunt of Senator Walsh into his own campaign slogan. Instead of "A vote for a Coolidge is a vote for chaos," Republicans successfully transformed the election into a referendum on "Coolidge or chaos." The president's rapid reassembly of a winning coalition, then, surprised observers like the *Times* correspondent because Coolidge did not mount a typical party campaign. To be sure, Coolidge did not ignore the tried-and-true tactics for seekers of the Republican presidential nomination. Following the playbook Mark Hanna and William McKinley had devised a generation earlier, Coolidge both raised a sizable war chest from business interests and assiduously courted delegates in the South—states with few Republican voters that nonetheless influenced the selection of the party's nominee. But for the most part Coolidge outmaneuvered his rivals through a carefully orchestrated media campaign that included flattering profiles in numerous magazines, radio broadcasts that exploited the incumbent's widely recognized skill at using the new medium, and films of the president in action at the White House. The campaign also conducted considerable outreach to organized interest groups, especially trade and professional associations connected to the emerging communications industries.[21]

Pundits like the *Times*'s Oulahan can hardly be faulted for their failure to recognize the rising politics of interest groups and mass media. Looming large in their frames of reference, the 1920 Republican convention had bequeathed to American politics an enduring symbol of party rule: the "smoke-filled room." That term entered the American political lexicon in 1920, in reference to the salon in Chicago's Blackstone Hotel where Republican leaders brokered the nomination of "the best of the second raters," Warren G. Harding.[22] According to a series of widely circulated, slightly sensational, and highly self-serving accounts, party leaders disregarded the regulars on the convention floor (and wholly ignored the preferences of the small number of primary voters), assembling the ticket in a back room amid cigar smoke and whiskey glasses. Exaggerated as it was, the story held some truth; 1920 became an archetype of the bossed convention.

Of course, the shifts in the style and structure of presidential campaigns that became manifest in 1924 were already under way four years earlier. The very nomination of Calvin Coolidge as vice president in 1920 gave the lie to the legend of party discipline. The denizens of the smoke-filled room had tapped Senator Irvine Lenroot (R-WI) as Harding's running mate, but the rank and file on the convention floor bristled. "Curiously," reflected Kansas delegate and longtime Republican insider William Allen White, "the delegates in the convention revolted." They "were disgusted" and "they rose and flouted the bosses."[23]

Four years later, Coolidge's campaign threw into sharp relief both the decay of the system of partisan competition in place for the previous generation and new developments in the structure of American presidential politics. Coolidge not only pioneered novel tactics of mobilization and communication, he also distanced himself from the Republican Party. Stressing his individual accomplishments and character, the Coolidge campaign depicted the president as a nonpartisan statesman. Not only did his handlers deploy the Coolidge Non-Partisan League, but they also deliberately used radio to burnish this image. They routinely broadcast Coolidge's appearances before nonpartisan audiences but did not record his more openly partisan speeches to explicitly Republican crowds. Under Barton's guidance, the campaign produced a series of testimonials from average citizens to, in the advertising man's words, "build up a wonderful Coolidge legend in the country." In what would become a staple of later presidential politics, the president surrounded himself with popular entertainers, casting himself, like the nation's most celebrated performers, as a celebrity. For example, under the aegis of the Coolidge Non-Partisan League, the president and first lady welcomed thirty prominent entertainers to a breakfast of sausages and hotcakes. Headlining the performance, Al Jolson performed an original song, "Keep Coolidge," and suggested that voters would heed the actors' endorsement of the president because "we members of the theater are perhaps in more intimate touch with the people than any other profession."[24]

Rather than tout a Republican era of peace and prosperity, the Coolidge campaign detached the candidate from his partisan affiliation. The "Coolidge political machine to all intents and purposes," explained the *Saturday Evening Post*, "has always been a one-man machine, and the one man is Calvin Coolidge."[25] As historians such as Greenberg and Balogh have demonstrated, that strategy pointed up long-term developments in presidential politics. Coolidge may well have moved in that direction even if his predecessor had been nothing but upright; he had already experimented with public relations and interest group outreach as governor of Massachusetts. But Coolidge's approach also reflected the exigencies of the 1924 election. With "Republican corruption" dominating the headlines, the prosecution of Harding administration perpetrators under way, the squeaky-clean La Follette in the field (Battlin' Bob had entered Wisconsin politics as an impassioned foe of bribery and graft), and the Singing Teapot on the road, Coolidge had to separate himself from his scandal-ridden fellow partisans. Thus Coolidge not only ran as an individual, he took steps to defuse and depoliticize the scandals, including the appointment of a pair of special counsels, one from each party, to investigate the wrongdoing; new leadership at the Republican National Committee; and a new director of the FBI with a reputation for honesty, J. Edgar Hoover.

At the recommendation of the special counsels, the government also launched criminal prosecutions of the wrongdoers and civil cases against companies that had illegally benefited from the shady dealings. The strategy even convinced the California Progressive Chester Rowell to support the president. "Deride the 'Coolidge Myth' all you like," Rowell warned, but the incumbent had "come through the greatest storm of scandal that has stirred our generation, not merely personally untouched, but with his vessel unwrecked." While conceding that Coolidge did not fit the Progressive mold, Rowell swallowed whole the campaign's bait: "I have confidence in his personal independence of reactionary influence. The 'Old Guard' may be for him, but he is not for them."[26]

Along with relentless attacks on the "radicalism" of the Progressive program, Coolidge's tactics helped take the starch out of Robert La Follette's insurgency. The Progressive campaign of 1924 has gone down as one of the most successful third-party efforts in American history. Since the Civil War, only Theodore Roosevelt in 1912 and Ross Perot in 1992 have exceeded the 16.6 percent of the popular vote that La Follette tallied. Most accounts of his candidacy have focused around the persistence or demise of Progressivism. Suggesting explanations ranging from the exhaustion of reformers, to the distractions of consumer society, to the divisions within the American liberal community, to the lukewarm support of organized labor, to the apathy that widespread prosperity provoked, historians have largely depicted the campaign as a failure. In states with strong Progressive traditions, such as California and Washington (both of which went for TR in 1912), Coolidge won more votes than his two opponents combined. And except for Wisconsin, La Follette lost every state across the Midwest and the northern plains, even running mate Burton Wheeler's home state of Montana and the Farmer-Labor redoubts of Minnesota and South Dakota. While the American Federation of Labor (AFL) gave La Follette its first-ever endorsement, it furnished little material assistance, and other unions, including the United Mine Workers, actually supported Coolidge. One syndicated cartoonist depicted AFL chief Samuel Gompers riding simultaneously toward and away from La Follette.[27]

But like Perot's Reform Party, La Follette's campaign barely constituted a third party. Not only did the Progressives fail to run candidates for offices below the national ticket, they established no functioning state or local organizations, raised few funds, and failed to rally sympathetic interest groups to their standard. While the ticket made it onto the ballot in every state but Louisiana, state election officials listed La Follette and Wheeler under various party designations—Farmer-Labor, Labor, Progressive/Socialist, and, in California, just Socialist.[28] Oddly, much of the debate within and about La Follette's candidacy centered on the nature and value of political parties themselves. Or perhaps this fascination should not be surprising given the widespread concern with corruption and the ties observers frequently drew between graft and party rule. Some wanted the Progressives to become a true party, not just a personal vehicle for La Follette (the candidate, for his part, suggested that a party would emerge after the election as an expression of the people's will). They viewed the 1924 insurgency as continuous with the Bull Moose campaign or linked it to the formation of the first Labour government in Great Britain; either way, they saw it as the engine of an enduring realignment in American politics. *New Republic* founder Herbert Croly explicitly compared the Progressives to the emergence of the GOP during the 1850s, suggesting that much as the Republican Party built itself in opposition to the extension of one coercive system, a new partisan organization should champion the cause of oppressed farmers and workers. In fact, Croly expressed little enthusiasm for La Follette's candidacy except as the instrument for creating a new party.[29]

Felix Frankfurter's endorsement of La Follette also looked forward to a new party system that would reflect the nation's principal ideological divisions instead of the "unreal cohesions" of the present-day Democrats and Republicans. But Frankfurter, who had previously described himself as "politically homeless," also criticized the parties themselves, linking them to corruption and to obsolete modes of governance. They represented, in Frankfurter's words, "organized appetites kept alive by the emotional warmth of past traditions."[30] Pro–La Follette newspapers echoed this critique of the major parties and the candidate's commitment to forging a "militant political movement, independent of the two old party organizations, and responsive to the needs and sentiments of the common people."[31]

Yet others, even prominent Progressives, opposed La Follette precisely because his effort undermined the two-party system and put at risk alliances that key interests had forged with the Democrats or Republicans. Chester Rowell, for example, defended his endorsement of Coolidge in large part because he believed the GOP remained the most likely vehicle for progressive policy making.[32] In a similar vein, numerous Republican-leaning newspapers that had supported TR in 1912 objected to La Follette's appropriation of the name "Progressive."[33] Answering Croly and Frankfurter in the pages of the *New Republic*, Walter Lippmann ridiculed the argument for partisan realignment. He expected the two major parties to survive and that any third party would be absorbed into one or both of the old ones; he found unbelievable the promises that the Progressives "will make a new party system." In the end, Lippmann asserted, the likely short-term policy outcomes of the election must trump any pie-in-the-sky hopes to replace the established parties, eliminate self-dealing in politics, or mimic the British system of government.[34] A number of interest groups echoed this reluctance to forsake the major parties. Even the AFL's endorsement described La Follette as an "independent Republican" and his running mate Wheeler as an "independent Democrat."[35]

Historians have neglected this debate for obvious reasons; it never amounted to anything. The Progressive Party of 1924, such as it was, faded along with its standard-bearer (who died soon after the campaign); no restructuring of the party system took place (at least not along the lines envisioned in 1924). But the specific contents of this debate revealed less than the mere fact of its existence. The fascination with the nature, function, and future of political parties displayed a widespread recognition that major changes in presidential politics were already under way.

Ostensibly, John W. Davis and the Democrats seem like the bystanders to this drama, an insignificant sideshow to the transformations that Coolidge's and La Follette's campaigns highlighted. Not only did Davis perform poorly on Election Day, but the epic Democratic convention of 1924 revealed complete disarray. Although humorist Will Rogers would not utter his immortal description of the party until six years later, his words seemed apt: "I belong to no organized political party. I'm a Democrat." To be sure, some observers viewed the nomination of the amiable West Virginia–born corporate lawyer as a victory for the supporters of Al Smith and a portent of the direction the party would soon take (the Smith forces found the compromise candidate somewhat more appealing than McAdoo's people did). But the selection of Charles Bryan, brother of the Great Commoner William Jennings Bryan, for vice president made clear that the ticket barely patched over the party's divisions.

And nothing, according to the standard accounts, dramatized those rifts so baldly as attitudes toward the Ku Klux Klan. From 1920 to 1925, between three million and six million Americans joined the Klan. With widespread support from "respectable" segments of society—clergymen, law enforcement officers, business leaders—the Klan began exerting influence in state and local politics. Not only did KKK-affiliated candidates win election in southern states such as Georgia and Tennessee, Klan-backed slates swept the major offices in Oregon and beat back determined opposition to capture both the governorship and two Senate seats in Colorado. As the Democrats gathered for their national convention, a large encampment of Klansmen assembled across the Hudson in New Jersey, and the organization's imperial wizard, Hiram Wesley Evans, warned that he would allow no political party to disown his followers. For many southern and western Democrats in 1924, whatever their personal views, attacking the Klan amounted to political suicide.[36]

At the Madison Square Garden convention, Al Smith's supporters introduced a platform plank condemning "secret societies of all kinds" and pledging to oppose the Klan by name. A passionate and lengthy debate ensued; newspapers began referring to the conclave as the "Klanbake." When the final vote was tallied, the plank failed by one vote—543 to 542. Instead a vague affirmation of the constitutional protections for religious liberty went into the platform. The Klan declared victory.

During the general election campaign, La Follette expressed unequivocal opposition to the Klan, calling himself "unalterably opposed" and insisting that the KKK "can not long survive." Davis took a similarly outspoken stance: "If any organization . . . whether [called] Ku Klux Klan or by any other name, raises the standard of racial and religious prejudice . . . it does violence to the spirit of American institutions and must be condemned by all those who believe as I do in American ideals." Republican vice presidential candidate Charles Dawes conceded that the Klan's way "is not the right way to forward law enforcement," but he made excuses for the organization, saying he could understand its appeal and implying that it was a natural response to lawlessness and corruption. In the words of Fiorello La Guardia, Dawes "praised it with faint damn." However, most newspapers gave Dawes as much credit as La Follette and Davis for opposing the KKK. Despite Davis's frequent calls for the president to join him in condemning the Klan, Coolidge remained silent.[37]

To be sure, the Klanbake and the broader debate over the legitimacy of the KKK dramatized broad cultural conflicts between country and city, drys and wets, native Protestants and ethnic Catholics and Jews. But especially in the North and West, the Klan of the 1920s functioned as a vehicle of political mobilization outside of and often arrayed against established party organizations. In Kansas, according to *Emporia Gazette* editor and longtime Republican kingmaker William Allen White, the Klan operated almost like a third party, dissolving partisan attachments and challenging the authority of the party hierarchy. When Klan supporters wrested control of the gubernatorial nomination from mainline Republicans, Allen ran as an independent in a failed effort to restore the party regulars.[38] Recognizing the political strength of the KKK—especially the ways it weakened party affiliation and created space for interest groups and public relations efforts to mediate between candidates and voters—no doubt contributed to Coolidge's reluctance to say anything about the controversial secret society.

On the face of it, the election of 1924 seems like a bundle of curiosities, a collection of unrelated developments. Yet the innovations of Coolidge's campaign, the debate over the nature and purposes of a third party that bedeviled La Follette, and controversy over the Klan that split the Democrats all pointed toward a newly modern model of presidential politics—one in which interest groups and the mass media would compete with and even supplant party organizations as the principal vehicles of political mobilization and communication. The emphasis on "corruption" functioned as a proxy for a critique of party politics, a decline in voter turnout, and the emergence of new modes of political organization. Although hardly anyone noticed it at the time or after, in 1924 those long-simmering shifts in the structure and the style of national politics reached critical mass.

CHAPTER 8

The New Deal in 1940: Embattled or Entrenched?

Gareth Davies

By 1940 the New Deal as active reform crusade was moribund, the victim of a variety of ailments whose cumulative impact had been to annihilate the optimism with which Franklin Roosevelt had embarked on his second term in 1937. Back then, hard on the heels of the greatest electoral victory in American history, FDR perceived a mandate not simply to build on the policy legacy of his first term but to transcend some of the institutional constraints that had stood in his way—to make the Democratic Party firmly an instrument of liberalism, to bring to heel a recalcitrant Supreme Court, to make the administrative machinery of the executive branch more smoothly responsive to his will. Astonishingly quickly, though, things had fallen apart, in a dramatic series of reverses: bids to "pack" the Supreme Court and "purge" the Democratic Party ended in humiliating failure; FDR's grand executive reorganization plans were repudiated; a renewed slide in industrial production during 1937–38 (the so-called Roosevelt recession) diminished his standing; to his closest associates, the president sometimes conveyed a sense of demoralization and listlessness, a keen desire to retire to Hyde Park.

This much is clear, but determining the historical significance of the "end of reform" is a tricky business. For some, the failure of the New Deal to achieve its more social democratic aspirations—for economic planning, labor regulation, social provision—was portentous, ensuring that politics during the 1940s and 1950s (or even beyond) would have a constricted, complacent character, and that the fundamental problems of American democracy and

American capitalism would go unattended. To the extent that the New Deal yielded an enduring political era, it is notable primarily for its limits.[1] For other historians, the New Deal break with the nation's antistatist past was more impressive: it was during the Depression decade that Americans came, however uneasily, to look to government to protect them from adversity, and this constituted a historic change in political culture. According to this view, all presidents during the post–World War II era, Republican as well as Democrat, conservative as well as liberal, lived "in the shadow of FDR," and the new legitimacy of the state, this new habit of looking to Washington for help, constituted the lasting and vitally important consequence of the New Deal.[2]

That the emergency of the Great Depression should have been followed in such short order by World War II and the Cold War complicates one's task in attempting to characterize the distinct legacy of the New Deal. How does one separate out the respective contributions of reform politics and national security politics to American state building during the middle decades of the twentieth century? In statistical terms, the answer is straightforward: government spending, tax revenues, and the federal workforce all grew significantly during the 1930s, but they then increased massively during World War II, and those increases were maintained during the early Cold War period. Similarly, and despite the initial impression that politics moved right during the war, statistical evidence demonstrates that it had vastly more "progressive" socioeconomic consequences than had the New Deal: income differentials between rich and poor narrowed, taxation became much more sharply redistributive, women and African Americans enjoyed greater economic opportunities, labor union membership massively accelerated.[3] Reviewing these data, one might easily wonder whether the debate about the New Deal legacy really matters quite so much. Have participants in this debate not missed a much larger story, namely, the fact that, as so often in the United States, state expansion and portentous social change came about as by-products of war and national security politics rather than by design?[4]

A substantial body of literature exists that would tend to support this proposition, or at least to suggest that there is no point in making judgments about the long-term legacy of the New Deal unless one brings World War II in to the equation.[5] Thoroughly persuaded by this literature, my purpose in the present chapter is nevertheless to assert the dramatic changes in American political culture that the New Deal had already accomplished by Pearl Harbor. My vantage point for attempting this task is the presidential election of

1940, which falls conveniently between the end of the New Deal as an active reform movement and U.S. intervention in the war. The war in Europe was already the largest issue in American politics throughout 1940, yet its socially and politically transformative effects still lay mostly in the future. And while the war occupied far more campaign time than the history or future of the New Deal, the collapse of democracy across Europe in some respects encouraged reflection on the Roosevelt administration's domestic record over the past eight years.

The present chapter begins with an overall assessment of the political temper of the American people in 1940. How did they view FDR's record and his having consented to run for a third term? To the extent that they had had enough of the New Deal, did they wish to see it repealed, or did they simply wish for a breathing space? Next, we will consider why a seemingly conservative political temper, a marked reaction against the reformist ferment of the New Deal, should have spawned what is quite possibly the most progressive presidential matchup in American political history: FDR and Henry Wallace for the Democrats against Wendell Willkie and Charles McNary for the Republicans. What, if anything, does this tell us about the legacy of the New Deal? The third section discusses the contexts within which the New Deal was discussed in the subsequent campaign, focusing in particular on the marked tendency of both candidates to treat it as a living program rather than as one that belonged to the past. And the conclusion makes an overall assessment of the political standing of the New Deal in November 1940.

The Political Temper in 1940

A variety of poll data during the latter half of Roosevelt's second term confirmed the generally conservative mood of the American people: they favored strong moves to erase the federal budget deficit; they overwhelmingly opposed further New Deal experimentation; they were suspicious of "reliefers" and organized labor; they hoped that the Democratic nominee in 1940 would be a conservative; outside of the South, Republicans enjoyed a distinct partisan advantage over Democrats; and FDR's popularity was only a shade above 50 percent, well below the 62.5 percent approval rating he had enjoyed at the time of his reelection in 1936.[6] Conservative Republicans were further buoyed by the tremendous gains they had made in the 1938 midterm elections (eighty-one seats in the House, almost doubling their representation) and in recent gubernatorial contests (a net thirteen gains in 1938); they had a number of attractive young officeholders, such as New York's "racket-busting" district attorney Thomas Dewey and Minnesota's "boy governor," Harold Stassen; in concert with increasingly disenchanted conservative Democrats, they were regularly defeating FDR's legislative agenda.[7] Seemingly a lame duck, Roosevelt had no obvious Democratic successor, leaving the Republicans well placed for a return to power in 1940: there was talk of their retaking the House and every likelihood of their winning the White House.[8] The American people, it appeared, like the British people at the end of William Gladstone's great reforming ministry of 1868, had "tired of being improved."[9]

With the start of the European war, Roosevelt's political fortunes began to revive, and he appeared to regain some of his vitality, energized rather than overwhelmed by the enormity of the global crisis, perhaps relishing this new opportunity to display the qualities of emergency leadership that had made him such a commanding and inspirational leader during his first term. That said, popular opposition to a possible third term remained strong during the early months of 1940, diminishing only in the aftermath of the German conquest of Norway and the Low Countries in May, a month or so before the Republican convention.[10] It was at this point that Democratic prospects for the fall improved in another respect: for the past two years or so, Republicans had been assailing Roosevelt for his supposedly alarmist, belligerent international stance and opposing his preparedness moves; now, public opinion was increasingly persuaded that Roosevelt had been correct, and that left the principal GOP candidates for the presidency newly vulnerable, especially in the event that FDR were persuaded to run again.[11]

Nominating Willkie

The first Republican front-runner in 1940 was the charismatic Thomas Dewey, who had won national attention when he nearly defeated the popular Herbert Lehman in their 1938 Senate race. That so young and inexperienced a figure should have seemed politically attractive was remarkable, with the nation still mired in recession (there was talk of a further downward lurch in the early months of 1940) and in the context of the Nazi advance across western Europe: FDR's acerbic interior secretary, Harold Ickes, sought to make the idea incongruous when he quipped that Dewey had "thrown his diaper into the ring."[12] One astute foreign observer saw in Dewey's rise a tribute to

Roosevelt's impact on the presidency, an institution that had now become "too good for the average man."[13]

Seemingly more substantial than Dewey, but entirely lacking in charisma, were the other two leading aspirants for the GOP nomination. Robert Taft may have only been elected to the Senate in 1938, but he had commanded attention from the start, partly because he was the son of a president whom many conservatives held dear (William Howard Taft, among other attributes, had written a closely argued defense of the limited presidency),[14] but mainly because of a series of effective, modulated critiques of the New Deal. A strong opponent of FDR's domestic record, and skeptical too of what he took to be the president's saber-rattling, Taft was still less isolationist than many of his midwestern colleagues and could see some good in the New Deal too.[15] As for Arthur Vandenberg, the former Grand Rapids newspaper publisher had been in the Senate for a dozen years and was a member of the Foreign Relations Committee. Critical of the second New Deal and a leading opponent of court packing, he had also been a member of the Nye Committee and was a strong member of the "peace bloc."[16]

By the time that the Republican Party convened in Philadelphia to choose its nominee, the near-isolationism of Taft and Vandenberg was a political problem. While there was no more appetite than before for intervention (only 7 percent of those polled supported this course, according to Gallup), the passionate desire to stay out of war now coexisted with a growing recognition that the terrible events in Europe had powerful implications for the United States, as well as with a greater desire to aid the Allies.[17] That left Taft and Vandenberg less attractive than before, and perhaps—now that the "phony war" was over—it made Thomas Dewey less attractive too, on grounds of sheer youth (he was thirty-eight) and inexperience. Nevertheless, one of the three would have been nominated had not Taft's and Dewey's unwillingness to share the ticket created a route to the nomination for Wendell Willkie, a rank outsider. His rise constitutes one of the most improbable stories in the history of presidential politics.

What made his nomination improbable? First, Willkie had come to prominence as a private utilities executive, battling the Tennessee Valley Authority (TVA) and opposing government regulation of private power companies. On the one hand, this commended him to the Republican Party faithful, for whom TVA was the single most socialistic feature of the New Deal. On the other hand, power bosses were the very embodiment of the Wall Street label that the party desperately needed to shed in order to win back the White

House. Second, it is doubtful if any leading Republican in 1940 was more strongly in favor of the United States taking a firm stand against Hitler: it is extraordinary that isolationists as implacable as Bruce Barton and Joseph Martin should have endorsed his candidacy. Third, Willkie had been a Democrat as recently as 1938, and on issues other than power—on the regulation of Wall Street, on social welfare, on labor regulation—he was broadly supportive of the New Deal. Here is what he said about the program in the *Fortune* article that did much to bring his name before the Republican faithful in April: "There has grown up a new concept of public welfare. Our new outlook must include this. Government, either state or federal, must be responsible not only for the destitute and the unemployed, but for elementary guarantees of public health, the rehabilitation of farmers, rebuilding of the soil, preservation of the national forests, clearance and elimination of city slums and so forth."[18] How could the Republicans possibly nominate such a man?

The answer is straightforward: the party mainstream's position on the New Deal and the global crisis was unpopular, and GOP delegates in Philadelphia were desperate to win—to see the back of FDR (whom they assumed would stand for a third term, though he had given no public encouragement to this idea), to prevent him from doing any more damage to the American system of government, above all perhaps to experience national political power again after the political debacle of the 1930s. Polls showed that Americans wanted the GOP to pick a candidate more liberal than Alf Landon, and that if there was little appetite for extending the New Deal, still less was there any support for rolling it back.[19] As for the war in Europe, Americans had come to the view that the key to staying out of war was not detachment but rather military preparedness and unflinching opposition to Nazism. Before the fall of France, two days before the GOP convention, it had been smart politics to insist on strict neutrality, oppose Roosevelt's defense appropriation requests, and pooh-pooh his rhetoric about the Nazi threat as alarmist. Now, the opposite was the case: according to one poll, fully 60 percent of Republicans approved of FDR's international policies.

Perhaps Willkie's nomination might help to extricate the GOP from its predicament. Quite apart from his public policy positions, he was, one historian has noted, "both a hard fighter and a highly attractive personality, a tousled, rumpled figure, informal and folksy with his Hoosier twang, enthusiastic and very nearly indefatigable."[20] But it would not be straightforward. For one thing, how could Willkie achieve the distance that he needed to achieve from his party and its policy positions without fatally alienating the party faithful? For another, how would he transcend his past as a Wall Street lawyer and utilities magnate? (Harold Ickes, responding to his acceptance address, mocked him as a "simple, barefoot Wall Street lawyer.") What is more, when the Democrats met in Chicago, a few weeks after Philadelphia, they nominated Roosevelt—whose formidable campaigning skills led Willkie to label him "the Champ"—for a third term.

FDR and the New Deal in 1940

If the New Deal's permanence was already largely secure, then FDR's nomination, like that of Willkie, certainly helped to embed it further in American political culture. This is one of the respects in which the 1940 election not only provides a convenient way of taking the national political pulse at the end of the New Deal decade; also, this campaign, like many others considered in the present volume, changed American politics. That Roosevelt was the nominee ensured that the fall campaign would in substantial measure be fought over his record in office. Given the lowering clouds of European war, however, the leadership he had displayed in response to the great emergency of the Depression would inevitably be viewed through the prism of the ever-deepening global crisis. Had FDR displayed precisely the skills the nation needed in this new hour of need? Or did the record of his first two terms, and his decision to seek a third, disclose dictatorial instincts that left him peculiarly ill-equipped to defend American democracy?

To a greater degree than historians sometimes recognize, Roosevelt had often resisted the conservative trajectory of the late 1930s. True, he had suffered big defeats, and he sometimes exhibited a certain demoralization and frustration in their wake. But none of the president's principal defeats had been complete, whatever the headline story. Most familiarly, while the effort to pack the Supreme Court had been a fiasco, in its wake the Court had reformed itself, starting to construe the Constitution more broadly, in a way that left the New Deal newly secure. And then, between 1937 and 1940, Roosevelt—having made no nominations at all during his first term—was able to appoint no fewer than five New Deal justices to the Court. Spluttering with indignation at what they saw as frankly partisan and ideological appointments, conservative Republicans certainly did not feel themselves to be in control at these moments—and FDR's continued political authority was evident from the way conservative Democratic senators went along with the selections of these strong New Dealers, close associates of the president.[21] The jurisprudential impact of these appointments was felt almost immediately, most notably in the Carolene Products case and *Palko v. Connecticut*, which saw the emerging Roosevelt Court signal its new interest in civil liberties and civil rights. Little noticed at the time, and presaging an extension of the reform impulse to encompass matters that were of little concern to FDR, this was of course a development with the most profound long-term implications.[22]

Something of that same pattern—of the seeds of a liberal New Deal order being sown amid the seeming crisis of the reform impulse—is evident in relation to administrative reform. Again, the big political story was of bruising defeat. But even as Congress dismissed the Brownlow Commission's grand ideas for overhauling the executive branch, it ratified the creation of the Executive Office of the Presidency and overhauled the budgetary process.[23] Probably more important, though, was the way that New Deal agencies such as the Securities and Exchange Commission, the National Labor Relations Board, the Bureau of Public Assistance, the Rural Electrification Administration, and TVA were becoming part of the permanent fabric of American politics, together with the civil servants who administered them. Early on in his second term, FDR had seen the creation of an unambiguously liberal Democratic Party as being key to the survival of his reforms. In the event, though, as Sidney Milkis has shown, the New Dealers found an administrative rather than a partisan route to consolidating their achievement.[24] By the time the Republicans won back the White House, a long dozen years later, these New Deal bureaucrats had established formidable and largely bipartisan networks of support for the programs they administered, as well as agendas for expansion.[25] This pattern—developing incrementally and largely away from the public gaze—somewhat diminished the programmatic significance of FDR's failure to overhaul the Democratic Party.

That said, FDR did not give up on overhauling his party after the failure of the 1938 purge effort. Rather, whenever he addressed an explicitly partisan audience, he reiterated his strong view that the Democrats must develop greater ideological homogeneity—that they must become squarely a party either of conservatism or of reform. He did so in his annual Jackson Day address in January 1940; he did so again in a radio address to Young Democrats three months later; and the climax of the effort came in Chicago, when he made it clear to conservatives that he would not accept the nomination unless they accepted his choice of their bête noire, Henry Wallace, as vice president, in place of the conservative Texan John Nance Garner.[26] When it seemed that the convention might defy him (because delegates considered Wallace too forthrightly liberal, but also because they viewed him as eccentric in ways that could damage the ticket) and nominate House Speaker William Bankhead of Alabama, FDR drafted a remarkably direct message, to be released in the event that Wallace were rejected. In it, he declared that the Democrats had only been successful in the twentieth century when they had "been the champion of progressive and liberal policies," but that Wallace's rejection revealed the party to be still "divided on this fundamental issue." He went on:

> Until the Democratic Party makes clear its overwhelming stand in favor of liberalism, and shakes off all the shackles of control by conservatism and reaction, it will not continue its march to victory. It is without question that certain influences of conservatism and reaction have been busily engaged in the promotion of discord since this Convention convened. That being the fact and the case, I in all honor cannot and will not condone or go along with the fact of that party dissension. It would be best not to straddle ideals. It would be best for America to have the fight out. Therefore, I give the Democratic Party the opportunity to make that historical decision by declining the honor of the nomination for the presidency. I so do.[27]

Even in the context of the fall of France, therefore, FDR remained strongly committed to the long-term project of building a New Deal Democratic Party. More generally, Roosevelt's response to the terrifying collapse of democracy across Europe provides another instance of his continued determination to make the case for the New Deal. In the short term, the war only reinforced all the other circumstances that were serving to deaden the cause of reform; yet it also allowed him to argue that the New Deal had constituted a rebuilding of American democracy—against that desperate global backdrop, and despite its parlous condition at the end of Herbert Hoover's miserable presidency—and to make the case that enhancing the nation's capacity to defend Americans from insecurity and plutocracy must be an ongoing project if democracy were to stay healthy. In his acceptance address, for example, he argued that "the task of safeguarding our institutions" could be realized only in part through military preparedness. In addition, it required "the united effort of the men and women of the country to make our Federal and State and local Governments responsive to the growing requirements of modern democracy." Detecting "a constantly growing sense of human decency throughout our nation," he insisted that government must not fall prey to "reactions in the march of democracy." Rather, it must continue to strive for "social legislation," "human security," and the "wider and more equitable distribution of wealth." Among other things, Roosevelt identified "a war against poverty and suffering and ill-health and insecurity, a war in which all classes are joining in the interest of a sound and enduring democracy."[28]

Thereafter, until the very end of the contest, Roosevelt's formal campaigning was limited by his overwhelming responsibilities as commander in chief and doubtless too by his recognition that the execution of these responsibilities constituted his single greatest asset in the campaign—he could project qualities of statesmanship, command, reassurance, and determination, and partisan opponents risked looking trivial by comparison when they attacked him. For Wendell Willkie and his supporters, it must have been hard to know how best to counter Roosevelt's advantage: Should they try to knock him off his pedestal (present him as a warmonger, attack his record over the past eight years, accuse him of monarchical excess), or should they focus on packaging Willkie as a fresh, charismatic leader with an attractive and positive message?

The Willkie Campaign

Until the latter stages of the campaign, Willkie attacked FDR's domestic record more than his leadership in the present crisis. On the one hand, he deprecated the massive growth of government under the New Deal—the rise of bureaucracy, the centralization of power in the White House, the excessive regulation—and the persistence of high unemployment. On the other hand, during the course of the campaign he found himself endorsing nearly every significant New Deal initiative. He pledged, one historian of his campaign has noted, to "expand the Social Security Act; continue the Wagner Labor Relations Act and the Wages and Hours Act; give a Cabinet position to the North West; continue soil conservation, rural electrification, farm credit, commodity loans, and crop insurance; provide a job for every man and woman in the nation willing to work; and continue relief for all persons who could not find work."[29] Willkie's running mate, Senator Charles McNary of Oregon—a Western progressive, albeit a stronger party loyalist than some other members of that tribe—may have run a still more singular race: an admirer of his opposite number on the Democratic ticket, he and Wallace reportedly "often rode together to speaking engagements, and offered more praise than criticism of each other."[30]

One area where McNary clearly had an impact on Willkie's campaigning was in the area of public power. It was partly as a reward for McNary's strong support for TVA that FDR had authorized the building of the massive Bonneville Dam across the Columbia River, and in choosing the Oregonian as his running mate Willkie had hoped to neutralize attacks on his background as a utilities magnate. On the campaign trail, Willkie seems to have equably bid farewell to his anti-TVA past: he supported completion of Bonneville and the Grand Coulee Dams and backed public control over the electricity they would generate for the Pacific Northwest. In retrospect, this was the first presidential campaign to deploy the subsequently hallowed GOP practice of attacking "big government" in the abstract while endorsing its principal functions. At the time, the approach seemed incongruous. Socialist candidate Norman Thomas observed that Willkie had "agreed with Mr. Roosevelt's entire program of social reform and said it was leading to disaster."[31]

Republican activists were vexed by Willkie's approach and by his having opted to run largely independently of the party's machinery.[32] Like so many presidential candidates, he found himself torn between needing to appease his base and simultaneously reaching out to nonparty voters, without whose support he could not hope to win the White House. Willkie responded to this challenge, and to his frustrating inability to close FDR's narrow but persistent lead in the polls, by launching ever more outspoken attacks on the president's war leadership: while he approved of a destroyers-for-bases deal with Britain, FDR's failure to clear it properly with Congress was the greatest abuse of power in American history; if Roosevelt were victorious, American parents should expect their sons to be on the next transports to Europe; the Nazi seizure of the Sudetenland had been the result of secret presidential dealings with Hitler and Mussolini; if FDR were reelected, Americans would "be serving under an American totalitarian government before the long third term is up."[33]

It seemed to work. Strongly favoring aid to the Allies, and thoroughly convinced that the war in Europe had the most profound implications for American security, the voters were still desperately keen to avoid direct U.S. intervention, and they responded to Willkie's alarming and sometimes irresponsible charges. October polls showed Willkie and FDR running neck and neck, and some of the most staunchly isolationist Republicans, such as

Hamilton Fish, started expressing new approbation for their candidate. Frustrated by his inability to lure "the Champ" into the ring until this point, the tireless Willkie now had the satisfaction of provoking him to action: during the final week of the campaign, FDR made a series of five campaign speeches in which he explicitly repudiated Willkie's charges.

But this was a source of gratification for the president too: making the first of those speeches, in Philadelphia, he confessed: "I will not pretend that I find this an unpleasant duty. I am an old campaigner, and I love a good fight."[34] The single most important political purpose of these addresses was to blunt Republican claims about an irreversible drift to war under his leadership. In combatting those arguments, though, he also took the opportunity to sell the New Deal and even to sketch out some ideas for its future. His election eve speech in Cleveland started by asking, "Is the book of democracy now to be closed and placed away upon the dusty shelves of time?" Then, though, he went on to celebrate the "glories of democracy" as a living system, telling his audience that "it falls upon us now to say whether the chapters that are to come will tell a story of retreat or a story of continued advance." The rest of the speech sketched out what he meant by "advance" in a series of short paragraphs, each of which began "I see an America where . . ." and went on to envisage an end to poverty, the conservation of the nation's natural bounty, universal educational opportunity, fair taxation, and industrial democracy. Amid the "great storm raging now," his ultimate goal was "to stick by these people of ours until we reach the clear, sure footing ahead."[35]

Conclusion: The New Deal in 1940

Roosevelt's margin of victory in 1940 was very comfortable: he won by ten percentage points, and by 449 electoral votes to 82. If one's point of comparison is the landslide of 1936, then one can say that many Americans who had voted against Alf Landon had grown tired of FDR and were drawn to the candidacy of the attractive Willkie. In some large states (New York, New Jersey, Illinois, Ohio), FDR's margin was quite slight, and it is doubtful that any of the possible Democratic candidates whose names were being bruited in the spring—Garner, Paul McNutt, Cordell Hull, James Farley—could have won the election.

Still, if one's point of comparison is the various political defeats the New Deal had sustained during FDR's second term, the meaning of the election looks different. When the New Deal was discussed in 1940, the discussants were not simply conducting an autopsy on a program that had died. Rather, without significant exception, they took the permanence of the New Deal for granted and were debating its future. And, also without significant exception, they characterized Roosevelt's response to the Depression as having fundamentally transformed American political life. The harsh bitterness of the criticism that some conservatives leveled at FDR was a tribute not to their new power in national politics, but precisely to the disappearance of Calvin Coolidge's America: the language of individualism endured, as did the antistatist impulse, and—deeply embedded in American political culture—would continue to permeate campaign politics, right through the twentieth century, and indeed into the twenty-first. But that rhetorical world no longer described how Americans were governed, nor did it capture their deepest political attitudes, which now featured an expectation of governmental protection from adversity that had hitherto been conspicuous by its absence.

Accordingly, while scholars who point to the massive state-building impact of World War II on American political institutions and culture are perfectly correct, the politics surrounding the 1940 election reveal how firmly embedded a dramatically new role for government had already become, a year before Pearl Harbor. The extent of the change is easily missed if we compare the public policy record of the New Deal to grandiose visions of economic planning or welfare provision that came to naught, or focus narrowly on the multiple legislative disappointments of Roosevelt's second term, or for that matter if our primary reference point for judging reform is the minority rights revolution of the 1960s, or Scandinavian social democracy. Yet it comes clearly into view when we revisit the Roosevelt third-term election of 1940.

Each party's choice of candidate was significant, and so too was the way Willkie and FDR chose to conduct their respective campaigns. Deeply hostile to FDR and to the New Deal, for the most part, Republican activists nevertheless felt constrained to nominate the one candidate whose personality and public policy positions most closely resembled those of the president. Although that decision was overwhelmingly attributable to the fall of France, it would not have been possible had the GOP—pinching its collective nose—not by now come to terms with the permanence of the New Deal (even the most conservative Republican candidate, Taft, had mostly done so). More to the point, Willkie's subsequent campaign embrace of nearly every substantial New Deal measure disclosed not only his mostly liberal political ideology but his tactical judgment that these programs enjoyed deep, broad support in the country. The rhetoric of antistatism still touched a chord, and Willkie strove to exploit that fact too in some of his stump speeches, but its effective deployment required the speaker to simultaneously reassure Americans that Social Security, rural electrification, guaranteed bank deposits and mortgages, the minimum wage, and emergency public employment were safe with them.

What of Roosevelt? What do their nomination and campaign reveal about the status and prospects of the New Deal in 1940? That so little presidential timber should have grown in his shadow in one sense highlights the limited impact of his tenure on the Democratic Party—the conventional wisdom in Philadelphia seems to have been that no other potential candidate would have anything like so good a prospect of defeating Willkie.[36] Still, that he was nominated, that he forced the convention to endorse Henry Wallace as his running mate, and that the party ran on an avowedly liberal platform, drafted in the White House (it even made a tentative embrace of African American civil rights), all showed that conservative Democrats had not succeeded in wresting the political initiative from FDR since 1937, and that they too—like the Republicans—had no alternative but to acknowledge Roosevelt's personal authority and the popularity of his policy legacy. As for the subsequent campaign, FDR's inescapable immersion in his grave responsibilities as president was made easier by Willkie's ready embrace of virtually his entire policy record. And when the Republican jabbed harder at his opponent in the latter stages of the contest, forcing a (not-too-reluctant) Roosevelt out of his corner, FDR sought not just to parry Willkie's thrusts about the lurch to war but to transcend them, by relating the parlous global state of democracy to a broadened vision of political democracy and socioeconomic security at home. During the remainder of the war, he would have little opportunity to advance that vision through purposeful reform. Yet, just as the partisan battles of Roosevelt's second term had failed to extinguish the New Deal idea, and just as the advent of war in Europe had resulted in an FDR versus Willkie contest that served to embed that sensibility still more firmly in the American body politic, so too the subsequent U.S. prosecution of the war would powerfully strengthen the idea that it was fundamentally the job of government to protect the American people from the "hazards and vicissitudes of fate."[37]

CHAPTER 9

"Why Don't You Just Get an Actor?": The Advent of Television in the 1952 Campaign

Kevin M. Kruse

The standard story of the 1952 presidential election is fairly straightforward: after two long decades wandering the wilderness, the Republicans that year finally discovered a formula for winning back the White House. Early in the campaign, the GOP identified the essential elements of Korea, communism, and corruption as their main themes and then combined them as the scientifically expressed solution "K_1C_2." Republicans followed that formula with single-minded determination, highlighting those three issues on the campaign trail above all others. In so doing, they made full use of not only the partisan advantage they developed in the peak years of McCarthyism but also the personal strengths of that year's presidential ticket—General Dwight D. Eisenhower, the war hero who could solve the Korean conundrum, and Senator Richard M. Nixon, a crusader against communists and corrupt Democrats. Ultimately, this story concludes, the formula worked as intended: the Republicans won.

This K_1C_2 story has become so engrained in the narrative of the 1952 campaign that it now stands as a central theme in countless written works and undergraduate lectures. Indeed, a number of prominent histories, on both the postwar era in general and the Eisenhower administration in particular, simply present the anecdote as common knowledge, without any documentation in the footnotes.[1] Despite the thin trail of documentation, the K_1C_2 story likely had its origins in research conducted by Princeton University historian Eric Goldman for *The Crucial Decade: America, 1945–1955*, a first-draft history published in 1956. In the spring of 1955, Goldman wrote to Republican officials about the most recent presidential campaign, asking, among other things, about the K_1C_2 formula. In response, Robert Humphreys, the Republican National Committee official who directed public relations during the 1952 race, explained the phrase but downplayed its importance. "The symbols stood for 'Korea, Communism and Corruption,'" he told Goldman. "They were never formally used in the campaign, either by letter or by literature, so far as I know. I do not think the symbols were ever seriously used in any discussion." Humphreys referred the historian to Senator Karl Mundt, a cochairman of the speakers' bureau, who had coined the phrase. Mundt likewise asserted that "use of the symbol was largely limited to communications and statements among Headquarters people," with no use of it on the campaign trail.[2] Despite their caveats, Goldman could not resist the colorful detail. He played up the K_1C_2 story in his work,[3] inspiring other scholars to follow suit for decades after.[4]

While few studies have bothered to track down the lineage of the K_1C_2 story, fewer still have assessed its accuracy. Despite the common claim that the 1952 ticket faithfully followed this formula throughout the election, neither the Eisenhower camp nor the Republican Party displayed a firm commitment to its components. The Korean War was certainly an important topic late in the campaign, but its primacy in the Republican strategy has been exaggerated considerably. The campaign's main initiative on this matter—Eisenhower's dramatic announcement that he, the hero of D-Day, would travel to Korea and personally inspect the front—was an unplanned, last-minute gamble. As polls tightened during the closing weeks of the election, speechwriters on the campaign train came up with the idea independently of the party apparatus and brought it to the candidate for his approval. The result of their efforts, the famous "I Shall Go to Korea" speech delivered in Detroit on October 24, 1952, ultimately proved to be a success, with many claiming it sealed the election for Eisenhower. ("That does it," reporters on the Republican train remarked after seeing the text. "Ike is in!")[5]

But this spontaneous speech at the end of the election has been taken, in a historical teleology, as evidence that Korea was the most important issue of the GOP campaign from the start. It was not. When Eisenhower announced his candidacy in his hometown of Abilene, Kansas, in June 1952, for instance, he never mentioned the war. The general devoted a great deal of attention to foreign affairs in his formal address, offering thoughts on everything from the "evil" plans of the Kremlin and China to the current state of Western responses like the Marshall Plan and the NATO alliance. But not a word on Korea. In the same vein, when Eisenhower accepted his party's nomination at the Republican National Convention in Chicago in July, he once again made no mention of the war, devoting almost all of his time to domestic matters instead. The candidate and his surrogates mentioned it later, of course, but Korea was never the prominent issue—or even *a* prominent issue—for the Republican ticket at the outset. It may have well been that campaign strategists simply assumed that the hero of World War II had no need to address the current conflict because his military credentials spoke for themselves. But whatever the reason, the fact remains that Korea played only a slight role on the presidential campaign trail.[6]

Communism was an equally complicated component in the K_1C_2 formula. While anticommunist agitation proved a political godsend for Republican congressmen and senators during the late 1940s and early 1950s, Eisenhower found it much more difficult to exploit the issue himself. Because of diplomatic demands placed upon him during the prosecution of World War II, the general had left behind a trail of positive statements about—and even smiling photo ops with—Russian military leaders. He realized that accusations about Democrats having Soviet sympathies might seem questionable when coming from a recent working ally of the Russians. More pressing for Eisenhower was his close relationship with a military figure from his own side: General George C. Marshall. As secretary of state in the Truman administration, Marshall became a prime target for the anticommunist witch hunters in the GOP. In September 1950, for instance, Senator William Jenner of Indiana infamously denounced Marshall as "a front-man for traitors . . . a living lie . . . an errand boy, . . . a stooge, or a co-conspirator for this administration's crazy assortment of collectivist cutthroat crackpots and Communist fellow traveling appeasers." A year later, Senator Joseph McCarthy of Wisconsin revived the attack on Eisenhower's old friend, condemning him as "part of a conspiracy so immense as to dwarf any previous such venture in the history of man, a conspiracy of infamy so black that when it is finally exposed, its principals shall be forever deserving of the maledictions of all honest men."[7]

Eisenhower was disgusted by the attacks but realized that the needs of the campaign had to dictate his response. Senator Jenner and Senator McCarthy were both up for reelection that year, and each expected their party's standard-bearer to endorse and campaign alongside them. Because the two represented battleground states in the Midwest that Republicans needed in the presidential contest, Eisenhower's advisers persuaded him to make some effort. The general ultimately did his duty, though with barely concealed disgust. He urged Indiana voters to support the entire Republican slate, for instance, but refused to endorse Jenner by name. The senator was undeterred. Hamming it up alongside Eisenhower during a speech at Butler University, Jenner threw his arm around the GOP nominee at the end, just as the photographers popped their flashbulbs. Eisenhower's face grew red and he rushed off stage, later telling a speechwriter he "felt dirty at the touch of the man." Likewise, when the campaign came to Wisconsin, Eisenhower made his disdain for McCarthy clear. Learning that Eisenhower would praise Marshall's patriotism and his long career of service in his stump speech, the senator sneaked onto the candidate's train to ask him to remove the passage. Eisenhower refused and, moreover, told McCarthy in no uncertain terms how little he thought of the senator's grandstanding. As a longtime aide recalled, the meeting was the only time he ever saw Eisenhower speak "in red-hot anger."[8]

Despite his personal distaste for the anticommunist crusaders, however, Eisenhower did make occasional alliances with them. After a great deal of debate with his advisers, for instance, he excised the Marshall lines from his Wisconsin speeches, just as McCarthy had asked. In Green Bay, Eisenhower told crowds that he and their junior senator differed only in the "methods" they wanted to use to ferret out the "subversive and the disloyal" from government; in Milwaukee, the general again stressed the dangers of communist infiltration. Still, Eisenhower moved carefully on the issue, understanding that his internal tension was replicated throughout the Republican Party. Conservatives from the Midwest and the West were demanding an aggressive push on the anticommunist issue, but liberal and moderate members of Congress from the Northeast were insisting in equally strong terms that the nominee repudiate extremists in their midst. Eisenhower felt he needed to strike a delicate balance or risk alienating one side or the other. He ultimately made anticommunist comments, but in a tone that suggested he was merely going through the motions.[9]

The last component of the K_1C_2 formula was equally volatile. While most accounts of the 1952 election give much greater emphasis to the elements of Korea and communism than they do to corruption, such a stress comes not from the realities of the campaign but from the overwhelming shadow that McCarthyism and the Cold War still cast on our understanding of this era. Indeed, in terms of the frequency of mentions and the ferocity of the charges levied, corruption was actually the *most* important of these three issues. As noted earlier, the new Republican nominee never mentioned Korea and only broadly referred to the global menace of communism in his acceptance speech at the Republican National Convention. Corruption, however, was front and center. Calling on the delegates to join him in a "great crusade" on the campaign trail, Eisenhower stated their goals in no uncertain terms: "Our aims—the aims of this Republican crusade—are clear: to sweep from office an administration which has fastened on every one of us the wastefulness, the arrogance and corruption in high places, the heavy burdens and anxieties which are the bitter fruit of a party too long in power." Eisenhower pressed the issue repeatedly in the early months of the campaign. But in September he had to soften his emphasis on the issue once news leaked that some California businessmen had created a slush fund for running mate Richard Nixon's use. With Nixon's integrity called into question, accusations of Democratic corruption lost their power.[10]

The importance of the famed K_1C_2 formula is, in the end, greatly exaggerated. Despite assertions and assumptions to the contrary, it was not a carefully constructed blueprint that was followed coherently throughout the campaign. Corruption was a key issue early on but faded down the stretch. Korea had been largely absent at the start, meanwhile, but it rose to prominence in the final weeks. And communism remained a tricky issue throughout the campaign, one that was as likely as not to alienate crowds and antagonize internal Republican relationships. In the end, however, the real problem with a narrative that stresses Korea, communism, and corruption is not that there were other issues that were more important (though there were). The problem, rather, is that issues *in general* were unimportant. The 1952 campaign was first and foremost about image, with ideas running a distant second.

In many ways, the triumph of image over ideas is a perennial in presidential elections. Indeed, to jaded eyes, the entire history of American presidential campaigns might seem little more than an extended exploration of the cult of personality, with aspirants to the Oval Office spending a considerable amount of time on grandiose self-mythologizing and simple sloganeering. But in 1952 this traditional image making took on a new scale and scope. As the first presidential election to embrace the powerful new medium of television—and to be enveloped by it in return—the 1952 race represented a sea change in politics. It elevated the role of advertising experts and media consultants to unprecedented heights in campaigns as it simultaneously debased the content of their messages, with complex political issues distilled into short "spot ads" of a minute or even thirty seconds in length. Stump speeches and campaign publications faded in importance, with the old reliance on pages of oratory replaced by a quick string of sentences, a few catchy words, or even just an image. Personal contacts and retail campaigning—which had still seemed important just the election before, when Harry Truman tirelessly rode the rails on his famous "whistle-stop campaign" to meet voters face to face across America—were replaced by a wholesale approach in which candidates communicated with voters largely through their TVs. From 1952 on, the only messages that truly mattered were the ones filtered through those screens.

Appropriately enough for a man who loved to paint, Dwight Eisenhower entered politics as a blank canvas. Those who had witnessed his rise to power in World War II and the considerable charm and ambition he displayed in the conflict were convinced the general had political ambitions. As General George Patton observed in 1943, "Ike wants to be president so badly you can taste it." Still, Eisenhower tried to remain coy. Soon after the war's end, for instance, General Douglas MacArthur hosted a lavish dinner for Eisenhower at his Tokyo headquarters. When they were alone together after the meal, MacArthur speculated that one of them would be president in the near future. Eisenhower recoiled from the implication that he had political ambitions and lectured his colleague about the dangers of military leaders who pursued civilian offices. When he finished, MacArthur condescendingly patted his knee. "That's all right, Ike," he said. "You go on like that and you'll get it for sure."[11]

When Eisenhower returned to the United States and assumed the presidency of Columbia University, such speculation only increased. With his political sensibilities still inscrutable, Eisenhower faced calls from both Republicans and Democrats to run as their presidential nominee in 1948. When he issued a clear, Sherman-like statement that he was not interested in the office, efforts to draft him only increased. Walter Winchell, for instance, instructed his listeners to send cards and letters to Eisenhower urging him to seek the Republican nomination. Roughly twenty thousand pieces of mail poured in the first week, with so many more following that stacks soon filled up Eisenhower's spacious office at the university and forced him to take a vacation until they could be moved. (In the end, Columbia's Bureau of Applied Social Research took custody of the letters, hoping to gain insight into the "psychological reactions of people in the mass" through studying them.) At the same time, Democrats sought to draft Eisenhower to be *their* nominee. It began at the top, with President Truman encouraging the general to run and even offering to step aside and run as his vice president if he desired. Even after Eisenhower demurred and Truman decided to run for reelection in 1948, many in his party kept alive the Draft Eisenhower movement well into the convention.[12]

As the 1952 election drew near, the calls for Eisenhower only increased. His political appeal was so strong that New York governor Thomas Dewey, the Republican nominee in 1944 and 1948, dubbed Eisenhower a "public possession" and begged him to run. But even then the enigmatic general refused even to confirm whether or not he was a Republican. Inquiries to the county clerk in Abilene showed that Eisenhower had never registered there. "I don't think he has any politics," the clerk reported apologetically. Word later leaked that Eisenhower had voted for Republicans in 1932, 1936, 1940, and 1948, with his sole vote for the Democrat in 1944 owing to the war. Despite this voting record, Eisenhower still refused to confirm his party affiliation. A representative from *McCall's* magazine offered him $40,000 if he would simply give a yes or no to the question "Are you a Republican?" He still refused. In the end, only the requirements of the New Hampshire primary forced his hand. To be eligible there, Eisenhower finally announced that he was a Republican in January 1952.[13]

Though he was now formally a Republican, Eisenhower still seemed distant and detached from the party orthodoxy. He dutifully offered statements aligning himself with its positions on most domestic issues, but his commitment to the cause paled in comparison to that of his chief rival for the presidential nomination, Senator Robert Taft. The son of President William Howard Taft, the Ohio politician personified the lineage of the GOP. But in the eyes of many, the man known as "Mr. Republican" embodied not just the past of the party, but its present and future. At the height of his political powers, the *New Republic* marveled that "Congress now consists of the House, the Senate and Bob Taft." With more than a decade of experience in Congress, Senator Taft understood the issues that animated the Republican caucus. In sharp contrast, the novice Eisenhower appeared adrift and unprepared. The conservative *Chicago Tribune*, for instance, mercilessly mocked his campaign announcement speech in an editorial titled "Five Star Generalities." The address, the editors chided, was an "array of vacuities, contradictions, platitudes, and non sequiturs" that was so devoid of substance that any additional comment would be "superfluous."[14]

But ultimately, Eisenhower's poor performance on the issues was unimportant. While he could never compete with Mr. Republican in his command of the detailed legislative initiatives of congressional conservatives, Eisenhower proved much more able in the category that truly mattered in presidential politics: charisma. On this point, Taft was badly outmatched. A cold and calculating man, the Ohio senator resisted all efforts to polish his public image. Even when he acquiesced to advisers and grudgingly played to the crowds, the end results were unconvincing. Once, they tried to pose him with a dead turkey to make it look as though Taft had shot it while hunting, but the senator showed up for the photo session dressed in a drab business suit. On a second occasion, his aides arranged another sporting image, this time trying to make it seem as though the senator had landed a giant sailfish on a fishing trip. But the photo was another failure: the fish was clearly dead, the boat obviously tied to the dock. During the Republican National Convention in Chicago, the contrast between Taft and Eisenhower became clear. Party leaders began to worry openly that the colorless Ohioan would do little to win over voters and ultimately doom down-ticket candidates as well, while the war hero with the blazing smile seemed likely to have real coattails. Despite Taft's sizable lead in delegates coming into the convention, his support steadily eroded during the contentious gathering until Eisenhower pulled out the nomination. Republicans ultimately chose image over ideas.[15]

This choice was replayed in the general election. As he prepared to leave Chicago, Eisenhower signaled to the press corps that his coming speeches would be light on policy and heavy on platitudes. "I'm not eloquent," he said apologetically. "I wish I were eloquent—but I am sincere. I hope to bring a message of militant faith and hope to the American people in what they have got the capacity to do, gol darn it, rather than go into the details of a specific program." Just two weeks later, the Democrats set up their convention at the same amphitheater in Chicago that the Republicans had used, hoping to set a useful contrast between that party and their own. In his welcoming address, Illinois governor Adlai E. Stevenson mocked the GOP for its meaningless convention rhetoric. "For almost a week," he joked, "pompous phrases marched over this landscape in search of an idea." Witty, urbane, and intelligent, Stevenson delighted the Democratic delegates with his ability to articulate the policies of the New Deal in smooth tones and still attack their opponents with cutting remarks. The Republican Party had been "devoid of new ideas for almost 70 years," the governor insisted. "As to their platform, well, nobody can stand on a bushel of eels." With no clear favorite before the convention, delegates steadily lined up behind their erudite host. On the third ballot, they selected Stevenson as the party's nominee.[16]

Republicans initially thought Eisenhower would beat Stevenson as easily as Taft, and for the same reasons. (The general watched Stevenson's acceptance speech at his friend George Allen's Colorado ranch. "He's too accomplished an orator," Allen said; "he'll be easy to beat.") But those who assumed Eisenhower's plainspoken charm would simplify the election were soon disillusioned. In his first month on the trail, Eisenhower seemed a weak speaker who rambled until he ran out of platitudes. His stump speeches were uninspiring, Republican leaders complained; but more important, his tendency to speak in generalities and to invoke a vague "middle way" of politics gave voters the impression that he was perfectly content with the philosophy and policies of the New Deal, when most in his party longed to see them roundly rejected. As the summer wore on, his supporters' patience wore thin. On August 25, the Scripps-Howard newspaper chain, an early supporter of Eisenhower, ran a panicked editorial headlined "Ike, When Do We Start?" "Ike has not done anything lately to fortify our belief that he can win," the editors worried. His campaign was "running like a dry creek." Recently, the piece observed, Eisenhower issued "a statement of middle-road political philosophy which, considered in the abstract, was a noble pronouncement of principles to which most Americans can adhere. Yet, evaluated in the context of this campaign, it was such a statement that his adversary, Gov. Stevenson—a shrewd and seasoned politician—used it conveniently and happily to label Ike as just another 'me-too' candidate." As the panic grew, the candidate assured his staff that a new sense of direction and new energy would come soon. "Right after Labor Day," he told them, "I'll really start swinging."[17]

The new sense of direction came to the Eisenhower campaign via television. At first glance, the flashy new medium seemed a poor fit for the old-fashioned general. When Eisenhower made his campaign announcement in Abilene, for instance, the event devolved into a public relations nightmare. The candidate's plan to speak from a local baseball diamond was ruined as heavy rains came down just before the scheduled start. The old soldier doggedly tried to plod through the mud, with his pant legs rolled up and the rain soaking through to his suit. But ultimately he was unable to read the prepared text through his fogged-up glasses. As the candidate grew visibly irritated, his public relations aide looked on nervously. When the rain let up, Eisenhower gave it another go, but by then all the energy seemed to have been washed out of him. Buttoned up in a drab raincoat, with a few long strands of hair flying loose over his bald dome, he looked nothing like the hard-charging hero of D-Day.[18]

Despite his inauspicious debut, Eisenhower understood that television would be a key part of the coming campaign. Robert Humphreys, a former journalist and the Republican National Committee's director of public relations, insisted that television offered the best route to victory. "Both Republican candidates have warm and winning personalities," he wrote. "Obviously the thing to do is to gain entrance for them into the homes of America by every means possible so that the warmth of their personalities can be felt." Formal speeches would not do it, Humphreys insisted. "Informal, intimate television productions addressed directly to the individual American and his family, their problems and their hopes, are necessary to make the most of the ticket's human assets." A newcomer to politics without any preconceptions, Eisenhower accepted this advice. He soon sought tips on television from David Schoenbrun, an old wartime acquaintance who had since become a reporter with CBS. But Eisenhower proved an uninterested pupil. When Schoenbrun broached the subject of how the general's bald pate looked on camera, Eisenhower barked out: "I know I'm bald. What do you want me to do, put on a wig?" When the reporter offered that Eisenhower simply needed to learn to position himself correctly for the cameras and apply a little makeup and powder to reduce the glare from the lights, the general lashed out again. "Why don't you just get an actor?" he snapped. "Get a double to do my interviews for me."[19]

Despite his discomfort with the medium, Eisenhower acquiesced to its demands, thanks largely to the influence of the advertising firm Batten, Barton, Durstine and Osborn (BBD&O). Its legendary partner Bruce Barton had been advising Republican presidential candidates on their image for nearly four decades, informally at first for Calvin Coolidge and Herbert Hoover, but later in official campaign positions for Alf Landon and Tom Dewey. In this role, Barton regularly urged Republican candidates to strike a nonpolitical pose to seem above "the plane of partisan politics." They should "humanize" themselves in order to reach what Barton called, as early as 1919, "the great silent majority of Americans." This approach meant meeting voters on their own terms, through the media they enjoyed. "The radio audience is different from the assembled crowd," Barton cautioned Coolidge in 1924. "The radio audience tires quickly and it can walk out on you without you knowing it."[20]

When BBD&O secured the radio and television accounts for the Republican National Committee and the independent Citizens for Eisenhower-Nixon in early 1952, they applied Barton's old lessons to their new client. They imposed strict discipline on the campaign, letting it be known that every single television appearance had to be first approved by BBD&O. The ad men carefully scripted these public appearances, ensuring that audiences at home were treated to the dramatic entrance of the candidate and his wife and repeated shots of them walking through, and working, an adoring crowd of admirers. Even though the campaign bought thirty-minute blocks of TV programming, the agency ordered the candidate to keep his addresses to just twenty minutes so that they could package the speech with this visual drama. With such tight message control, BBD&O crafted a grand campaign theme that presented Eisenhower as a noble war hero who was detached from the petty concerns of common politicians. Still, they cautioned, the general had to avoid appearing aloof. As BBD&O president Ben Duffy noted, the secret to their campaign's success would be "merchandising Eisenhower's frankness, honesty and integrity, his sincere and wholesome approach."[21]

The fall campaign constructed around this image almost fell apart at the start. In mid-September word leaked that some business allies of Senator Nixon had put together what the liberal *New York Post* described as an $18,000 "slush fund" for his personal use. Republicans scrambled to control the damage, urging Nixon to make a major television address to rebut the charges, an appearance that would soon be famous as the "Checkers speech." As with the rest of the campaign, BBD&O orchestrated the entire event. With $75,000 from the Republican National Committee, they stitched together a network of 250 NBC and CBS television stations and the 500 radio stations of the Mutual network. They even paid top rates to secure the time slot immediately after the popular *Milton Berle Show*. In the end, more than 58 million Americans—about a third of the country's population and the single largest television audience to date—tuned in to see Nixon give a detailed, if corny, speech on the state of his finances.[22]

Bruce Barton, who had told Ben Duffy that the Republican presidential candidate needed to be "expertly stage managed" in his response to Nixon's address, created the necessary script and stagecraft for Eisenhower's reaction. In a letter to Duffy, he wrote:

> My suggestion is that he announce, in time for the evening papers, that he will be looking at Senator Nixon on TV alone—just he and Mrs. Eisenhower—no advisors, no managers, just the two of them. Then, at the conclusion of Nixon's speech, let the reporters and photographers wait for 15 minutes and then have the general come out with the following memo in his own handwriting: "I have seen many

> brave men perform brave duties. I have seen them march up to the cannon's mouth not knowing whether they would live or die. But I do not think I have ever known a braver act than I witnessed tonight."

The candidate should read the script "slowly and with deep feeling" so that it seemed sincere, Barton urged. That night, Eisenhower followed Barton's directions. He and his wife watched the speech alone and then waited a half hour before emerging with his response. "I have been a warrior and I like courage," he said. "I have seen many brave men in tough situations. I have never seen any come through it in better fashion than Senator Nixon did tonight." In the end, both Nixon and Eisenhower emerged from the crisis seeming to have displayed frankness, honesty, integrity, and sincerity, just as the ad men had scripted.[23]

While the BBD&O strategy worked, its greatest success came at the hands of an ad man at a rival firm, Rosser Reeves of the Ted Bates Agency. The innovative Reeves, in the words of a competitor, created ads "without subtlety and without concern for anyone's gentler feelings. He also proves that advertising works." His claim to fame was developing an approach called the "U.S.P."—for "unique selling proposition." When other ad campaigns offered competing claims that their product was the "best" or "brightest" of its kind, Reeves urged his clients to instead make bold claims that stood out from the pack, as he did when he convinced the makers of M&M candies to assert that their product "melts in your mouth, not in your hands." The ads Reeves made for his corporate clients were powerful and direct: an Anacin spot that depicted a headache as an animated set of pounding hammers; a Rolaids ad that showed stomach acid burning its way through cloth; a campaign depicting Bic pens being shot out of rifles and crossbows. He believed Dwight Eisenhower could be sold the same way.[24]

When a group of oilmen hired him to craft an independent television campaign for the candidate, Reeves had his chance to put his plan into action. The key, he decided, would be the spot advertisement. Traditionally, corporations purchased long blocks of time on a TV network—a full hour, or perhaps a half hour—and then sponsored the entire program. As Reeves explained to Eisenhower, this was incredibly wasteful. "A big advertiser . . . puts on a one-hour television show. It may cost him $75,000—for that one hour. Immediately after, another big advertiser follows it with another big expensive show," he noted. "But between the two shows comes the humble 'spot.' If you can run *your advertisement* in this 'spot,' for a very small sum *YOU GET THE AUDIENCE BUILT AT HUGE COSTS BY OTHER PEOPLE*." As Reeves recalled, Eisenhower had to be sold on the spot campaign because he worried that such short ads would not seem dignified. So Reeves asked Eisenhower if he had any reservations about the thirty-minute televised speeches that BBD&O was airing. The candidate had no problems with that approach, so Reeves pressed on, determining that he would be likewise fine with a fifteen-minute speech or even a five-minute one. "If we cut that speech to *one minute*," the ad man finally asked, "is there anything wrong with that?" "O.K.," Eisenhower grinned, "let's go ahead."[25]

Accordingly, Reeves worked to determine what the "unique selling proposition" for the Eisenhower spot ads would be. The candidate's speeches, to that point, were all over the place. "He was talking about three thousand things, and you don't do that in advertising," one observer noted. "You lose penetration." Even Reeves's crack research staff could only narrow it down to a dozen or so important topics, but Reeves wanted to have an even tighter focus. As always, he wanted to find one point of emphasis, but his clients demanded he come up with at least three. To find them, Reeves tried a variety of approaches. Using a contact at the Reader's Digest Corporation, for instance, he sent out three separate mailings of ten thousand inquiries to its subscribers, asking about their concerns. Later, he held a meeting with George Gallup at his offices in Princeton, New Jersey, "to find out what were the broad, basic *interests* of the electorate as a whole." In the end, Reeves settled on three topics that he would highlight in the coming campaign: the high cost of living, political corruption, and the war in Korea.[26]

On September 11, the Republican nominee entered the Transfilm Studios in Manhattan to create the spot ad campaign known as Eisenhower Answers America! As the title suggested, the spots depicted ordinary Americans asking the general some pointed questions. In truth, the questioners never saw the candidate in person; picked from the next day's tour groups at Radio City Music Hall, they were filmed separately. As for the man with the answers, Eisenhower sat in the studio alone. Hoping to avoid the tired image the general presented in Abilene, Rosser Reeves asked him to take off his glasses and read his lines off giant, hand-painted poster boards. When they were edited together, the illusion of a frank Q&A was created. In a typical ad, for instance, a young mother of two read her script to complain, "High prices are just driving me crazy." "Yes," Eisenhower replied with a knowing smile, "my Mamie gets after me about the high cost of living. It's another reason why I say, 'It's time for a change. Time to get back to an honest dollar, and an honest dollar's worth!' "[27]

Despite the attention given to the themes of Korea, communism, and corruption in the literature on this campaign, the famous ads of the Eisenhower Answers America! series were largely devoted to other topics. Indeed, of the twenty-eight ads aired, just two were focused on Korea, and only four more addressed graft, corruption, or scandal in some way. Communism, most notably, was not mentioned in *any* of the ads. In sharp contrast, the twenty-two remaining ads focused overwhelmingly on the concerns of pocketbook politics, with almost all involving complaints about high taxes or the high cost of living. "Food prices, clothing prices, income taxes," complained one citizen. "Won't they ever go down?" "Not with an eighty-five billion dollar budget eating away on your grocery bill, your clothing, your food, your income," the candidate replied. "General," another pled, "this suit costs sixty dollars. I used to buy the same for thirty dollars!" "You paid one hundred and one taxes on that suit," Eisenhower answered. "And next year you may pay two hundred unless you vote for a change." Others offered complaints about their debts, their inability to live off their pensions or Social Security, and the high cost of cars and homes and groceries. As Rosser Reeves saw it, the voting public was concerned with their own economic fortunes above all else. If Eisenhower had any kind of U.S.P., it would need to target these pocketbook problems.[28]

While the spot campaign was originally conceived as complementary to the main campaign being run by BBD&O, Reeves's messaging soon came to dominate everything. The spot ads became a central theme of the Eisenhower strategy, with over $1.5 million spent to air them in sixty-two targeted counties across the Northeast and the Midwest. "We have no idea how much was actually spent," Reeves later reflected, because countless Republican organizations ran local versions of the ads as well. As it became clear that the spot ads would be the main message of the Republican campaign, one of Reeves's colleagues, Alman Taranton, sent the campaign a memo with the headline "This is Urgent!" Taranton warned that the writers who were "determining the content" of the GOP ticket's speeches needed to be briefed about the spot campaign, because it would soon debut "with a tremendous roar" on October 21. "During this deluge," the executive noted, "anything that General Eisenhower or Senator Nixon or other Republicans will say [in person] on the subject of high prices, taxes, and corruption will represent a marginal supplementation to these short . . . almost 'on-the-hour-every-hour' Eisenhower broadcasts." But, he reminded them, the ads said nothing about communism. Therefore, "it would be extremely wise" if the candidates focused their attention on that issue while they were on the stump, to be sure it received some attention at least. Such work, he offered, would be helpful "plugging the gap" on this issue when the spot ads directed the spotlight elsewhere.[29]

When the Eisenhower Answers America! ads became public, they shook up the campaign considerably. "This is the worst thing I've ever heard of," Adlai Stevenson complained to an official at CBS. "Selling the presidency like cereal. How can you talk seriously about issues with half-minute spots?" In a press conference, his campaign chair, George Ball, mocked the idea as a "supercolossal, multimillion dollar production designed to sell an inadequate ticket to the American people in precisely the same way they sell soap, ammoniated toothpaste, hair tonic and bubble gum." "From morning to night, during interludes normally throbbing with the merits of Follicle shampoo or some new, improved detergent that takes the drudgery out of your Laundromat," Ball continued, "the air waves and the TV screens will be filled with the omnipresent General Eisenhower, every hour on the hour." Reeves had wanted to sell Eisenhower, but Democrats argued that being sold diminished and disgraced him. "The box tops this time are ballots," Ball mocked. "Send in enough of them and you get not only the general, you also get as an extra bonus a political space cadet with built-in secret code-breaker, atomic muscles made by U.S. Steel and smile by Barbasol." In the end, even Rosser Reeves admitted that Ball's tirade had been "skillfully done."[30]

The mockery of Madison Avenue's hold on the Eisenhower campaign continued in highbrow publications like the *Reporter*:

> Eisenhower hits the spot.
>   One full general, that's a lot.
> Feeling sluggish, feeling sick?
>   Take a dose of Ike and Dick.
> Philip Morris, Lucky Strike.
>   Alka Seltzer, I like Ike.

As luck had it, Harlan Cleveland, executive editor of the *Reporter*, lived next door to Rosser Reeves, giving the ad man a chance to interrogate his critic directly. Reeves asked why he hated the spots. "It was selling the President like toothpaste," Cleveland complained. "You can't say anything in a fifteen-second speech." Reeves disagreed and offered some examples. "Do you remember that old radio speech of Franklin Roosevelt, his first acceptance speech? And the phrase about the only thing we have to fear is fear itself?" "Of course." "Harlan," Reeves said, "that's a fifteen-second spot." Lincoln's Gettysburg Address was essentially a spot, he said, and so was Churchill's Iron Curtain speech. Churchill was "very good at spots," Reeves noted. And so was Eisenhower.[31]

When it came to television and the campaign, the contrasts between Eisenhower and Stevenson were incredibly pronounced. While the Republicans were spending over $2 million on an array of TV ads from top firms on Madison Avenue, the Democrats spent only a paltry $77,000 for spots created by a second-tier consultant from Baltimore. Unlike the spot ad strategy of Reeves, the Democratic plan revolved around half-hour slots they purchased for long speeches by Stevenson and other leaders. The slots were scheduled in the fall at 10:30 p.m. on Tuesday and Thursday nights. Airtime came fairly cheap, but largely because so few people tuned in at that hour; indeed, in the end, the Stevenson spots averaged just 3.8 million viewers each. The public seemed to know what it was missing. Stevenson's high-minded politics and high-flown language proved to be a poor fit for the new medium, making him seem distant if not arrogant. "Even after watching him for several weeks," the *New York Times* television critic reflected, "a viewer could hardly say that he felt he knew Governor Stevenson very well as an individual. There was an aloofness, one might say almost a loneliness, that came between him and a viewer." Stevenson's tone was off, but his timing was even worse. On several occasions, the networks were forced to cut him off midsentence when his time ran out. Eisenhower had mastered making his pitch in thirty seconds, but Stevenson could not make the sale in thirty minutes.[32]

In the end, Eisenhower's victory was sweeping and definitive, as he retook the White House for the Republican Party in commanding style. Nearly 61 million Americans voted in the election, a significant increase over the last race's total of 48 million voters that attested to broad interest in the campaign. Nearly 34 million voted for the general, giving him an impressive 55 percent of the popular vote. But thanks to the spot ad campaign's strategy of targeting sixty-two pivotal swing counties across the nation, the Republican campaign took in even larger percentages in the Electoral College, racking up a massive margin of 442 to 89 electoral votes there.[33]

The size of the victory had one downside, in that it became impossible to judge the effectiveness of the ad men and their television campaign. "Did they do any good?" Rosser Reeves asked shortly after the election. "Of course they did, but the election was such a landslide no one will ever be able to know." Three different social science studies tried to determine the impact of the ads as well, but ultimately decided that in light of the blowout result, the ads could not have been "decisive" in any sense. In the end, however, the overwhelming victory of Eisenhower in a televised campaign was decisive in another sense. From then on, presidential candidates in both parties would increasingly be drawn to television as an essential tool for their political success, with the short, thirty-second spot ad becoming one of the most reliable tools in the trade. Campaign officials in the 1952 race may have had doubts about the effectiveness of their image-making efforts before, during, and even after the election, but those in subsequent presidential elections had none. Indeed, in time they even followed Eisenhower's advice and hired an actor for the starring role.[34]

CHAPTER 10

Giving Liberalism a Window: The 1964 Election

Julian E. Zelizer

The 1964 election had a transformative impact on American political history.[1] Much of the literature on the Great Society has focused on Lyndon Johnson and how he was able to move bills as a result of his political wizardry. The Johnson-centered interpretation of the Great Society places such great emphasis on what the president was able to do—how the so-called Treatment, the moments when Lyndon Johnson literally invaded the personal space of other legislators and advisors to physically cajole them into supporting his policies, remade American politics—that scholars have greatly downplayed the environmental context that allowed a president with his skills to succeed.

The greatest challenge Johnson faced was the conservative coalition of southern Democrats and Republicans who dominated the committee system and who opposed most of the liberal programs that emerged in the late 1930s, especially on issues related to race and civil rights. After taking over the presidency following the assassination of John F. Kennedy, Johnson had been able to push the Civil Rights Act of 1964 through Congress, largely as a result of the pressure that the civil rights movement had placed on legislators to end public segregation. The movement created the same kind of pressure to pass this piece of legislation as a landslide election. The Eighty-Eighth Congress also passed the Economic Opportunity Act, though initially this was an inexpensive, small-scale measure that attracted the support of a number of southern Democrats who wanted money for their white rural constituencies. The buildup to the 1964 election also mattered to this bill. Johnson had told Democrats that a vote on this program was a vote of confidence on his presidency, since it was the first measure that was his rather than Kennedy's. Many Democrats agreed that passage of the bill would help Johnson be victorious.

The election created a policy-making window by bringing in huge liberal Democratic majorities and branding conservative Republicanism as far off center. While political scientists have effectively demolished the concept of critical, realigning elections,[2] it is important to understand how certain major elections still have been able to create short-term opportunities for policy making. After the 1964 election, no Republican wanted to be the next Barry Goldwater. Until the midterm elections of 1966, during which the conservative coalition regained its strength and was able to start checking Johnson's moves, liberals enjoyed extraordinarily favorable legislative conditions under which to push through an agenda that ranged from federal hospital insurance for the elderly to federal assistance for education. While not just any Democratic president could have done what Johnson did after 1964, their odds would certainly have been quite favorable.

Perhaps the most important moment in the 1964 campaign was when the Republicans selected their candidate. Throughout the 1940s and 1950s, the Republicans balanced the competing interests of a moderate wing led by politicians such as Henry Cabot Lodge and Nelson Rockefeller and a right wing faction that gained steam during the early Cold War.[3] In the summer of 1964, the right wing took control of the delegates as moderate candidates faced a series of problems that made their candidates less likely to succeed.

The nominee for the GOP was Arizona senator Barry Goldwater, who had served in the upper chamber since 1952 when he defeated Senate Minority Leader Ernest McFarland. With close ties to the business community of Arizona, Goldwater quickly attracted strong support from antiunion and antiregulation Republicans who were thirsting for their party to take a tougher stand against the New Deal. Goldwater had firmly identified himself as from the right, disappointing many of his own supporters, when he voted against the Civil Rights Act of 1964 the summer of the campaign, justifying his position on constitutional arguments. Still, Goldwater had the potential to be an effective candidate. He had an ideological zeal that was attractive to Republicans who were tired of compromise. He offered a strident anticommunism and defense of free-market principles that captured the attention of local grassroots activists who had been working in areas like southern California to build their political base.

The GOP met at the Cow Palace in San Francisco, and Goldwater did not disappoint. Their convention started on July 14. Republicans selected William Miller, a New York Republican who was known for his connections to right-wing organizations, as his running mate. There was a bit of regional balance, but not much ideological balance. The so-called Arizona Mafia, the supporters of Goldwater who had lined up the delegates, prepared them for the speeches they were going to hear and made certain that nobody would bolt toward the center.[4] When New York governor Nelson Rockefeller spoke to the convention, warning about an embrace of extremists who played on "fear, hate and terror," Goldwater struck back hard. In his acceptance speech, the Arizona senator indicated little tolerance for the center and instead called on the party to move toward the right. "Extremism in the defense of liberty is no vice," Goldwater said. "Moderation in the pursuit of justice is no virtue." The delegates went wild. "Waves of sound beat down upon him from 14,000 throats," one reporter noted. "The roar of acclaim did not lessen. It continued for minutes, an unabashed outpouring of human emotions."[5] After hearing the remarks, Rockefeller expressed "amazement and shock," believing Goldwater's words to be "dangerous, irresponsible, and frightening."[6] "It's not my personal choice," former president Dwight Eisenhower said of the ticket, but he would still support it.[7]

During the run-up to the Democratic convention, the party's nominee, President Johnson, did everything possible to protect himself from right-wing attack, especially on matters of national security. After watching Republicans win control of the White House and Congress in 1952 by using anticommunism against the Democratic Party, claiming that President Truman had not done enough to fight communism in Asia and in the United States, the Texan had vowed to never again allow the GOP to be victorious with this issue.[8] The campaign took place at a time when the pressures on foreign policy were mounting. Goldwater warned that Johnson would be weak on defense. He argued that Johnson was not willing to use necessary force against communist adversaries in Vietnam at the same time that he charged that the Johnson administration was secretly preparing to escalate the ground war.

Unwilling to let Goldwater tag him as weak on defense, Johnson wanted to send a signal to the Soviet Union—and the U.S. electorate—that he was willing to use force against the North Vietnamese. In early August, with just weeks remaining before the Democratic convention in Atlantic City, New Jersey, there were reports of an attack on navy ships that had been stationed in the Gulf of Tonkin, right off the coast of North Vietnam. The evidence that this was a concerted military attack was flimsy. Johnson understood this, admitting to advisers that fishermen were probably to blame or, at a maximum, some low-level military commander who had made a mistake. On the morning of August 4 there was another attack. Johnson told Secretary of Defense Robert McNamara that they needed to respond with a show of force. Still dubious privately that an attack had taken place, Johnson asked Congress to pass a resolution granting him authority to expand military operations in the region if necessary. Although many legislators were uncertain about the request, Arkansas senator William Fulbright—a renowned internationalist—worked the halls and convinced most senators that this was politically essential and that Johnson would not abuse the power. Many senators were also comforted by the fact that several resolutions of war that had been passed in previous years had not resulted in actual conflict. On August 7, Congress passed the Gulf of Tonkin Resolution with only two dissenters in the Senate.

Johnson also continued to push forward on the domestic front, hoping to bolster his policy record, which in his mind was the best argument for voting for the Democrats. On August 7, the same day that Congress passed the Gulf of Tonkin Resolution, the House passed the Economic Opportunity Act, which created what became known as the War on Poverty, by a vote of 226 to 185, a sizable margin. Johnson had urged all Democrats to vote for the legislation based on the fact that it would help to distinguish his presidency from Kennedy's and serve as a symbol of what the Democrats stood for. With Goldwater as the Republican nominee, many Democrats had agreed that the War on Poverty would help to highlight the differences between the parties, with Democrats seeking to help the disadvantaged and Republicans moving to the extremes and hoping to dismantle the social safety net.

The Democratic convention turned out to be as contentious as the Republican convention, though for very different reasons. Holding the convention in Atlantic City was an unpopular choice, reached when several other major cities were unable to host the event. The convention was the first major test of whether Johnson would be able to hold together the coalition he needed to win election and to govern. Despite all his fears of the right, liberals gave him the most trouble, particularly the civil rights community. The civil rights movement had been challenging the racial practices of the country at every level of society. An interracial delegation from Mississippi—the Mississippi Freedom Democratic Party (MFDP)—traveled to the Democratic convention to protest the seating of the all-white delegation. Joseph Rauh, a prominent Cold War liberal and founder of the Americans for Democratic

Action, agreed to represent the delegation and to fight for their right to be seated. According to the rules, the MFDP needed to obtain eleven votes from the one-hundred-person credentials committee. Then they could produce a minority report, and eight states could allow the report to be voted on.

Johnson was furious that the delegation was causing so much trouble. Since the original Mississippi delegation had supported the party ticket, it was in compliance with the rules, and there were no grounds to remove them. He also did not think the MFDP would help the cause of civil rights since it would only generate a backlash in the South and get moderates from the region in trouble. But for African Americans who were being swept up in the civil rights movement, the battle over Mississippi turned into a powerful symbolic and emotional issue. Johnson asked Hubert Humphrey, whom he would soon name as his vice presidential nominee and who had handled the civil rights bill in the Senate, to guide the negotiations with Rauh. Humphrey appealed to Rauh's sense of party loyalty and warned about the consequences if Rauh undermined the convention. Others involved in the negotiations included Mayor Richard J. Daley of Chicago and Senator Walter Mondale of Minnesota. The negotiations were tough. During the televised credential committee hearings, one of the Mississippi organizers, Fannie Lou Hamer, provided riveting testimony during which she spoke about the violence she had endured in the fight for voting rights. "Is this America," she asked, "the land of the free and the home of the brave, where we have to sleep with our telephones off the hooks because our lives be threatened daily, because we want to live as human beings, in America?"

In the end, organized labor, playing the vital role it often did in this period for the Democratic coalition, found a breakthrough. UAW leader Walter Reuther helped to resolve the issue, pressuring Rauh, who greatly respected him and depended on him, to reach a deal. Under the compromise, the official Mississippi delegation would be seated, while two members of the MFDP would participate in the floor debate without voting rights. The convention also would enact rules that in 1968 racial discrimination would be prohibited in state delegations. Many civil rights activists were furious with the agreement, feeling that the administration and the civil rights leadership had betrayed them. But they lived with it.

During the rest of the convention, Democrats boasted of the policy accomplishments of the administration. Central to the president's strategy was emphasizing the theme of an unfulfilled Kennedy legacy, and Johnson being the only person who could complete the agenda. When seated at the conven-

Figure 6. LBJ at campaign rally, 1964. Courtesy LBJ Archives.

tion hall, delegates were inundated with images of the deceased president. Democrats also started to stress the theme of Goldwater as an extremist, exactly what moderates in the GOP had feared. The convention reached a conclusion on August 27 with a blistering speech by Hubert Humphrey. He talked about the legislative record of the president and stressed how Goldwater had voted no on every issue. President Johnson's speech was not as memorable, overshadowed by a speech from Robert F. Kennedy, his potential competitor in 1968, that brought the crowd to its feet in thunderous applause and tears.

The entire fall campaign revolved around eviscerating Barry Goldwater as too far to the right, too off-center to govern the nation. While Johnson had been worried about a potential backlash in the South to the civil rights bill, he now concentrated on the possibility of a "frontlash" whereby many mainstream Republicans would find Goldwater too extreme for the White House. The goal of the campaign was to depict Goldwater as a radical extremist.[9] The president's campaign also disseminated material claiming that a big victory offered the best chance for Democrats to achieve their legislative agenda (see Figure 6).

Campaign officials wanted to focus on the positive—the bills Johnson had signed and would propose if reelected. The campaign, however, took a negative turn. The administration spread information about the people who were behind the Republican campaign, suggesting that Goldwater's advisers were shady characters with ties to dangerous organizations. The Democratic National Committee (DNC) worked with an advertising firm headed by Ned Doyle, Maxwell Dane, and William Bernbach to produce a series of frightening spots that played on the emotions of voters. The Johnson campaign spent about $3 million for local spots and $1.7 million for local programming. The centerpiece of the campaign aired on September 7, 1964, when the DNC broadcast the now infamous "Daisy" ad on prime-time television in the middle of a popular Monday night movie. The spot began with the image of a little girl picking the petals off a daisy. Viewers watched as the girl counted the petals to ten, then they heard the booming voice, in an official tone, of a man counting from ten to one. The camera zoomed in on one of her eyes, then a nuclear explosion filled her eyeball and the screen. The viewer then heard the voice of Lyndon Johnson say: "These are the stakes—to make a world in which all of God's children can live, or go into the dark. We must either love each other, or we must die." The ad never mentioned Barry Goldwater, but the focus of the frightening spot was clear.

Republicans complained bitterly about the ad, urging that it be pulled off the air. Dean Burch, the head of the Republican National Committee, blasted the "horror-type commercial" and said it should not be aired. "What will we see next?" asked Senator Thurston Morton, chairman of the Republican Senatorial Campaign Committee. "Herr Goebbels in his heyday could not compete with such gruesome, panic-inspiring falsehoods calculated to instill fear into our citizenry." Arizona Republican John Rhodes said that the Democrats were "callously playing on the fears of the American people by deliberately trying to picture Sen. Barry Goldwater as a man who would get this country into nuclear war."[10] Democrats obliged by taking the ad out of rotation, but they never intended for it to play very much. Bill Moyers, the presidential speechwriter, and advisers who had helped launch the ad admitted that it was never meant to be played more than once. They wanted it out there; they wanted to stimulate the discussion that Goldwater was "reckless" and force the GOP to defend him. The ad, Moyers noted in a memo, had "hung the nuclear noose around Goldwater and finished him off."[11]

Other ads also painted Goldwater as an extremist. One ad showed images of Ku Klux Klan members marching in their regalia as they burned crosses, with the narrator saying: "'We represent the majority of the people in Alabama who hate niggerism, Catholicism, Judaism, and all the -isms of the world.' So said Robert Creel of the Alabama Ku Klux Klan. He also said, 'I like Barry Goldwater. He needs our help.'" Another advertisement reviewed statements that Goldwater had made about his plan to "wreck" Social Security. Goldwater's running mate played right into the campaign strategy. When one reporter confronted Miller about Creel's statement that he would support Miller, the vice presidential candidate responded that he would accept anyone's support. The organizational structure of the campaign was also poor. Johnson's adviser John Barlow Martin reported in late September that Goldwater's campaign was falling apart; he "scattered his shots too widely, hit too many issues, and thus diffused his impact; . . . when he hit little issues, he seemed too far beneath the presidential level, particularly since the headlines posed such awesome perils and problems; and . . . on the big issues he scared people."[12]

Desperate to gain traction, Republicans played hardball. In Texas, some employers distributed a handout to employees showing a polished white boy, who had been fired from his job, and an "arrogant" African American who was grinning about the fact that he was hired instead.[13] The handout was called "LBJ Civil Rights Bill and You." Johnson called the handout the "most revolting" thing in the world. J. Evetts Haley, a conservative writer, published a book called *A Texan Looks at Lyndon* that offered a blistering portrait of the president as corrupt and too far to the left. Johnson tried to respond to the morality attacks by coining the term "smearlash" to characterize a dynamic whereby Republican voters were turned off by these kinds of tactics. "It's not the backlash," Johnson told a group of twenty-five people in downtown St. Louis. "That's gone. It's not the frontlash. It's the smearlash, because when some people get desperate they get dangerous, and when they are dangerous they are not cautious; and when they get to smearing and fearing, some of their own people do not want to go along with them."[14]

Notwithstanding such public displays of confidence, White House officials were terrified when one of Johnson's top advisers, Walter Jenkins, was arrested at the YMCA for being part of a sexual act with another man. It was soon discovered that this was not the first arrest. While Johnson officials tried to say that Jenkins had a nervous breakdown and worked hard to suppress the story in the media, it nevertheless expanded. The UPI ticker picked up on the arrest, which was reported in papers like the *Chicago Tribune*. Some Republicans, though not Goldwater, played on the story. Dean Burch, who felt burned by the Daisy ad, struck back. "The Walter Jenkins episode," he said, "raises grave questions of national security which only the President can—and must—answer." He added, "Knowing, as he must, the vulnerability of morals offenders to blackmail, the President should tell us whether Mr. Jenkins was permitted to sit in on meetings of the National Security Council, meetings of the Cabinet and otherwise given access to top military secrets."[15]

Johnson, who dismissed Goldwater as a "mud slinger" for engaging in these kinds of political attacks, had a bit of luck come his way when foreign policy pushed the Jenkins scandal off the map. First, the Soviet Union announced that Nikita Khrushchev had been removed from power, a coup that captured the attention of the world and raised questions about what would come next in the Cold War. Second, the Chinese exploded their first nuclear bomb. The Jenkins scandal fizzled rather quickly. Republicans also decided, based on Goldwater's opposition, not to release an ad called "Choice" that depicted African Americans rioting in the street. At the end of a forty-four-state campaign, Johnson stopped in New York to attack Goldwater as a radical who would endanger the country.[16]

The only positive moment of the fall for Goldwater came with a television ad by Ronald Reagan, former spokesman for General Electric and president of the Screen Actors Guild. On October 27, Goldwater's campaign premiered a commercial in which Reagan appeared to be giving a speech to an audience of Goldwater supporters. In the speech, called "A Time for Choosing," Reagan proclaimed that Goldwater's supporters should be proud about their ideals and that conservatism offered a road map to the future. Reagan attacked liberal domestic programs and called for a more vigorous stand against the Soviet Union. The delivery was perfect from this former actor and brought some enthusiasm to a party that was otherwise moribund.

The election, though, was a stunning victory for the Democrats and, at least temporarily, a huge blow to conservatism. Johnson won 486 electoral votes and 43,129,566 popular votes. Goldwater secured only 52 electoral votes and 27,178,188 popular votes. Goldwater had temporarily devastated the GOP by tarnishing the party with the label of extremism at a time when polls showed that Americans were supportive of many of the bills Johnson promised to propose. With Johnson losing in only six states, Democrats surged in the House and Senate—outnumbering Republicans 295–140 in the lower chamber and 68–32 in the upper chamber, enough to break a filibuster. The biggest sign of hope for Republicans came with victories in southern states like Alabama, South Carolina, or Georgia, where civil rights seemed to be having the kinds of effects that Johnson had always feared, alienating white southern

Democrats. Democrats did very well, though, in the Midwest, including in Iowa, Missouri, Minnesota, and North Dakota. Looking at the polls, Republicans were morose that they had done so poorly with a number of key constituencies, such as professional workers, women, college-educated voters, and African Americans. The Goldwater-Miller ticket lost by a margin of two to one in sixty-one of the largest cities, while suburban voters went against the GOP by a margin of three to two. The impact of the 1964 election would be significant in American political history on a number of levels. The first and perhaps most lasting consequence was that it broke the back of the southern Democratic–Republican coalition in Congress that had exercised immense control since the late 1930s, preventing progress on major policy innovations.

Whereas President Kennedy had faced a legislative playing field that offered little room for progress, Johnson now had incredibly favorable circumstances before him. Johnson's herculean effort to ratchet up his congressional majorities had worked perfectly. Not since the New Deal had liberal Democrats commanded such a sizable congressional majority. The president's legislative liaison Larry O'Brien estimated that the number of Great Society opponents in the House had fallen from over ninety to under sixty.[17] The members of the Democratic Caucus were more loyal to the party leadership than at any time since 1938, when the conservative coalition had emerged. For veterans of Washington, the new math meant everything. Administration officials breathed a sigh of relief. They stopped talking about the "southern Democratic–Republican coalition," a phrase that had loomed large in Washington since FDR's second term. "I can't remember when Southern influence in Congress was at this low point," noted one commentator.[18]

In addition to reforms passed in January 1965 that weakened the ability of committee chairs to block bills from being voted on, as well as changes to the party ratios of committees that allowed Democrats to stack key panels with members favorable to social legislation, the bloc of freshman votes in the House—the "Coattail Class of 1964," as they were sometimes called in the media—were crucial to the passage of the Great Society. The seventy-one new Democrats supported the president 89 percent of the time on a dozen major bills in the Eighty-Ninth Congress. Many Republicans, who were now on the defensive, were willing to vote for bills like Medicare, fearing that their opposition to the proposals before 1964 had cost them support. Nobody wanted to be a right-wing extremist anymore. The result would be a huge transformation in the infrastructure of public policy, with the passage of federal aid to education, Medicare and Medicaid, voting rights, and much more.

This was legislation, much of which passed by sizable majorities and bipartisan support in the final roll call votes, that would survive over the next few decades, proving to be the most enduring legacy of the election.

The second consequence of the election was to push back any kind of sweeping conservative revolution in American politics for fourteen years. The election was seen as a mandate against a candidate who ran too far to the right. Barry Goldwater had taken a strong stand for conservatism, proudly boasting of the ideals that had shaped him and which had been circulating in conservative networks in the nation. He urged delegates to accept the right rather than to constantly run from it.

But by most accounts the strategy had failed. Goldwater had been defeated by a frontlash of voters who saw him as too dangerous and who felt that conservative principles were not the kind through which the nation should be governed. As one author has documented, the defeat temporarily bolstered the standing of Republican moderates, who remained a significant part of the GOP.[19] In 1966 the most successful candidates would run to the center, and Richard Nixon in 1968 ran a campaign in which he worked hard to broaden his coalition—rather than just catering to the right. Though Nixon took a detour in his campaign for Republican candidates in the 1970 midterms, trying to divide the nation on a liberal versus conservative axis, he shifted back to the center in 1972 in his effort to build a lasting coalition.

The result of this delay in the conservative revolution was that between 1966 and 1980 the legislative accomplishments of Lyndon Johnson generally remained intact, very often growing, and there was enough support within the Democratic Congress to continue to grow government. Even after Johnson left the White House and was replaced by a Republican, domestic policies expanded with regard to the environment, workplace safety, consumer protections, antipoverty measures, and much more. This continuation of domestic policy making, which was made possible in part by the Republican retreat from extremism, resulted in a much more sizable domestic policy infrastructure being in place when conservatives finally gained power in 1980.

The third consequence of the election of 1964 was essential to the expansion of a war that, over the long term, would be very costly to the Democratic Party and in the short term would be devastating to the nation. During the campaign, Johnson had taken a number of steps, including calling on Congress to pass the Gulf of Tonkin Resolution, that accelerated the nation's presence in Southeast Asia. Johnson had refused to be outhawked by the GOP, as had happened to Adlai Stevenson in the presidential election of 1952.

Once the campaign ended, though, it was hard to go back. Johnson now had the authority he needed from Congress and made a series of tough statements on the campaign trail that would be difficult to retract. Even more, Johnson himself had become convinced of the political logic behind taking a tough stand against the Soviets in this region. Even as he heard from colleagues about the dangers of the war, and from some about the lack of necessity to go into battle, he believed that his tough stance helped insulate him from the right. After the election, the potential for massive domestic victories, which was really his main objective in politics, made him even more determined that he would not allow the GOP to use national security arguments to undercut his domestic progress.

Finally, the Daisy ad introduced a new kind of political spot that would be hugely consequential in the way that Americans conducted their elections for decades to come. It shifted the nature of the campaign spot away from ads that were primarily informational and that tried to feature the character and substance of the candidate toward highly emotional and visceral productions that tapped into the fears and anxieties of the electorate. "It was like the Bauhaus of advertising," said one of the executives who produced it. The Daisy ad was also a spot meant to stimulate discussion as much as it was intended to convey information. Johnson's advisers knew it would be played only a few times at most, but by putting the controversial material on the air they could get reporters and politicians to keep talking about it, and in turn, to keep talking about the flaws in Barry Goldwater that they wanted to highlight. The 1964 election had a direct impact on the future contours of public policy and movement politics by creating a legislative and electoral environment conducive to liberalism.

CHAPTER 11

The 1980 Election: Victory Without Success

Meg Jacobs

In 1980 Ronald Reagan swept the presidential election. The election, it seemed, was one of the most significant in the twentieth century—the GOP answer to 1912, 1932, 1964. Talk was in the air of a Reagan Revolution, or if not a revolution, then at least an important realignment. Gone was the New Deal; here was the New Right.

However, within the White House, Reagan's team of advisers was worried: Was there really a new Republican majority? Could the country be counted on to support conservative policy in a predictable fashion? Would they vote for the GOP in such high numbers in future elections? In short, was the electoral victory built to last?

Reagan and his advisers had cause for concern. Reagan won in a stunning landslide. But this conservative took office in a new era of political polarization and divided government, at a moment of global economic dislocations, which further made it difficult for either party to solidify a loyal political following. In 1986 Sidney Blumenthal published *The Rise of the Counter-Establishment*. As he explained it, the counterestablishment of conservative think tanks, institutes, and journals "was a political elite aspiring to become a governing elite."[1] The era of economic uncertainty and policy gridlock would make that a considerable challenge.

Reagan's top team understood the difficulty of transforming their 1980 victory into a permanent governing majority. On the one hand, Reagan came into office with highly mobilized grassroots partisan support. As Lee Atwater, the White House political strategist, put it, "He's got more people committed to him than anyone else. They're ready, able and willing to go into action at a moment's notice." Yet conservatives understood that undoing at least half a century of liberalism and entrenched public policy inheritances would prove challenging, especially as they faced formidable foes in Congress, where liberal Democrats still controlled the House, and an electorate that was not yet firmly in the GOP camp.[2]

If there was one bloc of voters whom the parties thought could be moved in one direction or another, and indeed a group the party needed to recruit, it was women. Reagan's advisers were instantly aware, as was the media, of the so-called gender gap, the ten-percentage-point difference between male and female support of the new president. They also knew that women were voting in higher numbers, and that trend was likely to continue. Of greatest concern was the fact that women's ambivalence, as it unfolded in the first few years of Reagan's time in office, revealed and reflected a larger uncertainty about the GOP among the electorate. Rather than voting strictly on "women's issues," women, including white working women, often voted on economic issues. Without the ability to generate a permanent new prosperity of the sort that had sustained the New Deal coalition, the GOP would not be able to rest comfortably. In this way, the gender gap was part of a larger political puzzle confronting the new president and his allies as they sought to become a new Republican majority.

The Elusive Realignment

When Ronald Reagan took the inaugural oath on January 20, 1981, he was a leader whose time had come. For decades, the former movie star had forged connections at the grass roots and in the halls of California government with conservative groups who shared his anticommunist and antigovernment zeal and were growing in strength, number, and influence. In 1964, when Reagan's political capital soared as he delivered an election eve televised speech on behalf of Barry Goldwater, the young ideologue posed a fundamental question, which would animate his political thinking for decades, including from the White House. Turning to television viewers, Reagan asked "whether we believe in our capacity for self-government or whether we abandon the American revolution and confess that a little intellectual elite in a far-distant capitol can plan our lives better than we can plan them ourselves."[3] Several years later, from his platform as the newly elected governor of California in 1967, Reagan told his voters: "We are going to squeeze and cut and trim until we reduce the cost of government. It won't be easy, nor will it be pleasant."[4] But, as he said, "the time has come to match outgo to income." And, in 1981, as the just-sworn-in president, he issued his famous inaugural adage, "Government is not the solution to our problem, government is the problem."[5]

When Reagan ran in 1980, he took on an unpopular incumbent, Jimmy Carter. In 1976, running as an outsider, Georgia governor Jimmy Carter had barely defeated President Gerald Ford. Once in office, Carter had a hard time winning the loyalty and approval of American voters. Carter alienated Democratic Party regulars by his tepid embrace of traditional Democratic interests such as organized labor, especially in the face of rising unemployment and stagflation, which were making it harder for working-class Americans to make ends meet. And he left many questioning his competence when he failed to prevent a second oil shock in the summer of 1979 that sent inflation sky high and Americans reeling. The Iranian hostage crisis further undermined popular support for this Democrat, who looked at best incompetent and at worst culpable in these difficult times. The week before the election, during the campaign debate, Reagan landed a fatal blow when he asked viewers: "Are you better off than you were four years ago? Is it easier for you to go and buy things at the stores than it was four years ago? . . . Is America as respected throughout the world as it was?"[6]

On Election Day, Reagan received 43.9 million votes to Carter's 35 million, and in the Electoral College the victory was a landslide, with the GOP challenger garnering 489 votes to the president's 49. Reagan took forty-four states to Carter's six. In the House, Republicans gained 35 seats, giving them 191 seats to the Democrats' 242. And the Senate shifted to Republican control for the first time since 1954, with a 53 to 46 majority. Conservative southern Democrats also posted impressive gains, further strengthening the conservative coalition of southern Democrats and Republicans on Capitol Hill.

Reagan had sailed to victory on the wings of many different conservative groups. As the standard-bearer of conservatism, he won support of social conservatives, probusiness and antitax voters, and foreign policy hawks. Evangelical Christians turned out in record numbers, and Reagan also had a strong showing in the South and the Southwest, building on Richard Nixon's inroads in these previously Democratic strongholds. Alongside this southern switch to the GOP were blue-collar voters in the Northeast and the Midwest—the Reagan Democrats—who were also changing their party affiliation.

Throughout the election, Reagan had sounded the antigovernment themes upon which he had built his career. If Barry Goldwater, Phyllis Schlafly, and other conservative activists had urged voters back in 1964 to vote for "a choice, not an echo," then it appeared that Reagan was finally fulfilling this hope. As *New York Times* reporter Hedrick Smith commented: "The nation today arrived at a fascinating and quite remarkable moment in its political history: A 69-year-old citizen-politician who has spent most of his working life in another profession has entered the White House and won the opportunity to lead a conservative political renaissance. . . . [Reagan] is a crusader, the first missionary conservative to be elected with the aim of reversing the liberal New Deal revolution of government activism and Democratic Party dominance established by Franklin D. Roosevelt nearly half a century ago."[7]

The key item, the one upon which Reagan would demonstrate his strength and solidify the new direction of conservative governance, was his tax cut. During the campaign, Reagan had embraced a supply-side theory that held that tax cuts, especially those aimed at the upper income brackets and corporations, would stimulate investment and economic growth for every American citizen. During the primaries, before Reagan tapped him to join the ticket as the vice presidential candidate, George H. W. Bush had criticized Reagan's "voodoo economics," displaying skepticism that this trickle-down theory would indeed spur the economy. Once Reagan was in office, all groups of Republicans knew the tax cut was the first order of business as the centerpiece of a larger policy agenda that favored market mechanisms over government spending.

The strength of this proposal, which would be the largest single tax cut to date, was its packaging as a cure to all Americans' economic troubles, not just those in the highest income brackets. Since Richard Nixon and his quest for a new Republican majority, the GOP had sought to win the support of white, ethnic, traditionally Democratic working-class voters who had become disillusioned with Great Society spending that was aimed at minorities and the poor. In the early 1970s, a spate of books heralded the possibilities of what analyst Kevin Phillips called the "emerging Republican majority" by appealing not only to southerners but also to working-class Americans for whom tax cuts not only meant less money taken out of their paychecks but also symbolized a shift in public policy away from social spending.

Peggy Noonan, who became one of Reagan's favorite speechwriters, captured the GOP appeal. Growing up Irish Catholic in Brooklyn as part of a loyal Democratic family, Noonan had named her first two fish Jack and Jackie after the Kennedys. The first in her family to go to college, which she did at night, Noonan felt alienated from the party of her youth and the apparent radicalism of her fellow students. With Reagan, Noonan felt she was part of "the quiet realignment in the eighties, in which what had seemed in my youth the party of the rich dullards became, almost in spite of itself, the party of the people." Similarly, David Stockman, who would serve as Reagan's budget director and chief architect of his tax cut, shed the radicalism of his college days and became a free-market fundamentalist. "I began to feel as if I was part of a movement. My revolutionary fires had been rekindled once again."[8]

On August 13, 1981, Reagan signed the Economic Recovery Tax Act and the Omnibus Reconciliation Act. Together, these measures announced a radical new agenda for the government, the crowning achievement of this new Republican era. One measure cut taxes by 25 percent, significantly lowering the overall tax rates, and the other cut spending by $35 billion. Days earlier Reagan had fired striking air traffic controllers, signaling a major departure in the recognition and support of union rights. As a backdrop to these policy changes, Reagan supported Paul Volcker's move at the Federal Reserve to impose a tight monetary policy as a way of bringing inflation under control, even if it meant triggering high unemployment.

But still, as impressive and historic as these accomplishments were, did they signal a fundamental realignment of the electorate? That was not clear. To be sure, political scientists before and since have debated the idea of electoral realignments. In 1980 the idea of realigning elections had much traction in the academy, which in turn filtered into the popular press and helped generate a news story about the election as fulfilling a cyclical vision of history where voters, in regular intervals, turn out old regimes and replace them with a new and enduring coalition that supports a significant shift in public policy. A decade earlier Walter Dean Burnham had published *Critical Elections and the Mainsprings of American Politics*, his famous analysis of American political parties and the realignment theory.[9]

From the contemporary vantage point, the evidence was unclear. In an age when a majority of Americans got their news from television, part of Reagan's appeal was specific to him, the handsome, charismatic Hollywood actor who after the assassination attempt on his life in March 1981 had even greater popular support among the electorate. But giving Reagan favorable ratings did not mean that the majority of citizens were solid members of the

GOP. Indeed, exit polls for 1980 revealed that only 11 percent of voters pulled the lever for Reagan because "he is a real conservative." The majority who voted for him did so because they felt it was "time for a change."[10] And still, the number of registered Democrats was significantly greater than registered Republicans.

Even those who switched into the GOP column could not necessarily be counted on. In this era, partisan attachments were not as strong as they had been. In the past, partisan affiliations ran deep, reflecting attachments that, as in Noonan's family, carried through generations and received reinforcement from active urban machines that had a strong hold on their local constituents. New Deal largesse dispensed through local machines cemented partisan identities rather than diluting them. But the rise of middle-class suburban voters loosened these attachments and opened the way for the emergence of large swaths of unaffiliated voters. Many were as likely to identify with and take their cues from any number of public interest groups who were becoming politically active and powerful in this period. And many who switched over to the GOP, such as neoconservatives, white southerners, and the white working classes, did so hesitatingly, and their support could be reversed.

Moreover, the political support that catapulted Reagan into office did not translate into a significant realignment in Congress. The Republicans' hold on their newfound power was divided and tenuous, and indeed the GOP would once again be in the minority when Democrats strengthened their numbers in the House in 1982 and regained control of the Senate in 1986. And the Democrats outside the South who were elected to office were increasingly liberal, reflecting a growing polarization between the two parties. The congressional reforms of the 1970s undercut some of the power of the more conservative southern Democratic committee chairs, increased the number of subcommittee chairs who were often younger and more liberal Democrats, and strengthened the ability of the rank and file to influence party leadership. In this environment, public interest groups, just like business interests, had much greater access and influence. Moreover, the weakening of the New Deal coalition did not mean its disappearance. Even though conservatives had increased their numbers, the Speaker was Tip O'Neill, an old school New Deal liberal with little appetite for caving in to a conservative revolution.

Indeed, Kevin Phillips, who had once augured a new Republican majority, issued a warning. Americans, according to Phillips, were more populist than conservative. That is, as he put it, they "are hostile to the rich and to big business at the same time as they dislike minorities and the liberal politicians who seem to favor minority interests over those of the white working class." He cautioned the White House about jumping to the conclusion that the electorate shared Reagan's antigovernment ideology. Patrick Caddell, a Democratic pollster, had written the epitaph for the Democratic Party, calling support for Reagan and for his tax cut a "revolution against government." But Phillips was not too sure. If Reaganomics did not provide the tangible benefits it promised, such as renewed recovery, more jobs, and a reduction in inflation—in other words, more money in voters' pockets—then they might not be willing to pull the GOP lever again. The tax cut provided tangible benefits, allowing citizens to keep more of their income. But it was not yet clear that the larger promise of Reagan's economic policies would be fulfilled. And in that case voters might not feel as committed to the GOP in future elections as they had in 1980.[11]

Building a Majority

The White House understood the challenges they faced from day one. And so did Reagan himself. During his days as California governor, he had learned firsthand the difficulties of dismantling government, an idea that had appeal as campaign rhetoric but could prove lackluster when it came time to cutting actual programs. Aware of the institutional and even electoral strength of liberal policies and programs, top Republican aides projected a story line that would suggest that indeed the new president had a mandate for conservative reform. The idea of a "Reagan Revolution" was a creation of Republican insiders as part of a political strategy to translate the electoral victory into governing success.

From the early days in office, Reagan had to decide how to chart a political course forward. All presidents, at least since Franklin Roosevelt, have done this, setting an agenda, making some issues higher priorities than others. The challenge then is how to move aggressively in one area without losing support in others. Given that Reagan came to office with the support of a new coalition of voters, the challenge was especially acute. As Reagan invested all his energies in the Economic Recovery Act, he had to figure out ways to satisfy groups for whom tax cuts were not the paramount issue.

Part of the job of building a predictable and reliable following fell to the Office of Public Liaison (OPL), an executive-level office within the White

House that reached out to various constituencies as a way of winning their support. To head the OPL the White House recruited Elizabeth Dole. Dole came from a long line of political women who got their start in consumer issues, a traditionally female domain within American policy making. By the time of her appointment as head of the OPL, Dole was a skilled political operator, and she became the boss of her former mentor, Virginia Knauer, who had headed the Office of Consumer Affairs under Nixon and Ford and was also a member of the OPL. In the late 1960s and early 1970s, Knauer mentored Dole as she emerged from her background as a southern Democrat from a conservative North Carolina family to become a new and promising member of the GOP. A Harvard-trained lawyer, Dole was one of two dozen females out of 550 students in her 1965 graduating law school class. Her contemporaries included Elizabeth Holtzman and Patricia Schroeder. Even as women's liberation was reaching college campuses, the Harvard professors called on women on "ladies' day," as Dole recalled it. Upon graduating, Dole moved to Washington, where she entered public service, rising through the ranks until her appointment to the Federal Trade Commission. She resigned that position in 1976 to join the vice presidential campaign of her husband, Senator Robert Dole, the Kansas Republican whom she had married the previous year. When Reagan appointed her to the OPL, her job was, as she put it, "to develop a consensus for Reagan administration programs."[12]

At the OPL, Dole relied on a coterie of younger party activists, many of whom came from inside the Beltway and had been working since the 1970s on shifting the GOP and the electorate to the right. Her staffers included Aram Bakshian, Jr., who had worked for Republican William Brock in the 1960s and then for William Simon in the Ford administration, and Robert F. Bonitati, who had served as an aide to Senator Howard Baker (R-TN) and then moved to Nixon's Office of Management and Budget (OMB). Dole also worked with active members from the conservative think tank and intellectual circles, such as Morton C. Blackwell, who had been the editor of the *New Right Report* and a contributing editor of *Conservative Digest*, and Wayne Valis, the special assistant to the president of the American Enterprise Institute.[13]

In the first year of the administration, the approach to various organized interests and different demographics was similar, regardless of whether they were supporters or critics of the president. To the extent that the White House devoted the majority of its political capital to passing Reagan's budget measures, the White House built loyalty on other issues through the appointment process. The appeal of James Watt as secretary of the interior, for example, had as much to do with his background as a lawyer and lobbyist defending land claims of western miners as it did with his affiliation with the hard right and his outspoken stance on many of the leading conservative social issues of the day. If Reagan failed to move forcefully on issues like a constitutional ban on abortion, he could score political points through his backing of these kinds of high-level officials. Similarly, in the summer of 1981, Reagan nominated Judge Sandra Day O'Connor as the first female Supreme Court justice as a way to repay campaign commitments to Republican women.

But there were several problems with this approach. For one thing, conservative supporters wanted more. Richard Viguerie, the direct mail guru who had galvanized millions of conservative voters, openly criticized the administration, and the press was regularly reporting on the "uneasy coalition" of Reagan supporters that was becoming ever more shaky.[14] One year into her job, Elizabeth Dole was worried about these social conservatives. The decision to rally supporters behind the tax program had made sense, but she expressed concern that that move had, "in turn, relegated the conservative social agenda to the back burner." "To do little or nothing" on social issues such as busing or prayer in school, Dole warned White House counselor Edwin Meese and James Baker, "will lead to greater conservative dissatisfaction and diminished active support for the economic battles."[15]

These concerns became more pronounced as the 1982 midterm elections drew near. Everyone in Washington understood that the first midterms usually did not go well for the party of a new president. Based on history, Reagan's advisers knew they would probably suffer losses. Indeed, by the summer of 1982, Terry Dolan, the chairman of the National Conservative Political Action Committee, was sending the same warning to Baker. Dolan shared polling data that demonstrated a significant drop in the numbers of self-identified conservatives who regarded Reagan favorably, telling Baker, "Unless you stop this erosion immediately, Republican and conservative candidates could be facing another 1974 election, where sympathetic voters will stay home because of the signals being sent from Washington."[16]

Of equal concern, of course, was the growing dissatisfaction among those who either had not supported the president in the first place or, more worrisome, those who were newcomers to the GOP. In early 1982, Dole was contemplating a strategy of how to reach out to African Americans, similar in approach to how she strategized about Hispanics, Jews, and other ethnic and minority groups.

It was no secret that, as a group, no other constituency had given the new president less support. While the Civil Rights Act of 1964 and the Voting Rights Act of 1965 might have swung southern Democrats toward the GOP, as Lyndon Johnson had feared from the very start, they forged a durable alliance between African Americans and the Democratic Party. Carter won support from 90 percent of the black community. There were cynical reports within the White House of African American schoolchildren cheering in the streets when they heard the news that Reagan had been shot in the assassination attempt. Yet Dole was not willing to abandon any group of voters as the White House sought to build a lasting and durable coalition.

Perhaps most important was that the African American critique of Reagan, steeped largely in economic terms, resonated with many other groups of voters as the economy dove into a recession. By the fall of 1982, unemployment reached 10.8 percent, a level not seen since the Great Depression of the 1930s. Compounding this economic downturn was the fact that many Reagan budget cuts targeted precisely the kinds of social programs that usually assisted those in need and offset economic hardships. Given that 80 percent of the federal budget paid for the military, entitlement programs, and the financing of the national debt, the most vulnerable programs were the ones that benefited the needy. Dole explained to Baker the challenges that Reagan was facing. "We are now grappling with the larger issue of the President's image, reputation, and public esteem . . . a dangerous stereotype of a President who is unsympathetic to the plight of the poor and needy," said Dole. She laid out the larger stakes as she saw them. "These perceptual issues impact most negatively on Black Americans, but have serious ramifications for other groups as well. In particular, the 'lack of compassion' label is one which has harmful long-term implications for women, the elderly, and moderates of all parties."[17]

The Reagan recession underscored the tenuous hold the GOP had on a new political majority. When the economic bottom fell out, it was far from clear whether the coalition of 1980 would remain in place through these difficult times. In his first two years in office, Reagan had scored an impressive achievement with his tax and budget measures. But he had also seen the limits to his self-proclaimed revolution. When he attempted to cut Social Security benefits early in his presidency as a way to reduce the deficit and offset tax cuts, there was a revolt in Congress so strong that Bob Dole, as chairman of the Senate Finance Committee, was forced to push through a resolution denouncing the White House move. As the economy turned down, and as the spending cuts to Great Society programs that benefited low-income Americans went into effect, Reagan's standing in the polls declined.

In the November 1982 midterms, the Republicans lost twenty-six seats in the House, giving the Democrats an even stronger majority. Historically, parties in power tend to lose voters in the off years. But that was not always true, and that had not been true in 1934, the year that Roosevelt solidified his gains, a victory from which he was able to push forward and cement the New Deal. The story for Reagan was different. As much as his advisers had crafted the idea of a mandate for leadership, the president was now leading a country with a government that was more divided, an electorate unsure of its political leanings, and an economy in trouble. The *New York Times* reporter Tom Wicker wrote an epitaph for the White House, grimly concluding, "There is no Reagan Revolution."[18]

The Gender Gap

After the midterm losses, the issue of the gender gap captured White House attention. If there was going to be a revolution, the Republicans were going to have to win over a much larger percentage of women voters. The party no longer felt confident that they could write off voters who had not joined them two years earlier. Lee Atwater, Reagan's senior political strategist, was worried. Days after the 1982 losses, Atwater wrote, "One of the most severe challenges facing the Administration in the next two years is the 'gender gap.' Some observers speculate that a new sex based political realignment is occurring; one that could lock the GOP into permanent minority status," said Atwater in a nineteen-page memo to senior White House staffers. "Clearly we will have to take some action."[19]

As a candidate in 1980, Reagan had reached out to women. He did not support what were seen as the leading women's issues, including the Equal Rights Amendment (ERA), which was facing its final deadline for ratification in June 1982, and reproductive rights on abortion. But he did promise to eliminate statutes in federal regulations that discriminated against women. With his typical cowboy swagger, Reagan had said, in the debate against Jimmy Carter, "I would have someone ride herd on those regulations."[20]

The 1980 election had already revealed potential problems for the GOP, especially among women voters. As Richard Beal, special assistant to the president, explained to top advisers, "President Reagan's relative vote support among women (compared to men) was the lowest of any Republican presidential candidate in the last 30 years." Never before had there been a significant difference between the preference of men and women, and never before had women demonstrated such weak support for the GOP candidate. In 1976 women preferred Gerald Ford to Jimmy Carter, and in 1960 they had also chosen Richard Nixon by larger numbers than John F. Kennedy.[21]

In the afterglow of the 1980 victory, Republicans were not yet concerned with the vulnerability in their coalition. Reagan's victory was so overwhelming, and, after all, more women voted for Reagan than for Carter. Women's support of Reagan was considered weak only in comparison to the strong support Reagan had received from men. The numbers revealed that men voted for Reagan by a much greater margin (57 percent to 37 percent) than women (47 percent to 44 percent).[22] In Reagan's first year in office, the White House did not put forward proposals that were meant to address what had been commonly thought of as "women's issues," including the ERA, legal abortion, and equal pay for equal work.

Since the emergence of the women's liberation movement, the Democrats had been the party that more aggressively responded to these issues and solicited the support of women who pushed for equality and an end to discrimination in the workplace and in society. Since the party reforms of 1968, the Democratic leadership had included more women in the conventions, in the primaries, and even in Congress. In 1972 Democratic voters elected Dole's former classmates Elizabeth Holtzman and Patricia Schroeder as well as Bella Abzug and Barbara Jordan to the House of Representatives. In 1973, when a constituent questioned Schroeder's decision to run for office as the mother of two young children, she responded, "I have a uterus and brain, and they both work."[23]

Until 1982 the Republicans were so confident of their standing and had so little concern about winning over this constituency that they actively blocked initiatives to promote gender equality. Once in office, the president had created the Task Force on Legal Equity, which promised to rid federal statutes of sex discrimination. In conjunction with this executive effort, the White House also initiated the 50 States Project to root out discrimination in state-level regulations. But neither of these were top priorities, and they received little serious backing. At the same time, the White House slowed the enforcement of affirmative action guidelines for government-contracted companies in their hiring and promoting of female workers. Clarence Thomas, who would become the chairman of the Equal Employment Opportunity Commission, said he would not enforce laws with which he did not agree. Unlike in the Carter administration, Reagan's personnel team deliberately did not create separate staff for women's issues.

The White House worked hard to derail the signature women's issue, the ERA. It was a major disappointment to women's groups that Elizabeth Dole, upon joining the administration as the most senior woman in the White House, rescinded her support of ERA. The amendment had passed Congress in 1972, and the ten years that the legislators had allowed for ratification would expire in the summer of 1982. Eager to thwart any movements for an extension, instead the White House promoted its 50 States Project. This was not a high-profile program around which to cement widespread loyalty. Instead, it was the kind of initiative constructed to satisfy and keep mobilized a band of already well-organized and active conservative women and leaders, such as Phyllis Schlafly, who saw this regulatory reform as a way to kill the ERA. To lead the effort, the White House appointed Judy Peachee, a Republican Party operative in Virginia who had played a key role in building the GOP in that Democratic state and, in the 1970s, had served as a mentor to a young Karl Rove.

The White House looked favorably upon using the tax code and other regulatory reforms as a way to provide what Barbara Honegger, a special assistant in the Justice Department's civil rights division, called "the financial enfranchisement of women."[24] As in other areas of domestic policy, Republicans thought that using the tax code was the best way to provide tangible benefits to different constituencies, including women, without relying on direct government assistance. Reforms to remove the tax penalization for marriage for a dual-income family, for example, and to provide tax credits for dependent care, along with expanding the ability of women to participate in IRA accounts and giving widows the right to draw income from their husbands' pension funds, allowed wage earners and their families to keep more of the money they earned. In addition, the White House looked favorably on reforms to allow for stricter enforcement of court-ordered child support payments.

The Economic Equity Act, a bipartisan measure introduced by Patricia Schroeder and Senator Dave Durenberger, a moderate Republican from Minnesota who had replaced Hubert Humphrey, advanced all these measures. But in 1981 the White House was focused on its own tax initiative, which would include things like the repeal of estate taxes for spouses. Furthermore, the bipartisan measure included other provisions that conservatives opposed, such as gender-neutral health insurance, and as a result the White House worked against what associate director of the OMB Annelise Anderson referred to as "the legislative vehicle for liberal feminism."[25]

The 1981 recession would change the political forecast for the president and the Republican Party. The recession unsettled the Reagan White House. All the confidence that came out of the election started to fade. Whereas those in the White House could once dismiss anyone who had not joined them in November 1980, now, as the bottom fell out of the economy under their watch, they started to fret over which constituencies might leave them and how they could reach out to new voters. With Democrats pounding away at the White House for its economic record, the president's advisers started to take a close look at their coalition. Known as the Reagan Recession, the downturn lasted from July 1981 through November 1982. The unemployment rate began inching upward in the fall of 1981 after having lingered around 7 or 8 percent throughout the year. By March 1982, the rate was at 9 percent, and by year's end it would be as high as 10.8 percent.

The decline in support for Reagan was precipitous. As the economy collapsed, so too did the president's favorable approval ratings. In just a single month, February 1982, as unemployment worsened and the White House released its 1983 budget, the president's job rating dropped eight points, approval of his handling of the economy fell ten points, and an overall sense of whether he was on the right track declined by thirteen points.[26]

Polling showed the sharpest decline among women. In February 1982, men gave Reagan a 57 percent approval rating, whereas only 45 percent of women gave the president a favorable rating, with 49 percent disapproving.[27] By April the gender spread in approval rating was 19 percent. And more women than men continued to believe that Reagan's economic programs hurt the country and felt more pessimistic about the future.[28]

By the summer of 1982, as the recession continued, the White House had real anxiety about the electoral implications of the gender gap. "What is the gender gap?" asked senior political strategist Richard Wirthlin rhetorically. "About 10 percentage points on the presidential job rating."[29] Wendy Borcherdt, who was the White House staffer in charge of recruiting women into the administration and the former director of the conservative Pacific Legal Foundation, took her concerns to Reagan's chief of staff, James Baker. "The criticism of the president has become severe and vocal and the polls have shown a steady erosion of women's support for the president. The women's constituency has declined in support more than any other group. . . . Currently, we are *very vulnerable*," Borcherdt told Baker.[30] Even the president was worried about his standing. When the *New York Times* ran a piece criticizing the administration, Reagan saw it and sent it directly to Ed Meese for his attention.[31]

The largest group against Reagan were nonmarried women, who gave the president a 61 percent disapproval rating. They were most likely to be low income and less educated and to have jobs outside the home. They tended to be more liberal and registered to vote Democrat, though one in four was not registered to vote. While a disproportionate number of the unmarried women who disapproved of the president's job performance were African American, pollster Richard Beal pointed out that 70 percent of these women were white. "It would be a serious mistake to explain the President's poor showing among women as a factor of 'race.'" Two out of every five women were unmarried. These single women were pessimistic about their personal circumstances and felt that the president's budget cuts had gone too far.[32]

The White House understood this polling result as a reaction to its agenda of slashing the welfare state. "The Democrats' social programs have made most non-married women dependent on the government, and hence, most directly susceptible to the President's program changes," asserted pollster Richard Beal. To the extent that the Reagan budget targeted social services, single, impoverished female heads of households, including those who were divorced or widowed, would feel these cuts most sharply. And the White House understood this. "This group is the most vulnerable one in American society. . . . It is understandable why they hold such strong anti-Reagan views," said Beal. Their vulnerability, according to Beal, stemmed from their dependence on government assistance. "No major breakthroughs can be gained until . . . [they] are weaned from the government dependency."[33]

The OPL concluded the same thing. According to Wendy Borcherdt, who had become Dole's assistant, widows, poor single heads of households, and divorced homemakers were the GOP's greatest critics. "These were the women," explained Borcherdt, "who use the Federal financial support to aid them in their daily lives." They were the ones who would feel the cuts in Aid to Families with Dependent Children, food stamps, and job training funds. "The unmarried woman is opposed to this Administration and will continue to be since we are reducing her Federal largesse," explained Borcherdt. Given the direction of policy, she concluded, there was nothing to be done. "This proportion of the women's constituency will never be supportive of this Administration."[34]

Even as the White House regarded the gender gap as a functionalist response by this group of women, they understood that there were differences among women. "It is a mistake to conclude that women now represent a major, one-dimensional voting bloc," instructed Beal. Polling experts broke down female voters, like male voters, according to age, employment, marital status, and educational level. Yet, when the economy was in decline, collectively, support from female voters fell off substantially, and not just among the most economically disadvantaged.[35]

The issue that revealed the greatest difference between the genders related to whether the president, through his policies, "lacked concern for the people," or what pollster Richard Beal called the "compassion or fairness issue." In part, for some women, the impression came as a result of real budget cuts. Indeed, programs aimed at women, such as those housed in the Women's Bureau in the Department of Labor, the Women's Enterprise Program at the Small Business Administration, and health services for women, had come under the axe of Reagan's budget cutters. "Women's programs throughout government have generally been reduced in scope and funding—almost 50 percent more than those of other constituents," said Borcherdt.[36] But in part this view of Reagan as uncaring stemmed from a broader perception issue. And on this question the White House felt it was especially vulnerable to losing support it would need to count on.

The negative polls were unnerving precisely because they reflected a widespread disappointment, which could even be found among the most loyal supporters, conservative women. The White House had counted on the support of these conservative activists. For decades, these women had been integral to the networks that had built the conservative movement. At the local level, they had gathered supporters, published newsletters, and in 1980 mobilized voters at the polling booths. Reagan would need these "reliable women . . . [to] provide the effective opposition to active feminists." But now, reported Borcherdt, "their enthusiasm is waning, for they perceive that the president does not care about them in a personal sense."[37]

The crucial group of women were the ones in the political center, the so-called independents. The key, as the political team argued, was to switch the allegiance of voters who were "uncommitted" and "mildly disapproving." These women, according to White House officials, were independents and "soft" Democrats who suffered from perception problems. As Annelise Anderson explained, "The gender gap arises from two separate problems—perception problems and the economy." With the right communication, these independent women "could be convinced that the economic benefits which the President is seeking are in their self-interest."[38]

What most distressed the White House was the failure of women to appreciate the reduction in inflation. When Reagan came into office, the inflation rate was more than 12 percent, and a year later it was cut in half. Significantly more women than men believed that the inflation problem was not getting better. Even as women entered the workforce in unprecedented numbers, most were still the primary shoppers, and as a result, they faced the challenge of stretching dollars of the family budget. "Why women feel that 'inflation is not better' probably relates to their being the primary most frequent shopper for the family," concluded Edwin Harper. Harper informed Ed Meese, therefore, that "the most important message we need to get across to women is that even though prices are still increasing, they aren't going up as fast as they were a year ago before the President's program began to take hold."[39]

Most worrisome, many men also shared women's critique of Reagan's economic program. A month before the midterm elections, 57 percent of all Americans disapproved of Reagan's handling of the economy. Twice as many Americans trusted Congress to handle economic policy more than they trusted the president. And economic problems were at the top of the agenda of concerns, with 72 percent pointing to the economy as the most pressing problem. Perhaps most ominous was the fact that two out of three Americans regarded the midterm election as a referendum on the president's and the GOP's performance.[40]

The key issue was the economy. That was true for men and for women. In general, concluded Red Cavaney, Elizabeth Dole's aide, "Americans do not understand Reaganomics . . . or how the President's program will improve their everyday life."[41] And the differential in their support of the administration reflected their relative judgment on the economy. In what Cavaney called "the gender gap bottom line," he said, the gap "is not related to questions concerning abortion, ERA, a woman for president, unjust discrimination, etc." His conclusions were stark. "We know that economic concerns rather than social issues dominate women's attitudes today. Economic concerns are paramount for men and women in 1982." To the extent that the gender gap narrowed in the months leading up to the election, it was because male support for Republicans was declining.[42]

The election proved damaging for Republicans and for the president. Instantly, the conclusion was that the women's vote mattered. What had previously been an observation by pollsters was now an electoral reality. And the evidence suggested that in certain races, such as the governor's race in New York, which saw the election of Democrat Mario Cuomo, and that in Texas, which resulted in the defeat of the incumbent Republican Bill Clements, women provided Democrats with an important margin of support. These races did not augur well. "It is clear that the gender gap undermines the President's governing coalition and could have a major impact on the '84 presidential election," concluded the staff at the Office of Policy Development. It was women's negative approval rating on the economy that was significant.[43]

Within a week, the White House established the Coordinating Council on Women. "There is no question," Elizabeth Dole told the president, "that the role of women in America has changed dramatically in the past twenty years. It is our task to help your Administration respond effectively and sensibly."[44] The demographic changes of the 1970s, with the rise in the number of female-headed households, would likely increase the gender gap. The evidence suggested that Reagan's support was weakest among women born after World War II, who in 1982 would be between the ages of twenty-one and thirty-six, those who were just entering the workforce, having young children, and also, in larger numbers than before, separating from their spouses. These women tended to be the most vulnerable economically, having jobs in the service sector that were the least secure, provided few benefits, and were nonunionized. The conclusion, according to Republican pollster Ronald Hinckley, was that a continued strengthening of the gender gap "could cause serious trouble for Republicans in 1984."[45]

For the White House, the gender realignment was confounding chances for a Republican realignment. *New York Times* reporter Adam Clymer, before the election, said that the specific results did not matter because the demographic and resulting electoral shifts were long-term and irreversible. "This so-called gender gap . . . may influence American life in the 1980s as much as the civil rights revolution did in the 1960s."[46] Lee Atwater, the White House political analyst, concurred. "There is solid evidence," he wrote in the weeks following the election, "that Clymer's thesis of sexual realignment is correct." "The political party that 'gets the women' will be the majority, while the party of men will be the minority." In 1980, Atwater noted, 5.5 million more women had voted than men. "It is clear that if the sexes continue to realign, the Republicans will be once again locked into minority status."[47]

As all the polling revealed, women gave Reagan poorer marks on the economy. Atwater noted in his memo that women did not support budget cuts and more general "deregulatory laissez faire policies." To explain this, Atwater searched beyond rational economic explanations. In the 1970s, Jimmy Carter's pollster Pat Caddell was reading sociologists Robert Bellah and Christopher Lasch about the breakdown of the social fabric. Now Atwater was reading Harvard psychology professor Carol Gilligan on male-female differences. In 1982 Gilligan published *In a Different Voice*, a paradigm-shifting treatment that suggested a fundamental difference between the genders. Men thought about justice, whereas women thought about fairness; the former cared about individual rights, the latter about relationships. "Only a liberal female Harvard professor could get away with outlining these differences so bluntly," said Atwater. According to the qualities Gilligan listed, the Reagan administration and its rhetoric were strongly masculine. Atwater went as far as to suggest that perhaps the administration was not lacking in support of women, but just had a "masculine surplus." "After all, Ronald Reagan is a man's man," a view put forth in *Psychology Today* that explained the male attraction to Reagan as a result of "his image as an outdoorsman, his articulation of the benefits of freedom, his expansive view of human potential." A possible theme moving forward, meant to soften the president's image and appeal to women, Atwater suggested, could be "Reagan Cares."[48]

But Atwater was not a reductionist. His basic thinking rested on a profound demographic shift, the entry of women into the labor force. Twenty-eight million women were now in the workforce, which was fourteen million more than the number of homemakers who did not work outside the home. The Friday before the election, Elizabeth Dole had published a high-profile editorial, "The Real Gender Gap," which outlined her view that the gender gap stemmed from what she called the Quiet Revolution, in which more than half of women were working outside the home. Writing with empathy, Dole acknowledged that women had yet to reach financial and legal parity with men. This labor force participation led to what Dole characterized as "fresh expectations and attitudes." "Modern woman's new-found economic involvement has virtually guaranteed independence of thought and action."[49]

The challenge for Republicans was to convince working women that the party's free-market policies would best serve their interests. Dole argued that Reagan's fight against inflation resulted in real economic gains, as did his tax cuts, including the easing of the marriage tax penalty, the elimination of estate taxes for spouses, and increasing the child care tax credit. "These initiatives represent more than verbal solidarity with working women. They add up to compassion women can put in the bank." Altogether, Dole reported, the average working woman earning $11,000 a year received an additional $700 in her pocket.[50] But obviously, amid recession, this argument fell on deaf ears.

So what could the White House do? In 1982, 45 percent of married women voted Republican, and only 33 percent of nonmarried women did. It was working women who had to be won over. They could be seen, said Atwater, "as almost a new immigrant group of low-paid workers, earning on average 59 percent of what men make." The trick was to recruit them to the GOP, which, history suggested, would be hard. "The Democratic Party has always been the party of the working man; now apparently, it might become the party of the working woman" If the New Deal gave workers labor rights and a safety network, the Democrats' support of equal pay for equal work would be "the new redistributionist battle cry." "We will have to work hard, within the constraints of our beliefs, to show working women that Republican policies are more beneficial to them," explained Atwater.[51]

The real issue was economic growth. If the economy improved before 1984, then claiming credit for this upturn and selling Reagan's deregulatory, market approach would be easier, Atwater hoped. In addition, the party and the president could adopt a more caring, compassionate tone. The basic Republican ethos, as Atwater reminded his colleagues, was centered on notions of voluntarism and community, "soft" values that the White House had ignored at its own peril in its emphasis on market principles and individualism. Nothing would be more important in the 1984 election than economic recovery. But reframing the president as a more compassionate leader "would help us with men and women."[52]

In 1984 Reagan would repeat his 1980 electoral performance with another stunning victory, winning 59 percent of the popular vote. Reagan's victory rested on the substantial economic recovery that preceded the election. In the two years between the midterms and this election, the White House had supported policies such as tax subsidies for child care for working women, enforcement of child support laws, and pension reforms to remove gender inequities, all premised on market approaches to improving working women's economic standing and security. Years later George W. Bush would promote what he called compassionate conservatism, a political economic vision that blended the Republicans' market approach with gender-based appeals.

But the key thing in Reagan's 1984 victory, as in all future electoral successes, was that in the short term the economy was doing well, and this election year fact ameliorated some of the bread-and-butter concerns that had loomed large in parts of the electorate. In his "Morning in America" theme, Reagan stressed the renewed recovery that benefited working men and women alike. "Today more men and women will go to work than ever before in our country's history. With interest rates and inflation down, more people are buying new homes and our new families can have confidence in the future," said Reagan. Lee Atwater and Elizabeth Dole understood the importance of tangible economic benefits to the working classes. As Dole had said two days after the 1982 midterm losses, "We have two more years after '82 to impact positively the two most important groups for '84: women and blue collar workers."[53] The results of the economic upturn paid off at the voting booth.

Searching for Voters Since 1980

To be sure, Reagan's 1980 victory against Jimmy Carter signified an important moment in the history of American politics. Conservatives found a champion of their cause, and he made it into the White House. Republicans had taken control of the Senate, and the mood in Washington indicated that politics was shifting to the right. Reagan capitalized on this success, pushing through a tax cut that weakened the progressive tax system that had been in place for much of the century and had underwritten the expansion of the American welfare state.

But the notion that there had been a Reagan Revolution or a conservative sweep was more a creation of the White House than a reflection of reality. Officials worked hard to convince the media and even voters themselves that 1980 had been a realigning election akin to 1896 or 1932, and that the Democratic coalition of the New Deal was now broken. Reagan's team sought to create the narrative that the election signaled that a majority of the American public was not satisfied with the welfare state and wanted a radical turn in the character of American public policy.

Yet even Reagan's advisers privately understood that this was an incomplete picture, and one that vastly overstated the durability of the conservative victory. Underlying Reagan's successful election was evidence that conservatives had a long way to go if they were to build the kind of coalition that Roosevelt had built in 1932. Huge parts of the electorate were not convinced that public policy should move to the right. In certain cases the White House realized that it could never win over parts of the electorate who at all times remained skeptical, including African Americans.

However, if Republicans were going to succeed, there were other parts of the electorate that could not be written off. Most important were women, who constituted over half of the voting population and were a presence in both political parties. As soon as the election of 1980 was over and when Democrats scored important gains in 1982, Republicans started to worry about a gender gap, a bias in women voters to go with the Democratic Party. The gender gap was not solely about social and cultural issues, as many experts in both parties suggested, but also about economic issues and the vulnerability that working women, many of whom were new to the workforce and also recently single, felt in a recessionary economy. In that climate, working women remained unconvinced that Republican policies would benefit them. Elizabeth Dole worked hard to figure out if the GOP could do anything to allay these concerns. By 1984 the return of economic growth temporarily mitigated some of these fears.

The problems of the gender gap that arose in these elections pointed to a challenge that would continue to haunt the Republican Party: how to build a vibrant and strong electoral coalition. Since 1980 Republican economic policies have created a certain amount of vulnerability with the mass electorate. The perception that Republican economic policies did not benefit middle- and working-class Americans was something that the Democrats would continue to capitalize on, especially during downturns. When Republicans promised economic growth through markets, the Democrats promised fairness and a social safety net. The challenge for Republicans was how to build a stable coalition around free-market policies. Republicans did not forget what happened in 1982 and understood that they could not count on the perception of booming economic times over the long run. To build a dominant coalition in the White House and Congress, they would need to win over large blocs of voters who would stick with them, by and large, in good times and bad.

For all the talk about the culture wars and the ways in which social cleavages of the 1970s have dominated party politics, more attention needs to be paid to how economic issues were actually the fault line between the two parties. The gender gap reflected a larger problem of how to address economic concerns, especially in a transformed economy. As Reagan's advisers understood, the working woman's challenges were the challenges of all American families. Both parties would struggle with appealing to voters as globalization and growing inequality introduced ever greater economic uncertainty.

Historians need to look back to the history of elections and to unpack certain issues traditionally characterized as social, such as the politics of gender, to examine the ways in which growing economic divisions between the parties were at play, shaping electoral behavior as well as party strategy. Recent political science research by scholars such as Larry Bartels, Jacob Hacker, and Paul Pierson has placed emphasis on the centrality of political economy to the evolution of the GOP since the 1970s. What Bartels shows is that pocketbook politics really matters in elections, and the party that has put more money into the wallets and savings accounts of white working-class male Americans has often done better at the polls.[54] The same is even more the case for working women. With all the attention to issues such as abortion, in fact, these early elections showed the importance of the economic anxieties of women entering the workforce.

The gender gap has continued to pose a threat to the GOP since 1980. It has been a perennial source of weakness and turned out a vote that has continued to empower Democrats in Congress as well as in the White House. The conservative revolution fell short in 1980, never figuring out how to win over crucial parts of the electorate that continued to turn to Democrats for economic support and security even in the age of Reagan and George W. Bush. That continues to be true today as single mothers face economic hardships and vote disproportionately for Democrats.

Looking more closely at the gender gap and electoral politics helps us understand better why realignment theory is not particularly helpful for explaining American politics since 1980. The 1980 election was significant, but not in the ways we usually think. It was indeed the start of an age of Reagan. But just as significant, there was no permanent realignment of the electorate. Since the economic upheavals of the 1970s, economic issues for working Americans have remained a regular source of instability in the electorate, especially among women. The elections of the early 1980s were the first when a significant gender gap emerged, not just around women's or social issues, but also around economic issues. The demographic shift of women into the workforce has created instability and insecurity among a larger part of the voting public, and the result is an even greater unpredictability in electoral outcomes as voters search for the party that can provide the best buffer amid uncertain times.

CHAPTER 12

Beyond the Water's Edge: Foreign Policy and Electoral Politics

Andrew Preston

It was Barry Goldwater's crowning moment. In front of thousands of ardent supporters, the senator from Arizona and standard-bearer for an emerging grassroots conservative movement addressed the Republican National Convention in San Francisco. While Goldwater trailed the Democratic incumbent, President Lyndon B. Johnson, in virtually every national poll, he elicited nothing but adoration from his fellow Republicans. Even the disgruntled moderates in the party who sulked in the convention shadows reinforced the sense of triumph for Goldwater's strident brand of insurgent conservatism. Goldwater spoke to "thunderous applause," observed the journalist Tom Wicker, there to cover the convention for the *New York Times*, and "was constantly interrupted by the enthusiasm of the delegates, who had never given serious thought to choosing anyone else." Pledging to uphold freedom at home and around the world, which he saw as inextricably linked, Goldwater warned that the United States should make no peace with communism: "The Good Lord raised this mighty Republic to be a home for the brave and to flourish as the land of the free—not to stagnate in the swampland of collectivism, nor to cringe before the bullying of Communism." The speech's most memorable line both summed up Goldwater's own political philosophy and explained his popularity among conservative Republicans: "Extremism in the defense of liberty is no vice."[1]

A week later, Goldwater struck a very different tone. In a meeting with President Johnson at the White House, the Republican challenger vowed he would not politicize the nation's foreign policy. "I do not believe it is in the best interest of the United States to make the Vietnam War or its conduct a political issue in the campaign," Goldwater promised LBJ. "I have come to promise I will not do so."[2] Johnson must have been as grateful as he was surprised: Vietnam, he confided to National Security Adviser McGeorge Bundy, was "just the biggest damned mess that I ever saw," and he knew the war would certainly get much worse before it might possibly get any better.[3] It was in Johnson's interest to avoid Vietnam on the campaign trail, and Goldwater had promised to do just that. Foreign policy could not be kept off the campaign trail, of course, but not for lack of trying by the candidates themselves.

What role, if any, does foreign policy play in American elections? None, if Goldwater and Johnson are to be believed. Despite their different ideologies and partisan loyalties, both seemed to agree that the lofty goal of preserving America's national security stood above the fray of electoral politics. Yet this was true only on the surface. Rather than provide evidence of its unimportance, their quiet White House agreement reveals just how crucial the politics of national security was to their election campaigns. Goldwater and Johnson both knew that foreign policy issues are usually fraught and divisive on the campaign trail. They are also laden with uncertainty and risk: largely driven by the actions of others, foreign crises are impossible to predict or control, even for a superpower. Neither Goldwater nor Johnson wanted to emphasize foreign policy because both were afraid of making a mistake: Goldwater feared looking like an extremist, and Johnson feared getting bogged down in a prolonged debate over Vietnam that would distract from his domestic reform agenda. Both realized that while foreign policy was unlikely to help, it carried enormous potential to hurt.

That war and foreign policy should be treated on a bipartisan, even nonpartisan, basis, especially in times of national emergency, is a sacred cow of American politics. During World War I, Woodrow Wilson famously declared that "politics is adjourned."[4] Three decades later, after Pearl Harbor and the early Cold War convinced him to abandon isolationism, Arthur Vandenberg similarly declared that "politics stops at the water's edge." This is of course a fictive nonsense, as Wilson discovered after the 1918 midterms and during the fight over ratification of the Treaty of Versailles, or as Vandenberg's partner Harry Truman discovered after the fall of China and during the worst excesses of McCarthyism. As Julian Zelizer has pointed out, the Truman-Vandenberg bipartisan moment that has been celebrated ever since was a fleeting aberration.[5] Nonetheless, the ideal of a national foreign policy, as opposed to competing Republican and Democratic foreign policies, carries enormous appeal. For all the bickering about domestic issues, Americans want to present themselves to the world with a united front.

When it comes to the study of elections, the bipartisan ideal remains strong. In political science, realignment theorists have perpetuated the notion that foreign policy is uniquely consensual and thus irrelevant to the outcome of elections, particularly critical elections. According to James L. Sundquist, major controversies during the early Cold War and the Vietnam War lacked political traction because both parties tacked toward the center. "It is significant," Sundquist argues, "that none of the major realignments of the American party system in the past have been produced by a crisis in foreign policy" or that "cleavage on foreign policy has at no time been the basic rationale for the country's two-party system."[6]

Scholars in other fields have been less credulous, however, and have done an excellent job illustrating the links between foreign policy and domestic politics. Historians of American foreign relations and American domestic politics have been particularly productive.[7] Aside from realignment theorists, American political scientists have paid careful attention to what David Mayhew terms "bellicosity."[8] In International Relations, *Innenpolitik*, which perceives a nation's foreign policy as motivated almost entirely by domestic factors, is an old and distinguished idea;[9] most notable are the theories of constructivism and the democratic peace.[10] Even realism, a school of thought that has long denigrated the influence of domestic politics, is now willing to embrace internal factors under the guise of "neoclassical realism."[11] Others are blending security and ideology to produce a new synthesis of international and domestic forces,[12] what Campbell Craig and Fredrik Logevall have termed "intermestic" politics.[13] Still, for the most part, these have been recent innovations. If the continuing appearance of jeremiads is any indication, the fields of diplomatic history and American political development need to do much more to integrate war and foreign policy with domestic politics.[14]

Perhaps there is good reason for this traditional scholarly neglect, at least when it comes to electoral politics. When they cast their votes, do people really pay much attention to foreign affairs? Even if they know generally what the United States is doing abroad, do they actually vote for specific reasons of foreign policy? If foreign policy does matter to electoral behavior, is it more important than bread-and-butter domestic issues such as taxation, unemployment, crime, race relations, inflation, or health care? In the 1992 campaign, James Carville, a strategist and adviser to Bill Clinton, told Democratic campaign staff to focus on a single issue: "It's the economy, stupid!"[15] Perhaps he was not mistaken.

Two basic questions arise. First, did foreign policy influence elections? If so, then foreign policy issues must have attracted widespread attention and been important to voters. Second, conversely, did elections have an impact on the conduct of foreign policy?

In answering these questions, this chapter will take a deliberately post-1900 approach. Before the 1890s, foreign policy was about issues very close to home, such as British infringement of neutral shipping rights and encroachment on the frontier in the years before 1812, or westward expansion in the decades after. Foreign policy, in other words, was not particularly "foreign." But from the 1890s on, when the frontier closed and the United States had assumed unprecedented industrial power, U.S. foreign policy dealt with issues that had little intrinsic connection to the continental United States. Foreign policy issues now tested the political imagination as never before, and Americans had to ask themselves if Europe or Asia really mattered to them in the same way that California, Oregon, or Texas had. Thus I have chosen to focus on elections since 1900, when William McKinley and William Jennings Bryan battled over the annexation of the Philippines and thereby globalized the domestic politics of U.S. foreign policy. Relatedly, I have also not treated some politically salient issues, such as free trade or immigration, that to some extent fall under the category foreign affairs because of their inherent importance to life within the boundaries of the United States.

Foreign policy has not been a major issue in all elections since 1900, however, and so I mostly discuss those election years in which events abroad reached an obvious crisis point and foreign policy could be reasonably expected to have been, in political terms, not only salient but preponderant; this includes the presidential election campaigns of 1900, 1916, 1940, 1948, 1952, 1960, 1964, 1968, 1980, and 2004. But presidential campaigns are not the only elections that matter. Several midterm elections have had an intimate connection to foreign policy issues, and so I also examine congressional elections, including 1918, 1946, 1950, 1966, 2002, and 2006.

Presidential Elections and Foreign Policy

Few political issues are as dramatic as a crisis overseas. Few are also as important: the decision to take the country to war, or even to deploy troops in a humanitarian mission, involves the most fundamental questions of civil liberties, constitutional authority, physical safety, and territorial security. As commander in chief, the president has wielded disproportionate power in deciding these issues, particularly since World War II. So it would seem strange if foreign policy had only a marginal influence on the outcome of presidential elections. And, indeed, it might seem that way: since 1916, it is unlikely that a specific foreign policy controversy decided a single election.

However, when we construe political choice and behavior less narrowly, it becomes clear that foreign policy has mattered a great deal. Elections perform a vital function by providing a regular cycle that forces parties and candidates to articulate their views on a range of issues. When political pressure and media scrutiny mount, it becomes nearly impossible to avoid taking a strong stand. Unlike domestic issues, which can be contextualized (spun) endlessly and which rarely seem to require immediate solutions, foreign policy issues demand clarity and bold action. If candidates still try to skirt or fudge an issue, events abroad usually force them to take a clearer position or else risk appearing weak and indecisive. In this sense, elections do not provide a good forum for reasonable and thoughtful discussion of America's engagement with the world. In political terms, foreign policy issues are often not about the specifics of an issue per se but offer insights into a candidate's "character." Similarly, foreign policy provides fertile terrain for fighting out battles over what Americans feel they should stand for in the world, and whether candidates have the temperament and backbone to lead the country forward. Thus, while foreign policy crises pivot on the most important matters of life and death, their importance to U.S. domestic politics is largely about image. This has become especially prevalent in an era driven by the politics of personality, when television, the Internet, and social media simultaneously shape a candidate's image and demand quick responses to rapidly unfolding and confusing events.[16]

Foreign policy can serve as a key valence issue on which candidates demonstrate their effectiveness in handling important and complex matters of state. How presidential candidates handled or reacted to foreign policy crises helped shape their public image by projecting an image of either strength/weakness or competence/incompetence, particularly when the economy was growing and was not a controversial issue. This helps explain why George H. W. Bush could ride strength on national security to victory over Michael Dukakis in 1988 but see his resounding triumph in the Gulf War fall flat in 1992, during a deep recession; indeed, it was Bush's very preoccupation with foreign affairs that made him seem clueless to the electorate's economic pain.[17] For the average voter, who may not care about the finer points of international diplomacy or know much about the intricacies of arms control, foreign policy can still be a bellwether on tone and trust. In 1964, for example, voters preferred Johnson's apparent reasonableness on the Cold War to Goldwater's unpredictability, which in turn reinforced existing interpretations of the candidates' respective temperaments; this was why the infamous "Daisy ad," so provocative it only needed to run once, was so devastatingly effective.[18]

Given the symbolic power of the president's dual role as head of state and commander in chief, foreign policy can provide voters with a litmus test on whether they can trust a candidate to be president. If voters find it difficult to envisage a candidate as commander in chief, it is unlikely they will envisage him or her as president. (The exceptions occur when the imminence of national security threats seems to be waning or when a terrible economy is the overriding issue of the day—or when these two forces converge, as they did in 1992 when a harsh recession followed the end of the Cold War.) Perhaps the best example of the importance of style and tone came in 1976, when a slip of the tongue about the Cold War proved to be Gerald Ford's undoing. When asked to defend détente, which was politically unpopular, Ford replied that "there is no Soviet domination of Eastern Europe and there never will be under a Ford administration. . . . I don't believe that the Poles consider themselves dominated by the Soviet Union."[19] This seemed to confirm people's worst fears about Ford's inability to lead the nation on the world stage or protect America's core interests and national security at a sensitive moment in the Cold War. Pollster George Gallup called it "the most decisive moment" of the entire campaign.[20]

Style and tone can also matter as much as substance when there seems to be little to separate the candidates on the specifics of foreign policy, providing voters with little to choose between them even when world events are obviously a dominant political issue. Consider three elections in a time of war. In 1940 both the Democratic president, Franklin Roosevelt, and his Republican challenger, Wendell Willkie, adopted nearly identical positions of aiding Great Britain without committing the United States to war. To the dismay of his fellow Republicans, in the middle of the campaign Willkie even endorsed the first peacetime draft in American history, thus blunting one of his only effective campaign weapons.[21] In 1952 Republican Dwight Eisenhower and Democrat Adlai Stevenson—neither of them the incumbent—both hinted they would end the war in Korea.[22] And in 1968 voters facing a choice between Republican Richard Nixon and Democrat Hubert Humphrey—again, with neither running for reelection—had little to distinguish between them: though Humphrey was constrained by his reluctance to distance himself from LBJ's record, by Election Day both he and Nixon seemed committed to withdrawing from Vietnam even though neither of them put forward a coherent or detailed plan to do so.[23]

However, this is not to say that foreign policy was irrelevant in 1940, 1952, or 1968. In fact, foreign policy was the most important structural factor because it set the very context within which campaigns unfolded and elections occurred. Even if voters did not make a decision on the specifics of foreign policy issues, the election race itself took place in an environment created by events abroad and turned on who was trusted more to handle the crisis. In 1940, for example, it would have been unthinkable for Roosevelt to run for an unprecedented third term without the backdrop of the increasingly menacing world crisis. In this sense, the fall of France had a tremendous impact on the election, both by creating the conditions that made it feasible for FDR to run again and by highlighting his stature as a leader Americans could trust in a time of national emergency.[24] In 1952 and 1968, by contrast, foreign wars destroyed the presidencies of Harry Truman and Lyndon Johnson. Both had wanted to run for reelection, but both realized early in the year that they had no chance of winning because of their stewardship of an unpopular war. Had either actually run, the election would have been a referendum on foreign policy, and they almost certainly would have lost. Eisenhower and Nixon won in 1952 and 1968 because they appeared more credible on national security than Stevenson and Humphrey; voters wanted to end the war, and they chose the person they believed most likely to do so without it leading to a humiliating withdrawal.[25] Furthermore, Korea and Vietnam did tremendous damage to the party of the incumbent president: in both cases, the Democrats lost seats in Congress as well as the White House.[26]

Foreign policy played a large structural role in two other elections, 1960 and 1980, when Cold War tensions were running high. Historians have subdivided the Cold War into three phases: the First Cold War, which lasted from roughly 1946 to 1963; détente, 1963–79; and the Second Cold War, 1979–89.[27] The 1960 and 1980 elections thus occurred when national security threats seemed to be at their most severe, and both preceded the closest nuclear war scares of the entire era (the Cuban Missile Crisis in 1962 and Able Archer in 1983). Unsurprisingly, the challenger on both occasions placed the incumbent party's foreign policy at the heart of his campaign, and in both cases foreign policy proved to be a factor in November. In 1960 John F. Kennedy accused Richard Nixon of allowing the Soviet Union to build an advantage in nuclear missiles and of not preventing the fall of Cuba to communism; Nixon was not the incumbent, but he had been vice president for the past eight years and was associated with the incumbent's foreign policies.[28] One historian has even argued that the missile gap controversy allowed the Democrats to gain an advantage in swing states with large defense contractors and/or military installations.[29]

The role of foreign policy in the 1980 election campaign was both similar and different. Ronald Reagan strongly challenged incumbent Jimmy Carter's foreign policy record, especially over the Iran hostage crisis and, in a manner similar to JFK in 1960, for supposedly allowing the Soviets to gain a decisive strategic advantage over the United States. But Reagan did not need to spend much time focusing on foreign policy, and his main campaign themes were the recessionary economy and the energy crisis. With the saga in Tehran dominating news coverage all year, Reagan did not need to remind voters about the hostages; he only needed to fear the Carter administration pulling off an "October surprise" by securing their release right before the election.[30] Moreover, Reagan's biggest obstacle was his reputation for being a conservative hard-liner, even an extremist, much like Goldwater in 1964. It would have done him little good to confirm voters' worst fears by stressing his anticommunist credentials. His ability to appear statesmanlike contrasted sharply with Carter's apparent inability to deal with some of the worst challenges the United States had faced in the Cold War. It was that difference—a "statecraft gap"—that helped fuel Reagan's campaign to victory.[31]

The examples considered so far featured foreign policy mainly as symbol rather than substance; not coincidentally, all but one fell in the age of television. But substance has mattered as well. In fact, events overseas came closest to being decisive in two presidential elections in the early twentieth century—1900 and 1916—when foreign policy was only just beginning to become a major aspect of the federal government's activities and when national security had not yet acquired the capacious, global remit it would assume after 1941. Indeed, foreign policy probably assumed such importance in 1900 and 1916 *because* of its distance from the everyday lives of Americans. In the era before air power and nuclear weapons, the absence of a direct threat to the United States possibly created space for debate in a way that was not possible during the international crises of later years.

If most twentieth-century election campaigns offered an impenetrable sameness on foreign policy, with candidates differing on narrow degrees of implementation rather than on basic objectives, 1900 offered one of the sharpest contrasts possible. Though overseas expansion had featured in the elections of 1896, when the anti-imperialist Democrats opposed the annexation of Hawaii, it was not one of the primary issues; economics trumped almost all other issues, especially in the midst of the worst recession the country had experienced up to that point. But four years later, with the economy booming, imperialism was the most contentious and prominent issue. The Democrats, once again led by William Jennings Bryan, opposed expansionism with a moral fervor that—ironically, given that Bryan's stronghold was the Jim Crow South—echoed the abolitionist crusade of the 1850s. But when McKinley submitted the Treaty of Paris to the Senate for ratification in 1899, and with it the annexation of the Philippines, Bryan inexplicably muddied the waters by recommending that Democrats vote for it. Bryan calculated that the Philippines could be his winning weapon. As his biographer notes, "Opposing the war for empire seemed to offer Bryan a political opening that free silver and anti-trust could not match."[32] After ratification, he would be free to make the treaty the centerpiece of his 1900 campaign, and his promise to use America's colonial sovereignty to free the Filipinos from bondage would win him enough votes to capture the White House. He could not have been more mistaken.

McKinley had already sensed that imperialism was not as important as prosperity. But when voters did consider imperialism, it was a vote winner for the Republicans. In fact, central to McKinley's decision to annex the islands was that it would be popular, and that ceding them back to Spain or to another great power would be politically disastrous. During the midterm campaigns of 1898, which occurred in the wake of the Spanish-American War and when the question of the Philippines was becoming central, McKinley used his stump speech for Republican candidates as a test of imperialism's popularity. In Ohio, Illinois, Iowa, and Indiana, crowds enthusiastically applauded McKinley's cagey hints at assuming the burden of an overseas empire. In these prepolling days, he had a stenographer record his speeches and indicate the intensity of the applause for different parts; he found that imperialism generated the most excitement. Even in Bryan's home state of Nebraska, McKinley was greeted with passionate cries of "No!" when he asked of the Philippines, "Shall we deny to ourselves what the rest of the world so freely and so justly accords to us?"[33] McKinley humiliated Bryan in November, even beating the Great Commoner on his home turf by carrying Nebraska's eight Electoral College votes.

In 1916, even more than in 1900, events overseas became the defining issue of the campaign and almost certainly affected the outcome of the election. After the Great War broke out in Europe, only a small minority of Americans advocated U.S. intervention. President Woodrow Wilson, a Democrat, was not among them; in fact, with the vast majority of interventionists being prominent Republicans, led by former president Theodore Roosevelt, and with the vast majority of Democrats being resolutely opposed to intervention, the war had the potential to become a partisan issue. Wilson ran for reelection in 1916 on his record of maintaining neutrality and an implicit promise to continue adhering to nonintervention: though he never uttered the phrase himself, the ability of Democrats to argue that "he kept us out of the war" buoyed his campaign.[34] But Wilson could not appear aloof from the war, especially not with German submarines attacking shipping in the North Atlantic, sometimes resulting in American casualties. Thus he tried to balance two threats—from the Germans and the Republicans—by keeping out of the war without sacrificing American interests or prestige. Wilson may have been "too proud to fight," but he was also too proud to back down.[35] This delicate balancing act included demands that Germany cease its U-boat attacks, support for military preparedness at home, and a pledge that the United States would help underwrite European security by establishing a postwar League of Nations. When Wilson's Republican opponent, Charles Evans Hughes, refused to provide a foil and also favored neutrality, preparedness, and the League, Wilson campaigned against the jingoistic Teddy Roosevelt instead. As Democratic advertisements asked voters on the eve of Election Day, did Americans want "Wilson and Peace with Honor? or Hughes with Roosevelt and War?"[36] In the tightest election in thirty years, one that Wilson himself thought he had probably lost, the Democrats pushed his record on nonintervention more than any other issue.[37]

More recently, foreign policy dominated the presidential election of 2004. By the time Americans cast their votes, the Iraq War had been raging for nearly twenty months, and it had been a significant problem for George W. Bush since at least the fall of 2003, when inspectors had still not found any of Iraq's purported weapons of mass destruction and the insurgency sprang to life. By the time of the 2004 election, voters had been confronted with a continuing spectacle of shame and defeat in Iraq, including the WMD controversy, the battle of Fallujah, and the Abu Ghraib torture scandal. The war "may cost you the election," Republican Party grandee Newt Gingrich told White House aides. "I'm here to tell you that it is bad. . . . Losing a war is bad."[38] Throughout the campaign, Americans continually stated that the war was one of the most important issues at stake: in the spring, 58 percent said they disapproved of Bush's handling of the war (a figure that remained fairly stable throughout the year); shortly after the election, a plurality of 22 percent claimed that Iraq was the most important issue in deciding their vote.[39] Bush could hardly repudiate his own war policies, despite their lack of success, and his opponent, John Kerry, did so with relish. Thus voters were presented with a clear choice between two distinct foreign policy visions, possibly the clearest choice since 1900. Faced with similar political headwinds in Korea and Vietnam, Truman and Johnson could not even face the prospect of running for reelection. But Bush not only ran, he won. Even more remarkably, Bush's fellow Republicans increased their majorities in both houses of Congress. It was a clean sweep for the party in power, even though that party had presided over the most divisive foreign war since Vietnam.

How did Bush manage to pull off such a remarkable political feat? There were two reasons, almost certainly related, for the Republican triumph. The first was that while voters disapproved of Bush's handling of Iraq, they had little faith Kerry could do any better. Truman and LBJ would have been envious: Bush prevailed not *despite* Iraq but *because of* Iraq. After the candidates' televised debate on national security, 49 percent of Americans thought Bush had "a clear plan for handling the situation in Iraq," while only 41 percent thought the same of Kerry—and Kerry had used the debate to improve from his previous Iraq approval rating of a dismal 30 percent.[40] Right before Election Day, Gallup called the race a dead heat, yet in every one of its polls in October it recorded higher approval ratings for Bush on Iraq.[41]

The second reason for Bush's unlikely victory was the overwhelming importance of terrorism as a political issue, one that was visceral and difficult to separate from the war in Iraq. To be sure, large majorities did not believe that Saddam Hussein was responsible for 9/11, but similarly large majorities also gave Bush credit for the absence of a follow-up to 9/11. Here, Bush held an even larger advantage over Kerry than he did on Iraq. Only 33 percent of Americans thought Kerry could do a better job fighting terrorism, as opposed to 60 percent for Bush. An October poll found that while Bush ran behind Kerry on issues such as health care, the federal budget deficit, Social Security, and the economy, Bush had a 22 percent advantage on terrorism—by far the highest advantage in the survey (Kerry's highest was a 13 percent lead on Medicare).[42] Like trade and immigration, terrorism is one of those issues that is both intrinsically foreign and domestic. Yet terrorism also carries with it a much greater sense of threat to physical safety. People have strong opinions on trade and immigration, but at least there is room for debate, and many believe them to be beneficial rather than threatening. In this sense, terrorism could not be more different. Like communist subversion and espionage in the early Cold War, terrorism could bring no benefits, only danger. Against such a force, one that emanated from abroad but potentially had the most serious repercussions at home, voters seemed to err on the side of caution and to favor strength, even if that strength was not always adeptly used. As Bill Clinton observed after the 2002 midterms, which were also dominated by terrorism and war to the Republicans' advantage, "When people are feeling insecure, they'd rather have someone who is strong and wrong rather than somebody who is weak and right."[43] This boded just as well for Bush in 2004, in an election year when the economy was booming and voters ranked terrorism and Iraq as the two most important issues.[44]

The Iraq War election of 2004 stands out as an obvious instance of national security shaping, perhaps even deciding, an election result. Surprisingly, however, there have been moments when foreign policy should have been an overriding electoral factor but was not. The prevalence of international tension did not always mean that foreign policy shaped the election campaign or its outcome, and 1948 provides a perfect example of a dog that did not bark. At a time when the Cold War was coming to define American public life generally, Harry Truman ran mostly on domestic issues. Unlike any subsequent year of his presidency, he was still mostly safe on national security: the Truman Doctrine, the Marshall Plan, and the National Security Act, which most congressional Republicans and southern Democrats had supported, were all in place by the 1948 campaign, and the Soviet atomic bomb test and the fall of China were still a year away. Moreover, Truman was able to focus on domestic issues not only because of his anticommunist strategy of containment but because of the unusual nature of the election. In a four-candidate race, the Progressive Party's Henry Wallace to Truman's left ensured that the Democrats would not bear the worst of Republican red-baiting, while the defection of the Dixiecrats allowed Truman to run unequivocally on a liberal platform embodied in the Fair Deal. Rather than being an election about the emerging Cold War or about the wisdom of containment, 1948 was a referendum, skewed by the two additional candidates, on domestic New Deal–Fair Deal policies.[45]

Congressional Elections and Foreign Policy

Presidential elections draw most of the attention, but congressional midterms can also be shaped by foreign affairs. This is not necessarily obvious: midterms occur when voters are selecting not a commander in chief but legislators who normally campaign on local issues of social, cultural, and especially economic importance.[46] But midterms provide a plebiscitary function in American democracy, and their outcomes are sometimes reflective, or even the result, of the national mood and broader electoral trends.[47] While rare, these instances of pivotal foreign policy midterms are compelling.

The midterms of 1918 provide perhaps the best example. Two years earlier, Wilson had won reelection by a narrow margin, with a diminished share of the Electoral College and without a majority of the popular vote. He nonetheless interpreted it as a vindication of his noninterventionist policies, and in January 1917 he followed reelection with one of his most important foreign policy speeches, one that called for "peace without victory." This proved to be a deft political strategy at home, but diplomatically and militarily it meant relinquishing the initiative to others. Whether the United States intervened in the war was now up to Germany: if it resumed unrestricted submarine warfare, Wilson would have little choice but to respond by bringing the United States into the war.

This is exactly what happened between January and April 1917, when Congress declared war. Now, the American people expected peace *with* victory. So did Wilson, but he envisioned a new world order based on openness and reciprocal security. The nation, however, had moved far beyond such subtleties, as had the Republican Party, and they wanted something approaching a total victory over Germany. The midterms of November 1918, which took place as Wilson was sounding out a German peace offer based not on British and French war aims but on his own visionary and magnanimous Fourteen Points, proved to be a serious rebuke to the Democrats. Sensing his party's precarious situation, shortly before Election Day Wilson implied that a vote for the Republicans would bring aid and comfort to the enemy. The Republicans were not alone in their outrage, and even many Democrats thought their president had gone too far.[48] The Republicans' comprehensive victory—they regained control of both houses of Congress—had a profound effect on foreign policy, even on world history, because it meant that the Senate would not ratify a treaty based on a Wilsonian peace.

The impact of foreign policy as a valence issue was palpable in the congressional elections of 1946, 1950, and 1966, when the Democrats' fitness to manage international crises came under intense scrutiny and criticism. In these midterms, there was little partisan difference or voter uncertainty over the best general direction of foreign policy. Instead, Republican candidates wounded their Democratic opponents by linking them to the foreign policies of the Truman and Johnson administrations. Specifically at issue was whether Truman and Johnson were competently managing internal espionage, the escalation of tensions with the Soviet Union, and the wars in Korea and Vietnam.

The Cold War midterms of 1946 and 1950 occurred when worries about the spread of communism ran high. In 1946 the Republicans constantly hammered home the message that the Democrats were soft on communism, both at home and abroad; by linking that single major issue to nearly all other questions of policy (economics, industrial relations, race relations), the Republicans were able to win an overall majority in Congress after having been the minority party for the previous eight elections.[49] In 1950 the Democrats lost a large number of seats and were able to retain control of Congress only because of the overwhelming majorities they had piled up in 1948 (as we have seen, an election in which foreign policy played a minor role). Their biggest weakness was on national security. Truman's decision to intervene in Korea was not disputed, but his ability to win the war was; coming soon after the Alger Hiss trial, the fall of China, and the Soviet atomic bomb, the Cold War was not friendly political ground for liberal Democrats. Around the country, midterm campaigns were fought largely on the issue of who would fight communism more effectively, a dynamic that played to Republican strengths.[50] Moreover, the sheer number of Democratic seats lost does not convey the full story: the conservative coalition of Republicans and southern Democrats remained mostly untouched, while left-liberal Democrats perceived to be soft on communism suffered disproportionately.[51]

Vietnam was the key valence issue in the 1966 midterms: shortly before the midterms, pollsters ranked it as the "most important problem facing this country today," ahead of civil rights and the economy.[52] And it defined the atmosphere in which the campaigns took place: the Republican National Committee placed Vietnam at the heart of the party's campaigns, and George Gallup concluded that the war was "the great underlying issue and probably the prime reason why the G.O.P. did so well."[53] But the results were nonetheless ambiguous. The Democrats suffered modest losses in the Senate and a huge defeat in the House, yet were still able to maintain overwhelming majorities in both chambers. Some Democratic losses were virtually inevitable given the historically large majorities the party had racked up in the unusual election year of 1964. But even more, the equivocal mandate in 1966 probably stemmed from the unusual problems Vietnam posed. It was, in short, not an easy war to win, and while Johnson clearly had his difficulties, the Republicans had no coherent response of their own. Some high-profile GOP candidates ran as doves, some as moderates who supported the president, and some as hawks.[54] Voters did not like Johnson's strategy, but for the time being they were willing to continue supporting it in the absence of a viable alternative.[55]

The midterms of 2002 and 2006 also stand out for the starring role played by national security, though they produced dramatically different results. In 2002, flush with what seemed to be a successful war in Afghanistan and growing concerns about a possible threat from Iraq, the primacy of foreign policy enabled the Republicans to buck historical trends (the president's party usually loses ground in midterms) and cement their control of Congress. With the absence of another terrorist attack on U.S. soil, the Bush administration presented Congress with a war resolution on Iraq. The Democrats were terrified of appearing soft on terrorism (as they once had feared being soft on communism), and the resolution passed overwhelmingly in October 2002. But in supporting Bush's war, Democrats handed the Republicans a significant triumph. After that, a Republican victory in the midterms a month later was virtually a foregone conclusion, and otherwise popular Democrats who were tarred with the charge of being soft on terrorism—such as Georgia senator Max Cleland, a Democrat who voted against the Homeland Security Act—lost their bids for reelection.[56] The 2006 election, however, was a referendum on a failing war, and for the first time in a long time national security issues redounded to the Democrats' benefit. With a strong economy relegating domestic concerns to the political margins, the Iraq War was far and away the most important issue in voters' minds: on the eve of the midterms, 64 percent of respondents told pollsters that Iraq "should be the top priority for the president and Congress," while the economy came in second at 18 percent. With terrorism now effectively decoupled from the war, only 6 percent listed terrorism as the nation's main concern.[57] Ironically, then, the absence of another terrorist attack, arguably Bush's greatest achievement as president, undercut the Republicans' appeal on national security grounds. "People are fed up with this war," a prominent Republican said behind closed doors that fall. "Republicans are going to pay a huge price for this war in November. I think we're going to lose the election in November because of this war."[58]

The Foreign Policy of Domestic Politics

It is clear, then, that foreign policy has influenced presidential and congressional elections. But what about the reverse? Have elections affected the conduct of U.S. foreign policy? Here, the answer is also clear: America's policies overseas have been profoundly shaped by electoral politics. Bob Woodward's behind-the-scenes account of Robert D. Blackwill, the National Security Council officer for Iraq who was seconded to Bush's reelection campaign in 2004, is telling:

> Blackwill was struck that there was never any real time to discuss policy. In between the stops or in the air, whenever Iraq came up, it was always through the prism of the campaign. What had the Democratic nominee, Massachusetts Senator John Kerry, said that day about Iraq? What had happened on the ground in Iraq that might impact the president's bid for reelection? As the NSC coordinator for Iraq, Blackwill probably knew as much about the war as anybody in the White House. He had spent months in Iraq with [L. Paul] Bremer. But he was with the campaign only as part of the politics of reelection. Not once did Bush ask Blackwill what things were like in Iraq, what he had seen, or what should be done. Blackwill was astonished at the round-the-clock, all-consuming focus on winning the election. Nothing else came close.[59]

Blackwill may have found his experience unsettling but, in historical perspective, it was hardly unusual. However, a few caveats are important to remember. The first is the radical disjuncture between campaign rhetoric and presidential action. If election promises are the benchmark, one would probably conclude that elections actually bear no relation to subsequent foreign policy. After all, several presidents have campaigned for peace only to oversee a major war. Five months after winning reelection as the president who "kept us out of the war," Woodrow Wilson strolled down Pennsylvania Avenue to ask Congress for a declaration of war against Germany.[60] "Your boys," Franklin Roosevelt promised an audience in Boston during the last stages of the 1940 campaign, "are not going to be sent into any foreign wars."[61] And in 1964, in a memorable applause line that quickly became a standard part of his stump speech, Lyndon Johnson told a crowd in New Hampshire, "I have not thought that we were ready for American boys to do the fighting for Asian boys."[62] The 1968 election provides a similar example, when Nixon ran on an implicit promise to get the country out of Vietnam, yet took four agonizing years to do so—four years in which more than 20,000 U.S. soldiers and hundreds of thousands of Vietnamese died. Or consider Bill Clinton, who dismissed foreign policy in 1992 and yet spent as much of his time as president focusing on foreign affairs as he did on domestic policies.[63]

A second caveat is the striking degree of foreign policy continuity between presidencies, even when parties have changed. This does not mean that foreign policy is bipartisan or free of politics, but it does suggest that the application of many foreign policies does not emanate from political ideology. Eisenhower's pursuit of containment differed little from Truman's, just as Kennedy's differed little from Eisenhower's—despite the heated rhetoric of the 1952 and 1960 campaigns.[64] One might be tempted to attribute such continuity to a supposed "Cold War consensus," but the phenomenon has outlasted the Cold War: Clinton's foreign policy differed little from George H. W. Bush's, while Barack Obama continued, and even augmented, many of George W. Bush's national security and antiterrorism policies.[65] George W. Bush's wars seemed to mark a decisive break with his predecessor, but this was not apparent until the unprecedented shock of 9/11—after which many Democrats, including Clinton and Al Gore, supported the case for war in Iraq.[66]

These caveats are important, but they do not disprove the influence the political calendar has had on U.S. foreign policy. Elections matter in two structural ways. First, they set limits on what candidates can and cannot promise to do, and thereby close off certain foreign policy options. For example, with noninterventionism and outright isolationism still popular in 1940, neither party could run on an outright war platform. Similarly, elections also shape the contours of U.S. foreign policy by committing the winner to a certain course of action, from Eisenhower's 1952 vow to end the war in Korea to Barack Obama's 2008 promise to withdraw from Iraq. Elections can also provide a mandate for radical shifts in foreign policy. For example, despite Roosevelt's and Willkie's promises to stay out of the war, the 1940 election consolidated internationalism's defeat of isolationism, thus completely changing the character of America's engagement with the rest of the world.[67]

Second, elections shape foreign policy by compelling policy makers to act in certain ways, either from fear of being punished at the polls or in hope of gaining a winning edge. There are countless examples of presidents adjusting the implementation of their foreign policy in response to electoral considerations or the heat of an election campaign—indeed, far too many to examine or even list here—but consider two of the most important.

First and perhaps foremost is the Cuban Missile Crisis. Though the missile gap was quietly forgotten, Kennedy found himself a prisoner of his tough campaign rhetoric on Cuba, which narrowed his options when considering the flawed Bay of Pigs invasion plan. Communism survived, and JFK came under increasing pressure to dislodge Fidel Castro. Kennedy authorized a covert plan of sabotage and assassination, Operation Mongoose, to do just that, but, being secret as well as a failure, it did nothing to relieve his political pressures. When Senator Kenneth Keating, a Republican from New York, began (accurately) proclaiming that the Soviets had secretly placed medium-range nuclear missiles in Cuba in the fall of 1962, Kennedy felt he had to act despite the consensus of his advisers that the missiles made no strategic difference to the United States, resulting in the most dangerous confrontation of the entire Cold War.[68]

Vietnam provides several other examples because Johnson and Nixon constantly devised military and diplomatic strategy with one eye fixed on the election cycle. Johnson administration officials were instructed to keep Vietnam out of the spotlight during 1964, which constrained policy making considerably.[69] Four years later, after being humiliated in the New Hampshire primary, LBJ realized that running for reelection would be futile, and as a result he announced measures he had long resisted: a bombing halt and the opening of negotiations.[70] During the campaign that year, Nixon secretly encouraged South Vietnamese president Nguyen Van Thieu to scuttle the Paris negotiations between the United States and North Vietnam, which would have given a boost to Hubert Humphrey; in return, Nixon promised Thieu a better deal for South Vietnam, and four more years of war followed.[71] Four years after that, when Henry Kissinger emerged from negotiations in Paris to declare that "peace was at hand," Nixon (once again in tandem with Thieu) deliberately scuttled his administration's own peace plan. Kissinger's priority was geopolitics, and he produced a suitable settlement. But Nixon's priority was winning reelection, and he did not want Kissinger's negotiations to become a political liability. Nixon calculated that a peace settlement finalized before Election Day would help Democrat George McGovern, as it would validate his antiwar platform and remove an issue that was preventing many "hard-hat" prowar Democrats from voting for the dovish McGovern. Nixon "feels strongly," H. R. Haldeman recorded in his diary, "that, as far as the election's concerned, we're much better off to maintain the present position" rather than chase Kissinger's breakthrough.[72]

Which brings us back to Lyndon Johnson and Barry Goldwater. Just over a week after their private bargain not to politicize foreign policy in the 1964 election campaign, North Vietnamese torpedo boats appeared to attack U.S. naval ships in the Gulf of Tonkin. Johnson responded with a limited bombing reprisal against North Vietnam and asked Congress for a resolution of support. The combined effects of the retaliation and the resolution gave Johnson a massive political boost at Goldwater's expense. With a limited retaliatory strike and with overwhelming bipartisan support from Congress, LBJ could have it both ways: he could still appear to be the reasonable statesman while also proving that he was no pushover. With Vietnam now an asset, he went on the offensive and made it a central issue of his campaign, and the Daisy ad ran a month later.[73] Now heavily politicized, foreign policy proved to be a triumph for Johnson and a disaster for Goldwater.

The Republican would never forget the political lesson he had been given. Two years later, in October 1966, when Johnson announced he would convene a conference to explore a settlement in Vietnam, Goldwater's bitterness was evident: "No matter how piously the President may deny any domestic political considerations, the very fact that the meeting is scheduled so close to the congressional elections . . . makes it impossible to separate the trip from pure and simple Johnson politics."[74] As Goldwater belatedly realized, U.S. foreign policy and electoral politics have a long and intimate history.

CHAPTER 13

From Corn to Caviar: The Evolution of Presidential Election Communications, 1960–2000

Brian Balogh

This chapter examines the modern communications infrastructure of presidential elections. While most scholarly attention has been riveted on the way presidents communicate *to* the voters, I will pay close attention to the other side of that conversation: how candidates *discern* the preferences of voters. The chapter traces the shift from party- and interest group–mediated communications to a different kind of mediation: public opinion polling and the use of digital data, often referred to as "analytics" or "big data," to identify the concealed preferences of portions of the electorate. I then consider how this new kind of political intelligence was deployed in a landscape dominated by broadcast television. That ground was shifting even as the broadcast networks dominated the political airwaves during the 1960s and 1970s. Political operatives like Richard Viguerie employed America's oldest form of mass media—the U.S. Postal Service—to reach millions of would-be voters who responded favorably to more provocative messages than television could accommodate. While the humble letter was soon joined by telemarketing, sophisticated get-out-the-vote efforts, talk radio, and the Internet, the guidance system for all of these messages increasingly activated like-minded groups of individuals by directing provocative messages at them. In the hunt for sure bets, candidates entered into a direct dialogue with the voters that often marginalized the intelligence-gathering functions that interest groups and parties had once provided. This, in turn, undermined the key role that their leaders played in putting together coalitions capable not only of electing candidates, but of governing once elected. Aggressive messaging also contributed to the polarization and stalemate that gripped the nation by the end of the twentieth century.

Cutting Out the Middlemen

For much of the nineteenth century and well into the twentieth, political parties were crucial intermediaries between presidential candidates and the electorate. They recruited the candidates, publicized partisan planks, and connected the "party in the electorate" to the "party in government." Parties and their local machines provided tangible benefits to voters, most notably jobs. They also distributed government contracts and benefits to those districts and geographic regions that voted their way. And they called upon tens of thousands of supporters to help turn out the vote by organizing rallies, distributing literature, and canvassing neighbors on Election Day, providing a ride, a drink, a couple of dollars, or simply encouragement to vote for the party's candidates.[1]

Parties were also the best and often the only source of intelligence about what the voters were thinking. Parties conveyed voter preferences to candidates and elected officials through a highly localized apparatus. In a sprawling democracy, parties were a crucial way to narrow the distance between the candidates and their would-be constituents. Samuel Kernell captured the contrast between this highly mobilized electorate and late twentieth-century campaigns run by "increasingly self-reliant candidates." "With their limited reach into the electorate," Kernell contended, "the best the modern candidates could hope to do was fashion and communicate an attractive message to a receptive audience." Kernell contrasted the thick connections among candidate, party, and electorate in the nineteenth century to their more attenuated modern substitute—the public opinion poll. He also underscored the new connective tissue that disembodied forms of intelligence relied upon: "an attractive message."[2]

Political scientists have labeled elections characterized by the candidate's emphasis on the individual's record and personality "candidate-centered campaigns." Some political scientists date the emergence of candidate-centered presidential campaigns to the Eisenhower-Stevenson contests of the 1950s, and there is broad consensus that by the time that John F. Kennedy mounted his campaign for the White House, political parties had been displaced from their long-standing perch as essential intermediaries between voter and candidate in presidential elections.[3]

One other kind of organization emerged in the twentieth century that conveyed crucial political intelligence about voters to candidates and mobilized blocs of voters on behalf of candidates—the interest group. Some interest groups, ranging from huge federated organizations like the AFL and the CIO, or the American Farm Bureau Federation, commanded the allegiance of hundreds of thousands of members, subscribers, or supporters and could transmit voter preferences and signal candidate acceptance back to their members, just as political parties did. Other more narrowly drawn interest groups, such as business trade associations, compensated for smaller membership with disproportionate clout in the political economy. Interest groups often proved more adept than parties at conveying the preferences of a narrow slice of the electorate, which is precisely why politicians listened to them. A leading student of interest group politics in the 1920s, Harwood Childs, summed up his detailed study of the Chamber of Commerce and the AFL this way: "The Chamber and the Federation . . . play an important role in the policy-determining activities of the state. They are at the same time reservoirs of ideas, mirrors of desires, sifters of major from minor policies, agencies for leading and directing the legislative activities of the government." Interest groups could sometimes provide a more granular, timely portrait of portions of the candidate's constituency than political parties could in the middle of the twentieth century.[4]

As parties struggled to remain relevant in the1960s and 1970s, the number of interest groups exploded, their growth fueled by social movements advocating for civil rights, a cleaner environment, or second-wave feminism. The proliferation of such public interest groups triggered a countermobilization by businesses directly affected by the new social regulation advocated by many of these new groups. Interest groups stood guard over the legislative and regulatory process, ostensibly translating their members' preferences into public policy. Although political action committees (PACS) claimed to operate in nonpartisan fashion, they soon entered the electoral fray closely aligning with political parties. Despite congressional efforts to stanch the flow of campaign funding from interest groups to candidates, the number of PACs ballooned from roughly 600 in 1974 to 5,400 in 2010.[5]

Yet the growth in interest groups occurred against a backdrop of "diminished democracy" within these organizations themselves. As Theda Skocpol noted in her book by that title, "National public life is now dominated by professionally managed advocacy groups without chapters or members." These professional advocates were in no position to transmit the preferences of the rank and file, who now had little involvement beyond writing a check once a year. Besides, public opinion polling, especially when combined with database-driven analytics, could provide a far more objective portrait of segments of the population. Checkbook advocacy severed the connection between leaders and members, while public opinion polling displaced the political intelligence that effective interest group leaders had leveraged to gain access and influence.[6]

Before the advent of reliable public opinion polling, parties and interest groups were the *only* source of this political intelligence besides the candidate's own informal contacts and guesswork. Access to reliable poll numbers broke that monopoly and provided presidential candidates with an independent guide to voter preferences, encouraging the rise of the candidate-centered campaign.

When they lost their exclusive role as interpreters of public opinion, parties and interest groups also lost a powerful tool for governing. In America's mid-twentieth-century pluralist politics, party and interest group elites engaged in bargaining over legislation and public policy that required the construction of dense networks of common interest and that valued enduring reciprocal relationships. Effective bargaining rested upon a combination of the leader's institutional position and the electoral clout of the constituency that supported him or her. Because these elites were both conduits for and interpreters of their constituents' preferences, they had a great deal of discretion over how these opinions were characterized and conveyed. Washington insiders were insulated from plebiscitary pressure because they retained a monopoly over gathering and interpreting that opinion. Operating in a pluralist, bargaining fashion, elites were delegated the authority to cut deals and broker compromises. Their most potent weapon was their constituents' electoral clout—an asset to which interest group and party elites claimed privileged access. Like a good number of middlemen who have been cut out of the process because the raw data are now available directly online—think insurance brokers, travel agents, and no shortage of regulators!—party and interest group leadership lost a great deal of their clout, as candidates sought the data they needed directly from the source: in this case, the voters. A victory of sorts for direct democracy, this trend posed serious obstacles for governance.[7] Imperfect information, it turned out, was a powerful incentive for negotiation and compromise.

By the 1960s, public opinion polling gave candidates the opportunity to know voters better than party or interest group leaders did. Simultaneously, the penetration of television into virtually every household allowed politicians to broadcast messages back to voters directly, bypassing party and interest group channels. These new ways of communicating political preferences and signaling their reception back to constituents would soon replace the static-filled networks that parties and interest groups had monopolized. Politicians would finally be able to access and transmit this kind of intelligence independently, freed from the biases of partisan or special interest interference. Indeed, the diffusion of television and the embrace of frequent public opinion polling as crucial tools in presidential elections were two factors that further eroded party influence over campaigns and undermined interest groups' claims to any special knowledge about their base.

With candidates increasingly checking the latest polls and beaming messages directly to the voters, the latent power of public opinion that brokers in a pluralist system had wielded was fractured. So too were the reciprocity and insulation necessary for successful negotiations, free from the daily twists and turns of public opinion. Not quite direct democracy, the balance between the national will of the people and their representatives' delegated authority shifted dramatically toward the will of the people between 1960 and 2000. Ironically, this made translating that will into public policy more challenging. Delegation may have been bad for democracy, but it was good for translating the preferences of well-organized groups into public policy.

Meeting Average Voters at Their Own Level

From the 1950s through the 1970s, candidate-centered campaigns in both parties beamed their messages back to voters through three television networks. By the late 1950s, television displaced radio as the mass medium of choice for the vast majority of Americans. The three broadcast networks were, in effect, an oligopoly that reached roughly 90 percent of all viewers for much of this period. Whether they liked politics or not, most Americans were exposed to it through television, especially when all three networks carried a debate or press conference. Roughly 60 percent of American households tuned in to watch John F. Kennedy debate Richard M. Nixon in 1960. It was not uncommon for presidential speeches to attract 80 percent of those watching in the early days of television. Limited to three networks with roughly equal shares of viewership in the 1960s and 1970s, the savvy candidate aimed for the broad middle. When presidential aspirants diverged from that template, as Barry Goldwater and George McGovern did, they paid a hefty price.[8]

Accounts of the activities of early political consultants, the experts who replaced party functionaries in election campaigns by the late 1950s and early 1960s, offer a valuable portrait of campaign strategy in the early days of broadcast television and public opinion polling. The firm credited with creating the profession of campaign consulting, Whitaker and Baxter, noted that a campaign's theme "must be simple and have a strong human interest appeal" and "more 'corn than caviar.'" Whitaker and Baxter's advice is illustrative of the early days of candidate-centered campaigns that broadcasted their messages through radio, television, and other mass-market media.[9]

The candidate's message "must be directed to the many-sided interests of the individual voter," these professionals warned. "The particular voter is not only a union member, but also a father, a Catholic, a veteran, a member of the PTA, and a sports fan. Each of the individual's group loyalties must be appealed to in a special way." Like many successful advertising professionals in the late 1950s, Whitaker and Baxter were experts on the "mass mind." And the source of their expertise was their own "good average minds," which enabled them to "meet the average man at his own level and see things as he sees them." As political consultants replaced party operatives, the candidate-centered style that emerged emphasized the ways in which the candidate's "individual attributes and attachments," as Adam Sheingate has written, connected with the voter. It was these personalized qualities that began to replace "partisan loyalties and affiliations."[10]

The one-size-fits-all approach to broadcast television pursued by candidates simply conformed to the nature of this medium itself. As the historian of television James Baughman wrote in *Same Time, Same Station*, "Great disappointment came as the medium settled on a set of practices or 'rules' that in effect standardized the business of television in the late 1950s." One of the cardinal rules was to avoid controversy at any cost. That was because the networks required a national audience and a sizable market share of that national audience in order to make a profit.[11]

While television was a godsend for shoring up a presidential candidate's broad base, the inexorable march of special interests not only continued unabated; its pace quickened dramatically during the 1960s and 1970s, pressuring candidates to attend to minority interests while remaining "presidential." Presidents, presidential candidates, and their parties might have been stuck with corn when it came to televised communications. But that did not mean they could not experiment with a sophisticated array of variations on that staple, from cornbread to high fructose corn syrup.

Presidential Pollsters Come Out of the Closet

The extensive survey research that Lou Harris provided to the Kennedy campaign signaled a new phase in the use of polling. Harris began polling systematically for the campaign in 1959, covering twenty-seven states in the year and a half leading up to the election. The survey contained open-ended questions that asked voters to state the most important problem facing the country. Kennedy's team then promoted the popular issues that were most likely to burnish the "Kennedy image." The campaign's organization of private polling data, the number of polls conducted, and the strategic use of that data suggested that polling had arrived as a major component of presidential campaigns. Of equal significance, Harris continued to poll for Kennedy over the course of his administration.[12]

Although Lyndon Johnson had a strong personal interest in public opinion polling, the Nixon White House's voracious appetite for these data eclipsed even Johnson's commitment. Nixon took polling in the White House to unprecedented levels, conducting 40 percent more polls than Johnson. Nixon's team also drew upon the latest findings in *Public Opinion Quarterly* and leading university-affiliated research centers. Nixon replaced Johnson's open-ended questions about the president's personality with sophisticated constructs to explore interpersonal qualities and assess the voters' views of the president's image and appeal. Perhaps most importantly, Nixon trusted polls as no other president had before him. He made them an integral part of his campaign, relying upon them to provide strategic guidance and tactical insights. Nixon tapped his own chief of staff, H. R. Haldeman, who was conversant with polling from his days at the J. Walter Thompson Agency, to oversee polling for the White House. Whether measured by the frequency of polling, its sophistication, the speed with which these data were interpreted, or the breadth and depth of the questions asked, Nixon raised the bar.[13]

Nixon also put his internal polls to more explicit political use in campaigning for some of the public policies he cared about the most once he was in office. The historian Mark Nevin has documented the case of Nixon's campaign for the Safeguard antiballistic missile (ABM) defense system, for instance. After an April 1969 Gallup poll showed that only 25 percent of the American public supported Nixon's program, the president authorized his own internal polling on the matter. Providing those surveyed on the topic with information about the ABM proposal made all the difference in the world. Nixon's internal poll reported that once informed about the program, 73 percent of Americans believed that Congress should approve Safeguard. Nixon wasted no time in getting the word out, using Safeguard supporter William Casey's Citizens Committee for Peace and Security to publicize the findings of this White House poll. The White House even conducted a second internal poll aimed at Vermont voters in order to convince Republican senator Winston Prouty to vote for Safeguard.[14] The selective release of internal polls in order to convince elected officials became yet another weapon in the elected official's arsenal. As Nevin concludes, "In time, the White House developed a 'standard operating procedure' for distributing favorable polls on the Hill."[15]

Along with polls came pollsters. The "president's pollster" enjoyed a relatively steady rise in stature between the Kennedy administration and President Carter. Over the course of this period, pollsters moved from cloistered outside consultant to trusted visible adviser. Yet the very use of polls by presidents was a politically sensitive matter. As Robert M. Eisinger has argued, Congress viewed the interpretation of public opinion as its own constitutionally mandated responsibility and jealously guarded that charge in the first two decades following World War II. Members understood that political clout came with the claim to understand precisely what the voters wanted. For decades that prize had been the product of their own soundings combined with partisan and interest group intelligence. President Kennedy's fear of the negative reaction to polling drove him to store the Harris polls in his brother's (Attorney General Robert Kennedy) safe. As late as the Nixon administration, H. R. Haldeman continued to treat polls as political secrets to be sequestered in his own safe.[16]

President Gerald Ford institutionalized what previously had been a less formal set of practices. Within a month of taking office, Ford tapped Robert Teeter of Market Opinion Research to serve as his pollster. Like Nixon, Ford funneled these operations through his chief of staff, in this case Dick Cheney. Despite the turmoil that followed the Watergate scandal, Ford's White House institutionalized the role of presidential pollster, continuing the process that Nixon had begun.[17]

If the administration of Richard Nixon stood out for the number and pace of polls and the degree to which the president himself relied upon polls to identify image and appeal, President Jimmy Carter's administration marked the moment when the presidential pollster came out of the closet and enjoyed unparalleled direct access to the president. By the age of twenty-five, Patrick Caddell was directing polling for Jimmy Carter's campaign. After Carter was elected, Caddell served as the president's pollster and far more. Caddell used his close relationship with the president and his unprecedented access to offer Carter advice that ranged from political strategies to commentaries on policies and theories about leadership. It was Caddell's seventy-five-page 1979 memo to Carter entitled "Of Crisis and Opportunity" that preceded Carter's infamous "Crisis of Confidence" speech—also dubbed the "malaise" speech.[18]

Caddell's memos enjoyed greater circulation within the White House than those of previous pollsters due to his prominence as an adviser and Carter's belief in transparency, and because public opinion polling was gaining far more legitimacy as a scientific tool through which to take the pulse of the people. That legitimacy was underscored when major media outlets like the *New York Times* and the television networks began to conduct and report on their own polls. By the end of the Carter administration, public opinion polling was a standard part of any president's repertoire and a crucial ingredient of presidential campaigns.[19]

Serving Caviar with Corn: The Rise of "Priming"

As presidents grew more comfortable with polling, they sought more from the torrent of data that flooded in. Capturing a snapshot of broad public opinion that could also be broken down by cross-sectional analysis to home in on specific segments of the population without having to rely on intermediaries, be they political parties or interest groups, was simply too tempting to ignore. In this era, no politician viewed polling as a panacea. With broadcast television the only game in town, whatever a candidate might learn about the nuances of a sliver of the electorate would still have to be reconciled with a message that met average viewers at their own level. But polling might serve as a panopticon that could survey both majority perspectives and dissenting alternatives. Polling data might reveal the secret formula for balancing corn and caviar—discovering ways for candidates to serve both.

A group of historically informed political scientists have documented just such a menu. Presidential candidates, they argue, used survey research to "prime" voters on policy issues that played well with crucial segments of the population but that also enhanced the candidate's image, improving his overall positive standing in the polls. If the polls could be trusted, voters would not have to choose between corn and caviar: the two might go quite nicely together—perhaps even complement one another. Nor would this fare have to be served at a fancy restaurant. Priming was, quite literally, made for TV.

In some of the earliest literature on priming, Lawrence Jacobs and Robert Shapiro demonstrated the ways in which candidate John F. Kennedy drew the attention of voters to, or primed them toward, policy issues that the polling data identified as popular. While the voters might punish candidates for taking specific policy positions if they guessed wrong about where the majority of voters stood, Kennedy could afford to take these stands on public policy because the polling data assured him that majorities would react favorably to this select set of issues. The purpose of this priming, however, was not to promote these policies per se. Rather, it was to enhance Kennedy's image by associating him with policies the voters liked. Here was a way to enhance image that did not rely on the personality of the candidate. Indeed, it was an attempt to use polling data about voters' reactions to policy issues in order to embellish or downplay preexisting views of the candidate's personality.[20]

Jacobs and Shapiro demonstrated that issues receiving favorable ratings in the Harris polls, particularly "increasing Social Security, passing Medicare legislation, reforming education, fighting unemployment, combating the high cost of living, and such foreign policy issues as bolstering America's military spending and general prestige," were mentioned by Kennedy in his public statements frequently. The correlation between favorable poll results and priming increased in the waning days of the campaign. Poll results that showed a threefold increase in favorable responses on the issue of unemployment correlated with a fourfold increase in Kennedy's public statements on that same issue the following week. In the final analysis, Kennedy's campaign devoted "enormous resources to identifying the public's policy goals," but it used this information primarily to "influence evaluations of Kennedy's personal qualities."[21]

Jacobs and Melanie Burns subsequently examined the *changes* in polling and the kinds of questions asked from the Johnson administration through the Reagan administration. They found two significant developments: increased frequency of polling, as we have seen, and a shift from asking about policy preferences to questions about the candidate's image and appeal. Jacobs and Burns argued that the more-sophisticated questions about image and appeal and, more importantly, presidents' growing confidence in the findings allowed candidates to craft a strategy that would enhance their public standing with a majority of the voters. This, in turn, freed these candidates to support a select group of policies that were unpopular with a majority of voters but were crucial to motivating the activists and interest groups. Questions relating to image and appeal increased appreciably during the Nixon administration. This gave Nixon and the Reagan White House "confidence that [they] could knowingly defy the policy preferences of majorities of Americans . . . in order to pursue [their] desired policy goals and not suffer electoral punishment."[22]

Whether the findings from these latest twists and turns in priming studies are conclusive or not, it is clear that presidents running for reelection sought to maintain their broad appeal by associating themselves with issues known to be popular with voters at the same time that they signaled support to key coalition members who embraced less popular views. Political parties had accomplished this feat by taking advantage of their deep roots in localities and regions. Interest groups had cemented their access, regardless of electoral outcomes, by cultivating ties to both parties whenever possible. Yet, with the declining capacity of both parties and interest groups to mobilize their supporters, and with the allure of survey research offset by the limitations of television, presidents from Kennedy on sought to strike a delicate balance between majoritarian appeals and assurances to true believers who often cared most about issues that did not poll well. Priming was one way to talk about issues while improving one's image among less engaged voters who cared little about the details. But candidates soon discovered alternatives to television for disseminating views that might not play so well through that homogenous medium. That memo came in the mail.

"Like Using a Water Moccasin for a Watchdog": Direct Mail's Stealth Appeal

In contrast to the space-age use of broadcast television and sophisticated public opinion polling for campaigns from 1960 to 1980, the old-fashioned letter proved to be a powerful tool for raising funds and activating true believers. This was especially true for candidates who diverged from the mainstream. The most influential strategist who adapted the use of direct mail to political applications was Richard Viguerie. Viguerie, a committed conservative at a time when such views were marginalized, was passionate about politics. Viguerie served as the chair of the Harris County (Houston) Young Republicans, and then as Harris County campaign chair for John Tower's campaign for the Senate in 1960.[23]

Viguerie got his chance to make a "bigger mark," as he put it, in the summer of 1961—working as the public relations and fund-raising account manager for Young Americans for Freedom (YAF). The fledgling YAF fit Viguerie's hard-right political perspective and matched his passion for politics. Viguerie's boss, Marvin Liebman, was already renowned among conservative groups for his fund-raising acumen. While working for Liebman and the YAF, Viguerie grasped the potential power of fund-raising appeals through the mail. It was the presidential campaign of another dark horse candidate, Barry Goldwater, however, that demonstrated just how effective direct mail could be. The Goldwater campaign netted almost $5 million in contributions from its mailing operations. Even more impressive was the number of small contributions the campaign received—almost four hundred thousand under the sum of $100. Goldwater's defeat in 1964 only hardened Viguerie's sense that the establishment media and *both* parties were stacked against the views held by conservatives like Goldwater and himself.[24]

Although Goldwater did not win, his campaign's populist postal appeal proved that there were ways around intermediaries like parties and outlets for reaching voters beyond broadcast television. Viguerie left his position with the YAF, started his own direct mail company, and never looked back. Direct mail had been used by the private sector for some time. As Viguerie put it, "I didn't have to play Lewis and Clark." Viguerie studied the techniques of the major Madison Avenue firms and pored over "every page of *The Reporter of Direct Mail*."[25]

Viguerie applied the lessons he learned from the commercial sector to politics and fund-raising for single-issue groups. Lists were everything. That was because direct mail was all about activating true believers. Fortunately for Viguerie, campaign laws at the time required all candidates for federal office to report the names and addresses of supporters who contributed $50 or more. Viguerie walked into the office of the clerk of the House of Representatives, where these reports were filed, and copied by hand the information on Goldwater contributors. Viguerie combined the list of Goldwater supporters with names purchased from Liebman and other conservative organizations. Within fifteen years, Viguerie's company was sending roughly seventy million letters a year on behalf of conservative single-issue organizations.[26]

Viguerie effectively applied commercial techniques to the art of politics. But two developments, one political and the other technological, dramatically enhanced his prospects. Watergate was one of these developments. In 1974, as confidence in government plummeted, Congress passed campaign reform measures that restricted donations to individual campaigns to a maximum of $1,000. Suddenly, eliciting small donations from large numbers of supporters was an essential task for all presidential candidates.[27]

Computers were the other factor that helped turn direct mail into a political juggernaut. Computers allowed technicians like Viguerie to merge mailing lists, and over time, employ a variety of databases to pinpoint likely supporters. Far from determining the course of politics, the use of this technology was itself determined by a number of political variables. Viguerie noted that when it came to political infrastructure, from PACs to think tanks, the New Right was simply playing catch-up with the left. But there was one distinctive innovation by the movement that would help sweep Ronald Reagan into power by 1980. "The one thing that the New Right brought to the table that the Left had *not* was the marriage of computerized direct mail and the political process. Use of this new technology would make the New Right's foundations, PACs and special interest groups far more effective than those on the Left over the course of the Seventies."[28]

Viguerie's company provided technical and strategic support for single-issue groups that coalesced to form the New Right. Viguerie's bread-and-butter business provided direct mail campaigns for dozens of single-issue interest groups on the right, from busing to protecting the rights of gun owners. He also successfully adapted direct mail techniques crafted for the George Wallace campaign in 1968. Former Viguerie employee Bruce Eberle raised more money for Ronald Reagan's 1976 presidential campaign than was raised for any other campaign in history up to that time.[29]

Although Viguerie and his disciples carved out a distinct advantage for the application of direct mail to causes on the right, he did not hold a monopoly. Like Barry Goldwater, George McGovern was a candidate who won his party's nomination despite the antagonism of the party establishment. McGovern tapped into the direct mail skills of Morris Dees to finance his presidential campaign. Dees remained with the campaign and coordinated its direct mail efforts, bringing in a record-setting $24 million. This elicited praise from a knowledgeable opponent. As Richard Viguerie told the press, "Someone in the McGovern camp knew what he was doing." Once again a presidential candidate shunned by his own party and rejected by the vast majority of voters in the general election proved that direct mail was a powerful tool for reaching citizens who felt strongly about a set of issues, even if their views did not comport with those of a majority of Americans.[30]

Direct mail was a technology that bypassed traditional intermediaries, from parties to interest groups. Commenting on a mailing sent by Senator Robert Taft in his 1950 reelection campaign, Viguerie and David Franke discuss how this may have been the first documented instance of bypassing "the establishment (in this instance the union bosses)" in order to "go directly to constituents (the union workers themselves)." If the coauthor of the widely acknowledged antiunion Taft-Hartley Act could successfully bypass union leadership by targeting union members directly, the possibilities for unmediated communication with constituents were endless.[31]

Direct mail was not simply a fund-raising device. To be sure, it was handy that direct mail paid for itself. But its greatest value lay in advertising the message it carried. Contrasting direct mail to television advertising, Viguerie emphasized that "political direct mail advertising . . . through wise list selection goes almost entirely to people who are *predisposed* to agree with you on the issues or candidates, people who are open to persuasion to support your cause." The right message could activate these sympathetic voters.[32]

Viguerie insisted that direct mail was like a water moccasin because despite the staggering volume of correspondence, it operated silently and relatively invisibly, precisely because it was targeted at segments of the population often neglected or ignored by more established media. Despite the 1 billion pieces of mail sent to conservatives between 1974 and 1980, mainstream newspaper and broadcast television correspondents did not seem to appreciate the impact of this onslaught until Ronald Reagan's impressive victory in 1980. During the years in which broadcast television dominated all other forms of media, conservatives, according to Viguerie and Franke, "thought of direct mail as *our* TV, radio, daily newspaper, and weekly magazine combined." From the perspective of conservative activists, it was all the more effective for its ability to fly under the radar of what they perceived to be the liberal media establishment.[33]

The Data Arms Race

Because candidates could direct messages at a narrow slice of their audience and command the kind of selective attention that interest groups had once claimed for their members, the emergence of direct mail encouraged greater efforts to find even more creative ways to slice and dice the electorate. Ronald Reagan rode into the White House on a tidal wave of polling data that allowed him to pursue broader image-building strategies and target key segments of the electorate simultaneously. The Republican Party invested heavily in what today we call "big data" and at the time was usually labeled "technology," "computerized" (fill in the noun), or simply "high tech." That triggered what one veteran *Wall Street Journal* editor labeled a "data arms race."[34]

This is not to say that either side ignored conventional arms. Presidential pollsters were alive and well, and although they were now publicly identified, their methods remained shrouded in a veil of mystery. Reagan's pollster was Richard Wirthlin. "Just how his talents and his printouts will be used," Adam Clymer wrote in December 1980, "has not been defined." Clymer covered polling as part of his broader political beat for the *New York Times*, and his reporting, along with that of other political correspondents, offered some clear answers to his own question over the next eight years. Still confined to broadcast television as the only game in town when it came to mass communications, political strategists experimented with techniques beyond priming to craft messages that might appeal to a more select group of viewers without turning off the rest.[35]

They procured more qualitative data from their respondents by increasing the use of focus groups. Buoyed by their findings and confident that they could strike strategic targets without too much collateral damage, the George H. W. Bush campaign launched a series of negative advertisements that added a powerful new weapon to the poll-driven arsenal. All the while, candidates tinkered with the images they projected on television, employing the latest polling data to shore up chinks in their armor or take advantage of strategic opportunities.

Focus groups, a technique adopted directly from marketing, used short sessions with a small number of voters—often selected based on key demographic factors revealed by polling—to get answers to a series of questions or elicit responses to a political commercial. They provided room for commentary by members of the test group and offered a more finely drawn snapshot of voter preferences. Until the mid-1980s, focus groups were considered too expensive to use on a regular basis, but as Paul Taylor reported in the *Washington Post* in January 1989, "Now they're a standard feature."[36]

Building on the Republican Party's confidence in market research and message testing, the George H. W. Bush campaign deployed this process in the service of negative advertising in the 1988 election. Lee Atwater directed the attack. The campaign aired infamous negative ads such as the Willie Horton "revolving door" spot to highlight Dukakis's liberal position on prison furloughs. This and other negative ads were vetted in focus groups by a team of consultants working for the Bush campaign. Pollsters also used two techniques to follow up on the effectiveness of such ads. Daily tracking polls measured whether advertisements registered with voters. The other method was to assemble a set of carefully selected voters who watched the advertisement at home and took a telephone survey after.[37]

Democratic pollster Paul Maslin embraced the "arms war" metaphor to explain this development. "The techniques have gotten so refined, the weapons so powerful, that if you don't use them, you will lose them, because the other side will use them on you," Maslin told the *Post*. A Republican pro, former Ford campaign strategist Doug Bailey, was dismayed at just how successful his own profession had been since the 1970s. It was "no longer necessary for a political candidate to guess what an audience thinks," Bailey lamented. "He can do it with a nightly tracking poll."[38]

Even as negative advertising became a staple, political parties and candidates mined sophisticated polling data in a variety of other creative ways in order to get around the corn-fed fare that broadcast television encouraged. Again, the Republican Party led the way. *Washington Post* political correspondent Thomas Edsall reported in June 1984 that the party kept "extending the outer edges of political high technology, exploring new uses of computers . . . telemarketed voter registration and contribution solicitation, [and] highly targeted direct mail."[39]

Exhibit A was the New York advertising firm McCollum/Spelman, which was brought in to develop "psychometric" analysis of the party's strategies. It used polling data to identify those demographic groups—"such as women, abortion opponents, Hispanics, blue collar workers"—who might be persuaded to vote Republican. It was research director Elaine Morgenstein's job to craft the candidate's image in ways that might enhance his appeal to a group like women who were not naturally inclined to vote for him. While a Republican who suddenly advocated for women's rights would look foolish (and perhaps lose portions of his base), McCollum/Spelman sought ways to signal that the candidate stood for the "little guy," thus evoking more support from groups like women who could identify with the underdog. Morgenstein equated her campaign work to previous assignments on corporate accounts: "You try with a corporation to give it personality." Edsall noted that Morgenstein had extensive experience doing just that with "'imagery products'—perfume, liquors, cigarettes and the like." With branding techniques for luxury items such as perfume and liquor providing the template for political campaigns, perhaps serving caviar to discerning voters might make the difference in a close campaign.[40]

Adam Clymer documented just how such an advertising campaign might toy with the candidate's image in order to address the gender gap. Reporting on the congressional races in August 1982, Clymer pointed to a *New York Times/CBS News* poll that showed 42 percent of men but just 34 percent of women would vote for a candidate who favored President Reagan's policies. To the outspoken Republican chair of the National Women's Political Caucus, imagery was part of the problem. As she put it, "It doesn't seem to me that politics has changed that much. . . . There are still all those commercials of men talking to men sitting on tractors." Although they acknowledged limits to what they could do, pollster Robert Teeter and John Deardourff, a political advertising specialist, believed that subtle messages might help to close the gap. For mass advertising, indirect appeals were the most frequent approach to addressing this kind of challenge. Republican advisers created ads like the one for Governor Tommy Thompson that proclaimed that Wisconsin had the "most extensive inhome nursing program in the nation" using visual imagery that showcased a nurse checking the blood pressure of an elderly woman. The commercial closed with a scene of a daughter and her elderly mother in the kitchen. While mom fixes some food, the daughter tells the viewer, "With Governor Thompson having this program, she's able to stay in her own home and she doesn't have to go to a convalescent home."[41]

By the end of the twentieth century, polling expanded the candidates' capacity to discern the voters' preferences about as far as it could, while candidates crafted a variety of techniques for circumventing broadcast television or making the best of it through adjustments in the image projected and by lavishing attention on commercial placement.

Even as such efforts flourished, burgeoning databases and the plummeting costs of computers made the analysis of information that all voters inadvertently provided through their day-to-day activities the next frontier for identifying preferences. Such data included a voter's hobbies, gleaned from magazine subscriptions and patterns of consumption reported by credit card companies. When these data were combined with digitized census, voter registration, and polling data, they produced profiles that were snapped up by candidates. These profiles offered candidates even greater assurance that taking a position that was a bit out of the mainstream but that resonated forcefully with an identifiable minority might be worth considering. Rather than signaling preferences to party and interest groups elites—Washington insiders who used privileged knowledge of their constituents' preferences as crucial bargaining chips in a pluralist negotiation—voters displayed their proclivities through a variety of outlets. The proxies that intermediaries between the voter and the candidate once held were now replaced by direct communications. Like travel agents, video stores, and insurance agents, political middlemen were being replaced by consumers who could now order directly from the service provider. Governing, however, required far more room for negotiation between competing interests and perspectives than streaming a video or logging onto Orbitz to book a flight.

Once convinced of the advantages, candidates gambled on tactical flights to the margins for two reasons. The first, made famous by Karl Rove, was to "stir up the base." The other, however, could not have been more different. It entailed salvaging voters from the political wasteland of *in*attention (in contrast to that highly motivated base) or, even more boldly, poaching voters from the opposing party. Such sorties could be costly—both financially and politically—if the gambit alienated other voters in the candidate's coalition. But growing confidence in the kinds of data that could identify fruitful targets, combined with the growing range of mass-media alternatives to broadcast television, encouraged candidates on both sides of the aisle to roll the dice.

Polling remained an essential ingredient in the candidate's repertoire, just as cues from parties did.[42] Nevertheless, by the last decade of the twentieth century, the marginal advantage in what had become a highly competitive contest between the two parties appeared to go to the candidates who could leverage massive databases in order to "microtarget" selective audiences for narrowly tailored messages.[43]

Perhaps the most important thing a campaign could know about a citizen was simply whether he or she was registered to vote. This informed all subsequent decisions as to where the campaign should invest its resources. The quest for this kind of information received a huge, albeit inadvertent, boost in 2002 when the Help America Vote Act mandated that states maintain digital voter registration files. These files contain the essential ingredients needed to identify party affiliation and the voter's past turnout record. They also contain identifiers like street addresses. These voter registration files are the foundation of the huge databases that have been constructed by both parties. Voter registration information is then merged with data obtained from the census, consumer sources, and polling.[44]

Until recently, the database arms race had been a lopsided one. Writing in 2006, *Los Angeles Times* political correspondents Peter Wallsten and Tom Hamburger noted that "over two or three decades, the GOP has painstakingly built up a series of structural advantages that make the party increasingly difficult to beat. And in the last five years, it has strengthened its hold under President Bush and his political guru, Karl Rove." One of those advantages was "the most sophisticated vote-tracking technology around." When Ronald Reagan took office, he inherited a party that had been committed to developing state-of-the-art computer technology, voter lists, and a direct mail operation that still was far ahead of the Democratic Party's. According to Thomas Edsall, the Republicans still maintained that advantage as Reagan's first term came to a close. "The Republican technological advantage over the Democrats lies not in secret techniques," Edsall wrote in June 1984, "but in having the money to pay for the latest advances, most of which are developed for the commercial telemarketing and direct-mail world or by computer specialists producing programs for the political arena."[45]

While money helped, the political party that had suffered through decades at midcentury when it was a perennial underdog had every incentive to innovate and experiment when it came to finding and turning out voters. And as the political scientist Daniel Galvin has illustrated, Republican presidents had been particularly attentive to this aspect of party building. Watergate may have been the greatest political disaster of the twentieth century for the Republican Party, but in a move that underscored the commitment of Republican presidents to party building, precinct-level election data files painstakingly accumulated by Richard Nixon's Committee to Reelect the President (CREEP) 1972 campaign were merged with the Republican Party's files from the 1974 election and matched with census and other demographic data to create the first in-house capacity for either party. The Republican National Committee (RNC) made these data available to all Republican candidates and to the state parties.[46]

By the time that Frank Fahrenkopf assumed the chairmanship of the RNC in 1983, Republicans had been perfecting their in-house database for eight years. Fahrenkopf built on the Republican advantage by adding novel information like fishing and hunting license records. Although Reagan won both of his elections by commanding majorities of electoral votes, and even though

Republicans took control of the Senate in 1980 for the first time since 1952, there was good reason to believe that the Republican Party was not taking full advantage of its potential support in the electorate. For instance, Reagan outpaced two-thirds of the Republicans running for Congress in both of his elections, continuing a long tradition of Republican presidents running far ahead of their fellow party members.[47]

Many Republicans believed that the long Democratic dominance at the local and state levels, which continued through the 1980s, along with the opportunities it offered for gerrymandering, was the problem. Under Reagan, the RNC set up a new redistricting division, which leveraged the Republican digital advantage and focused these resources on turning the tables by the next reapportionment. President George H. W. Bush's Republican Party intensified the digital support for redistricting. As Galvin has recounted, "Thanks to continual upgrades in the party's computer technology since the mid-1970s, vast stores of data on voting patterns and demographic information for every county in the country were already on hand at the RNC and easily manipulated. Once the new census data arrived, the RNC would be ready to merge the new data with its preexisting data and offer sophisticated analyses to help state and local party leaders redraw district lines in ways that favored Republican candidates."[48]

By the mid-1980s, recognizing that they trailed badly when it came to targeting, the Democrats sought to close the gap. The Democratic National Committee (DNC) contracted with the Claritas Corporation to catch up. Claritas had "geocoded" every ZIP code in America, sorting each into one of forty clusters that best represented the mix of data humming through the firm's computers. These data included income, lifestyle, race, and a range of other demographic factors. Neighborhoods in wealthy suburbs like Houston's River Oak, for instance, were tagged as "furs and station wagons" kinds of places, whereas less toney sections of Los Angeles were consigned to the "Hispanic mix cluster."[49]

While geocoding represented an expensive Democratic step forward, the Republicans were hardly standing still. The National Republican Senate Committee signed a deal with CACI Incorporated to perform a more fine-grained analysis. Not content to settle for ZIP code zones, which might contain up to 2,250 households, thus diluting the character of the "cluster," CACI bought census data that allowed it to apply its forty-four labels to blocks rather than ZIP code zones. CACI aggregated its data down to units of 260 households—producing a much more homogenous slice of the population and one that was more reliable when it came to targeting the distilled set of characteristics that both parties were searching for.[50]

Even more impressive than the services the Republican Party was contracting for was its growing in-house capacity. The RNC invested in powerful computers of its own that were capable of breaking census data down to the block level. "We have it right here, and we can tell any candidate the demographics of any block in his district," a Republican political strategist told Edsall. "[We are] able to focus on almost any specific block and tell you who lives in that house and what they do for a living, how many kids they have and what their income is." The Democrats chased a moving target for the next two decades when it came to targeting. The Republican capacity to microtarget any block in a candidate's district had been the product of a sustained party-building commitment.[51]

Programs like Voter Vault, rolled out in 2006, were built on the legacy of that effort. That Republican database enabled party activists at the ground level to identify potential supporters by "personal hobbies, professional interests, geography—even their favorite brands of toothpaste and soda and which gym they belong to." The year 2006 was a big one for the Democrats too. After a tortured process that did not begin in earnest until the dawn of the twenty-first century, the Democrats tested their first national, centralized voter file.[52]

While the growing speed and capacity of computers and the ubiquitous nature of personal data available in digital form were clearly catalysts for the data arms race, technology was only one of several factors that encouraged this contest. As we have already seen, deep changes in the nature of political parties and interest group membership altered their role as "mirrors of desires." Candidate-centered races left politicians to fend for themselves when it came to political intelligence, and from the 1960s onward they had become accustomed to turning to pollsters for such information. Data-driven targeting no doubt seemed like the next logical step. Political reform even played an unanticipated role when the Help America Vote Act mandated easily accessible statewide voter registration information. The "permanent opposition" tag that had burdened the Republican Party in the wake of the powerful New Deal coalition that dominated Congress and the White House during the middle decades of the twentieth century provided a powerful incentive for the Republicans to innovate.

Perhaps the most significant contextual factor that encouraged the data arms race, however, was the success that the Republican Party had in narrowing the gap between Democrats and Republicans by the 1980s. Close competition had developed between the two parties, especially in presidential races. The gap between those who identified as Republicans and those who called themselves Democrats between 1952 and 1980 had averaged twenty-one percentage points. By 1988 the Democratic advantage had narrowed to six percentage points. Between 1972 and 2004 the gap between those who identified as Republicans and those who identified as Democrats narrowed from 11 percent to zero. The 2000 election, decided by the Supreme Court of the United States, epitomized this competitive environment. Under such conditions, candidates had good reason to believe that every vote counted and that voters who previously might have seemed long shots, either because of their party registration or the fact that they were not registered at all, were worth another look.[53]

Republicans believed that Democrats had only come this close to the presidency because they outperformed the GOP in the "ground game." The GOP increased its investment in database development, honing its capacity to target politically conservative, pro-Israel Jews or to pick off socially conservative Latinos. Data that could identify alienated Democratic blue-collar workers were particularly valued.[54]

Lost in the logistics was the underlying condition that made these initiatives worth the effort and expense: the intensely competitive state of presidential politics. The Democrats understood the changing stakes too. "A lot of the consumer data helps at the margins," the DNC's director of special projects, Keith Goodman, told Peter Wallsten. And as Goodman noted, "Many elections are decided in the margins." Voters who in a period of Democratic or Republican hegemony might have been ignored were now attracting more attention than ever due to the competitive state of presidential politics.[55]

Under these competitive conditions, registering new voters became a top priority for both parties. The Republican Party put its capacity to microtarget voters to use in the service of a massive voter registration drive for the 1984 campaign. The party invested $4 million to sign up 3 million new Republicans. Meanwhile, the Reagan-Bush 1984 campaign focused on converting the Democratic blue-collar workers labeled Reagan Democrats by pundits into enduring Republicans by having them change their registration. The party also worked with American Coalition for Christian Values chairman Tim LaHaye, who claimed that he signed up two million new Republicans, primarily through church groups. Edsall and Haynes Johnson labeled the effort "a 1984 version of the American political machine." It was driven by "sophisticated, expensive and impersonal computer equipment bearing such names as NCR 'Mentor' and Honeywell 'Ultimate.'" An RNC aide described how the campaign targeted one potentially rich vein of voters. "We at the Republican National Committee have developed a Hispanic-surname extract," the operative told Edsall and Johnson. "If we take those tapes and cross-tab them against the voter lists, then cross-tab it against the county assessor lists, we'll be able to identify unregistered Hispanics who are homeowners. Then we can run that list against car-buyer lists, mailing lists for financial newspapers, Hispanic business lists." "Our initial target has to be the upwardly mobile Hispanic who has a vision of the future that is similar to Ronald Reagan's," the aide continued. "That takes a very sophisticated effort."[56]

That effort was far more challenging for Republicans. Byron Nelson, a Texas Republican, complained that the low-hanging fruit had already been harvested. "The thing about Republican precincts," Nelson noted, "everybody is registered." "I walked my precinct, and 90 percent of the people were registered. We have to be selective." Edsall and Johnson contrasted this to the situation that Democrats faced. As they put it, Democrats "can easily go door to door in a black or poor neighborhood and find a large pool of unregistered voters who lean toward the Democratic Party. The GOP, in contrast, faces the risk in almost every neighborhood of registering as many Democrats as Republicans." That is why the Republicans placed a special premium on signing up the right kind of voters in independent or even Democratic-leaning districts. But they did not give up on those few voters living in heavily Republican neighborhoods who had not yet registered—Nelson's missing 10 percent. In those wards, the party paid for lists of citizens who had requested new utility connections, contacting these newly arrived voters to urge them to register. Writing on November 4, 1984, Edsall concluded that in what should have been an easy win for the Democrats when it came to signing up new voters, the GOP "held its own."[57]

By the twenty-first century, both parties were combining voter registration information with polling, census, and marketing data. Data that revealed gun ownership or church attendance could often provide clues to a voter's political preference, as did information about household size and whether the voter owned or rented. At its most sophisticated, microtargeting could identify the most unlikely voters as prospects. The Republican Voter Vault, for instance, identified a suburban African American woman who tended to vote Democratic in the past. Yet she was bombarded with waves of e-mail messages, phone calls, and other communications from the Republican Party.

Why target her? Voter Vault apparently had discerned that despite her otherwise left-leaning profile, she was also "a mother with children in private schools, an active church attendee, an abortion opponent and a golfer."[58]

While there were plenty of reasons to pursue microtargeting for its powerful ability to identify voters who might make the difference in close races, the changing mass-media environment also encouraged this trend. Long before microtargeting, candidates had more data about voters from polls and other sources than they could use selectively to reach certain voters in an age dominated by broadcast television. Direct mail and then telemarketing had provided an opportunity to target messages to such voters. But as David Paul Kuhn pointed out it was not just the ability to categorize preferences into narrower gradations that was changing. So too were the ways in which candidates acknowledged receipt of these preferences. "Mastering the art of microtargeting is increasingly important to the parties," Kuhn noted, "as the more traditional forms of communication become less and less effective in campaigns." The explosive growth of DVRs had dented the effectiveness of traditional political advertising. The number of Americans who got most of their campaign news online was growing. And the rapid shift to cell phones meant that traditional phone banks were less effective. With increased use of the Internet and social media, it was not just the cues that candidates received from voters that were delivered in narrower slices. So too were the messages that campaigns "narrowcast" back to voters.[59]

Conclusion

Presidents in the second half of the twentieth century increasingly have "gone public," continuing their campaigns for policies ranging from tax cuts to health care reform long after the voting stops. However, going public has proved to be a poor substitute for the kinds of incremental negotiated settlements that formed the New Deal and World War II generation's social contract, from the expansion of Social Security to Medicare. The most underappreciated reason for the declining capacity of intermediaries to negotiate as pluralist theory predicted they would is the displacement of parties and interest groups as the primary means of taking the pulse of the voters, and the rise of direct communications between candidates and the electorate.[60]

This is not to argue that parties and interest groups are irrelevant to the electoral process. Far from it. They finance much of the political intelligence and messaging that candidates rely upon. And parties, unlike a generation earlier, have distilled clearly distinguishable ideological brands and exercise far more discipline over their members in Congress.

Mastering communications unmediated by party or interest group should have finally liberated candidates from these go-betweens—at least when it came to political intelligence. It failed to do so, however, because of the cost of the new communications infrastructure. Polling and microtargeting were expensive, as were advertisements on broadcast television and then cable. And as the Democratic Party discovered, aggregating national voter databases was no easy task. The party's institutionalized stake in painstaking incremental improvements to the database, compared to the ephemeral nature of any single candidate's stake, proved to be a key factor in the successful development of this resource. Just when candidates might have freed themselves from the self-interested agendas of parties and interest groups, they found themselves more indebted—literally—than ever to the fund-raising capacity of both parties and interest groups and the longer-term investment horizon of parties.

Yet today's parties and interest groups are crippled when it comes to the actual business of governing, as the job of reassembling the odd-shaped coalitions that elect a president for the far less dramatic business of passing legislation has proved nearly impossible. In the absence of key brokers who can both claim access to a unique perspective on their constituents' preferences and the authority to reach a deal on their behalf, presidents are often left with the option of tailoring bite-sized policies that will poll well without activating too much opposition, or exhorting Congress to take bold actions even as such calls are used to enflame segments of the loyal opposition.

Had interest groups and parties served solely as pure conduits of their members' diverse interests, this displacement would have barely registered a ripple. These two intermediaries, however, did far more than convey preferences to candidates. Partisan and interest group leaders mixed and matched their members' preferences, adapting them to the politically possible. The key to their flexibility was the broad deference that members granted party and interest group leadership when it came to cutting deals with other elites. These insiders translated broad voter demand into narrowly drawn policy outcomes. Ironically, these bite-sized compromises added up to a broad social contract—at least for those Americans who were well represented at the ballot box and on K Street.

Public opinion polling, which by the 1980s was increasingly combined with big data, cut out the middlemen. Increasingly secure in the likelihood of garnering a favorable response from a properly chosen fragment of the population, candidates were tempted to direct provocative messages at ever-narrowing slivers of the electorate, confident that a properly targeted appeal would be limited to that receptive audience. And as presidential elections became more competitive, turning out key fragments in battleground states could often mean the difference between winning and losing. It also meant the rise of polarized politics and the decline of pluralist bargaining.

Candidates no longer needed to work through the intermediaries of party and interest groups to discern the preferences of voters. Instead, they could commission polls or combine polling data with a range of demographic data, voting histories, and consumption patterns in order to intuit directly what voters preferred. The political world we inhabit today is the product of this shift—a world in which candidates know more details about individual voters than they ever have, yet a world in which the ability to build the kind of coalitions that party and interest group intermediaries were once talented at crafting eludes the grasp of public officials as they seek to placate, or at least neutralize, the relatively unmediated and often nonnegotiable demands of their key constituents.

NOTES

Introduction

1. Twain dictated the first quote for his autobiography on January 23, 1906. The second is commonly attributed to him but has no published source.

2. For an outstanding analysis of presidential election politics before the Civil War, see M. J. Heale, *The Presidential Quest* (London: Longman, 1982). For British elections during the same period, see Frank O'Gorman, *Voters, Patrons, and Parties: The Unreformed Electoral System of Hanoverian England, 1734–1832* (Oxford: Oxford University Press, 1989), and, for the later nineteenth century, H. J. Hanham, *Elections and Party Management: Politics in the Time of Disraeli and Gladstone* (London: Longmans, 1959). For recent scholarship on the roots of mass elections, see the following: John L. Brooke, *Columbia Rising: Civil Life on the Upper Hudson from the Revolution to the Age of Jackson* (Chapel Hill, NC, University of North Carolina Press, 2010); Donald J. Ratcliffe, *Party Spirit in a Frontier Republic: Democratic Politics in Ohio, 1793–1821* (Columbus: Ohio State University Press, 1998); Johann N. Neem, *Creating a Nation of Joiners: Democracy and Civil Society in Early National Massachusetts* (Cambridge, MA: Harvard University Press, 2008); Andrew W. Robertson, "The Tortuous Trajectory of American Democracy," in *Era of Experimentation: American Political Practices in the Early Republic*, ed. Daniel Peart and Adam I. P. Smith (Charlottesville: University of Virginia Press, 2014).

3. Charles Dickens, *American Notes for General Circulation* (1842; Harmondsworth, UK: Penguin, 2000), 73.

4. Alex Keyssar, *The Right to Vote: The Contested History of Democracy* (New York: Basic Books, 2009).

5. See Michael McGerr, *The Decline of Popular Politics: The American North, 1865–1928* (New York: Oxford University Press, 1986).

6. Stephen Skowronek, *The Politics Presidents Make: Leadership from John Adams to Bill Clinton* (Cambridge, MA: Harvard University Press, 1993).

7. See Arthur M. Schlesinger, Jr., *The Age of Jackson* (Boston, MA: Little Brown, 1945), and idem., *The Cycles of American History* (Boston, MA: Houghton Mifflin, 1986).

8. See, for example, Samuel P. Hays, "The Social Analysis of American Political History," *Political Science Quarterly* 80 (1965): 373–94; Paul Kleppner, *The Cross of*

Culture: A Social Analysis of Midwestern Politics (New York: Macmillan, 1970); Joel Silbey, Allan G. Bogue, and William H. Flanigan, eds., *The History of American Electoral Behavior* (Princeton, NJ: Princeton University Press, 1978).

9. Skowronek, *Politics Presidents Make*; Theda Skocpol, *Protecting Soldiers and Mothers: The Political Origins of Social Policy in the United States* (Cambridge, MA: Harvard University Press, 1992).

10. Scott C. James, *Parties, Presidents, and the State: Electoral College Competition, Party Leadership, and Democratic Regulatory Choice, 1884–1936* (Cambridge: Cambridge University Press, 2000).

11. For the most devastating attack on alignment theory, see David R. Mayhew, *Electoral Realignments: A Critique on American Genres* (New Haven, CT: Yale University Press, 2004).

12. These factors are discussed in John Sides and Lynn Vavreck, *The Gamble: Choice and Chance in the 2012 Presidential Election* (Princeton, NJ: Princeton University Press, 2013).

13. William E. Leuchtenburg, "The Pertinence of Political History: Reflections on the Significance of the State in America," *Journal of American History* 73, no. 3 (December 1986): 600.

14. See also the work of Mark Wahlgren Summers, *Rum, Romanism and Rebellion: The Making of a President, 1884* (Chapel Hill: University of North Carolina Press, 2000); Joel Silbey, *Party over Section: The Rough and Ready Presidential Campaign of 1848* (Lawrence: University Press of Kansas, 2009); Andrew E. Busch, *Reagan's Victory: The Presidential Election of 1980 and the Rise of the Right* (Lawrence: University Press of Kansas, 2005); Lewis Gould, *Four Hats in the Ring: The 1912 Election and the Birth of Modern American Politics* (Lawrence: University Press of Kansas, 2008).

15. For a representative sample of this work, see Meg Jacobs, William Novak, and Julian Zelizer, eds., *The Democratic Experiment: New Directions in American Political History* (Princeton, NJ: Princeton University Press, 2003).

1. The Devolution of 1800

1. Quotations from "Republicans Rejoice!," New York *American Citizen*, February 21, 1801; Vera Brodsky Lawrence, *Music for Patriots, Politicians, and Presidents: Harmonies and Discords of the First Hundred Years* (New York: Macmillan, 1975), 165; "Selected Toasts," Boston *Constitutional Telegraphe*, March 11, 1801; Hartford *American Mercury*, March 19, 1801.

2. Henry Adams, *History of the United States of America During the Administrations of Thomas Jefferson* (New York: Literary Classics of the United States, 1986), 145–47, 164, 226; Dumas Malone, *Jefferson the President: First Term, 1801–1805*, (Boston: Little, Brown, 1970), 27–28. Among the socially oriented scholars should be included the vote-counting "new political historians" of the 1960s and 1970s, whose developmental model for the rise of "mass democracy" virtually required the universal white male suffrage laws that the election of 1800 helped usher in, and who were in any case

almost exclusively concerned with voting levels and patterns rather than governmental or constitutional changes. See William Nisbet Chambers and Walter Dean Burnham, *The American Party Systems: Stages of Political Development* (New York: Oxford University Press, 1967); Ronald P. Formisano, *The Birth of Mass Political Parties: Michigan, 1827–1861* (Princeton, NJ: Princeton University Press, 1971); Ronald P. Formisano, "Deferential-Participant Politics: The Early Republic's Political Culture, 1789–1840," *American Political Science Review* 68 (1974): 473–87; Ronald P. Formisano, *The Transformation of Political Culture: Massachusetts Parties, 1790s–1840s* (New York: Oxford University Press, 1983); Paul Kleppner et al., *The Evolution of American Electoral Systems* (Westport, CT: Greenwood Press, 1981). The most extreme argument for a "revolution of 1800," Daniel Sisson, *The American Revolution of 1800* (New York: Alfred A. Knopf, 1974), went several bridges too far in trying to remove the election of 1800 from the context of party politics and put it in the pantheon of world revolutions. Reviews of the book commonly took the opportunity to condemn not just Sisson's but also Jefferson's description of the event. Perhaps the most common move has been that made by James Roger Sharp, *American Politics in the Early Republic: The New Nation in Crisis* (New Haven, CT: Yale University Press, 1993), 276–88, emphasizing that Jefferson's victory did not mean acceptance of a permanent two-party system and treating the "Republican ascendancy" as essentially the continuation of Founder Rule without fundamental changes except that the ruling faction was more southern-based. This interpretation has much more merit and a stronger factual basis than others that follow the Federalist critics of Jefferson's administration in setting out to prove that he was just a hypocrite who eagerly contradicted his own principles in office, such as Leonard W. Levy, *Jefferson and Civil Liberties: The Darker Side* (Chicago: Ivan R. Dee, 1989). I do not mean to suggest that I am the only recent historian to defend the reality of a "revolution of 1800." For other recent and not so recent works making the case for the importance of the election of 1800, usually in the form of a narrative, see John Ferling, *Adams and Jefferson: The Tumultuous Election of 1800* (New York: Oxford University Press, 2004); Susan Dunn, *Jefferson's Second Revolution: The Election Crisis of 1800 and the Triumph of Republicanism* (Boston: Houghton Mifflin, 2004); Bernard A. Weisberger, *America Afire: Jefferson, Adams, and the Revolutionary Election of 1800* (New York: William Morrow, 2000). Richard Hofstadter, *The Idea of a Party System: The Rise of Legitimate Opposition in the United States, 1780–1840* (Berkeley: University of California Press, 1969), 128–40, accords proper importance to the election of 1800, but does so in the service of a developmental argument that relies far too much on an unstated functionalist teleology about how parties were supposed to evolve, toward the professionalized "responsible" model of something along the lines of the British Labour Party. For a critique, see Kenneth Kolson, "Party, Opposition, and Political Development," *Review of Politics* 40 (1978): 163–82. For a much fuller version of my take on the historiography of the "revolution of 1800," see Jeffrey L. Pasley, "1800 as a Revolution in Political Culture: Newspapers, Celebrations, Democratization, and Voting in the Early Republic," in *The Revolution of 1800: Democracy, Race, and the New Republic*, ed. James

Horn, Jan Ellen Lewis, and Peter S. Onuf (Charlottesville: University of Virginia Press, 2002), 121–52. Another increasingly popular line of argument, reflected in a number of other essays in the previously cited book, holds that the election of 1800 actually represented a step backward for democracy, with slaveholders taking command of the national government and a politics based on courting the votes of common white male voters pressing against the rights and political participation of blacks and women. For two versions of this argument, see Robin L. Einhorn, *American Taxation, American Slavery* (Chicago: University of Chicago Press, 2006), especially 113–15; and Rosemarie Zagarri, *Revolutionary Backlash: Women and Politics in the Early American Republic* (Philadelphia: University of Pennsylvania Press, 2007).

3. On the "celebratory politics" that characterized campaigning in the early Republic, see (among others) David Waldstreicher, *In the Midst of Perpetual Fetes: The Making of American Nationalism, 1776–1820* (Chapel Hill: University of North Carolina Press for the Omohundro Institute of Early American History and Culture, 1997); Andrew W. Robertson, "Voting Rites and Voting Acts: Electioneering Ritual, 1790–1820," in *Beyond the Founders: New Approaches to the Political History of the Early American Republic*, ed. Jeffrey L. Pasley, Andrew W. Robertson, and David Waldstreicher (Chapel Hill: University of North Carolina Press, 2004), 57–78.

4. Quotation from Thomas Jefferson to Judge Spencer Roane, September 6, 1819, in Thomas Jefferson, *Writings*, ed. Merrill D. Peterson (New York: Literary Classics of the United States, 1984), 1425. The seminal work on the change of political culture across the election of 1800 is Alan Taylor, "From Fathers to Friends of the People: Political Personas in the Early Republic," *Journal of the Early Republic* 11, no.4 (1991): 465–91.

5. James Morton Smith, *Freedom's Fetters: The Alien and Sedition Laws and American Civil Liberties* (Ithaca, NY: Cornell University Press, 1956); Marilyn C. Baseler, *"Asylum for Mankind": America, 1607–1800* (Ithaca, NY: Cornell University Press, 1998), 260–85; Edward C. Carter II, "A 'Wild Irishman' Under Every Federalist's Bed: Naturalization in Philadelphia, 1789–1806," *Pennsylvania Magazine of History and Biography* 94, no. 3 (1970): 331–46; Richard H. Kohn, *Eagle and Sword: The Beginnings of the Military Establishment in America* (New York: Free Press, 1975), 174–273.

6. Johann N. Neem, "Freedom of Association in the Early Republic: The Republican Party, the Whiskey Rebellion, and the Philadelphia and New York Cordwainers' Cases," *Pennsylvania Magazine of History and Biography* 127, no. 3 (2003): 259–90, quotations on 265 and 272. For more on the Democratic Societies, see Philip S. Foner, ed., *The Democratic-Republican Societies, 1790–1800: A Documentary Sourcebook of Constitutions, Declarations, Addresses, Resolutions, and Toasts* (Westport, CT: Greenwood Press, 1976); Albrecht Koschnik, "The Democratic Societies of Philadelphia and the Limits of the American Public Sphere, Circa 1793–1795," *William and Mary Quarterly* 3d ser., 58, no. 3 (July 2001): 615–36; Albrecht Koschnik, *"Let a Common Interest Bind Us Together": Associations, Partisanship, and Culture in Philadelphia, 1775–1840* (Charlottesville: University of Virginia Press, 2007); Eugene Perry Link, *Democratic-Republican Societies, 1790–1800* (New York: Octagon Books, 1973); William Miller, "The

Democratic Societies and the Whiskey Insurrection," *Pennsylvania Magazine of History and Biography* 62, no. 3 (1938): 324–49; Matthew Schoenbachler, "Republicanism in the Age of Democratic Revolution: The Democratic-Republican Societies of the 1790s," *Journal of the Early Republic* 18, no. 2 (1998): 237–61; Judah Adelson, "The Vermont Democratic-Republican Societies and the French Revolution," *Vermont History* 32, no. 1 (1964): 3–23; Jeffrey A. Davis, "Guarding the Republican Interest: The Western Pennsylvania Democratic Societies and the Excise Tax," *Pennsylvania History* 67, no. 1 (2000): 43–62; Marco Sioli, "Citizen Genet and Political Struggle in the Early American Republic," *Revue Française d'Etudes Americaines*, no. 64 (1995): 259–67; Marco M. Sioli, "The Democratic Republican Societies at the End of the Eighteenth Century: The Western Pennsylvania Experience," *Pennsylvania History* 60, no. 3 (1993): 288–304.

7. "Republicans Rejoice!"; Thomas Jefferson, "First Inaugural Address," in Jefferson, *Writings*, 493. On Federalist attitudes, see Marshall Smelser, "The Jacobin Phrenzy: Federalism and the Menace of Liberty, Equality, and Fraternity," *Review of Politics* 13 (1951): 457–82; Marc Lendler, "'Equally Proper at All Times and at All Times Necessary': Civility, Bad Tendency, and the Sedition Act," *Journal of the Early Republic* 24, no. 3 (2004): 419–44; James P. Martin, "When Repression Is Democratic and Constitutional: The Federalist Theory of Representation and the Sedition Act of 1798," *University of Chicago Law Review* 66, no. 1 (1999): 117–82; Neem, "Freedom of Association in the Early Republic"; Paul Douglas Newman, "The Federalists' Cold War: The Fries Rebellion, National Security, and the State, 1787–1800," *Pennsylvania History* 67, no. 1 (2000): 63–104; Whitman H. Ridgway, "Fries in the Federalist Imagination: A Crisis of Republican Society," *Pennsylvania History* 67, no. 1 (2000): 141–60.

8. "Selected Toasts"; Sharp, *American Politics in the Early Republic*, 276–88; Hofstadter, *Idea of a Party System*, 122–69.

9. Jeffery A. Smith, *War and Press Freedom: The Problem of Prerogative Power* (New York: Oxford University Press, 1999), 75–125 (91–92 quoted); John Nerone, *Violence Against the Press: Policing the Public Sphere in U.S. History* (New York: Oxford University Press, 1994), 53–83; Harold L. Nelson, ed., *Freedom of the Press from Hamilton to the Warren Court* (Indianapolis: Bobbs-Merrill, 1967), 41; Jeffrey L. Pasley, *"The Tyranny of Printers": Newspaper Politics in the Early American Republic* (Charlottesville: University of Virginia Press, 2001), 259–82. Even the radical abolitionists, whose voices were muffled by mail bans, congressional gags, and violence under the Federalists and the Jacksonian Democrats, were never subjected to a federal sedition law. The worst example of "false equivalence," with a dash of role reversal, can be found in Levy, *Jefferson and Civil Liberties.*

10. "Selected Toasts"; Jefferson, "First Inaugural Address," 494–95.

11. While trying to make a broader and different point, much of what follows draws freely on certain sections of my recent book, Jeffrey L. Pasley, *The First Presidential Contest: 1796 and the Founding of American Democracy* (Lawrence: University Press of Kansas, 2013); and an earlier article (never available to a scholarly audience), Jeffrey L. Pasley, "Popular Constitutionalism in Philadelphia: How Freedom of Expression Was Secured

by Two Fearless Newspaper Editors," *Pennsylvania Legacies* 8, no. 1 (May 2008): 6–11, which in turn represents an evolution of the thinking behind Pasley, "*Tyranny of Printers*," chaps. 4–8.

12. Popular constitutionalism is a much-debated issue in legal academia, and I do not really mean to engage it here or make any normative arguments for popular constitutionalism versus judicial review, but see Christian G. Fritz, *American Sovereigns: The People and America's Constitutional Tradition Before the Civil War* (New York: Cambridge University Press, 2008); Larry Kramer, *The People Themselves: Popular Constitutionalism and Judicial Review* (New York: Oxford University Press, 2004). I am more influenced by social historians of the American Revolution, as seen in such works as Alfred F. Young, "The Framers of the Constitution and the 'Genius' of the People," *Radical History Review* 42 (1988): 8–18; and Alfred F. Young, Gary B. Nash, and Ray Raphael, eds., *Revolutionary Founders: Rebels, Radicals, and Reformers in the Making of the Nation* (New York: Alfred A. Knopf, 2011). My claim would simply be that, historically, other than judicial means of constitutional enforcement were live options in the eighteenth century, and that the election of 1800 was the popular method by which the Federalist interpretation of the Constitution was struck down.

13. Edward Dumbauld, "State Precedents for the Bill of Rights," *Journal of Public Law* 7 (1958): 323–44, quotation on 328n27; Willi-Paul Adams, *The First American Constitutions: Republican Ideology and the Making of the State Constitutions in the Revolutionary Era* (Chapel Hill: University of North Carolina Press for the Institute of Early American History and Culture, Williamsburg, Virginia, 1980); Gordon S. Wood, *The Creation of the American Republic, 1776–1787* (New York: W. W. Norton, 1972), 271–73.

14. Wood, *Creation of the American Republic*, 536–43; Young, "Framers of the Constitution." For a sober view that makes a good case for what constitutional limitations Hamilton did believe in, see Max M. Edling, *A Revolution in Favor of Government: Origins of the U.S. Constitution and the Making of the American State* (Oxford: Oxford University Press, 2003).

15. Jacob E. Cooke, ed., *The Federalist* (Middletown, CT: Wesleyan University Press, 1961), 578–80.

16. Alexander Hamilton, "Opinion on the Constitutionality of a National Bank," February 23, 1791, in *The Papers of Alexander Hamilton*, ed. Harold C. Syrett and Jacob E. Cooke, 26 vols. (New York: Columbia University Press, 1961), 8:97–106.

17. Dumbauld, "State Precedents," 337–38. Many of Madison's fellow Constitution supporters were disgusted with his cave-in on the Bill of Rights question, so the committee that considered his amendments in the First Congress stripped them down even further in hopes of avoiding any reductions in the new government's powers or freedom of action. Kenneth R. Bowling, "'A Tub to the Whale': The Founding Fathers and the Adoption of the Federal Bill of Rights," *Journal of the Early Republic* 8, no. 3 (1988): 223–51.

18. Hamilton, "Opinion on the Constitutionality of a National Bank," and Jefferson to Washington, May 23, 1792, in Jefferson, *Writings*, 416, 988.

19. Quotations from "To Mr. George Latimer, Chairman of the Committee of Correspondence," *National Gazette*, August 25, 1792; "Rules," part 2, *National Gazette*, July 7, 1792; Philip M. Marsh, ed., *The Prose of Philip Freneau* (New Brunswick, NJ: Scarecrow Press, 1955), 284, 290.

20. James D. Tagg, *Benjamin Franklin Bache and the Philadelphia "Aurora"* (Philadelphia: University of Pennsylvania Press, 1991); Jeffery A. Smith, *Franklin and Bache: Envisioning the Enlightened Republic* (New York: Oxford University Press, 1990).

21. On the transatlantic radicals and their role in the Democratic-Republican opposition, and especially the press, see Michael Durey, *Transatlantic Radicals and the Early American Republic* (Lawrence: University Press of Kansas, 1997); Michael Durey, *"With the Hammer of Truth": James Thomson Callender and America's Early National Heroes* (Charlottesville: University of Virginia Press, 1990); Michael Durey, "Thomas Paine's Apostles: Radical Emigrés and the Triumph of Jeffersonian Republicanism," *William and Mary Quarterly* 3d ser., 44 (1987): 661–88; Kim Tousley Phillips, *William Duane, Radical Journalist in the Age of Jefferson* (New York: Garland, 1989); Seth Cotlar, *Tom Paine's America: The Rise and Fall of Transatlantic Radicalism in the Early Republic* (Charlottesville: University of Virginia Press, 2011); Richard N. Rosenfeld, *American Aurora: A Democratic-Republican Returns; The Suppressed History of Our Nation's Beginnings and the Heroic Newspaper That Tried to Report It* (New York: St. Martin's Press, 1997); Richard J. Twomey, *Jacobins and Jeffersonians: Anglo-American Radicalism in the United States, 1790–1820* (New York: Garland, 1989); and Marcus Daniel, *Scandal and Civility: Journalism and the Birth of American Democracy* (New York: Oxford University Press, 2009).

22. James D. Tagg, "Benjamin Franklin Bache's Attack on George Washington," *Pennsylvania Magazine of History and Biography* 100, no. 2 (1976): 191–230; Jeffrey L. Pasley, "Thomas Paine and the U.S. Election of 1796: In Which It Is Discovered That George Washington Was More Popular Than Jesus," July 2009, http://www.common-place.org/pasley/wp-content/uploads/2009/07/pasley_paine1796.pdf. Quotation from Thomas Paine, *Letter to George Washington, President of the United States of America. On Affairs Public and Private* (Philadelphia: Benj. Franklin Bache, 1796), 12.

23. The key document was Smith's widely reprinted newspaper series and two-part pamphlet, *The Pretensions of Thomas Jefferson to the Presidency Examined; and the Charges Against John Adams Refuted. Addressed to the Citizens of America in General; and Particularly to the Electors of the President* (Philadelphia: [John Fenno], 1796). For quotations, see Pasley, *First Presidential Contest*, 254, 272.

24. Pasley, *First Presidential Contest*, 262–63; James D. Richardson, *A Compilation of the Messages and Papers of the Presidents* (Washington, D.C.: Bureau of National Literature and Art, 1908), 1:220–21; John Fea, *Was America Founded as a Christian Nation? A Historical Introduction* (Louisville, KY: Westminster John Knox Press, 2011), 171–90; Douglass Adair, "Was Alexander Hamilton a Christian Statesman?," in Adair, *Fame and the Founding Fathers* (New York: W. W. Norton for the Institute of Early American History and Culture, 1974), 141–59.

25. J. M. Smith, *Freedom's Fetters*, 6; Richardson, *Messages and Papers of the Presidents*, 1:226, 240–41.

26. Annals of Congress, 5th Cong., 2d sess., House of Representatives, May 2, 1798, 1569–70; J. M. Smith, *Freedom's Fetters*, 26–29; Baseler, *"Asylum for Mankind,"* 267–78.

27. Annals of Congress, 5th Cong, 2d sess., House of Representatives, June 16, 1798, 1957–58, 1986–87; J. M. Smith, *Freedom's Fetters*, 68–75; Baseler, *"Asylum for Mankind,"* 277–83. The problem was that the Framers of the Constitution had failed to make any mention of powers over resident aliens at all, except for the euphemistic ban on the prohibition of the international slave trade, which referred to the "emigration or importation of such persons" as the states thought proper to admit. This created the somewhat nonsensical possibility that the states had charge of border control and also put the Federalists in the unintended position of seeming to directly threaten slavery.

28. J. M. Smith, *Freedom's Fetters*, 99–101; Alexander Addison, *Liberty of Speech and Press: A Charge to the Grand Juries of the County Courts of the Fifth Circuit of the State of Pennsylvania* (Washington, PA: John Colerick, for the Author, 1798), 18, 19; Alexander Hamilton, *Observations on Certain Documents Contained in No. V & VI of "The History of the United States for the Year 1796," in Which the Charge of Speculation Against Alexander Hamilton, Late Secretary of the Treasury, is Fully Refuted* (Philadelphia: Printed for John Fenno, by John Bioren, 1797), 3.

29. J. M. Smith, *Freedom's Fetters*, 99–111; Annals of Congress, 5th Cong., 2d sess., House of Representatives, June 16, 1798, 1957–58, 2093–94.

30. Philadelphia *Aurora General Advertiser*, July 19, 1798.

31. Vernon Stauffer, *New England and the Bavarian Illuminati* (New York: Columbia University Press, 1918); David Brion Davis, *The Fear of Conspiracy: Images of Un-American Subversion from the Revolution to the Present* (Ithaca, NY: Cornell University Press, 1971), 35–54. See also my entries for "Alien and Sedition Acts" and "Jedidiah Morse" in Peter Knight, ed., *Conspiracy Theories in American History: An Encyclopedia* (Santa Barbara, CA: ABC-CLIO, 2003), 49–55, 511–13.

32. *The Claims of Thomas Jefferson to the Presidency, Examined at the Bar of Christianity* (Philadelphia: Asbury Dickins, 1800); John M. Mason, *The Voice of Warning, to Christians, on the Ensuing Election of a President of the United States* (New York: G. F. Hopkins, 1800); William Linn, *Serious Considerations on the Election of a President: Addressed to the Citizens of the United States* (New York: John Furman, 1800), 20.

33. Annals of Congress, 5th Cong., 2d sess., House of Representatives, July 10, 1798, 2153; Mason, *Voice of Warning*, 26–27. On the Standing Order and the close relationship between the Congregational clergy and the Federalist Party, see Jonathan D. Sassi, *A Republic of Righteousness: The Public Christianity of the Post-Revolutionary New England Clergy* (New York: Oxford University Press, 2001); Richard J. Purcell, *Connecticut in Transition, 1775–1818*, vol. 2 (Middletown, CT: Wesleyan University Press, 1963); Christopher Grasso, *A Speaking Aristocracy: Transforming Public Discourse in Eighteenth-Century Connecticut* (Chapel Hill: University of North Carolina Press

for the Omohundro Institute of Early American History and Culture, 1999); Anson Ely Morse, *The Federalist Party in Massachusetts to the Year 1800* (Princeton, NJ: Princeton University Library, 1909); James King Morse, *Jedidiah Morse: A Champion of New England Orthodoxy* (New York: AMS Press, 1967); Peter S. Field, *The Crisis of the Standing Order: Clerical Intellectuals and Cultural Authority in Massachusetts, 1780–1833* (Amherst: University of Massachusetts Press, 1998).

34. On Lyon, see Aleine Austin, *Matthew Lyon: "New Man" of the Democratic Revolution, 1749–1822* (University Park: Pennsylvania State University Press, 1981).

35. Phillips, *William Duane*, 54–95; Pasley, *"Tyranny of Printers,"* 176–95.

36. Pasley, *"Tyranny of Printers,"* 176–95; Alan V. Briceland, "The Philadelphia *Aurora*, the New England Illuminati, and the Election of 1800," *Pennsylvania Magazine of History and Biography* 100, no. 1 (January 1976): 3–36; Robert J. Imholt, "Timothy Dwight, Federalist Pope of Connecticut," *New England Quarterly* 73, no. 3 (2000): 386–411.

37. "Republican Fete," New York *American Citizen*, March 6, 1801.

38. My admittedly "Jeffersonian" interpretation nevertheless aims to be consistent with recent seminal works recovering the lost history and influence of the American state, such as Brian Balogh, *A Government out of Sight: The Mystery of National Authority in Nineteenth-Century America* (New York: Cambridge University Press, 2009); William J. Novak, *The People's Welfare: Law and Regulation in Nineteenth-Century America* (Chapel Hill: University of North Carolina Press, 1996); Richard R. John, "Governmental Institutions as Agents of Change: Rethinking American Political Development in the Early Republic, 1787–1835," *Studies in American Political Development* 11 (1997): 347–80; and Richard R. John, *Spreading the News: The American Postal System from Franklin to Morse* (Cambridge, MA: Harvard University Press, 1995). My own small contribution to this literature, and a caveat to the argument presented in this chapter, can be found in Jeffrey L. Pasley, "Midget on Horseback: American Indians and the History of the American State," *Common-Place* 9, no. 1 (October 2008), http://www.common-place.org/vol-09/no-01/pasley/.

39. Jefferson, "First Inaugural Address," 493. On the speech, see Stephen Howard Browne, *Jefferson's Call for Nationhood: The First Inaugural Address* (College Station: Texas A&M University Press, 2003).

40. Noble E. Cunningham, Jr., *The Process of Government Under Jefferson* (Princeton, NJ: Princeton University Press, 1978); Balogh, *Government out of Sight*, 109–10; Alexander DeConde, *This Affair of Louisiana* (Baton Rouge: Louisiana State University Press, 1978), 139–41; Jan Lewis, "'The Blessings of Domestic Society': Thomas Jefferson's Family and the Transformation of American Politics," in *Jeffersonian Legacies*, ed. Peter S. Onuf (Charlottesville: University of Virginia Press, 1993); Drew R. McCoy, *The Elusive Republic: Political Economy in Jeffersonian America* (New York: W. W. Norton, 1982), chaps. 8 and 9.

41. Kyo Ho Youm, "The Impact of 'People v. Croswell' on Libel Law," *Journalism Monographs* 113 (June 1989): 1–24; Robert W. T. Martin, "Reforming Republicanism:

Alexander Hamilton's Theory of Republican Citizenship and Press Liberty," *Journal of the Early Republic* 25, no. 1 (2005): 21–46; William E. Nelson, *Marbury v. Madison: The Origins and Legacy of Judicial Review* (Lawrence: University Press of Kansas, 2000); R. Kent Newmyer, *John Marshall and the Heroic Age of the Supreme Court* (Baton Rouge: Louisiana State University Press, 2001).

42. Baseler, *"Asylum for Mankind,"* 287–310; ed. Barbara Oberg, *The Papers of Thomas Jefferson*, vol. 36, *1 December 1801 to 3 March 1802*, (Princeton, NJ: Princeton University Press, 2009), 253–58; John Keane, *Tom Paine: A Political Life* (Boston: Little, Brown, 1995), 469–74; John B. Boles, *The Great Revival: Beginnings of the Bible Belt* (Lexington: University Press of Kentucky, 1996); Noble E. Cunningham, Jr., *The Jeffersonian Republicans in Power: Party Operations, 1801–1809* (Chapel Hill: University of North Carolina Press for the Institute of Early American History and Culture, 1963); Pasley, *"Tyranny of Printers,"* 196–228; Taylor, "From Fathers to Friends."

43. Chilton Williamson, *American Suffrage: From Property to Democracy, 1760–1860* (Princeton, NJ: Princeton University Press, 1960); Alexander Keyssar, *The Right to Vote: The Contested History of Democracy in the United States* (New York: Basic Books, 2000). On the party press of the nineteenth century, see Culver H. Smith, *The Press, Politics, and Patronage: The American Government's Use of Newspapers, 1789–1875* (Athens: University of Georgia Press, 1977); Gerald J. Baldasty, "The Press and Politics in the Age of Jackson," *Journalism Monographs* 89 (1984): 1–28; Mark Wahlgren Summers, *The Press Gang: Newspapers and Politics, 1863–1878* (Chapel Hill: University of North Carolina Press, 1994).

2. The Bombshell of 1844

1. Lee Benson, *The Concept of Jacksonian Democracy: New York as a Test Case* (Princeton, NJ: Princeton University Press, 1961).

2. Daniel Walker Howe, *What Hath God Wrought: The Transformation of America, 1815–1848* (New York: Oxford University Press, 2007), 682. Howe draws heavily on Gary Kornblith's "Rethinking the Coming of the Civil War: A Counterfactual Exercise," *Journal of American History* 90 (2003): 76–105. See also Amy S. Greenberg, *A Wicked War: Polk, Clay, Lincoln, and the 1846 U.S. Invasion of Mexico* (New York: Alfred A. Knopf, 2012). Numerous essential older studies cover or otherwise illuminate the election. Those on which I have relied most heavily, albeit selectively, include James C. N. Paul, *Rift in the Democracy* (Philadelphia: University of Pennsylvania Press, 1951); Charles G. Sellers, *James K. Polk, Continentalist, 1843–1846* (Princeton, NJ: Princeton University Press, 1966) ; Sellers, "Election of 1844," in *History of American Presidential Elections, 1789–1968*, ed. Arthur M. Schlesinger, Jr. (New York: Chelsea House, 1971), 745–861; Frederick Merk, *Fruits of Propaganda in the Tyler Administration* (Cambridge, MA: Harvard University Press, 1971); Merk, *Slavery and the Annexation of Texas* (New York: Alfred A. Knopf, 1972); William J. Cooper, Jr., *The South and the Politics of Slavery, 1828–1856* (Baton Rouge, LA: Louisiana State University Press, 1978); Norma Lois Peterson, *The Presidencies of William Henry Harrison and John Tyler* (Lawrence, KS:

University Press of Kansas, 1989); William W. Freehling, *The Road to Disunion: Secessionists at Bay, 1776–1854* (New York: Oxford University Press, 1990); Michael A. Morrison, "Westward the Curse of Empire: Texas Annexation and the Whig Party," *Journal of the Early Republic* 10 (1990): 221–49; Morrison, "Martin Van Buren, the Democracy, and the Partisan Politics of Texas Annexation," *Journal of Southern History* 61 (1995): 695–722; Michael F. Holt, *The Rise and Fall of the American Whig Party: Jacksonian Politics and the Onset of the Civil War* (New York: Oxford University Press, 1999); and Joel H. Silbey, *Storm over Texas: The Annexation Controversy and the Coming of the Civil War* (New York: Oxford University Press, 2005). In addition, I have benefited from John Niven, *John C. Calhoun and the Price of Union: A Biography* (Baton Rouge, LA: Louisiana State University Press, 1988); Irving H. Barlett, *John C. Calhoun: A Biography* (New York: W.W. Norton, 1993); Donald B. Cole, *Martin Van Buren and the American Political System* (Princeton, NJ: Princeton University Press, 1984); Merrill D. Peterson, *The Great Triumvirate: Webster, Clay, and Calhoun* (New York: Oxford University Press, 1987); and Robert V. Remini, *Henry Clay: Statesman for the Union* (New York: W.W. Norton, 1991). I have also adapted and modified my interpretation in *The Rise of American Democracy: Jefferson to Lincoln* (New York: W.W. Norton, 2005), 566–76.

3. Joel H. Silbey, *The Shrine of Party: Congressional Voting Behavior, 1841–1852* (Pittsburgh, PA: University of Pittsburgh Press, 1967).

4. On "revisionists" versus "fundamentalists," see Edward L. Ayers, *What Caused the Civil War: Reflections on the South and Southern History* (New York: W. W. Norton, 2005), 132–33, as supplemented by Elizabeth R. Varon, *Disunion! The Coming of the Civil War* (Chapel Hill, NC: University of North Carolina Press, 2009), 3–5.

5. John Quincy Adams Diaries, February 20, 1820, vol. 31, 269, Massachusetts Historical Society, at http://www.masshist.org/jqadiaries/doc.cfm?id=jqad31_269.

6. Michael F. Holt, *The Political Crisis of the 1850s* (New York: John Wiley & Sons, 1978), 37.

7. Clay quoted in Remini, *Clay*, 593.

8. On Calhoun's preparing Upshur to become secretary of state, see Calhoun to Duff Green, February [March] 19, 1843, in *The Papers of John C. Calhoun*, ed. Robert L. Meriwether et al., 28 vols. (Columbia: University of South Carolina Press for the South Caroliniana Society, 1959–2003), 17:125.

9. Clay to John J. Crittenden, December 5, 1843, in Robert Seager II, ed., *The Papers of Henry Clay*, 10 vols. (Lexington, KY: University Press of Kentucky, 1988), 9:897–98.

10. Clay to Leverett Saltonstall, ibid., 9:896. It seems unlikely that Clay and Van Buren reached any formal agreement, although Clay did later assume that Van Buren, like himself, would not endorse immediate annexation. As Van Buren had been ducking the Texas issue since the beginning of his presidency, the assumption would have been reasonable even without a mutual promise. See Remini, *Clay*, 613.

11. Merk, *Slavery*, 22.

12. Calhoun to [Abel P.] Upshur, August 27, 1843, in Meriwether et al., *Papers of John C. Calhoun*, 17:381–83. Covering his tracks, Calhoun also instructed Upshur on how to ensure that the propaganda campaign appeared to be emanating from Virginia rather than from the Calhoun camp, which "would do more harm than good" (quotation on 382). It is highly likely, as was widely believed at the time, that Upshur himself wrote some of the pro-Texas articles in the Tyler administration's chief organ, the *Madisonian*, especially the most fiery of them. See Merk, *Slavery*, 35.

13. On February 15, Clay reported with surprise of learning that forty-two senators supported annexation, comfortably more than the two-thirds necessary to ratify the treaty. A month earlier, Upshur had assured the U.S. chargé in Texas, William S. Murphy, that the necessary Senate votes were there. Clay to John J. Crittenden, February 15, 1844, in Seager, *Papers of Henry Clay*, 10:6–7.

14. Senator Thomas Hart Benton, a fierce opponent of Calhoun, later reported seeing Gilmer carrying Jackson's letter into the House of Representatives, "with many expressions of now confident triumph over Mr. Van Buren." Benton also charged that the letter was a cog in an elaborate Calhounite conspiracy, hatched early in 1843 if not before, to get Jackson on record in favor of immediate annexation. As Benton offered scant evidence for some of his claims, historians have been skeptical. Given the timing, though, it is almost certain that Gilmer and Brown were coordinating their efforts in order to get Jackson's endorsement; it is even likely that Gilmer wrote his original published remarks with the aim of having Brown solicit Jackson's views. Benton was convinced that Gilmer was working on Calhoun's behalf from the start. Whatever the truth of that, Benton's remark about seeing Gilmer with Jackson's letter is entirely credible. Benton, *Thirty Years' View; or, A History of the Workings of the American Government for Thirty Years, from 1820 to 1850*, 2 vols. (185456; New York: D. Appleton & Co., 1873), 2:584.

15. Letcher to Martin Van Buren, September 23, 1843, Martin Van Buren Papers, Library of Congress. On the Calhounites' plotting over Texas in 1843, see also Andrew Stevenson to Van Buren, October 17, 1843; W[illiam] H. Roane to Van Buren, October 17, 1843; J[ohn] Bragg to Van Buren, October 28, 1843; ibid. In December, the Calhounites obtained a letter from Calhoun warmly supporting immediate annexation; see note 16 in this chapter.

16. For Upshur informing Calhoun through Maxcy, as well as on Gilmer and Upshur supporting Calhoun, see R[obert] M. T. Hunter to John C. Calhoun, September 1, 1844; Calhoun to Hunter, September 12, 1843; and Virgil Maxcy to Calhoun, December 10, 1843 (quotation on 602), in Meriwether et al., *Papers of John C. Calhoun*, 17:393, 433, 599–603. For related machinations, see Hunter to Calhoun, May 23 and September 1, 1843; Calhoun to Hunter, December 22, 1843; Maxcy to Calhoun, December 10, 1843; ibid., 17:186, 392–94, 636–37. In mid-December, Gilmer, now firmly if secretly in Calhoun's camp, undertook a stilted, formulaic exchange with Calhoun, in part to inform him that negotiations with the Texans had begun and in part to solicit a pro-annexation letter. The exchange, which almost certainly was prearranged, could only have been

part of the preparations for the Democratic National Convention. Calhoun requested that Gilmer not send his letter to any newspaper, but he added that he wanted his views known and that Gilmer "should show this to any friend you may think proper." Much as Brown and Gilmer were holding off publishing Jackson's response to Gilmer's pro-annexation letter, so Calhoun wanted to make sure his views went unpublished—at least for the time being. Thomas W. Gilmer to Calhoun, December 13, 1843; Calhoun to Gilmer, December 25, 1843; in Meriwether et al., *Papers of John C. Calhoun*, 17:605–6, 640–42 (quotation on 642). See also Peterson, *Presidencies*, 187.

17. Maxcy to Calhoun, December 3, 1843; Hunter to Calhoun, January 19, 1844; in Meriwether et al., *Papers of John C. Calhoun*, 17:585–86 (quotation on 586), 714–16 (quotation on 715); Van Buren to Andrew Jackson, January 13, 1844, Van Buren Papers.

18. Lewis to [Richard K. Crallé], March 19, 1844, in Meriwether et al., *Papers of John C. Calhoun*, 17: 879. See also Lewis to Calhoun, March 6, 1844; Hunter to Calhoun, March 8, 1844; ibid., 17:821–25, 842–45. Lewis, among others, told Calhoun bluntly that "a ground swell from the people themselves growing out of the Texas question may roll you into the position of a Candidate." The Senate helped to force Calhoun's hand by unanimously confirming his appointment before he even learned he had been selected. (Benton was absent, or there would certainly have been one negative vote.) Historians have long disagreed over Tyler's attitude toward Calhoun and whether Wise's advice was decisive in getting the president to select him. Clearly, though, Wise was among the first to raise the possibility, as, immediately after the *Princeton* disaster, he sought out the South Carolina congressman and Calhoun protégé George McDuffie to ask about Calhoun's availability. Given Wise's perceived closeness to Tyler, that approach would have been interpreted as an inquiry from Tyler himself—and so by the time Wise spoke to Tyler, Calhoun's appointment was something of a fait accompli. See Henry A. Wise to Hunter, March 7, 1844, ibid., 17:844. When Tyler's choice to replace Upshur as secretary of the navy, David Henshaw, failed to win Senate confirmation in February 1844, the president considered both Maxcy and Gilmer for the job and finally decided on Gilmer. Ten days later, Gilmer and Maxcy died in the *Princeton* explosion.

19. James Wishart to Calhoun, March 28, 1844, ibid., 17:899–902 (quotation on 901).

20. Walker to F. P. Blair, April 13, 1844, Robert J. Walker Papers, Darlington Collection, Special Collections Department, University of Pittsburgh. Walker had been pressing Jackson on Texas since January. See Walker to Jackson, January 10, 1844, ibid. For Clay's sense of Van Buren's position at this point in the drama, see Clay to John J. Crittenden, April 21, 1844, in Seager, *Papers of Henry Clay*, 10:47–48.

21. Blair to Van Buren, March 18, 1844, Van Buren Papers.

22. Pakenham to Upshur, February 26, 1844, in Meriwether et al., *Papers of John C. Calhoun*, 28:52–55 (quotation on 53).

23. Calhoun to Pakenham, April 18, 1844, ibid., 28:273–78 (quotation on 277).

24. Historians, including virtually all of those mentioned in note 2 in this chapter, have long argued over Calhoun's motivations in writing the letter and then sending it

to the Senate. In line with the multivalent ways that Calhoun normally operated, he probably had several motives all at once. He was certainly troubled about how the southern Whigs would vote on the annexation treaty, and one of his motives was to force them into line, as Calhoun himself disclosed in a private letter to then governor of South Carolina, James H. Hammond (Calhoun to [James H.] Hammond, May 17, 1844, ibid., 18:533–34). In the same letter, Calhoun also stated that he hoped to attract western as well as southern Whigs to the treaty's cause. Had he managed that—and if all of the Whigs from the slaveholding border states are included—he would have been assured of eighteen out of the twenty-eight Whig votes in the Senate, bringing the total (if combined with all of the Democratic senators outside the North) within shouting distance of ratification. Many observers, then and since, however, have argued that by cracking the whip over slavery, Calhoun's letter actually destroyed the treaty's chances by alienating otherwise sympathetic northerners. This view, however, slights the political context as well as Calhoun's longtime tactics of choice vis-à-vis the North. Before Calhoun wrote his letter to Pakenham, the treaty's chances of gaining the Senate's approval had grown slender. Even if Calhoun managed to unite the South and win over the western Whigs, the tiny margins would have required gaining the votes of on the order of four to six northern senators, a difficult but not impossible proposition. And given that intimidation of the North had proven so successful in the past, Calhoun may have hoped that the Pakenham letter would achieve that too. By replying to Pakenham (and Aberdeen) so discordantly, he might also have hoped to provoke a strong British response, which in turn would push the country, in its customary Anglophobia, to support the treaty. In addition, he also might well have aimed simply, with his usual syllogistic logic, to make explicit the fears of British abolitionism that underlay the administration's argument in favor of immediate annexation. But as William J. Cooper, among many others, contends, whatever else Calhoun hoped to accomplish, "without any doubt he wanted to hurt Van Buren in any way he could." See appendix A in Cooper, *The South*, 375–76, as well as the judicious interpretation in Peterson, *Presidencies*, 229–60.

25. Webster to Robert Charles Winthrop, April 28, 1844, in Charles M. Wiltse, ed., *The Papers of Daniel Webster: Correspondence*, vol. 6 (Hanover, NH: University Press of New England for Dartmouth College, 1984), 46.

26. Stephens quoted in Holt, *Rise and Fall*, 172.

27. Butler to Van Buren, March 29, 1844, Van Buren Papers.

28. Wright to Van Buren, April 11, 1844, Van Buren Papers. Since his defeat in 1840, Van Buren had been increasingly entertaining the view, expressed by one associate in connection to Texas, that the experience of the previous four decades had proved that "the more the Northern Democracy yields to the South, the more she demands." Jabez D. Hammond to Van Buren, April 7, 1844, ibid.

29. The timing raises an abiding if unanswerable question: What would Van Buren have done had he been privy to Calhoun's provocative letter to Pakenham, dated two days before his own letter to Hammet? Might Calhoun's explicit connection of annexation and proslavery brought out the old placater in Van Buren and pushed him to

write a marginally pro-annexation letter, albeit with the many qualifications he included in the letter he did write? Or might he have written a letter that took personal as well as political offense at Calhoun's proslavery manipulation, opposed immediate annexation with heavy qualifications, and tried to use the Pakenham letter as a means to discredit Calhoun and his supporters, even in the South, as divisive extremists? Either course, though, would have entailed enormous risks, which underscores the effectiveness of Calhoun's maneuver.

30. Calhoun to Hunter, May [1], 1844, in Meriwether et al., *Papers of John C. Calhoun*, 18; 384.

31. Bancroft to Van Buren, May 21, 1844; Roane to Van Buren, April 30, 1844, Van Buren Papers.

32. Benton quoted in Sellers, *Polk, Continentalist*, 59; Mangum to Paul Cameron, February 10, 1844, quoted in Holt, *Rise and Fall*, 165. Continuing battles in the Congress over the House's gag rule (which finally fell in 1844) as well as over the tariff had further alienated southern Democrats from Van Buren as well as from northern Democrats generally. With the gag rule fight, slavery and antislavery entered into the 1844 election in more ways than one.

33. Johnson, who had served as Van Buren's vice president, had taken as his common law wife an octoroon slave whom he had inherited from his father, and who bore him two daughters. Johnson's open arrangement scandalized much of the slave South.

34. Saunders had supported and advised Calhoun during the latter's presidential bid and after. See R[omulus] M. Saunders to Calhoun, August 26, October 9, 1843, and March 8, 1844, in Meriwether et al., *Papers of John C. Calhoun*, 17:380–81, 494, 845–46.

35. Calhoun quoted in Barlett, *Calhoun*, 316.

36. O'Sullivan to Van Buren, May 29, 1844, quoted in Sellers, *Polk, Continentalist*, 93.

37. Remarks of S.W. Trotti (1844), reported in Congressional Globe, Appendix, 31st Cong., 1st sess., 178; Pickens to James Edward Calhoun, September 14, 1844, quoted in Cooper, *The South*, 206. After Wright refused, the convention, in order to balance the ticket, nominated the conservative Pennsylvanian George Dallas, who happened to be related by marriage to Robert J. Walker.

38. In fact, it was the Calhounites who first demanded that Polk pledge himself to a single term, given, as Dixon Lewis wrote, that "we mean to run [Calhoun] in 1848, if alive"; Lewis to F[ranklin] H. Elmore, May 9, 1844, quoted in Sellers, *Polk, Continentalist*, 113.

39. Wright to Benjamin F. Butler, June 8, 1844, Wright-Butler Letters, New York Public Library. Wright also agreed to resign from the Senate and run for governor of New York, a move that would improve Polk's prospects in the all-important Empire State by enlarging Democratic turnout.

40. Pickens to Calhoun, September 9, 1844, in Meriwether et al., *Papers of John C. Calhoun*, 19:728. Several weeks after the convention, Calhoun rejoiced at the rejection of what he called "the New York Dynasty," whose "restoration . . . would well near have

ruined the party and the country." But as Polk was not one of his own, Calhoun would not support him publicly without some assurances and agreements. See Calhoun to Francis Wharton, July 14, 1844, ibid., 19:357.

41. Regular southern Democrats as well as Calhounites echoed Mississippi governor Albert Gallatin Brown's insistence that annexation was necessary to secure "peace in the exercise of [the South's] domestic policy," meaning slavery; Brown quoted in Cooper, *The South*, 196. For a fine interpretation of the ideology of Manifest Destiny among the Democrats, see Edward L. Widmer, *Young America: The Flowering of Democracy in New York City* (New York: Oxford University Press, 1998).

42. Northern Democrats made particularly effective use of the enormously popular pro-annexation pamphlet by Robert J. Walker, *Letter of Mr. Walker, of Mississippi, Relative to the Annexation of Texas*, originally published as an article in the Washington *Globe*, February 3, 1844. Walker was an especially strong advocate of the "diffusion" idea. See Merk, *Fruits*, 95–128.

43. George S. Yerby to Willie P. Mangum, June 29, 1844; Weed to Francis Granger, September 3, 1844; quoted in Holt, *Rise and Fall*, 173, 186.

44. John K. Kane to James K. Polk, July 2, 1844, quoted in Sellers, *Polk, Continentalist*, 121.

45. On Clay and naturalization, see Clay to Thomas Ewing, June 19, 1844, in Seager, *Papers of Henry Clay*, 10:71. Even when he distanced himself from the nativists, Clay was less than unequivocal about allying with them, telling one associate privately only that "I do not belong to the Native American Party, nor have I expressed any opinion in favor of their particular creed." He was certainly happy when the nativists persuaded their backers to support Whig candidates. See Clay to Andrew G. Burt, October 9, 1844; Clay to Peter Sken Smith, October 16, 1844; ibid., 10:131, 133.

46. These figures and those in the next two paragraphs are drawn from Thomas B. Alexander, "The Dimensions of Voter Partisan Constancy in Presidential Elections from 1840 to 1860," in *Essays on American Antebellum Politics, 1840–1860*, ed. Stephen Maizlish and John J. Kushma (College Station, TX: Texas A&M University Press, 1982), 78, 92–93, 116; and Holt, *Rise and Fall*, 195–206.

47. S. M. Chester to Clay, November 13, 1844, quoted in Holt, *Rise and Fall*, 196.

48. In New York, for example, nearly twenty-five thousand more voters voted Democratic in 1844 than four years earlier, compared to only about sixty-five hundred more for the Whigs—a difference almost five times as large as the Democrats' winning margin in the state, and considerably larger than the total vote in New York for the Liberty Party. Similar figures held in Pennsylvania. In April 1845, Clay observed that although "many causes, no doubt concurred to defeat the Whigs last fall," he believed, above all, that except for "the existence of the Native American party," the Whigs would have won. Clay to Dudley Selden, April 23, 1845, in Seager, *Papers of Henry Clay*, 10:218.

49. Holt, *Rise and Fall*, 200.

50. After 1840, the Democratic gains were especially impressive in New York, Pennsylvania, Ohio, Indiana, and Illinois. The massive shift of new voters helps explain why

the Democrats increased their total in 1844 compared to 1840 in every northern state but three and outstripped the Whigs among new voters in every northern state except Rhode Island. Between 1840 and 1844, the Massachusetts Whigs actually lost, overall, a sizable number of voters. But at the very end of that period, during the 1844 campaign, the Whigs increased their vote total by upward of ten thousand, whereas the Massachusetts Democrats' vote *declined* by just more than two thousand. Even in New York, where new voters broke to the Democrats in staggering numbers, overall, between 1840 and 1844, the Whigs captured roughly 60 percent of new voters after the Texas controversy began. The Whigs made similar late gains in all of the other northern states except Maine, Indiana, and Illinois.

51. Silbey, *Storm*, 79.

52. The annexation treaty went down to crushing defeat in the Senate by thirty-five nays to fifteen ayes, along strict party lines. Every senator voting in favor was a Democrat; every Whig voted against, along with six antislavery northern Democrats. Congressional Globe, 28th Cong., 1st sess., June 8, 1844, 652.

53. Calhoun to Wharton, November 20, 1844, in Meriwether et al., *Papers of John C. Calhoun*, 20:335–36.

54. Polk to Cave Johnson, December 21, 1844, in "Letters of James K. Polk to Cave Johnson, 1833–1848," *Tennessee Historical Magazine* 1 (1915): 254.

55. On the Calhoun party, the Kansas-Nebraska Act, and the repeal of the Missouri Compromise, see, for example, Charles Eugene Hamlin, *The Life and Times of Hannibal Hamlin* (Cambridge, MA: Riverside Press, 1899), 263–74, esp. 263, 265, 271.

56. Adams Diaries, November 8, 25, 1844, Diary 44, 504, 521, at http://www.masshist.org/jqadiaries/doc.cfm?id=jqad44_504 and http://www.masshist.org/jqadiaries/doc.cfm?id=jqad44_521.

3. Beyond the Realignment Synthesis

1. Examples of the New Political History that made extensive use of realignment theory include Michael F. Holt, *Forging a Majority: The Formation of the Republican Party in Pittsburgh, 1848–1860* (New Haven, CT: Yale University Press, 1969); Mark L. Berger, *The Revolution in the New York Party Systems, 1840–1860* (Port Washington, NY: National University Publications, 1973); Dale Baum, *The Civil War Party System: The Case of Massachusetts, 1848–1876* (Chapel Hill: University of North Carolina Press, 1984); Joel H. Silbey, *The Partisan Imperative: The Dynamics of American Politics Before the Civil War* (New York: Oxford University Press, 1985).

2. Some scholars working within the realignment synthesis argued that the realignment continued into the late 1860s, although usually still nevertheless seeing 1860 as a "critical" election. See, for example, Steven Hansen, *The Making of the Third Party System: Voters and Parties in Illinois, 1850–1876* (Ann Arbor: Michigan University Press, 1980). Most, however, saw voter loyalties as fixed into new patterns after 1860. See Joel Silbey, *A Respectable Minority: The Democratic Party in the Civil War Era, 1860–1868* (New York: W. W. Norton, 1977).

3. The pioneering work establishing the ethnocultural approach to the analysis of antebellum politics was Lee Benson, *The Concept of Jacksonian Democracy: New York as a Test Case* (Princeton, NJ: Princeton University Press, 1961).

4. See, for example, Morris Fiorina, *Retrospective Voting in American National Elections* (New Haven, CT: Yale University Press, 1981).

5. David R. Mayhew, *Electoral Realignments: A Critique of an American Genre* (New Haven, CT: Yale University Press, 2002), 153.

6. Walter Dean Burnham, "Party Systems and the Political Process," in *American Party Systems*, ed. Walter Dean Burnham and William A. Chambers (New York: Oxford University Press, 1967), 294.

7. Joel Silbey, *Party over Section: The Rough and Ready Election of 1848* (Lawrence: University Press of Kansas, 2010), nevertheless makes the case that the 1848 election can be fitted into the second party system paradigm.

8. See Michael F. Holt, "An Elusive Synthesis," in *Writing the Civil War: The Quest to Understand*, ed. James McPherson and William J. Cooper, Jr. (Columbia: University of South Carolina Press, 1998), 112–34; Holt, "Change and Continuity in the Party Period," in *Contesting Democracy: Substance and Structure in American Political History, 1775–2000*, ed. Byron E. Shafer and Anthony J. Badger (Lawrence: University Press of Kansas, 2001), 93–115; Holt, *The Political Crisis of the 1850s* (New York: Wiley, 1980); Holt, *The Rise and Fall of the American Whig Party and the Onset of the Civil War* (New York: Oxford University Press, 1999); Holt, *The Fate of Their Country: Politicians, Slavery Extension, and the Coming of the Civil War* (New York: Hill and Wang, 2005).

9. Glenn C. Altschuler and Stuart M. Blumin, *Rude Republic: Americans and Their Politics in the Nineteenth Century* (Princeton, NJ: Princeton University Press, 2000).

10. For critiques, see Richard L. McCormick, *The Party Period and Public Policy: American Politics from the Age of Jackson to the Progressive Era* (New York: Oxford University Press, 1986), 64–88; David R. Mayhew, *Electoral Realignments: A Critique of an American Genre* (New Haven, CT: Yale University Press, 2002).

11. Lincoln to Simeon Francis, Springfield, August 4, 1860, quoted in Roy P. Basler, ed., *The Collected Works of Abraham Lincoln*, 9 vols. (New Brunswick, NJ: Rutgers University Press, 1953–55), 4:90.

12. There were a few exceptions to the sectionalization of the election into a Lincoln/Douglas race in the free states and a Breckinridge/Bell race in the South. In Missouri, California, and Oregon all four main candidates had a realistic chance. There were two northern states in which Breckinridge was strong: Pennsylvania and Connecticut. And in northern Alabama, Douglas polled well, winning four counties (Lauderdale, Lawrence, Madison, and Marshall) in the Tennessee valley.

13. See, for example, *Campaign Plain Dealer and Popular Sovereignty Advocate* (Cincinnati), July 7, 1860, 2.

14. Lincoln to Simeon Francis, Springfield, August 4, 1860, in Basler, *Collected Works*, 4:90.

15. All but 80,000 of the 395,000 Fillmore voters appear to have supported Lincoln in 1860. See William E. Gienapp, "Who Voted for Lincoln?," in *Abraham Lincoln and the American Political Tradition*, ed. John L. Thomas (Amherst: University of Massachusetts Press, 1986), 507; and Gienapp, "Nativism and the Creation of a Republican Majority in the North Before the Civil War," *Journal of American History* 72 (1985): 529–59.

16. "Logical Results of Republicanism," *Democratic Review* 43 (October 1859): 201–17.

17. Peter Knupfer, "A Crisis in Conservatism: Northern Unionism and the Harpers Ferry Raid," in *His Soul Goes Marching On: Responses to John Brown and the Harpers Ferry Raid*, ed. Paul Finkelman (Charlottesville: University of Virginia Press, 1995), 119–48.

18. "Anti-party Glee," in *The Lincoln and Hamlin Songster of the Continental Melodist* (Philadelphia: Fisher and Brother, 1860), 49.

19. Quoted in Douglas R. Egerton, *Year of Meteors: Stephen Douglas, Abraham Lincoln, and the Election That Brought on the Civil War* (New York: Bloomsbury, 2010), 188.

20. Alexis de Tocqueville, *Democracy in America* (New York: Library of America, 2004), chap. 10, 155.

21. *The Ruin of the Democratic Party: Reports of the Covode and Other Committees* (Washington, DC: Republican Congressional Committee, 1860). See also Young Men's Republican Union, *Lincoln and Liberty!*, vol. 2 (June 26, 1860), 4. For a summary of the role of the corruption issue in the election, see Mark W. Summers, *The Plundering Generation: Corruption and the Crisis of the Union* (New York: Oxford University Press, 1987), 270–80.

22. David E. Meerse, "Buchanan, Corruption, and the Election of 1860," *Civil War History* 12 (1966): 124.

23. Quoted in Daniel W. Crofts, *Reluctant Confederates: Upper South Unionists in the Secession Crisis* (Chapel Hill: University of North Carolina Press, 1993), 76–77. On expectations of the creation of a new Union Party, see Michael F. Holt, "Abraham Lincoln and the Politics of Union," in *Abraham Lincoln and the American Political Tradition*, ed. John L. Thomas (Amherst: University of Massachusetts Press, 1986). On Whiggery in the South in 1860, see Holt, *Rise and Fall*, 978–85; Thomas B. Alexander, "Persistent Whiggery in the Confederate South, 1860–1877," *Journal of Southern History* 27, no. 3 (1961): 305–29.

24. Only in California did the Bell vote (7.6 percent) exceed Lincoln's margin of victory. And only in Massachusetts among the free states did the Bell vote replicate the Fillmore total in 1856 (13.2 percent for Bell; 11.5 percent for Fillmore). Conservatives in Massachusetts were more inclined to stick with the party that resembled the Whigs partly because of the strong Whig tradition of that state (Bell's running mate was Edward Everett, a Massachusetts Whig) and partly because of the exceptional radicalism of the Massachusetts Republican Party.

25. As shown most clearly in Jean H. Baker, *James Buchanan* (New York: Times Books, 2004).

26. *New York World*, October 23, 1860.

27. August Belmont to John Forsyth, New York, November 22, 1860, in Belmont, *Letters, Speeches and Addresses of August Belmont*: Privately printed, N.p. 1890), 23–24.

28. *North American*, November 28, 1860.

29. The concept of valence issues was introduced by Donald E. Stokes, "Spatial Models of Party Competition," *American Political Science Review* 57 (1963): 368–77. See also Donald E. Stokes, "Valence Politics," in *Electoral Politics*, ed. Dennis Kavanagh (Oxford: Clarendon Press, 1992).

30. Two recent accounts of the 1860 campaign are Egerton, *Year of Meteors*, and Michael S. Green, *Lincoln and the Election of 1860* (DeKalb: Southern Illinois University Press, 2011).

31. *Illinois State Journal* (Springfield), September 1, 1860; Michael Burlingame, *Abraham Lincoln: A Life*, 2 vols. (Baltimore: Johns Hopkins University Press, 2008), 1:666.

32. *New York Times*, August 28, 1860.

33. *Campaign Plain Dealer and Popular Sovereignty Advocate*, October 17, 1860.

34. Quoted in Egerton, *Year of Meteors*, 187. See also Robert McKnight, *Mission of Republicans: Sectionalism of Modern Democratic Party; Speech of Robert McKnight of Penn., Delivered in the House of Representatives, April 24, 1860* (New York: Republican National Committee, 1860).

35. This point is made in correspondence between Manton Marble and his friend, the lieutenant governor of Rhode Island, Samuel G. Arnold. See, for example, Arnold to Marble, March 20, 1861, Marble Papers, Library of Congress.

36. *New York Times*, July 2, 1860.

37. Abraham Lincoln, [September 16–17, 1859], Notes for speech in Kansas and Ohio, Abraham Lincoln Papers, Library of Congress.

38. Ollinger Crenshaw, *The Slave States in the Presidential Election of 1860* (Baltimore: Johns Hopkins University Press, 1945), 89–111.

39. New York Young Men's Republican Union, *Lincoln and Liberty!*, vol. 3 (July 3, 1860), 3.

40. Republican National Committee, *Homesteads: The Republicans and Settlers Against Democrats and Monopoly* (New York: Republican National Committee, 1860), 1.

41. *New York Tribune*, June 11, 1860.

42. Robert Kelley, *The Transatlantic Persuasion: The Liberal-Democratic Mind in the Age of Gladstone* (New York: Alfred A. Knopf, 1969), xix.

43. Studies of the impact of European political ideas on U.S. politics in the 1850s include Andre M. Fleche, *The Revolution of 1861: The American Civil War in an Age of Nationalist Conflict* (Chapel Hill: University of North Carolina Press, 2012); Timothy Mason Roberts, *Distant Revolutions: 1848 and the Challenge to American Exceptionalism* (Charlottesville: University of Virginia Press, 2009); Mischa Honeck, *We Are the Revolutionists: German-Speaking Immigrants and American Abolitionists After 1848*

(Athens: University of Georgia Press, 2011); Yonatan Eyal, *The Young America Movement and the Transformation of the Democratic Party, 1828–1861* (Cambridge: Cambridge University Press, 2007).

44. Arthur M. Schlesinger, Jr., *The Cycles of American History* (Boston: Houghton Mifflin, 1986).

45. The call for the Republican Party convention in 1860 had gone out not just to "pure" Republicans, as the radicals had wanted, but also to "members of the People's Party of Pennsylvania and of the Opposition Party of New Jersey, and all others who are willing to co-operate." *Proceedings of the Republican National Convention, Held at Chicago, May 16, 17 and 18, 1860* (Albany, NY: Weed, Parsons and Co., 1860), 1.

46. See Adam I. P. Smith, *No Party Now: Politics in the Civil War North* (New York: Oxford University Press, 2006).

47. *Harper's Weekly*, February 25, 1865.

48. George E. Baker, ed., *The Works of William H. Seward*, 5 vols. (Boston; Houghton, Mifflin, 1884), 5:513–14. On expectations of realignment in the aftermath of the war, see LaWanda Cox and John Cox, *Politics, Principle, and Prejudice, 1865–1866* (New York: Free Press, 1963).

4. Markets, Morality, and the Media

For assistance in the preparation of this chapter, I am grateful to Gareth Davies, John Evans, Nancy R. John, Jeffrey Nichols, Walter Nugent, Mark Walgren Summers, Richard Samuel West, and Julian E. Zelizer.

1. Richard R. John, *Network Nation: Inventing American Telecommunications* (Cambridge, MA: Belknap Press of Harvard University Press, 2010), 172.

2. The structural significance of disenfranchisement for post–Civil War electoral politics is a major theme of two monographs by Mark W. Summers: *Rum, Romanism, and Rebellion: The Making of the President, 1884* (Chapel Hill: University of North Carolina Press, 2000), and *Party Games: Getting, Keeping, and Using Power in Gilded Age Politics* (Chapel Hill: University of North Carolina Press, 2004).

3. Cited in Scott C. James, *Presidents, Parties, and the State: A Party System Perspective on Democratic Regulatory Choice, 1884–1936* (Cambridge: Cambridge University Press, 2000), 36.

4. Emil Pocock, "Wet or Dry? The Presidential Election of 1884 in Upstate New York," *New York History* 54 (April 1973): 185.

5. The partisan allegiance of workers in the late nineteenth-century industrial city should not be taken for granted. It would be a mistake, for example, to assume that, all things being equal, workers could be expected to vote the Democratic ticket. Like businessmen, workers had a vested interest in high tariffs, a winning issue for Republicans. In addition, many were Irish Catholics, which, or so party leaders assumed, might predispose them to vote for Blaine. Though Blaine was a Protestant, his mother was a devout Irish Catholic, a fact widely reported in the immigrant press.

6. Summers, *Rum, Romanism, and Rebellion*, 229–35; Edward T. James, "Ben Butler Runs for President: Labor, Greenbackers, and Anti-Monopolists in the Election of 1884," *Essex Institute Historical Collections* 113 (April 1977): 65–88.

7. John, *Network Nation*, chap. 5.

8. Lee Benson, *Merchants, Farmers, and Railroads: Railroad Regulation and New York Politics, 1850–1887* (Cambridge, MA: Harvard University Press, 1953), chap. 8.

9. Francis B. Thurber, *Remarks of F. B. Thurber at the Anti-Monopoly Meeting Held at Tammany Hall New York, October 3, 1881* (New York: n.p., 1881), 7.

10. "The Railroad Bills," *New York Times*, March 10, 1882, 2.

11. Thurber, *Remarks*, 7; James, "Ben Butler," 70.

12. Edwards & Critten, ed., *New York's Great Industries* (New York: Historical Publishing Co., 1885), 112.

13. Pamela Walker Laird, *Advertising Progress: American Business and the Rise of Consumer Marketing* (Baltimore: Johns Hopkins University Press, 1998), 90, 118.

14. Summers, *Rum, Romanism, and Rebellion*, 113–14.

15. Francis B. Thurber, *Democracy and Anti-Monopoly* (New York: n. p., 1883), 9.

16. Cited in David McCullough, *Mornings on Horseback: The Story of an Extraordinary Family, a Vanished Way of Life, and the Unique Child Who Became Theodore Roosevelt* (New York: Simon and Schuster, 1981), 269.

17. "The Anti-Monopolists Do Not Like Mr. Cleveland and His Friends," *Chicago Daily Tribune*, July 15, 1884, 1.

18. "The Other Mr. Thurber's Reasons," *New York Times*, October 11, 1884, 5.

19. "The Anti-Monopoly View," *New York Times*, July 24, 1884, 4.

20. "Serious Suggestions for Workingmen," *Brooklyn Daily Eagle*, October 29, 1884, 4.

21. Francis B. Thurber, "Steam and Electricity," *International Review* 2 (September 1875): 631.

22. "How to Crush Monopoly," *New York Times*, September 22, 1883, 3.

23. Thurber, "Steam and Electricity," 631.

24. "Not Business, but Monopoly," New York *Daily Graphic*, October 11, 1884, 754.

25. Albert C. E. Parker, "Beating the Spread: Analyzing American Election Outcomes," *Journal of American History* 67 (June 1980): 77–78; Geoffrey Blodgett, "The Emergence of Grover: A Fresh Appraisal," *New York History* 73 (April 1992): 165; Lee Benson, *Toward the Scientific Study of History* (Philadelphia: Lippincott, 1972), 14–40.

26. Pocock, "Wet or Dry?," 174–90.

27. Michael E. McGerr, *The Decline of Popular Politics: The American North, 1865–1928* (New York: Oxford University Press, 1986), chaps. 4–5.

28. Summers, *Rum, Romanism, and Rebellion*, 14–17; "Gould, Roach, and Thurber's Trap for Workingmen," *New York Herald*, October 27, 1884, 4.

29. "The Press on the Dinner," *New York Herald*, November 1, 1884, 4. "This is the first time in the history of any party," opined one journalist, "that Jay Gould has openly lent his influence for a particular candidate, and it is only the second or third time that he has ventured to appear at a public banquet."

30. "A Feast of Soap," New York *World*, October 26, 1884, 4.

31. "The Millionaire's Banquet," New York *World*, October 29, 1884, 4.

32. "The Press on the Dinner," *New York Herald*, November 1, 1884, 4.

33. Walt McDougall and Valerian Gribayedoff, "The Royal Feast of Belshazzar Blaine and the Money Kings," New York *World*, October 30, 1884, 1.

34. The circumstances surrounding the composition of the "Royal Feast" remain somewhat mysterious. According to an account published over a decade later in *Printers' Ink*, the cartoon originated as a pen-and-ink mockup, drawn by McDougall, that was around four feet long. The mockup was then photographed so that Gribayedoff could engrave it in a format suitable for mass reproduction in the *World*. McDougall had presumably prepared the mockup well in advance of the dinner, though it is impossible to determine when. The account of its composition that McDougall published many years after the event in his memoir is unreliable. In his memoir, McDougall reminisced that the *World* had run in the previous June an elaborate cartoon of his after he had tried unsuccessfully to sell it to *Puck*. A page-by-page inspection of the *World* for June 1884 failed to locate this cartoon. It is conceivable that McDougall floated this story to conceal the similarity in conception between his cartoon and Joseph Keppler's "Writing on the Wall," an anti-Blaine cartoon on an identical theme that *Puck* featured in June. McDougall envied Keppler's artistry, which far exceeded his own, and may have floated his alternative story in order to distance himself from his rival. Donald Dewey, *The Art of Ill Will: The Story of American Political Cartoons* (New York: New York University Press, 2007), 35; "The Beginning of Illustrated Newspaper Work on New York Papers," *Printers' Ink* 33 (October 1900): 16–17; Walt McDougall, *This Is the Life!* (New York: Alfred A. Knopf, 1926), 96–97.

35. Joseph Keppler, "The Writing on the Wall," *Puck* 15 (June 18, 1885): 199.

36. Thomas Nast, "At His Old Tricks Again out West," *Harper's Weekly* 28 (October 4, 1884): 654; Thomas Nast, "The 'Great American' Game of Public Office for Private Gain," *Harper's Weekly* 28 (August 9, 1884): 523.

37. "Mr. Blaine's Spots," New York *World*, June 18, 1884, 4; "Let Us Hope Not," New York *World*, June 25, 1884, 7; Samuel J. Thomas, "The Tattooed Man Caricatures and the Presidential Campaign of 1884," *Journal of American Culture* 10 (Winter 1987): 1–20.

38. Valerian Gribayedoff, "Pictorial Journalism," *Cosmopolitan* 11 (August 1891): 472.

39. Walt McDougall, "Liberty, Equality, Honesty!," New York *World*, November 8, 1884, 1.

40. James, *Presidents, Parties, and the State*, chap. 2. If one defines "mugwump" narrowly to refer *only* to Republicans who opposed Blaine and backed Cleveland in the 1884 presidential election, then this characterization would exclude both Thurber and Sterne. Thurber backed Butler rather than Cleveland in 1884, and Sterne was a Democrat. If, on the contrary, one follows James and lumps together as "business" mugwumps every New York antimonopolist, then Thurber and Sterne would clearly be included.

41. Rebecca Edwards, Richard R. John, and Richard Bensel, "Forum: Should We Abolish the 'Gilded Age'?," *Journal of the Gilded Age and the Progressive Era* 8, no. 4 (2009): 461–85.

42. Francis B. Thurber, "What Will Bring Prosperity?," *North American Review* 164 (April 1897): 430.

43. Francis B. Thurber, "The Right to Combine," *Journal of Social Science* 37 (December 1899): 225–26.

5. Anglophobia in Nineteenth-Century Elections, Politics, and Diplomacy

1. Sam W. Haynes, *Unfinished Revolution: The Early American Republic in a British World* (Charlottesville: University of Virginia Press, 2010), 2.

2. For a provocative overview, see A. G. Hopkins, "The United States, 1783–1861: Britain's Honorary Dominion?," *Britain and the World* 4, no. 2 (2011): 232–46.

3. Kariann Yokota, *Unbecoming British: How Revolutionary America Became a Postcolonial Nation* (New York: Oxford University Press, 2011).

4. *Oxford English Dictionary*, http://www.oed.com/view/Entry/7599?redirectedFrom=anglophobia#eid.

5. Quoted in Lance Banning, *The Jeffersonian Persuasion: Evolution of Party Ideology* (Ithaca, NY: Cornell University Press, 1978), 238.

6. Peter S. Onuf, *Jefferson's Empire: The Language of American Nationhood* (Charlottesville: University of Virginia Press, 2000), 80–108.

7. Lawrence A. Peskin, "Conspiratorial Anglophobia and the War of 1812," *Journal of American History* 98, no. 3 (December 2011): 647–69.

8. Haynes, *Unfinished Revolution*, 114.

9. Daniel Walker Howe, *The Political Culture of the American Whigs* (Chicago: University of Chicago Press, 1979), 88.

10. Julian Go, *Patterns of Empire: The British and American Empires, 1688 to the Present* (Cambridge: Cambridge University Press, 2011), 48–49.

11. Roy P. Basler (ed.), *The Collected Works of Abraham Lincoln*, 9 vols. (New Brunswick, NJ: Rutgers University Press, 1953–55), 2:324 (October 15, 1858).

12. *Journal of the Convention of the People of South Carolina* (Charleston, SC: Evans and Cogswell, 1861), 334.

13. Stephen Tuffnell, "'Uncle Sam Is to Be Sacrificed': Anglophobia in Late Nineteenth-Century Politics and Culture," *American Nineteenth Century History* 12, no. 1 (March 2011): 77–99; William C. Reuter, "The Anatomy of Political Anglophobia in the United States, 1865–1900," *Mid America* 61 (1979): 117–32.

14. *Diary of George Templeton Strong*, ed. Allan Nevins and Milton Halsey Thomas, 4 vols. (New York: Macmillan, 1952), 3:196–98.

15. Marc-William Palen, "Foreign Relations in the Gilded Age: A British Free-Trade Conspiracy?," *Diplomatic History* 37, no. 2 (March 2013): 217–47; Edward P. Crapol, *America for Americans: Economic Nationalism and Anglophobia in the Late Nineteenth Century* (Westport, CT: Greenwood Press, 1973).

16. Mark W. Summers, *Rum, Romanism, and Rebellion: The Making of a President, 1884* (Chapel Hill: University of North Carolina Press, 2000), 210–22; Palen, "Foreign Relations in the Gilded Age," 239.

17. Democratic Party Platform, 1884.

18. T. C. Hinckley, "George Osgoodby and the Murchison Letter," *Pacific Historical Review* 27, no. 4 (November 1958): 359–70; Lewis L. Gould, "Tariffs and Markets in the Gilded Age," *Reviews in American History* 2, no. 2 (June 1974): 269; Palen, "Foreign Relations in the Gilded Age," 238.

19. Peter Onuf, "Imperialism and Nationalism in the Early American Republic," in *Empire's Twin: U.S. Anti-Imperialism from the Founding Era to the Age of Terrorism*, eds. Ian Tyrrell and Jay Sexton (Ithaca, NY: Cornell University Press, 2015).

20. Yokota, *Unbecoming British*.

21. The classic example here is John Quincy Adams's oration on the Fourth of July, 1821. See *Niles' Weekly Register*, July 21, 1821.

22. Robert J. Walker, "Letter of Mr. Walker," January 1844, in Frederick Merk, *Fruits of Propaganda in the Tyler Administration* (Cambridge, MA: Harvard University Press, 1971), 221–52.

23. Calhoun to Pakenham, April 18, 1844, in *The Papers of John C. Calhoun*, ed. Robert L. Meriwether et al., 28 vols. (Columbia: University of South Carolina Press for the South Caroliniana Society, 1959–2003), 18:273–81; William Freehling, *The Road to Disunion*, vol. 1, *Secessionists at Bay, 1776–1854* (New York: Oxford University Press), 409.

24. Jay Sexton, *Debtor Diplomacy: Finance and American Foreign Relations in the Civil War Era* (Oxford: Oxford University Press, 2005), 69.

25. Walker, "Letter of Mr. Walker."

26. Theodore Roosevelt, "The Monroe Doctrine," March 1896, in Theodore Roosevelt, *The Works of Theodore Roosevelt*, vol. 13 (New York: Scribner's, 1926), 168–81.

27. Jay Sexton, *The Monroe Doctrine: Empire and Nation in Nineteenth-Century America* (New York: Hill and Wang, 2011), 97–111.

28. See, for example, Frederick Merk, *The Monroe Doctrine and American Expansionism, 1843–1849* (New York: Alfred A. Knopf, 1966).

29. This point is argued in Steven Heath Mitton, "The Free World Confronted: The Problem of Slavery and Progress in American Foreign Relations, 18331844," Ph.D. dissertation, Louisiana State University, 2005.

30. David Sim, *The Union Forever: The Irish Question and U.S. Foreign Relations in a Victorian Age* (Ithaca, NY: Cornell University Press, 2013).

31. Mike Sewell, "Political Rhetoric and Policy-Making: James G. Blaine and Britain," *Journal of American Studies* 24 (April 1990): 61–84.

32. Charles Sumner, *Our Claims on England* (Washington, DC: Rives and Bailey, 1869).

33. Gerald Eggert, *Richard Olney: Evolution of a Statesman* (University Park: Penn State University Press, 1974); Robert Kagan, *Dangerous Nation: America and the World, 1600–1898* (London: Atlantic Books, 2006), 368–74.

34. Bulwer to Clayton, April 21, 1850, Clayton Papers, Library of Congress.

35. Other examples would include the Treaty of Ghent of 1815 (which said nothing concerning the British practice of impressment), the Webster-Ashburton Treaty of 1842 (which sidestepped controversial issues, including the Oregon border), and the 1871 Treaty of Washington (which was not clear as to whether U.S. "indirect claims" would be reviewed at the Geneva Arbitration of 1872).

36. Crapol, *America for Americans*, 11.

37. Buchanan to McClernand, April 2, 1850, in "Letters of Bancroft and Buchanan on the Clayton-Bulwer Treaty, 1849, 1850," *American Historical Review* 5, no. 1 (October 1899): 95–102.

38. Sexton, *Monroe Doctrine*, 181–82.

39. Henry C. Carey, *The Way to Outdo England Without Fighting Her* (Philadelphia: H. C. Baird, 1865).

40. Christian J. Maisch, "The Falklands/Malvinas Islands Clash of 1831–32: U.S. and British Diplomacy in the South Atlantic," *Diplomatic History* 24, no. 2 (Spring 2000): 185–209.

41. William Howard Russell, *My Diary North and South*, ed. Eugene H. Berwanger (Baton Rouge: Louisiana State University Press, 1988), 132.

42. *Niles' Weekly Register*, July 21, 1821.

43. David L. Anderson, *Imperialism and Idealism: American Diplomats in China, 1861–1898* (Bloomington, IN: Indiana University Press, 1985), 10 ("jackal"); Frank Ninkovich, *The United States and Imperialism* (Oxford: Blackwell's, 2001), 158 ("hitchhiking").

44. Alexander DeConde, "Washington's Farewell, the French Alliance, and the Election of 1796," in *Washington's Farewell Address: The View from the 20th Century*, ed. Burton Ira Kaufman (Chicago: Quadrangle Books, 1969).

45. Edward Crapol, "John Quincy Adams and the Monroe Doctrine: Some New Evidence," *Pacific Historical Review* 48 (August 1979): 413–18.

46. Gale W. Magee, "The Monroe Doctrine—A Stopgap Measure," *Mississippi Valley Historical Review* 38, no. 2 (September 1951): 233–35.

47. John Moser, *Twisting the Lion's Tail: Anglophobia in the United States, 1921–1948* (Basingstoke: Macmillan, 1999).

6. The War and Peace Election of 1916

1. Ross Gregory, *The Origins of American Intervention in the First World War* (New York: W. W. Norton, 1971), 104–5.

2. Lawrence Goodwyn, *Democratic Promise: The Populist Movement in America* (New York: Oxford University Press, 1976); Elisabeth S. Clemens, *The People's Lobby: Organizational Innovation and the Rise of Interest Group Politics in the United States, 1890–1925* (Chicago: University of Chicago Press, 1997); Gretchen Ritter, *Goldbugs and Greenbacks: The Antimonopoly Tradition and the Politics of Finance in America* (New

York: Cambridge University Press, 1997); and Elizabeth Sanders, *Roots of Reform: Farmers, Workers, and the American State, 1877–1917* (Chicago: University of Chicago Press, 1999).

3. Sanders, *Roots of Reform* , 78–81, 149–53.

4. Eleanor Flexner and Ellen Fitzpatrick, *Century of Struggle: The Woman's Rights Movement in the United States* (Cambridge, MA: Harvard University Press, 1996), 255–62; and Steven M. Buechler, *The Transformation of the Woman Suffrage Movement: The Case of Illinois, 1850–1920* (New Brunswick, NJ: Rutgers University Press, 1986), 6–19.

5. Kirk H. Porter, *National Party Platforms* (New York: Macmillan, 1924), 361–68, 403–11; Sanders, *Roots of Reform*, 55–71; and James Weinstein, *The Decline of Socialism in America, 1912–1925*, New Brunswick, NJ: Rutgers University Press, 1984), 39–111.

6. Stephen Skowronek, *Building a New American State: The Expansion of National Administrative Capacities, 1877–1920* (New York: Cambridge University Press, 1982); Jerome M. Clubb, *Congressional Opponents of Reform, 1901–1913* (Ann Arbor, MI: UMI Dissertation Publishing, 1963); David Sarasohn, *The Party of Reform: Democrats in the Progressive Era* (Jackson: University Press of Mississippi, 1989); Robert Harrison, *Congress, Progressive Reform, and the New American State* (New York: Cambridge University Press, 2004); and Sanders, *Roots of Reform.*

7. Sanders, *Roots of Reform*, 290–97, 356–59.

8. Ibid., 294; and Arthur S. Link, *Woodrow Wilson and the Progressive Era, 1910–1917* (New York: Harper Torchbooks, 1954), 79.

9. Elizabeth H. Davidson, *Child Labor Legislation in the Southern Textile States* (Chapel Hill: University of North Carolina Press, 1939), 251–57; Arthur S. Link, *Wilson*, vol. 5, *Campaigns for Progressivism and Peace* (Princeton, NJ: Princeton University Press, 1965), 38–39; and Sanders, *Roots of Reform*, 314–38, 364–65.

10. Sanders, *Roots of Reform*, 365.

11. Link, *Wilson*, vol. 3, *The Struggle for Neutrality, 1914–1915* (Princeton, NJ: Princeton University Press, 1960), chaps. 2–6.

12. The House-Grey Memorandum was an agreement forged by Wilson adviser and emissary Edward House and British foreign secretary Sir Edward Grey in February 1916 to propose a conference of belligerents at a time chosen by the Allies, anticipating that Germany would refuse to attend or not accept the conditions favored by the Allies (in which case the United States would probably enter the war against Germany). See Link, *Wilson*, vol. 4, *Confusions and Crises* (Princeton, NJ: Princeton University Press, 1964), 133–41; and Link, *Wilson*, 5:16–23. The word "probably" was inserted by Wilson in deference to American constitutional processes, according to Link.

13. The most complete accounts of 1916–early 1917 Wilsonian diplomacy are those of Arthur Link, *Wilson*, vols. 3, 4, and 5 (cited fully in notes 11, 12, and 9, respectively, in this chapter), supplemented with Link's short but more recent volume, *Woodrow*

Wilson: Revolution, War, and Peace (Wheelan, IL: Harlan Davidson, 1979). The facts of the shunned 1916–17 German peace effort are there, though Wilson's desire to promote peace is not questioned. A detailed chronology and uniquely critical account of Wilson's foot-dragging wartime diplomacy, written in the isolationist 1930s, is Walter Millis, *Road to War: America 1914–1917* (Boston, MA: Houghton Mifflin, 1935). Other incisive accounts of the issues and moves of 1916 diplomacy can be found in Karl E. Birnbaum, *Peace Moves and U-Boat Warfare* (Stockholm: Almqvist and Wiksell, 1958); Ernest R. May, *The World War and American Isolation, 1914–1917* (Cambridge, MA: Harvard University Press, 1959); Justus Doenecke, *Nothing Less Than War* (Lexington: University Press of Kentucky, 2011); Gregory, *Origins of American Intervention*; David Stephenson, *The First World War and International* Politics (New York: Oxford University Press, 1988); Donald E. Schmidt, *The Folly of War: American Foreign Policy, 1898–2005* (New York: Algora Publishing, 2005); Konrad H. Jarausch, *The Enigmatic Chancellor: Bethmann Hollweg and the Hubris of Imperial Germany* (New Haven, CT: Yale University Press, 1973); Johann-Heinrich Bernstorff, *My Three Years in America* (New York: Charles Scribner's Sons, 1920); and Patrick B. Devlin, *Too Proud to Fight: Woodrow Wilson's Neutrality* (New York: Oxford University Press, 1974).

14. John Milton Cooper, Jr., *Woodrow Wilson* (New York: Alfred A. Knopf, 2009), 297. For Wilson's speeches on the preparedness tour, see *The Messages and Papers of Woodrow Wilson*, ed. Albert Shah and Woodrow Wilson, vol. 1 (New York: Review of Reviews, 1924), 155–215.

15. Link, *Wilson*, 5:23.

16. Harold Sprout and Margaret Sprout, *The Rise of American Naval Power, 1776–1918* (Annapolis, MD: Naval Institute Press, 1967), 335 (quoting the Navy Department annual report of 1915). "Incomparably the greatest navy in the world," Wilson pledged in a February 3 speech in St. Louis, the last city of his preparedness-advocacy tour (ibid., 336).

17. Quoted in ibid., 343–44.

18. Link, *Wilson*, 4:chap. 11 and 327–34; Skowronek, *Building a New American State*, 228–32; George C. Herring, Jr., "James Hay and the Preparedness Controversy, 1915–1916," *Journal of Southern History* 30, no. 4 (November 1964): 383–404.

19. Richard F. Bensel, *Sectionalism and American Political Development* (Madison: University of Wisconsin Press, 1982), 121.

20. Ibid., 122–24; Link, *Wilson*, 4:167–94.

21. Link, *Wilson*, 4:167–94; Cooper, *Woodrow Wilson*, 312–14; Doenecke, *Nothing Less Than War*, 159–66. The majority of Republicans in the House, along with five Progressives and one Socialist, voted against tabling the McLemore resolution. Democrats, under enormous pressure from the president, voted 181–32 to table the resolution to ban Americans from traveling in war zones on armed merchant ships of belligerent countries. The Senate version of the resolution would have denied passports for such travel. *The Eagle and the Dove: The American Peace Movement and American Foreign Policy*, ed. John Whiteclay.Chambers (Syracuse, NY: Syracuse University Press, 1991), 67–68.

22. The early preparedness agitators of 1914–15 were mostly northeastern elites, distinguished men who organized societies to promote military expansion and reorganization (including the National Security League) and even ran private training camps. They received strong support (and their critics, vicious attacks) from the large metropolitan newspapers. Sprout and Sprout, *Rise of American Naval Power*, 322–23.

23. Sanders, *Roots of Reform*, 402–5.

24. The United Mine Workers were active in the antipreparedness movement, and the AFL, at its annual convention at the end of 1916, "ignored its own presidnt, Samuel Gompers, by deciding to oppose 'militarism.'" Doenecke, *Nothing Less Than War*, 195–96.

25. Wilson, intent on his own mediation project, was not friendly to private peace efforts. The president "viewed the pacifists' persistent appeals with a mixture of weariness and amusement," writes David S. Patterson in *The Search for a Negotiated Peace: Women's Activism and Citizen Diplomacy in World War I* (New York: Routledge, 2008), 153–57 (quote from 153).

26. Chambers, *Eagle and the Dove*, xlvii.

27. Ibid., xv–xvi, and documents from a meeting of American Union Against Militarism leaders Lillian Wald and Max Eastman with President Wilson, 70–74; Thomas J. Knock, *To End All Wars: Woodrow Wilson and the Quest for a New World Order* (Princeton, NJ: Princeton University Press, 1992), 63–64; Blanche Wiesen Cook, "Democracy in Wartime: Antimilitarism in England and the United States, 1914–1918," in *Peace Movements in America*, ed. Charles Chatfield (New York: Schocken Books, 1993), 39–56.

28. Knock, *To End All Wars*, 52–58; David Steigerwald, *Wilsonian Idealism in America* (Ithaca, NY: Cornell University Press, 1994), 1–17.

29. In the summer of 1918 the League to Enforce Peace called for "a complete victory over German militarism" as the necessary first step toward a new peace organization. *New York Times*, July 22, 1918.

30. Link, *Wilson*, 5:39. An abbreviated copy of the text of Wilson's speech is included in Chambers, *Eagle and the Dove*, 74–76.

31. Sanders, *Roots of Reform*, 60–69.

32. Link, *Wilson*, 5:39–40.

33. Knock, *To End All Wars*, 49.

34. Ibid.

35. Link, *Wilson*, 5:41–42.

36. Ibid., 42 and Ray Stannard Baker, *Woodrow Wilson, Life and Letters: Facing War* (Garden City, NY: Doubleday, Doran, 1937), 249–50.

37. "How the Convention Woke Up: Languid over 'America' Until Glynn Struck Peace Keynote," *New York Times*, June 15, 1916.

38. Martin H. Glynn, "Address to the Democratic National Convention," June 14, 1916, official report of the proceedings of the Democratic National Convention of 1916,

typescript copy of Carter Glass, secretary, St. Louis, Missouri [henceforth cited as Proceedings], 18.

39. Ibid., 20.

40. Ibid., 21.

41. Ibid.

42. Ibid., 22.

43. Ibid., 24.

44. Ibid., 25.

45. Ibid., 28.

46. Ibid., 39.

47. Ibid., 33.

48. Ibid., 43.

49. Ibid., 51.

50. Ibid., 56–63.

51. Ibid., 71–76.

52. Ibid., 81–82.

53. Ibid., 83. According to Arthur Link (and House's diary), Colonel House had seen and approved Glenn's speech, and sent it to the president. Wilson and House would have appreciated Glenn's praise of the president and the remarks about preparedness and Mexico, which may have been suggested by House. The president could not have anticipated the riotous embrace of keeping out of war by the other speakers and convention delegates. Link, *Wilson*, 5:38.

54. "How the Convention Woke Up," *New York Times*.

55. Proceedings 198–213; Michael Kazin, *A Godly Hero* (New York: Alfred A. Knopf, 2006), 250–51.

56. "Delegates Hasten Action: Threat to Go Home and Not Wait for Saturday," *New York Times*, June 16, 1916; Link, *Wilson*, 5:45–46; and Glynn, "Address to the Democratic National Convention," Proceedings 183–84.

57. James, Proceedings 186–87.

58. Ibid., 174, 170.

59. Ibid., 183.; and Link, *Wilson*, 5:45–47. James's reference is probably to the Sussex Pledge by Germany in early May, 1916.

60. Link, *Wilson*, 5:48.

61. Ibid.

62. Ibid., 60–64.

63. Sanders, *Roots of Reform*, 37–81.

64. Link, *Wilson*, 5:109–11; Kazin, *Godly Hero*, 251–52. Wilson's regard for Bryan was not high, and he was no doubt relieved—as were most of the cabinet—to be rid of him. But Bryan's well-received convention speech and the prospect of an extremely close election led Wilson to ask his help in the campaign (ibid., 248–49, 251).

65. Link, *Wilson*, 5:99–100, 140.

66. Ibid., 110–11.

67. Ibid., 111, 135.

68. Merlo J. Pusey, *Charles Evans Hughes*, vol. 1 (New York: Macmillan, 1951), 90–270; Betty Glad, *Charles Evans Hughes and the Illusions of Innocence* (Urbana: University of Illinois Press, 1966), 11–99; S. D. Lovell, *The Presidential Election of 1916* (Carbondale: Southern Illinois University Press, 1980), 22–36; James A. Henretta, "Charles Evans Hughes and the Strange Death of Liberal America," *Law and History Review* 24, no. 1 (Spring 2006), 115–171. Hughes also won the nomination of the Progressive Party.

69. Link, *Wilson*, 5:100–104.

70. Pusey, *Charles Evans Hughes*, 315–49.

71. Ibid., 161; and "Votes of Women and the Bull Moose Elected Wilson," *New York Times*, November 12, 1916.

72. Lovell, *Presidential Election of 1916*, 137–47, 177.

73. Link, *Wilson*, 5:162.

74. See Christine A. Lunardini and Thomas J. Knock, "Woodrow Wilson and Woman Suffrage: A New Look," *Political Science Quarterly* 95, no. 4 (1981): 362–63.

75. Flexner and Fitzpatrick, *Century of Struggle*, 269–72; "Votes of Women and the Bull Moose Elected Wilson"; Lunardini and Knock, "Woodrow Wilson and Woman Suffrage," 361; and Porter, *National Party Platforms*, 385, 402.

76. Link, *Wilson*, 5:162.

77. "Wilson was a little startled by this development" is the way Patrick Devlin puts it in *Too Proud to Fight*, 527.

78. If the president had not broken off diplomatic relations and then asked Congress for a declaration of war after the German chancellor and the German ambassador to the United States lost their bets with the militarist faction in Berlin, the exhausted and hungry belligerents would probably have very soon called for a peace conference to end the war. Germany would have become a republic within a year or so, with a Social Democratic government. There would have been a "peace without victory" and without the humiliation, land losses, and bankrupting reparations imposed on Germany. Without those conditions, it is quite possible there would have been no Chancellor Adolf Hitler and no World War II. At the very least, another million and a half soldiers (including over a hundred thousand Americans) would not have lost their lives. The flu epidemic might have been less severe in a less exhausted population. And sooner or later the United States—perhaps under a more reasonable president—would have joined the League of Nations.

7. Farewell to the "Smoke-Filled Room"

1. *Presidential Elections, 1789–1996* (Washington, DC: Congressional Quarterly), 57, 109.

2. "La Follette and the German Vote," *Literary Digest*, October 11, 1924, 10–11.

3. "The Democracy States Its Case," *Literary Digest*, July 12, 1924, 6.

4. Reprinted in *Literary Digest*, August 23, 1924, 7.

5. *Richmond Times-Dispatch,* quoted in "The Democratic Line of Attack," *Literary Digest,* July 5, 1924, pp. 1011.

6. "The Democratic Line of Attack," *Literary Digest,* July 5, 1924, 10–11.

7. "The Democratic Platform," *Literary Digest,* July 12, 1924, 8.

8. "Women to Tour in 'Teapot,'" *New York Times,* October 18, 1924, 2; "'Singing Teapot' off on Tour Tomorrow," *New York Times,* October 19, 1924, 4.

9. "Hulbert Angered, Quits as Speaker," *New York Times,* October 21, 1924, 8.

10. Arthur M. Schlesinger, Jr., ed., *History of American Presidential Elections,* vol. 6 (New York: Chelsea House, 1985), 2518.

11. Robert La Follette, address in New York City, September 18, 1924, reprinted in ibid., 6:2545.

12. "Comment of the Press on Coolidge's Speech," *New York Times,* August 15, 1924, 3.

13. "Voter Turnout in Presidential Elections, 1828–1928," http://www.presidency.ucsb.edu/data/turnout.php.

14. William E. Leuchtenburg, *The Perils of Prosperity, 1914–1932* (Chicago: University of Chicago Press, 1958), 120–39; Lynn Dumenil, *The Modern Temper* (New York: Hill and Wang, 1995), 15–16, 202–3; Amity Shlaes, *Coolidge* (New York: Harper, 2013), 301–10.

15. David Burner, "Election of 1924," in Schlesinger, *History of American Presidential Elections,* 6:2464.

16. Samuel Lubell, *The Future of American Politics* (New York: Harper and Row, 1951), 43–55.

17. Brian Balogh, "'Mirrors of Desires: Interest Groups, Elections, and the Targeted Style in Twentieth Century America," in *The Democratic Experiment,* ed. Meg Jacobs et al. (Princeton, NJ: Princeton University Press, 2003), 223.

18. David Greenberg, *Calvin Coolidge* (New York: Times Books, 2006), 99–107.

19. Ellis Hawley, *The Great War and the Search for a Modern Order,* 2d ed. (New York: St. Martin's Press, 1992), 60–61.

20. Richard V. Oulahan, "Party Chaos Left by Loss of Harding as Chosen Leader," *New York Times,* August 4, 1923, 1.

21. Greenberg, *Calvin Coolidge,* 99–107.

22. To be sure, few contemporary historians believe the story of the smoke-filled room in 1920, but that phrase remains a colorful shorthand for the influence of party organizations. For the current scholarship on 1920, see John A. Morello, *Selling the President, 1920* (Westport, CT: Praeger, 2001). For an example of the continuing resonance of the smoke-filled room, see Rick Beyer, "Where There's Smoke, There's . . . Political Intrigue?," *Politico,* March 3, 2008, http://www.politico.com/news/stories/0308/8803.html.

23. William Allen White, The *Autobiography of William A. White (N.Y.: Simon Publications, 1946),* 588. For an account of the convention, see David Pietrusza, *1920: The Year of the Six Presidents* (New York: Carroll and Graff, 2007), 236–41.

24. "Actors Eat Cakes with the Coolidges," *New York Times*, October 18, 1924, 1. See also Greenberg, *Calvin Coolidge*, 103. On celebrity mobilization and presidential politics more generally, see Kathryn Brownell, *Showbiz Politics* (Chapel Hill: University of North Carolina Press, 2014).

25. Quoted in Greenberg, *Calvin Coolidge*, 106.

26. Chester H. Rowell, "Why I Shall Vote for Coolidge," *New Republic*, October 29, 1924, reprinted in Schlesinger, *History of American Presidential Elections*, 6:2577.

27. *Literary Digest*, August 16, 1924, 13; Leuchtenburg, *Perils of Prosperity*, 135.

28. Nathan Fine, *Labor and Farmer Parties in the United States, 1828–1928* (New York: Russell and Russell, 1961), 412.

29. Herbert Croly, "Why I Shall Vote for La Follette," *New Republic*, October 29, 1924, reprinted in Schlesinger, *History of American Presidential Elections*, 6:2563–69.

30. Felix Frankfurter, "Why I Shall Vote for La Follette," *New Republic*, October 22, 1924, reprinted in Schlesinger, *History of American Presidential Elections*, 6:2570–73. The "politically homeless" description comes from a 1916 letter to Henry Stimson, quoted in Michael Alexander, *Jazz Age Jews* (Princeton, NJ: Princeton University Press, 2003), 82.

31. Robert M. La Follette, letter to the Conference for Progressive Political Action, Cleveland, Ohio, July 3, 1924, http://www.fofweb.com/History/MainPrintPage.asp?iPin=E14385&DataType=AmericanHistory&WinType=Free. On the pro–La Follette press, see Nancy Unger, "Lessons for the Nader Camp: 'Fighting Bob' La Follette in 1924," History News Service, August 22, 2000, History News Service, http://historynewsservice.org/2000/08/lessons-for-the-nader-camp-fighting-bob-la-follette-in-1924/.

32. Rowell, "Why I Shall Vote for Coolidge," 2576.

33. "The New 'Progressive' Party," *Literary Digest*, August 16, 1924, 11.

34. Walter Lippmann, "Why I Shall Vote for Davis," *New Republic*, October 29, 1924, reprinted in Schlesinger, *History of American Presidential Elections*, 6:2578–80.

35. Kenneth MacKay, *The Progressive Movement of 1924* (New York: Octagon Books, 1966), 152.

36. Rory McVeigh, "Power Devaluation, the Ku Klux Klan, and the Democratic National Convention of 1924," *Sociological Forum* 16, no. 1 (2001): 1–30.

37. "The Klan and the Candidates," *Literary Digest*, September 6, 1924, 10–11. For La Guardia quote, see Donald R. McCoy, *Calvin Coolidge: The Quiet President* (New York: Macmillan, 1967), 257.

38. White, *Autobiography*, 625–30.

8. The New Deal in 1940

I am grateful to Edward Berkowitz, Nigel Bowles, Martha Derthick, Larry DeWitt, Peter Ghosh, Otis L. Graham, Charles O. Jones, Ira Katznelson, Iwan Morgan, Byron Shafer, and Tom Packer for their helpful reactions to earlier versions of this chapter.

1. See Steve Fraser and Gary Gerstle, eds., *The Rise and Fall of the New Deal Order* (New York: Basic Books, 1989); Alan Brinkley, *The End of Reform: New Deal Liberalism*

in Recession and War (New York: Alfred A. Knopf, 1995). See also Ira Katznelson, *Fear Itself: The New Deal and the Origins of Our Time* (New York: Liveright, 2013), which sees the emergence of the New Deal "procedural state" as having been portentous in terms of the ideological alternatives that it foreclosed.

2. David Kennedy, *Freedom from Fear: The American People in Depression and War, 1929–1945* (New York: Oxford University Press, 1999); William E. Leuchtenburg, *In the Shadow of FDR: From Harry Truman to Ronald Reagan* (Ithaca, NY: Cornell University Press, 1983); Jennifer Klein, *For All These Rights: Business, Labor, and the Shaping of America's Private-Public Welfare State* (Princeton, NJ: Princeton University Press, 2003).

3. U.S. Department of Commerce, *Historical Statistics of the United States: Colonial Times to 1957* (Washington, DC: Government Printing Office, 1960), 43, 46–47 (black migration), 73 (unemployment), 88 (expansion of labor movement), 139 (GNP), 166 (distribution of wealth), 710 (federal employment), 718 (federal spending).

4. Bruce Porter, *War and the Rise of the State: The Military Foundations of Modern Politics* (New York: Free Press, 1994); Geoffrey Perret, *A Country Made by War: The Story of America's Rise to Power* (New York: Vintage, 1990); Michael Sherry, *In the Shadow of War: The United States Since the 1930s* (New Haven, CT: Yale University Press, 1995); Robert Saldin, *War, the American State, and Politics Since 1898* (New York: Cambridge University Press, 2011).

5. In addition to Porter, see Robert Higgs, *Crisis and Leviathan: Critical Episodes in the Growth of American Government* (New York: Oxford University Press, 1987): Barry D. Karl, *The Uneasy State: The United States from 1915 to 1945* (Chicago: University of Chicago Press, 1983); Katznelson, *Fear Itself*; and James Sparrow, *Warfare State: World War II Americans and the Age of Big Government* (New York: Oxford University Press, 2011).

6. Gallup polls dated January 14, 1940 (partisan affiliation), January 17, 1940 (Wagner Act), July 18, 1940 (WPA), July 26, 1940 (organized labor; regulation of business), reproduced in George Gallup, *The Gallup Poll: Public Opinion, 1935–71*, vol. 1 (New York: Random House, 1972), 202–3, 233–34; Roper Poll, March 1940 (future of New Deal), taken from iPOLL database.

7. The best account remains James T. Patterson, *Congressional Conservatism and the New Deal: The Growth of the Conservative Coalition in Congress, 1933–1939* (Lexington: University Press of Kentucky, 1967).

8. Susan Dunn, *1940: FDR, Willkie, Lindbergh, Hitler—The Election amid the Storm* (New Haven, CT: Yale University Press, 2013), 3.

9. Robert Blake, *Disraeli* (London: Eyre and Spottiswoode, 1966), 535.

10. In January 1940, 54 percent still opposed a third term; by June, 57 percent approved. Gallup, *Gallup Poll*, 1:200, 226.

11. Herbert Parmet, *Never Again: A President Runs for a Third Term* (New York: Macmillan, 1968), 41.

12. Robert Burke, "Election of 1940," in *History of American Presidential Elections, 1789–1968*, ed. Arthur M. Schlesinger, Jr., vol. 4 (New York: Chelsea House, 1971), 2923.

13. D. W. Brogan, "The American Election," *Political Quarterly* 11, no. 4 (October 1940): 328. "Too Good for the Average Man" was the title of a 1936 song by Lorenz Hart.

14. William Howard Taft, *The Chief Magistrate and His Powers* (New York: Columbia University Press, 1925).

15. See James T. Patterson, *Mr. Republican: A Biography of Robert A. Taft* (Boston: Houghton Mifflin, 1972), 183–94.

16. C. David Tompkins, *Senator Arthur H. Vandenberg: Evolution of a Modern Republican, 1884–1945* (Lansing: Michigan State University, 1970).

17. Poll dated May 29, 1940, in Gallup, *Gallup Poll*, 1:226.

18. Burke, "Election of 1940," 2927.

19. Poll dated February 11, 1940, in Gallup, *Gallup Poll*, 1:207. Even some archconservatives felt constrained to accommodate this sentiment. Representative Hamilton Fish of New York, a vitriolic opponent of the New Deal, told the chairman of the Republican National Committee, "Liberalize your leadership and policies or the Republican Party dies." Dunn, *1940*, 155.

20. Burke, "Election of 1940," 2925.

21. They were, in order, Hugo Black, Stanley Reed, Felix Frankfurter, William O. Douglas, and Frank Murphy. During his third term, FDR would make a further four appointments. Eight of his appointees had directly served the New Deal, while the ninth, Wiley Rutledge, had supported court packing while dean of the University of Iowa law school. See Rayman Solomon, "Franklin D. Roosevelt," in *Oxford Companion to the Supreme Court*, ed. Kermit Hall, 2d ed. (New York: Oxford University Press, 2012), online edition.

22. Tucked away in footnote 4 of *U.S. v. Carolene Products* (304 U.S. 144), Justice Harlan Fiske Stone anticipated that state laws affecting the rights of "discrete and insular minorities" would now receive the "strict scrutiny" of the court. *Palko v. Connecticut* (302 U.S. 319) was a crucial milestone in the process of incorporation, whereby the Supreme Court made elements of the Bill of Rights binding on the states as well as on the federal government. In general, see Henry Abraham, *Freedom and the Court: Civil Rights and Liberties in the United States* (New York: Oxford University Press, 1968).

23. Referring to Congress's 1939 reorganization measure, Frank Freidel remarks that it "seemed at the time little more than a meaningless sop," but that it ended up giving him all the authority that he required "to begin substantial modernization of the federal administration." He goes on to observe that FDR "was as delighted with it as with a new toy." Freidel, *Franklin D. Roosevelt: A Rendezvous with Destiny* (Boston: Little, Brown, 1990), 278.

24. Sidney Milkis, *The President and the Parties: The Transformation of the American Party System Since the New Deal* (New York: Oxford University Press, 1993).

25. The classic case is Social Security, on which see Martha Derthick, *Policymaking for Social Security* (Washington, DC: Brookings Institution, 1979), and Edward Berkowitz, *America's Welfare State: From Roosevelt to Reagan* (Baltimore, MD: Johns Hopkins University Press, 1991).

26. Address at Jackson Day Dinner, January 8, 1940, and Radio address to the Young Democratic Clubs of America, April 20, 1940, in *The Public Papers and Addresses of Franklin D. Roosevelt: 1940 Volume*, ed. Samuel Rosenman (London: Macmillan, 1941), 25–35, 166–70.

27. He asked his speechwriter, Samuel Rosenman, to "smooth it out and get it ready for delivery," and Rosenman reproduces FDR's draft in *Working with Roosevelt* (New York: Harper, 1952), 216. Kenneth S. Davis provides Rosenman's version, including a sharper statement of the need for ideological clarity: "The party must go wholly one way or wholly the other. It cannot face in both directions at the same time." Davis, *FDR: Into the Storm, 1937–1940* (New York: Random House, 1993), 601.

Writing to his progressive Republican ally, George Norris, after the convention, FDR confessed, "I was, frankly, amazed by the terrific drive which was put on by the old-line conservatives to make so many things adverse to liberalism occur," and denounced "their stupidity in making a violent issue out of Wallace." By the same token, he was delighted by the outcome, feeling that "from a purely political point of view, a great victory was won in Chicago." Wallace, in his view, was "a true liberal—far more so than any of the others suggested for Vice President." FDR to Norris, July 21, 1940, reproduced in *FDR: His Personal Letters, 1928–1945*, ed. Elliott Roosevelt, vol. 2 (New York: Duell, Sloan and Pearce, 1950), 1046–47.

28. "The President Accepts the Nomination for a Third Term," radio address to the Democratic National Convention, July 19, 1940, in Rosenman, *Public Papers . . . 1940*, 298–300.

29. Donald Johnson, *Wendell Willkie and the Republican Party* (Urbana: University of Illinois Press, 1960), 138.

30. *American National Biography*, s.v. "Charles L. McNary," www.anb.org.

31. Ibid., 124. FDR's labor secretary and longtime associate, Frances Perkins, recalls his having subsequently told her: "You know, Willkie would have made a good Democrat. Too bad we lost him." Perkins, *The Roosevelt I Knew* (London: Hammond, 1946), 96.

32. See Henry Evjen, "The Willkie Campaign: An Unfortunate Chapter in Republican Leadership," *Journal of Politics* 14, no. 2 (May 1952): 241–56.

33. Burke, "Election of 1940," 2942.

34. Address at Philadelphia, October 23, 1940, in Rosenman, *Public Papers . . . 1940*, 488.

35. Address at Cleveland, November 2, 1940, in ibid., 545–50.

36. See Dunn, *1940*, 135.

37. From Roosevelt's August 14, 1935, remarks on signing the Social Security Act, American Presidency Project, www.presidency.ucsb.edu.

9. "Why Don't You Just Get an Actor?"

1. For a sampling of major works on the era that assert the importance of the K_1C_2 formula to the election without providing *any* sourcing, see Herbert S. Parmet,

Eisenhower and the American Crusades (New York: Macmillan, 1972): 141; Stephen Ambrose, *Eisenhower*, vol. 1, *Soldier, General of the Army, President-Elect, 1890–1952* (New York: Simon and Schuster, 1983), 553; David Halberstam, *The Fifties* (New York: Fawcett Columbine, 1993), 233; James T. Patterson, *Grand Expectations: The United States, 1945–1974* (New York: Oxford University Press, 1996), 256; Lee Edwards, *The Conservative Revolution: The Movement That Remade America* (New York: Simon and Schuster, 1999), 57; Robert Dallek, *Harry S. Truman* (New York: Macmillan, 2008), 143; Jean Edward Smith, *Eisenhower in War and Peace* (New York: Random House, 2012), 547.

2. Robert Humphreys to Eric F. Goldman, March 21,1955, and Karl E. Mundt to Eric F. Goldman, March 29, 1955, Box 1109, Record Group VII, Karl E. Mundt Archives, Dakota State University, Madison, South Dakota.

3. In his account, Goldman significantly exaggerated the internal emphasis on K_1C_2 and implied that the entire campaign, including the presidential ticket's public addresses, was drawn from it: "From the beginning of the campaign the top Republican strategists had more or less agreed that there were three key issues. One day at a conference, Senator Karl Mundt, cochairman of the Speakers' Bureau, lightheartedly referred to the trio of points by the formula K_1C_2 and the phrase was becoming more and more common in GOP strategy letters and conversations. The campaign addresses for Eisenhower were also increasingly focusing on K_1C_2—the Korean War and charges of corruption and of Communism in the government." See Eric F. Goldman, *The Crucial Decade: America, 1945–1955* (New York: Alfred A. Knopf, 1956), 224–25.

4. While Goldman elevated the inside joke to an informal campaign theme, later scholars stretched the truth even further, stating as fact that the Republican campaign adopted the formula as its official slogan or even that Eisenhower's supporters wore campaign buttons with the slogan on them. See Michael Kazin, Rebecca Edwards, and Adam Rothman, *The Princeton Encyclopedia of American Political History* (Princeton, NJ: Princeton University Press, 2011), 316, and David Halberstam, *The Coldest Winter: America and the Korean War* (New York: Hyperion, 2008), 626, respectively.

5. Sherman Adams, *Firsthand Report: The Story of the Eisenhower Administration* (New York: Harper and Brothers, 1961), 42–44; *New York Times*, October 29, 1952; *Wall Street Journal*, October 27, 1952. For further analysis of the Korea speech, see Martin J. Medhurst, "Text and Context in the 1952 Presidential Campaign: Eisenhower's 'I Shall Go to Korea' Speech," *Presidential Studies Quarterly* 30:3 (September 2000): 464–84.

6. *New York Times*, June 5, 1952; Dwight D. Eisenhower, "Acceptance Address," July 11, 1952, transcript, Box 1, Speech Series, Dwight D. Eisenhower Papers as President (Ann Whitman File), Dwight D. Eisenhower Presidential Library, Abilene, Kansas.

7. Quoted in Smith, *Eisenhower in War and Peace*, 527.

8. Parmet, *Eisenhower and the American Crusades*, 126–31.

9. Ibid., 132.

10. Eisenhower, "Acceptance Address."

11. Robert A. Divine, *Eisenhower and the Cold War* (New York: Oxford University Press, 1981), 4; Halberstam, *The Fifties*, 208–9.

12. Dwight D. Eisenhower, *Mandate for Change: The White House Years, 1953–1956* (New York: Doubleday, 1963), 9; David McCullough, *Truman* (New York: Touchstone, 1992), 584, 632–36.

13. Halberstam, *The Fifties*, 209–10.

14. Ibid., 208; *Chicago Tribune*, June 5, 1952.

15. Halberstam, *The Fifties*, 208.

16. Parmet, *Eisenhower and the American Crusades*, 106–7, 118; Goldman, *Crucial Decade*, 222.

17. Halberstam, *The Fifties*, 234; Parmet, *Eisenhower and the American Crusades*, 114–15; *New York Sun*, August 25, 1952; Smith, *Eisenhower in War and Peace*, 526.

18. David Greenberg, "A New Way of Campaigning: Eisenhower, Stevenson, and the Anxieties of Television Politics," in *Liberty and Justice for All? Rethinking Politics in Cold War America*, ed. Kathleen G. Donohue (Amherst: University of Massachusetts Press, 2012), 194.

19. Edwin Diamond and Stephen Bates, *The Spot: The Rise of Political Advertising on Television*, 3d ed. (Cambridge, MA: MIT Press, 1992), 51; Sig Mickelson, *The Decade That Shaped the News: CBS in the 1950s* (Westport, CT: Greenwood Press, 1998), 88; Gary Edgerton, *The Columbia History of American Television* (New York: Columbia University Press, 2010), 206–7.

20. John E. Hollitz, "Eisenhower and the Admen: The Television 'Spot' Campaign of 1952," *Wisconsin Magazine of History*, 66 (Autumn 1982): 27–28.

21. Diamond and Bates, *The Spot*, 51, 59; Halberstam, *The Fifties*, 224–25; *Manchester Guardian*, October 31, 1952.

22. Jeffrey Frank, *Ike and Dick: Portrait of a Strange Political Marriage* (New York: Simon & Schuster, 2013): 50–62; Smith, *Eisenhower in War and Peace*, 531–42; Parmet, *Eisenhower and the American Crusades*, 135–39.

23. Hollitz, "Eisenhower and the Admen," 29–30.

24. Halberstam, *The Fifties*, 226; Diamond and Bates, *The Spot*, 39.

25. Hollitz, "Eisenhower and the Admen," 31, 34.

26. Martin Mayer, *Madison Avenue, U.S.A.* (New York: Harpers and Brothers, 1958), 295–96; Stephen C. Wood, "Television's First Political Spot Ad Campaign: Eisenhower Answers America," *Presidential Studies Quarterly* 20 (Spring 1990): 270; Hollitz, "Eisenhower and the Admen," 34.

27. Hollitz, "Eisenhower and the Admen," 35–37.

28. Wood, "Eisenhower Answers America," 275–79.

29. Hollitz, "Eisenhower and the Admen," 34–37.

30. *Christian Science Monitor*, October 2, 1952; *New York Times*, October 2, 1952; Wood, "Eisenhower Answers America," 272.

31. Smith, *Eisenhower in War and Peace*, 544–45; Halberstam, *The Fifties*, 231–32.

32. Greenberg, "New Way of Campaigning," 202–4; Diamond and Bates, *The Spot*, 45–47. See also Douglas Slaybaugh, "Adlai Stevenson, Television and the Presidential Campaign of 1956," *Illinois Historical Journal* 89 (Spring 1996): 2–16.

33. Smith, *Eisenhower in War and Peace*, 548–49; Parmet, *Eisenhower and the American Crusades*, 145–50.

34. Hollitz, "Eisenhower and the Admen," 38; Greenberg, "New Way of Campaigning," 209n5.

10. Giving Liberalism a Window

1. Robert David Johnson, *All the Way with LBJ: The 1964 Presidential Election* (New York: Cambridge University Press, 2009). This chapter builds on arguments that I present in my book, *The Fierce Urgency of Now: Lyndon Johnson, Congress, and the Battle for the Great Society* (New York: Penguin Press, 2015). See that book for a fuller treatment of the election, and the Johnson presidency.

2. David Mayhew, *Electoral Realignments: A Critique of an American Genre* (New Haven, CT: Yale University Press, 2002).

3. Geoffrey Kabaservice, *Rule and Ruin: The Downfall of Moderation and the Destruction of the Republican Party, from Eisenhower to the Tea Party* (New York: Oxford University Press, 2012).

4. Rick Perlstein, *Before the Storm: Barry Goldwater and the Unmaking of the American Consensus*, 2d ed. (New York: Nation Books, 2009).

5. Willard Edwards, "Return to Liberty: Barry," *Chicago Tribune*, July 17, 1964.

6. Robert J. Donovan, "Barry Speech Re-opens Deep GOP Split," *Boston Globe*, July 18, 1964.

7. Vincent J. Burke, "Ticket 'Not My Choice,' Says Ike, but He'll Support It," *Boston Globe*, July 17, 1964.

8. Julian E. Zelizer, *Arsenal of Democracy: The Politics of National Security—From World War II to the War on Terrorism* (New York: Basic Books, 2010).

9. Jack Valenti to President Johnson, September 7, 1964, Lyndon Baines Johnson Presidential Library, Austin Texas (LBJL,) WHCF Ex PL2 9/6/64–9/14/64, Box 84, File: PL 2 9/6/64–9/14/64.

10. "Democrats' TV Ad Draws G.O.P Rebuke," *Chicago Tribune*, September 13, 1964; "TV Ads Hit by Morton," *The Baltimore Sun*, September 17, 1964.

11. Zelizer, *Arsenal of Democracy, 190.*

12. John Bartlow Martin to Bill Moyers, September 22, 1964, LBJL, Aides, Office Files of Bill Moyers, Box 6, File: Pre-election Material—September.

13. Telephone conversation, Lyndon Johnson and McGeorge Bundy, October 24, 1964, LBJL, White House Presidential Tapes.

14. Fendall W. Yerxa, "Johnson Finds 'Smearlash' Costing Goldwater Voters," *New York Times*, October 22, 1964.

15. "Johnson Denies Any Cover-Up in Jenkins Case," *The Baltimore Sun*, October 16, 1964.

16. "Johnson Hurls Hardest Attack at Goldwater," *Los Angeles Times*, November 1, 1964.

17. James T. Patterson, *Grand Expectations: The United States, 1945–1974* (New York: Oxford University Press, 1996), 564.

18. David Kraslow, "Southern Power Fades in Current Congress," *Los Angeles Times*, January 6, 1965.

19. Geoffrey Kaba service, *Rule and Rain: The Downfall of Moderation and the Destruction of the Republican Party, from Eisenhower to the Tea Party* (New York: Oxford University Press, 2013).

11. The 1980 Election

1. Sidney Blumenthal, *The Rise of the Counter-Establishment: From Conservative Ideology to Political Power* (New York: Times Books, 1986), 5.

2. Hedrick Smith, "Taking Charge of Congress," *New York Times Magazine*, August 9, 1981, 17. For a longer treatment of Reagan's challenges in office, on which this chapter draws, see Meg Jacobs and Julian Zelizer, *Conservatives in Power: The Reagan Years, 1981–1989* (Boston: Bedford / St. Martin's Press, 2010).

3. Ronald Reagan, "A Time for Choosing," October 27, 1964, Ronald W. Reagan Speeches and Articles (1950–1964), Ronald Reagan Presidential Library, Simi Valley, California.

4. Ronald Reagan, "California and the Problem of Governmental Growth," January 5, 1967, Pre-presidential Speeches, Ronald Reagan Presidential Library.

5. Ronald Reagan, "Inaugural Address," January 20, 1981, in *Public Papers of the President of the United States: Ronald Reagan, 1981* (Washington, DC: U.S. Government Printing Office, 1982), 1:1–4.

6. Commission on Presidential Debates, "Debate Transcript: The Carter-Reagan Presidential Debate," October 28, 1980, http://www.reagan.utexas.edu/archives/reference/10.28.80debate.html.

7. Hedrick Smith, "Reformer Who Would Reverse the New Deal's Legacy," *New York Times*, January 21, 1981.

8. Peggy Noonan, *What I Saw at the Revolution: A Political Life in the Reagan Era* (New York: Ballantine, 1990), xvi, 10–11; David A. Stockman, *The Triumph of Politics: Why the Reagan Revolution Failed* (New York: Harper and Row, 1986), 40.

9. Even as scholars such as David Mayhew pose fundamental empirical challenges to this view, the notion of realignment retains popular support, including among officials in Washington. David R. Mayhew, *Electoral Realignments: A Critique of an American Genre* (New Haven, CT: Yale University Press, 2002).

10. Michael Schaller, *Reckoning with Reagan: America and Its President in the 1980s* (New York: Oxford University Press, 1992), 33.

11. Kevin Phillips, "Post-Conservative America," *New York Review of Books*, May 13, 1982.

12. Elizabeth Bulmiller, "The Other Dole—A Special Report," *New York Times*, July 16, 1996.

13. Ronald Reagan, "Appointments to the White House Office of Public Liaison," March 17, 1981, http://www.presidency.ucsb.edu/ws/index.php?pid=43552.

14. David Shribman, "Neoconservatives and Reagan: Uneasy Coalition," *New York Times*, September 28, 1981.

15. Memo, Elizabeth H. Dole to Edwin Meese III and James A. Baker III, March 9, 1982, Folder: Conservatives—General 1982 (2 of 6), Box 20, Elizabeth H. Dole Files, Ronald Reagan Presidential Library.

16. Letter, John T. (Terry) Dolan to James Baker, August 12, 1982, Folder: Conservative Issues—General, Box 19, Edwin Meese Files, Ronald Reagan Presidential Library.

17. Memo, Elizabeth H. Dole to James A. Baker III, February 24, 1982, Folder: Black Strategy 1982, Box 5, Elizabeth H. Dole Files, Ronald Reagan Presidential Library.

18. Tom Wicker, "The End of the Affair," *New York Times*, November 5, 1982.

19. Memo, " 'The Gender Gap': A Post-Election Assessment," Lee Atwater to James A. Baker III, November 23, 1982, Folder: Women—Gender Gap [1 of 2], Box 77, Elizabeth H. Dole Files, Ronald Reagan Presidential Library. For a recent study that draws on many of the same documents cited here and explores the debate over the proper policy response to the gender gap, see Marisa Chappell, "Reagan's 'Gender Gap' Strategy and the Limitations of Free-Market Feminism," *Journal of Policy History* 24, no. 1 (2012): 115–34.

20. Memo, Barbara Honegger to Martin Anderson, April 28, 1981, Folder: Women's Rights, Box CFOA 87, Martin Anderson Files, Ronald Reagan Presidential Library.

21. Memo, Richard Beal to Edwin Meese, James Baker, Michael Deaver, and Elizabeth Dole, May 6, 1982, Folder: Women's Issues, Box 23, Edwin Meese Files, Ronald Reagan Presidential Library.

22. Ibid.

23. Quoted in Kathleen Hall Jamieson, *Beyond the Double Bind: Women and Leadership* (New York: Oxford University Press, 1988), 69.

24. Memo, Barbara Honegger to Martin Anderson, April 28, 1981.

25. Memo, Annelise Anderson to Ken Cribb, January 12, 1982, Folder: Women's Issues, Box OA 9461, Edwin Meese Files, Ronald Reagan Presidential Library.

26. Memo, Edwin Harper to Edwin Meese, August 8, 1982, Folder: Women's Issues, Box 23, Edwin Meese Files, Ronald Reagan Presidential Library.

27. Memo, Richard Beal to Edwin Meese, James Baker, Michael Deaver, and Elizabeth Dole, May 6, 1982.

28. Memo, Red Cavaney to Elizabeth Dole, October 22, 1982, Folder: Women—Gender Gap [2 of 2], Box 77, Elizabeth H. Dole Files, Ronald Reagan Presidential Library.

29. Memo, Richard Wirthlin to Edwin Meese, July 15, 1982, Folder: Women—Gender Gap [2 of 2], Box 77, Elizabeth H. Dole Files, Ronald Reagan Presidential Library.

30. Memo, Wendy Borcherdt to James A. Baker, May 21, 1982, Folder: Women—50 States Project [April 1–May 1982], Box 76, Elizabeth H. Dole Files, Ronald Reagan Presidential Library.

31. Memo, Kenneth Cribb to Craig L. Fuller, June 2, 1982, Folder; Women's Issues, Box 23, Edwin Meese Files, Ronald Reagan Presidential Library.

32. Memo, Richard Beal to Edwin Meese, James Baker, Michael Deaver, and Elizabeth Dole, May 6, 1982.

33. Ibid.

34. Memo, Wendy Borcherdt to James A. Baker, May 21, 1982.

35. Memo, Red Cavaney to Elizabeth Dole, October 22, 1982.

36. Memo, Wendy Borcherdt to James A. Baker, May 21, 1982.

37. Ibid.

38. Ibid.

39. Memo, Edwin Harper to Edwin Meese, August 8, 1982.

40. Memo, Red Cavaney to Elizabeth Dole, October 22, 1982.

41. Ibid.

42. Ibid.

43. Memo, Office of Policy Development, November 19, 1982, Folder: Women—Gender Gap [1 of 2], Box 77, Elizabeth H. Dole Files, Ronald Reagan Presidential Library.

44. Memo, Elizabeth H. Dole to Ronald Reagan, November 13, 1982, Folder: Women—Gender Gap [2 of 2], Box 77, Elizabeth H. Dole Files, Ronald Reagan Presidential Library.

45. Memo, Ronald Hinckley to Ed Harper and Emily Rock, November 5, 1982, Folder: Women—Gender Gap [1 of 2], Box 77, Elizabeth H. Dole Files, Ronald Reagan Presidential Library.

46. Adam Clymer, "Before the Votes Are Counted, Some Conclusions Seem Clear," *New York Times*, October 31, 1982, E1.

47. Memo, " 'The Gender Gap': A Post-Election Assessment," Lee Atwater to James A. Baker III, November 23, 1982.

48. Ibid.

49. Elizabeth Dole, "The Real Gender Gap," *Christian Science Monitor*, October 29, 1982.

50. Ibid.

51. Memo, " 'The Gender Gap': A Post-Election Assessment," Lee Atwater to James A. Baker III, November 23, 1982.

52. Ibid.

53. Memo, Elizabeth H. Dole to Richard Wirthlin, November 4, 1982, Folder: Women—Gender Gap [2 of 2], Box 77, Elizabeth H. Dole Files, Ronald Reagan Presidential Library.

54. Larry M. Bartels, *Unequal Democracy: The Political Economy of the New Gilded Age* (Princeton, NJ: Princeton University Press, 2008).

12. Beyond the Water's Edge

1. Tom Wicker, "Convention Ends: Extremism in Defense of Liberty 'No Vice,' Arizonan Asserts," *New York Times*, July 17, 1964.

2. Quoted in Jon Margolis, *The Last Innocent Year: America in 1964—The Beginning of the "Sixties"* (New York: William Morrow, 1999), 277. See also Robert David Johnson, *All the Way with LBJ: The 1964 Presidential Election* (New York: Cambridge University Press, 2009), 140–42.

3. Telephone conversation, Lyndon B. Johnson and McGeorge Bundy, May 27, 1964, in Michael R. Beschloss, ed., *Taking Charge: The Johnson White House Tapes, 1963–1964* (New York: Simon and Schuster, 1997), 370.

4. Seward W. Livermore, *Politics Is Adjourned: Woodrow Wilson and the War Congress, 1916–1918* (Middletown, CT: Wesleyan University Press, 1966).

5. Julian E. Zelizer, *Arsenal of Democracy: The Politics of National Security—From World War II to the War on Terrorism* (New York: Basic Books, 2010), 5.

6. James L. Sundquist, *Dynamics of the Party System: Alignment and Realignment of Political Parties in the United States*, rev. ed. (Washington, DC: Brookings Institution, 1983), 337–42, 379–82 (quote on 379). One reason for realignment theory's dismissal of foreign policy is that it was not a major issue in any of the elections deemed "critical" (1828, 1860, 1896, 1932). For examples of the almost total absence of foreign wars and foreign policy in realignment theory, see, in addition to Sundquist, V. O. Key, Jr., "A Theory of Critical Elections," *Journal of Politics* 17 (February 1955): 3–18; V. O. Key, Jr., "Secular Realignment and the Party System," *Journal of Politics* 21 (May 1959): 198–210; E. E. Schattschneider, *The Semisovereign People: A Realist's View of Democracy in America* (New York: Holt, Rinehart and Winston, 1960); Walter Dean Burnham, "The Changing Shape of the American Political Universe," *American Political Science Review* 59 (March 1965): 7–28; Walter Dean Burnham, *Critical Elections and the Mainsprings of American Politics* (New York: W. W. Norton, 1970); Jerome M. Clubb, William H. Flanigan, and Nancy H. Zingale, *Partisan Realignment: Voters, Parties, and Government in American History* (Beverly Hills, CA: Sage, 1980); and David W. Brady, *Critical Elections and Congressional Policy Making* (Stanford, CA: Stanford University Press, 1988).

7. For a selection of historical overviews of the domestic political influence on U.S. foreign policy, see Melvin Small, ed., *Public Opinion and Historians: Interdisciplinary Perspectives* (Detroit: Wayne State University Press, 1970); Robert A. Divine, *Foreign Policy and U.S. Presidential Elections, 1940–1960*, 2 vols. (New York: New Viewpoints, 1974); Melvin Small, *Democracy and Diplomacy: The Impact of Domestic Politics on U.S. Foreign Policy, 1789–1994* (Baltimore: Johns Hopkins University Press, 1996); Robert David Johnson, *Congress and the Cold War* (New York: Cambridge University Press, 2006); Campbell Craig and Fredrik Logevall, *America's Cold War: The Politics of Insecurity* (Cambridge, MA: Harvard University Press, 2009); and Zelizer, *Arsenal of Democracy*. For a selection of interesting case studies, see Livermore, *Politics Is Adjourned*; John Lewis Gaddis, *The United States and the Origins of the Cold War, 1941–1947* (New York: Columbia University Press, 1972); Steven Casey, *Cautious Crusade: Franklin D. Roosevelt, American Public Opinion, and the War Against Nazi Germany* (New York: Oxford University Press, 2001); Jeremi Suri, *Power and Protest: Global*

Revolution and the Rise of Detente (Cambridge, MA: Harvard University Press, 2003); Melvin Small, *At the Water's Edge: American Politics and the Vietnam War* (Chicago: Ivan R. Dee, 2005); Steven Casey, *Selling the Korean War: Propaganda, Politics, and Public Opinion in the United States, 1950–1953* (New York: Oxford University Press, 2008); Andrew L. Johns, *Vietnam's Second Front: Domestic Politics, the Republican Party, and the War* (Lexington: University Press of Kentucky, 2010); and Curt Cardwell, *NSC 68 and the Political Economy of the Early Cold War* (New York: Cambridge University Press, 2011).

8. David R. Mayhew, *Electoral Realignments: A Critique of an American Genre* (New Haven, CT: Yale University Press, 2002), 157–58. For other examples that take war and foreign policy seriously, see Stephen Skowronek, *The Politics Presidents Make: Leadership from John Adams to Bill Clinton*, rev. ed. (Cambridge, MA: Harvard University Press, 1997); David R. Mayhew, *Parties and Policies: How the American Government Works* (New Haven, CT: Yale University Press, 2008); and William J. M. Claggett and Byron E. Shafer, *The American Public Mind: The Issues Structure of Mass Politics in the Postwar United States* (New York: Cambridge University Press, 2010).

9. See, for example, Robert D. Putnam, "Diplomacy and Domestic Politics: The Logic of Two-Level Games," *International Organization* 42 (Summer 1988): 427–60; Jack S. Levy, "Domestic Politics and War," in *The Origin and Prevention of Major Wars*, ed. Robert I. Rotberg and Theodore K. Rabb (New York: Cambridge University Press, 1989), 79–101; Jack Snyder, *Myths of Empire: Domestic Politics and International Ambition* (Ithaca, NY: Cornell University Press, 1991); Peter B. Evans, Harold K. Jacobson, and Robert D. Putnam, eds., *Double-Edged Diplomacy: International Bargaining and Domestic Politics* (Berkeley: University of California Press, 1993); Richard Rosecrance and Arthur A. Stein, eds., *The Domestic Bases of Grand Strategy* (Ithaca, NY: Cornell University Press, 1993); Helen V. Milner, *Interests, Institutions, and Information: Domestic Politics and International Relations* (Princeton, NJ: Princeton University Press, 1997); and Edward D. Mansfield and Helen V. Milner, *Votes, Vetoes, and the Political Economy of International Trade Agreements* (Princeton, NJ: Princeton University Press, 2012).

10. See, respectively, Alexander Wendt, *Social Theory of International Politics* (New York: Cambridge University Press, 1999); and Bruce Russett, *Controlling the Sword: The Democratic Governance of National Security* (Cambridge, MA: Harvard University Press, 1990).

11. For the canonical articulation, see Gideon Rose, "Neoclassical Realism and Theories of Foreign Policy," *World Politics* 51 (October 1998): 144–72. For specific examples, see Fareed Zakaria, *From Wealth to Power: The Unusual Origins of America's World Role* (Princeton, NJ: Princeton University Press, 1998); William C. Wohlforth, "Measuring Power—and the Power of Theories," in *Realism and the Balancing of Power: A New Debate*, ed. John A. Vasquez and Colin Elman (Upper Saddle River, NJ: Prentice Hall, 2002), 250–65; Randall L. Schweller, *Unanswered Threats: Political Constraints on the Balance of Power* (Princeton, NJ: Princeton University Press, 2006); Steven E. Lobell, Norrin M. Ripsman, and Jeffrey W. Taliaferro, eds., *Neoclassical Realism, the*

State, and Foreign Policy (New York: Cambridge University Press, 2009). But for an earlier realist account that links domestic ideology to external behavior, see Stephen M. Walt, *Revolution and War* (Ithaca, NY: Cornell University Press, 1997).

12. See, for example, Peter Trubowitz, *Politics and Strategy: Partisan Ambition and American Statecraft* (Princeton, NJ: Princeton University Press, 2011).

13. Craig and Logevall, *America's Cold War*, 10.

14. For diplomatic history, see Jussi M. Hanhimäki, "Global Visions and Parochial Politics: The Persistent Dilemma of the 'American Century,'" *Diplomatic History* 27 (September 2003): 423–47; Fredrik Logevall, "Politics and Foreign Relations," *Journal of American History* 95 (March 2009): 1074–78; and Thomas Alan Schwartz, "'Henry, . . . Winning an Election Is Terribly Important': Partisan Politics in the History of U.S. Foreign Relations," *Diplomatic History* 33 (April 2009): 173–90. For American Political Development (APD), see Mayhew, *Parties and Policies*, 288. But for an important exception to the APD literature, see Ira Katznelson and Martin Shefter, eds., *Shaped by War and Trade: International Influences on American Political Development* (Princeton, NJ: Princeton University Press, 2002).

15. Quoted in Sean Wilentz, *The Age of Reagan: A History, 1974–2008* (New York: Harper, 2008), 321.

16. In addition to Brian Balogh's chapter in this volume, see Joshua Meyrowitz, *No Sense of Place: The Impact of Electronic Media on Social Behavior* (New York: Oxford University Press, 1985); Kiku Adatto, *Picture Perfect: The Art and Artifice of Public Image Making* (New York: Basic Books, 1993); and Jason Gainous and Kevin Wagner, *Rebooting American Politics: The Internet Revolution* (Lanham, MD: Rowman and Littlefield, 2011).

17. Zelizer, *Arsenal of Democracy*, 384–85.

18. Fredrik Logevall, *Choosing War: The Lost Chance for Peace and the Escalation of War in Vietnam* (Berkeley: University of California Press, 1999), 193–213; Johnson, *All the Way with LBJ*, 201–3.

19. Quoted in Dominic Sandbrook, *Mad as Hell: The Crisis of the 1970s and the Rise of the Populist Right* (New York: Alfred A. Knopf, 2011), 207.

20. Gallup quoted in "Gallup Says 2nd Debate Key," *Lowell Sun*, November 9, 1976.

21. Robert Dallek, *Franklin D. Roosevelt and American Foreign Policy, 1932–1945* (New York: Oxford University Press, 1995), 247–50.

22. Casey, *Selling the Korean War*, 326–36.

23. Robert D. Schulzinger, *A Time for War: The United States and Vietnam, 1941–1975* (New York: Oxford University Press, 1997), 269–73.

24. Lynne Olson, *Those Angry Days: Roosevelt, Lindbergh, and America's Fight over World War II, 1939–1941* (New York: Random House, 2013), 263; Susan Dunn, *1940: FDR, Willkie, Lindbergh, Hitler—The Election amid the Storm* (New Haven, CT: Yale University Press, 2013).

25. On Korea in 1952, see Casey, *Selling the Korean War*, 332–35. On Vietnam in 1968, see Johns, *Vietnam's Second Front*, 234–36.

26. In 1952 the Democrats not only lost control of the White House, they also became the minority in both houses of Congress for only the second time in two decades. The Democrats lost seats in 1968 as well, although they did maintain majorities in both the House and the Senate. This can be explained in part by the narrowness of Nixon's victory over Humphrey—his margin of victory in the popular vote was only 0.7 percent—which meant that Republican candidates had trouble riding the coattails of their presidential standard-bearer.

27. See, for example, Vladislav Zubok and Constantine Pleshakov, *Inside the Kremlin's Cold War: From Stalin to Khrushchev* (Cambridge, MA: Harvard University Press, 1996), 236–37; John Lewis Gaddis, *We Now Know: Rethinking Cold War History* (New York: Oxford University Press, 1997), 291–92; Marc Trachtenberg, *A Constructed Peace: The Making of the European Settlement, 1945–1963* (Princeton, NJ: Princeton University Press, 1999), 352, 379–82, 398–402; James G. Hershberg, "The Crisis Years, 1958–1963," in *Reviewing the Cold War: Approaches, Interpretations, Theory*, ed. Odd Arne Westad (London: Frank Cass, 2000), 319–20; Jennifer W. See, "An Uneasy Truce: John F. Kennedy and Soviet-American Détente, 1963," *Cold War History* 2 (January 2002): 161–94; and Andrew Preston, *The War Council: McGeorge Bundy, the NSC, and Vietnam* (Cambridge, MA: Harvard University Press, 2006), 54–74. For more radical periodizations, see Fred Halliday, *The Making of the Second Cold War*, 2d ed. (London: Verso, 1986), 3–7, which divides the Cold War into four phases; and Anders Stephanson, "Cold War Degree Zero," in *Uncertain Empire: American History and the Idea of the Cold War*, ed. Joel Isaac and Duncan Bell (New York: Oxford University Press, 2012), 19–49, which argues that the Cold War actually ended in 1963.

28. Robert Dallek, *An Unfinished Life: John F. Kennedy, 1917–1963* (Boston: Little, Brown, 2013), 295; Craig and Logevall, *America's Cold War*, 191–92.

29. Christopher A. Preble, *John F. Kennedy and the Missile Gap* (DeKalb: Northern Illinois University Press, 2004).

30. Which may have encouraged Reagan to engineer his own "October surprise" by undermining negotiations between the Carter administration and Tehran, though no hard evidence for this theory exists. On the hostage crisis and the election, see David Farber, *Taken Hostage: The Iran Hostage Crisis and America's First Encounter with Radical Islam* (Princeton, NJ: Princeton University Press, 2005), 176–80.

31. Robert Dallek, *Ronald Reagan: The Politics of Symbolism* (Cambridge, MA: Harvard University Press, 1984), 56–59. More generally, see Gil Troy, *Morning in America: How Ronald Reagan Invented the 1980s* (Princeton, NJ: Princeton University Press, 2005).

32. Michael Kazin, *A Godly Hero: The Life of William Jennings Bryan* (New York: Alfred A. Knopf, 2006), 97.

33. Quoted in Warren Zimmermann, *First Great Triumph: How Five Americans Made Their Country a World Power* (New York: Farrar, Straus and Giroux, 2002), 319. See also Ernest R. May, *Imperial Democracy: The Emergence of the United States as a Great Power* (New York: Harcourt, Brace and World, 1961), 252–62.

34. John A. Thompson, *Woodrow Wilson* (London: Longman, 2002), 125–31, 219–20.

35. Patrick Devlin, *Too Proud to Fight: Woodrow Wilson's Neutrality* (New York: Oxford University Press, 1975); John Milton Cooper, Jr., *The Warrior and the Priest: Woodrow Wilson and Theodore Roosevelt* (Cambridge, MA: Harvard University Press, 1983), 288–302.

36. Quoted in Thompson, *Woodrow Wilson*, 129.

37. John Milton Cooper, Jr., *Woodrow Wilson: A Biography* (New York: Knopf, 2009), 355–59. Yet as Cooper also points out, the result of the Electoral College vote turned on the swing state of Ohio, where the war was not much of a factor and which Wilson probably carried because of organized labor's support for Progressivism. See also Thompson, *Woodrow Wilson*, 91.

38. Quoted in Bob Woodward, *State of Denial* (New York: Simon and Schuster, 2006), 253.

39. Polling data, May 12 and December 16, 2004, Alec M. Gallup and Frank Newport, eds., *The Gallup Poll: Public Opinion, 2004* (Lanham, MD: Rowman and Littlefield, 2006), 197, 498.

40. Polling data, October 6, 2004, ibid., 401.

41. Polling data from five October 2004 polls, reported November 1, 2004, ibid., 437.

42. Polling data, May 12 and October 19, 2004, ibid., 197, 420.

43. "Clinton Says Party Failed Midterm Test over Security Issue," *New York Times*, December 4, 2002.

44. In an October 27, 2004, poll, Gallup asked voters whether ten issues were "extremely important," "very important," or "somewhat important." Terrorism ranked first with 46 percent of respondents rating it as "extremely important," while Iraq came second with 41 percent; the economy came in third with 39 percent. Gallup and Newport, *Gallup Poll, 2004*, 431.

45. Alonzo L. Hamby, *Man of the People: A Life of Harry S. Truman* (New York: Oxford University Press, 1995), 452–66; James T. Patterson, *Grand Expectations: The United States, 1945–1974* (New York: Oxford University Press, 1996), 155–63.

46. For an overview, see Barbara Hinckley, *Congressional Elections* (Washington, DC: Congressional Quarterly Press, 1981).

47. Barry C. Burden and David C. Kimball, *Why Americans Split Their Tickets: Campaigns, Competition, and Divided Government* (Ann Arbor: University of Michigan Press, 2002); Mayhew, *Parties and Policies*, 180–97. For precisely this reason, some realignment theorists portray certain midterms as presaging or confirming critical presidential elections. See, for example, Sundquist, *Dynamics of the Party System*; and Brady, *Critical Elections and Congressional Policy Making*.

48. Thompson, *Woodrow Wilson*, 177–78.

49. Jonathan Bell, *The Liberal State on Trial: The Cold War and American Politics in the Truman Years* (New York: Columbia University Press, 2004), 14–45; Zelizer, *Arsenal of Democracy*, 103–7.

50. Bell, *Liberal State on Trial*, 198–237; Casey, *Selling the Korean War*, 109–20.

51. Mayhew, *Electoral Realignments*, 93.

52. Polling data from October 19, 1966, George H. Gallup, *The Gallup Poll: Public Opinion, 1935–1971*, vol. 3 (New York: Random House, 1972), 2034.

53. Johns, *Vietnam's Second Front*, 114; Zelizer, *Arsenal of Democracy*, 195–201 (Gallup quoted on 200). See also G. Calvin Mackenzie and Robert Weisbrot, *The Liberal Hour: Washington and the Politics of Change in the 1960s* (New York: Penguin Press, 2008), 331–32.

54. Johns, *Vietnam's Second Front*, 121–24.

55. Lloyd C. Gardner, *Pay Any Price: Lyndon Johnson and the Wars for Vietnam* (Chicago: Ivan R. Dee, 1995), 306–8.

56. Zelizer, *Arsenal of Democracy*, 463–65; Michael Isikoff and David Corn, *Hubris: The Inside Story of Spin, Scandal, and the Selling of the Iraq War* (New York: Crown, 2006), 157–58.

57. Polling data, November 3, 2006, 2006, Alec M. Gallup and Frank Newport, eds., *The Gallup Poll: Public Opinion, 2006* (Lanham, MD: Rowman and Littlefield, 2007), 458.

58. Quoted in Bob Woodward, *The War Within: A Secret White House History, 2006–2008* (New York: Simon and Schuster, 2008), 82–83. See also Wilentz, *Age of Reagan*, 448–49.

59. Woodward, *State of Denial*, 335–36.

60. On how this happened, see Thomas J. Knock, *To End All Wars: Woodrow Wilson and the Quest for a New World Order* (New York: Oxford University Press, 1992), 105–22.

61. Quoted in Casey, *Cautious Crusade*, 38.

62. Quoted in Gardner, *Pay Any Price*, 131.

63. See Derek Chollet and James Goldgeier, *America Between the Wars: From 11/9 to 9/11* (New York: PublicAffairs, 2008), esp. 38–43, 57–59, 148–49, 286–89.

64. As John Gaddis has pointed out, containment remained the goal of all presidents between Truman and Reagan even if its method of implementation varied across the presidencies: John Lewis Gaddis, *Strategies of Containment: A Critical Appraisal of American National Security Policy During the Cold War*, rev. ed. (New York: Oxford University Press, 2005).

65. On the similarities between George H. W. Bush and Clinton, see Andrew J. Bacevich, *American Empire: The Realities and Consequences of U.S. Diplomacy* (Cambridge, MA: Harvard University Press, 2002). On the similarities between George W. Bush and Obama, see James Mann, *The Obamians: The Struggle Inside the White House to Redefine American Power* (New York: Viking, 2012). This is not, of course, to say that the foreign policies of all these presidents were the *same*—merely *similar* in several key respects, and more so than one would expect from their party affiliations and campaign rhetoric.

66. See, for example, Al Gore, "A Commentary on the War Against Terror: Our Larger Tasks," speech at the Council on Foreign Relations, New York, February 12, 2002, http://www.cfr.org/terrorism/commentary-war-against-terror-our-larger-tasks/p4343.

67. A point made by Mayhew, *Electoral Realignments*, 126–27.

68. The definitive account is Zelizer, *Arsenal of Democracy*, 148–77.

69. Robert Dallek, *Flawed Giant: Lyndon Johnson and His Times, 1961–1973* (New York: Oxford University Press, 1998), 143–44.

70. Larry Berman, *Lyndon Johnson's War: The Road to Stalemate in Vietnam* (New York: W. W. Norton, 1989), 186–202.

71. Larry Berman, *No Peace, No Honor: Nixon, Kissinger, and Betrayal in Vietnam* (New York: Free Press, 2001), 32–36. Incredibly, Lyndon Johnson and several of his top national security officials knew about the Nixon-Thieu back channel but kept it quiet because they trusted Nixon to remain faithful to an independent South Vietnam more than they did their fellow Democrat, Hubert Humphrey. See David Milne, "The 1968 Paris Peace Negotiations: A Two Level Game?," *Review of International Studies* 37 (April 2011): 577–99.

72. Jeffrey Kimball, *Nixon's Vietnam War* (Lawrence: University Press of Kansas, 1998), 323–48 (Kissinger quoted on 346); Robert Dallek, *Nixon and Kissinger: Partners in Power* (New York: HarperCollins, 2007), 400–436 (Haldeman quoted on 420).

73. Logevall, *Choosing War*, 193–213; Randall B. Woods, *LBJ: Architect of American Ambition* (New York: Free Press, 2006), 547–49.

74. Quoted in Johns, *Vietnam's Second Front*, 124.

13. From Corn to Caviar

The author would like to thank Sheila Blackford, Doug Blackmon, Emily Charnock, Paul Freedman, Dan Galvin, David Greenberg, Sarah Igo, Katherine Krimmel, Evan McCormick, Mark Nevin, Brian Rosenwald, Lynn Sanders, Michael Schudson, Robert Shapiro, Adam Sheingate, and the editors for their assistance with this chapter.

1. Benjamin Ginsberg, Walter R. Mebane, Jr., and Martin Shefter, "The Presidency, Social Forces, and Interest Groups: Why Presidents Can No Longer Govern," in *The Presidency and the Political System*, ed. Michael Nelson, 5th ed. (Washington, DC: CQ Press, 1998), 358–61.

2. See Susan Herbst, *Numbered Voices* (Chicago: University of Chicago Press, 1993), 120, for a summary of how party bosses provided this kind of intelligence themselves. See Gil Troy, *How They Ran: The Changing Role of the Presidential Candidate* (Cambridge, MA: Harvard University Press, 1996), and Samuel Kernell, "Life Before Polls: Ohio Politicians Predict the 1828 Presidential Vote," *Political Science and Politics* 33, no. 3 (September 2000): 473 (for quote), 569–74.

3. On the candidate-centered system, see Adam Sheingate, "Politics as a System of Professions: Political Consulting and American Political Development," draft paper, 2013, 2–3. For timing, see John Herbert Aldrich, *Why Parties? A Second Look* (Chicago:

University of Chicago Press, 2011), 295. See also Bruce A. Bimber, *Information and American Democracy: Technology in the Evolution of Political Power* (New York: Cambridge University Press, 2003), 76–77.

4. On the ways in which major labor and business political action committees intervened in electoral politics from the 1940s through the 1960s, see Emily J. Charnock, "From Ghosts to Shadows: Parties, Interest Groups, and the Rise of Political Action" (PhD diss., Woodrow Wilson Department of Politics, University of Virginia, 2013). For quote see Harwood L. Childs, *Labor and Capital in National Politics* (Columbus: Ohio State University Press, 1930), 247. See Brian Balogh, "'Mirrors of Desires': Interest Groups, Elections and the Targeted Style in Twentieth Century America," in The Democratic Experiment, ed. Meg Jacobs, William Novak, and Julian Zelizer (Princeton, NJ: Princeton University Press, 2003), and Bimber, *Information and American Democracy*, 71.

5. On the explosion of interest groups, see Jeffrey M. Berry, *The Interest Group Society* (Boston: Little, Brown, 1984), and Jack L. Walker, *Mobilizing Interest Groups in America: Patrons, Professions, and Social Movements* (Ann Arbor: University of Michigan Press, 1991). On the countermobilization, see David Vogel, *Kindred Strangers: The Uneasy Relationship Between Politics and Business in America* (Princeton, NJ: Princeton University Press, 1996), and Kimberly Phillips-Fein, *Invisible Hands: The Making of the Conservative Movement from the New Deal to Reagan* (New York: W. W. Norton, 2009). On the role of the PACs, see Charnock, *Ghosts*. On the increase in PACs, see Paul S. Herrnson, "Reemergent National Party Organizations," in *The Parties Respond: Changes in the American Party System*, ed. L. Sandy Maisel (Boulder, CO: Westview Press, 1990), 136.

6. Theda Skocpol, *Diminished Democracy: From Membership to Management in American Civic Life* (Norman: University of Oklahoma Press, 2003), 7. See also Theda Skocpol, "Advocates Without Members: The Recent Transformation of American Civic Life," in *Civic Engagement in American Democracy*, ed. Theda Skocpol and Morris P. Fiorina (Washington, DC: Brookings Institution Press, 1999), 462. For a good summary of the organizational implications of Skocpol's thesis, see David Karpf, *The MoveOn Effect: The Unexpected Transformation of American Political Advocacy* (New York: Oxford University Press, 2012), 24–25.

7. Samuel Kernell, *Going Public: New Strategies of Presidential Leadership* (Washington, DC: CQ Press, 1993), 12–16.

8. On the role of television, see James L. Baughman, *Same Time, Same Station: Creating American Television, 1948–1961* (Baltimore: Johns Hopkins University Press, 2007), 202–3; see also Nicholas Lemann, "Tune In Yesterday," *New Yorker* 83, no. 10 (April 30, 2007): 80. On media oligopoly, see Kernell, *Going Public*, 138. For debate figures, see George C. Edwards III, *On Deaf Ears: The Limits of the Bully Pulpit* (New Haven, CT: Yale University Press, 2006), 188.

9. Robert J. Pitchell, "The Influence of Professional Campaign Management Firms in Partisan Elections in California," *Western Political Quarterly* 11, no. 2 (June 1958): 289.

10. Ibid.; 294 for Whitaker and Baxter quote. See also Sheingate, "System of Professions," 17.

11. On politics and television in this era, see David Greenberg, "A New Way of Campaigning: Eisenhower, Stevenson, and the Anxieties of Television Politics," in *Liberty and Justice for All? Rethinking Politics in Cold War America*, ed. Kathleen G. Donohue (Amherst: University of Massachusetts Press, 2012). See Baughman, *Same Station*, xiii (for quote) and 206, 209–11 (for examples of how this affected programming).

12. Robert Groves has identified three eras of survey research. The first, which we have already touched upon briefly, and which ran from 1930 to 1960, saw the emergence of systematic sampling and more structured questions that was generally conducted in concentrated geographic areas. The second phase, in Groves's periodization, ran from 1960 to 1990 and witnessed the proliferation of surveys for a variety of purposes. Its development was aided by the widespread use of telephones, and by the mid-1960s, computers which aided in the tabulation of results. Its scope expanded to national portraits of public opinion, although candidates often focused on battleground states. See Robert M. Groves, "Three Eras of Survey Research," *Public Opinion Quarterly* 75, no. 5 (2011): 861–71, 861–64 for citation. On Harris's polls, see Robert M. Eisinger, *The Evolution of Presidential Polling* (Cambridge: Cambridge University Press, 2003), 86, and Lawrence R. Jacobs and Robert Y. Shapiro, "Issues, Candidate Image, and Priming: The Use of Private Polls in Kennedy's 1960 Presidential Campaign," *American Political Science Review* 88, no. 3 (September 1994): 528, 536.

13. For an excellent analysis of the variety of ways in which Nixon deployed public opinion polling, see Mark Nevin, "Politicized Democracy: The Nixon Presidency and the Rise of Public Opinion Polling in American Politics" (PhD diss., Corcoran Department of History, University of Virginia, 2010). On Nixon, see also James M. Druckman, Lawrence R. Jacobs, and Eric Ostermeier, "Candidate Strategies to Prime Issues and Image," *Journal of Politics* 66, no. 4 (November 2004), 1180–1202 and Eisinger, *Evolution*, 62. On Johnson, see Eisinger, *Evolution*, 90, who cites Caro. On Nixon's adaptation of polling strategy, see Lawrence R. Jacobs and Melanie Burns, "The Second Face of the Public Presidency: Presidential Polling and the Shift from Policy to Personality Polling," *Presidential Studies Quarterly* 34, no. 3 (September 2004): 542, 551–52.

14. Nevin, "Politicized Democracy," chap. 2, 34–35.

15. Ibid., 18, 22–35, 35 for quote.

16. See Sheingate, "The Art and Science of Politics," draft manuscript, chap. 4 and D. Sunshine Hillygus, "The Evolution of Election Polling in the United States," *Public Opinion Quarterly* 75, no. 5 (2011): 962–81. Franklin D. Roosevelt was the first president to use public opinion polling in the White House. By his reelection campaign in 1944, FDR was receiving regular reports from the pioneering pollster Hadley Cantril. Cantril, in turn, worked closely with Sam Rosenman, a close adviser to the president and one of Roosevelt's speechwriters. The historian Richard Steele concluded that for Roosevelt, "the pulse of the people was seen more as a measure of the health of the physician than of the patient." See Richard Steele, "The Pulse of the People: Franklin D.

Roosevelt and the Gauging of American Public Opinion," *Journal of Contemporary History* vol. 9 no. 4 (October 1974): 216, cited in Sheingate, "Art and Science," 66. On the role of Congress, see Eisinger, *Evolution*, and on congressional prerogatives, see Julian E. Zelizer, *On Capitol Hill: The Struggle to Reform Congress and Its Consequences, 1948–2000* (New York: Cambridge University Press, 2004). On presidents treating polls as secret, see Jacobs and Burns, "Second Face," 542.

17. Eisinger, *Evolution*, 148, 153–54.

18. Ibid., 156, 158–59.

19. On circulation, see ibid., 157, and Herbst, *Numbered Voices*, 115. See Philip Meyer, *Precision Journalism: A Reporter's Introduction to Social Science Methods* (Bloomington: Indiana University Press, 1973), regarding how journalists can use social science to get at the truth.

20. Jacobs and Shapiro, "Issues," 529.

21. Ibid., 533, 537 for quote.

22. Jacobs and Burns, "Second Face," 538, 552 for quote.

23. On the second-class status of those political consultants who specialized in direct mail, see Sasha Issenberg, *The Victory Lab: The Secret Science of Winning Elections* (New York: Crown, 2012), 8. On Viguerie, see Alan Crawford, *Thunder on the Right: The New Right and the Politics of Resentment* (New York: Pantheon Books, 1980), 43, and Richard A. Viguerie and David Franke, *America's Right Turn: How Conservatives Used New and Alternative Media to Take Power* (Chicago: Bonus Books, 2004), 91.

24. Viguerie and Franke, *Right Turn*, 92, and Crawford, *Thunder*, 46–47.

25. Viguerie and Franke, *Right Turn*, 94–95.

26. Ibid., 84–85, 98–99, 134.

27. Zelizer, *On Capitol Hill*, 123, and Crawford, *Thunder*, 44.

28. Viguerie and Franke, *Right Turn*, 128.

29. Crawford, *Thunder*, 47–50.

30. Morris Dees and Steve Fiffer, *A Lawyer's Journey: The Morris Dees Story* (Chicago: American Bar Association, 2001), 133–38, 137 for Viguerie quote. See also Viguerie and Franke, *Right Turn*, 111.

31. Viguerie and Franke, *Right Turn*, 89. See also Walter Weintz, *The Solid Gold Mailbox: How to Create Winning Mail-Order Campaigns* (New York: Wiley, 1987).

32. Viguerie and Franke, *Right Turn*, 121.

33. Ibid., 109 (for quote), 135–36.

34. For examples, see Thomas B. Edsall and Haynes Johnson, "High-Tech, Impersonal Computer Net Is Snaring Prospective Republicans," *Washington Post*, April 22, 1984, and Thomas B. Edsall, "'An Extremely Fluid Electorate, Without Partisan Roots,'" *Washington Post*, November 4, 1984. "Arms race" quote is from personal correspondence with Doug Blackmon, May 3, 2013.

35. Adam Clymer, "Presidential Pollsters Are a Breed Apart," *New York Times*, December 14, 1980.

36. Paul Taylor, "Consultants Rise via the Low Road," *Washington Post*, January 17, 1989.

37. Ibid.

38. Ibid.

39. Thomas B. Edsall, "Donors, Voters Pinpointed; GOP Purchasing Technological Edge," *Washington Post*, June 18, 1984.

40. Ibid.

41. Adam Clymer, "Subtle Shifts in G.O.P Appeals Aimed at Women," *New York Times*, August 5, 1982.

42. Hillygus, "Evolution," 963.

43. Groves, "Three Eras," 861. See Hillygus, "Evolution," 976 for quote, along with Lawrence Jacobs and Robert Shapiro, "Polling Politics, Media, and Election Campaigns," special issue, *Public Opinion Quarterly* 69, no. 5 (2005): 635–41. In *Post-Broadcast Democracy: How Media Choice Increases Inequality in Political Involvement and Increases Polarization* (New York: Cambridge University Press, 2007), Markus Prior argues that media choice has allowed more citizens to avoid political discourse entirely, thus placing a premium on likely voters. This makes microtargeting efforts worth the effort. See also D. Sunshine Hillygus and Todd Shields, *The Persuadable Voter* (Princeton, NJ: Princeton University Press, 2008). For an excellent and highly engaging overview of the social science foundation on which microtargeting was built, see Issenberg, *Victory Lab.*

44. Hillygus, "Evolution," 977.

45. Peter Wallsten and Tom Hamburger, "The GOP Knows You Don't Like Anchovies," *Los Angeles Times*, June 25, 2006. On Republican uses of technology in the 1980s, see Daniel Galvin, *Presidential Party Building: Dwight D. Eisenhower to George W. Bush* (Princeton, NJ: Princeton University Press, 2010), 121. For Edsall quote see Edsall, "Donors, Voters Pinpointed."

46. Galvin, *Presidential Party Building*, 3–8, 104–5; for Reagan, see especially 15 and chap. 6.

47. Ibid., 120, 131.

48. Ibid., 146.

49. Edsall, "Donors, Voters Pinpointed."

50. Ibid.

51. Ibid.

52. Wallsten and Hamburger, "GOP Knows." See Galvin, *Presidential Party Building*, 141–42, on Democratic initiative; and David Paul Kuhn, "DNC Blunts GOP Microtargeting Lead," *Politico*, May 23, 2008, http://www.politico.com/news/stories/0508/10573.html.

53. Galvin, *Presidential Party Building*, 120, and, for poll, WashingtonPost.com, "The Independents," 2007, http://www.washingtonpost.com/wp-srv/politics/interactives/independents/data-party-identification.html.

54. Wallsten and Hamburger, "GOP Knows."

55. Ibid.

56. Galvin, *Presidential Party Building*, 131–34, and Edsall and Johnson, "High-Tech, Impersonal Computer Net."

57. Ibid.; for final quote, Edsall, "Extremely Fluid Electorate."

58. On the uses of data, see Kuhn, "DNC Blunts." On Voter Vault, see Wallsten and Hamburger, "GOP Knows."

59. Kuhn, "DNC Blunts."

60. On going public, see Kernell, *Going Public*, generally. For examples of such negotiated settlements, see Gareth Davies, *See Government Grow: Education Politics from Johnson to Reagan* (Lawrence: University Press of Kansas, 2007); Martha Derthick, *Policymaking for Social Security* (Washington: Brookings Institution, 1979); Julian Zelizer, *Taxing America: Wilbur D. Mills, Congress, and the State, 1945–1975* (New York: Cambridge University Press, 1998); and James T. Sparrow, Warfare State: World War II Americans and the Age of Big Government (New York: Oxford University Press, 2011).

CONTRIBUTORS

Brian Balogh is the Compton Professor at the Miller Center and the Corcoran Department of History at the University of Virginia. His most recent book is *A Government out of Sight: The Mystery of National Authority in Nineteenth-Century America*. Balogh is the cohost of *BackStory with the American History Guys*, a nationally syndicated radio show that airs on PBS stations across the United States.

Gareth Davies is University Lecturer in American History at St. Anne's College, Oxford University. He is the author of two books on the political legacy of the 1960s, most recently See Government Grow: Education Politics from Johnson to Reagan (2007). He is currently writing a book about the changing politics of disaster in the United States, from the early Republic to the creation of the Federal Emergency Management Agency.

Meg Jacobs is Associate Professor of History at MIT. She is the author of *Pocketbook Politics: Economic Citizenship in Twentieth-Century America*, winner of the OAH Ellis Hawley Award, and coauthor of *Conservatives in Power: The Reagan Years, 1981–1989*. She is currently completing a book on the energy crisis of the 1970s.

Richard R. John is a professor in the PhD program in communications at Columbia University and a core member of Columbia's history faculty. He has published widely on topics in American political development and is the author of two books: *Spreading the News: The American Postal System from Franklin to Morse* and *Network Nation: Inventing American Telecommunications*. At present he is writing a history of the antimonopoly tradition in American public life.

Kevin M. Kruse is Professor of History at Princeton University. He is the author of *White Flight: Atlanta and the Making of Modern Conservatism*, as well as the coeditor of three collections: *The New Suburban History*, with Thomas Sugrue; *Spaces of the Modern City*, with Gyan Prakash; and *Fog of War: The Second World War and the Civil Rights Movement*, with Stephen Tuck. His most recent book is *One Nation Under God: How Corporate America Invented Christian America* (Basic Books). He is also currently cowriting a textbook on U.S. history since 1974 with Julian Zelizer.

Jeffrey L. Pasley is Associate Professor of History at the University of Missouri and the author, most recently, of *The First Presidential Contest: 1796 and the Founding of American Democracy.*

Andrew Preston is Reader in American History and a Fellow of Clare College at Cambridge University, where he also serves as editor of the *Historical Journal.* He is the author of *The War Council: McGeorge Bundy, the NSC, and Vietnam,* and coeditor, with Fredrik Logevall, of *Nixon in the World: American Foreign Relations, 1969–1977.* His most recent book is *Sword of the Spirit, Shield of Faith: Religion in American War and Diplomacy.*

Elizabeth Sanders is a professor in the Government Department at Cornell University. Her book *The Regulation of Natural Gas Policy and Politics, 1938–1978* won the Kammerer Prize of the American Political Science Association in 1982. Her 1999 book *Roots of Reform: Farmers, Workers, and the American State, 1877–1917* was awarded the 2000 Greenstone Prize of the Politics and History Association of APSA.

Bruce J. Schulman is the William E. Huntington Professor of History at Boston University. He is the author of three books: *From Cotton Belt to Sunbelt*, *Lyndon B. Johnson and American Liberalism*, and *The Seventies*. He is also editor or coeditor of five books and a frequent contributor to newspapers and magazines.

Jay Sexton is University Lecturer and Tutorial Fellow in U.S. History at Corpus Christi College, the University of Oxford. He is the author of *Debtor Diplomacy: Finance and American Foreign Relations in the Civil War Era, 1837–1873* and *The Monroe Doctrine: Empire and Nation in Nineteenth-Century America*, and coeditor with Richard Carwardine of *The Global Lincoln* (2011).

Adam I. P. Smith is Senior Lecturer in History at University College London and is currently serving as the Honorary Secretary of the Royal Historical Society. He is the author of *No Party Now: Politics in the Civil War North* and of a forthcoming book about conservatism in American politics between 1848 and 1876.

Sean Wilentz is George Henry Davis 1886 Professor of American History at Princeton University. His books include *The Rise of American Democracy: Jefferson to Lincoln*, which was awarded the Bancroft Prize in 2006, and *The Age of Reagan: A History, 1974–2008*. A longtime contributing editor at the *New Republic*, his writing on contemporary American politics and political history appears regularly in a wide range of national publications, including the *New York Review of Books*, the *New York Times*, and *Rolling Stone*.

Julian E. Zelizer is the Malcolm Stevenson Forbes, Class of 1941 Professor of History and Public Affairs at Princeton University. He is the author and editor of fifteen books on American political history. His most recent book is *The Fierce Urgency of Now: Lyndon Johnson, Congress, and the Battle for the Great Society* (2015). He writes a popular column for CNN.Com.

INDEX

ACKNOWLEDGMENTS

The authors would like to thank the Boston University–Cambridge University–Princeton University political history conference for having hosted this event at Princeton University in June 2013. The conference where the chapters in this volume were first presented would not have been possible without the support of the Oxford University–Princeton University research fund or the generous assistance of the Department of History at Princeton. The authors want to thank Barbara Leavey for all her hard work making sure that logistics for the conference were in place. Finally, we want to thank Robert Lockhart and all of the editorial team at the University of Pennsylvania Press for their enthusiasm about this project.